PENNSYLVANIA BREWERIES

4TH EDITION

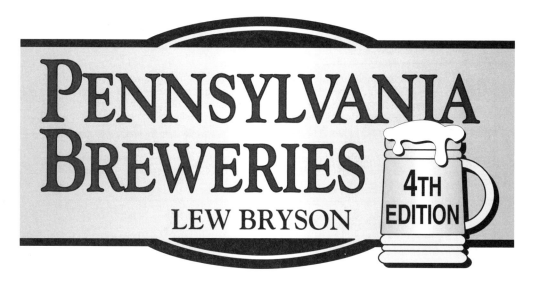

PENNSYLVANIA BREWERIES

LEW BRYSON

4TH EDITION

STACKPOLE
BOOKS

First edition published 1998. Second edition 2000. Third edition 2005
Fourth edition 2010

Published by
STACKPOLE BOOKS
5067 Ritter Road
Mechanicsburg, PA 17055
www.stackpolebooks.com

The author and publisher encourage readers to visit the breweries and sample their beers and recommend that those who consume alcoholic beverages travel with a nondrinking driver.

Printed in the United States of America

10 9 8 7 6 5

FIRST EDITION

Cover design by Tessa J. Sweigert

Labels and logos are used with permission of the breweries

Library of Congress Cataloging-in-Publication Data

Bryson, Lew.
Pennsylvania breweries / Lew Bryson. — 4th ed.
p. cm.
Includes index.
ISBN-13: 978-0-8117-3641-1 (pbk.)
ISBN-10: 0-8117-3641-5 (pbk.)
1. Bars (Drinking establishments)—Pennsylvania—Guidebooks. 2. Microbreweries—Pennsylvania—Guidebooks. 3. Breweries—Pennsylvania—Guidebooks. I. Title.
TX950.57.P4B79 2010
647.95748—dc22

2010022661

For my father,
Lewis M. Bryson II
Always at my side

CONTENTS

FOREWORD

B eer is pleasure. Whether it be the simple refreshment of a cool, pre-Prohibition lager while the hot dogs are grilling or the soul-satisfying contemplation of an imperial stout on the first raw night of November, beer speaks eloquently to those of us who listen.

But beyond the pleasure of the liquid, the beer geeks in us can readily admit to another pleasure to be found in beer. That pleasure is options. Glorious multitudes of flavor and character options are to be found in craft beer today. While students at Doemens Institute and the Technical University of Munich at Weihenstephan, we never savored a quadruppel or a double IPA. They simply didn't exist in the early nineties. Just as rauchbiers and weizenbocks did not exist in the United States in the seventies. What happened in between those decades?

What happened was that the intrepid thirst of a few avid beer lovers caused them to throw themselves into the craft of brewing and reinvigorate a moribund industry with flavor, style, and no shortage of guts. These pioneering craft brewers were beer lovers first, and then reluctant businessmen. Following their muse, they paved a golden road of pilsners and porters, stouts and saisons, as you cheered them on.

Your appreciation, as a consumer, was their reward. Your appreciation of these beers has sustained a fledgling industry and permitted families and businesses to flourish. Your appreciation took you to visit the sources of these beers, from across the nation to here in Pennsylvania.

In this book, *Pennsylvania Breweries*, Lew Bryson has captured the flavor, in every delicious detail, of what we as creators and consumers can be so proud of, the unabashed pleasure of the great beer we have to enjoy in Pennsylvania. You don't have to travel to every brewery in the state—Lew's already done that—but a great guide like this makes it easier to find the ones to put on your wish list.

So drink up this rich text and savor the success you've been an integral part of.

The pleasure is ours.

Bill Covaleski and Ron Barchet
Cofounders, Victory Brewing Company

ACKNOWLEDGMENTS

As I have done from the beginning, I have some acknowledgments to make in this, the fourth edition of *Pennsylvania Breweries*. Chris Trogner of Tröegs Brewing Company mentioned my name to an editor friend of his and got this whole series started back in 1997. Kyle Weaver, who has been my editor at Stackpole Books for all the *Breweries* books I've done, has been a huge help, has been understanding with my problems, and has become, over the years, a good friend (and a more adventurous beer drinker!).

Beer is not just a drink, it's the people you drink it with; that's why I've always included good bars in the book. I'd like to thank the folks who make those bars great: the owners and managers, the bartenders, and the folks sitting on my side of the bar too. To the mid-Atlantic forum on BeerAdvocate and the readers of my blog, Seen Through a Glass, who had great advice on bars (and even bought me a beer or two): thanks, and keep those e-mails coming! A special thanks to Bil Corcoran at MyBeerBuzz for help with the Wyoming Valley bars. Bob Batz Jr. at the *Post-Gazette* graciously shared contacts and news on the Pittsburgh scene. Thanks to Rich Pawlak for his help with the regional foods section: the smoked duck at Dietrich's is on me, brother.

My thanks to all the brewers of Pennsylvania, who have never let me down. You all came through in spades on this one. There have been many changes in the business since the first edition, and we all know each other better, even those who are new to this edition. We've seen Pennsylvania become home to the largest American-owned brewery (whether you count that as Yuengling or the Boston Beer brewery down the road), and we've got a couple tiny places brewing on a shoestring. I'm proud to call them all Pennsylvania breweries.

Special thanks once more to the people who have made me what I am. To my father, Lew, who couldn't be with me this time but was only a cell phone call away with helpful advice. To my mother, Ruth, who gave me the tools. To my children, Thomas and Nora, who are a great reason to come back home when the journey's done. And finally, always, to Cathy, who keeps me going when I wonder why I do this.

To all of you: Cheers!

INTRODUCTION

Welcome again to Pennsylvania and its breweries! You will find plenty of beer here these days, even though it's a far cry from the glory days of beer making over a hundred years ago. Almost every Pennsylvania town had a brewery then; some, like Philadelphia and Lancaster, had ten or more. You'll still find beautiful old bars in many small Pennsylvania towns, relics of the days when Pennsylvania's German and East European laborers crowded into taprooms in search of cool lager to relieve the heat of a day's hard work in forges and factories.

Pennsylvania still has five of its old breweries in one form or another, but the state has grown a new crop of breweries today—almost seventy, and more are on the way. They are called microbreweries or craft breweries, and they are notable not for their size, but for the broad variety of beer they make. This variety is not really a new thing; it is a return to the way beer used to be in America.

To understand where these new breweries came from, we need to take a look at our country's history, during which American brewing went from a broad, vibrant industry to a fossilized oligopoly of brewers making one style of beer, take it or leave it. What happened?

The Rise and Fall of American Brewing
The history of the Europeans in America goes like much of human history since the discovery of alcohol. As soon as they got ashore, the early settlers started looking for something to ferment and distill: pumpkins, corn, pine needles—anything for a jolt. The most popular alcoholic drink in early America was cider, followed closely by rum brought in from the West Indies.

Americans drank a lot of these beverages and a lot of alcohol in general. Per capita annual consumption of alcohol was over ten gallons by the 1840s. That's gallons of pure alcohol, not gallons of rum at 40 percent alcohol or cider at 7 percent. Americans drank pretty much all the time.

When Americans did drink beer, they mostly drank imported British ales. And when Americans began brewing, they mimicked the English by producing similar unfiltered ales.

Cider was still the most popular drink through Andrew Jackson's presidency, but things changed rapidly in the 1840s. There were three complementary components to this change. In Philadelphia in 1840, a brewer named John Wagner is believed to have been the first to brew German-style lager beers in America. This refreshing beer became very popular with laborers because it could be drunk quickly to quench a thirst.

Paradoxically, the temperance movements that swept the nation in the 1840s accelerated the rise of lager beer. Temperance had strong effects on many suppliers, retailers, and drinkers. One of its major "successes" was wiping out America's cider-producing orchards almost entirely. The 1840s saw fields of stumps on many farms; woodcut illustrations of the devastated orchards are a bemusing legacy. The demand for drink did not go away, of course, and lager brewers picked up the shifting market.

The third thing that drove lager's popularity was the rise in immigration to America after the squashed German rebellions of 1848. Germans and other beer-drinking Europeans came to America by the thousands, and they wanted their beer. America was happy to supply it.

There were plenty of breweries in Pennsylvania, and some of the names survive in labels brewed by other brewers—Stegmaier, Schmidt's, Gibbon's—or merely in memory. You or your father (or mother) may remember Old Reading, Koehler of Erie, F&S out of Shamokin, Ortlieb's from Philadelphia, Lancaster's Rieker-Star, or DuBois Budweiser.

There were more than two thousand breweries in America at the turn of the century, mostly small local breweries producing almost every style of beer, although lager was a clear favorite. The temperance movements, however, had not gone away. The Great Killer of breweries in America was the little social experiment called Prohibition (1920–33). By 1939, when this fanaticism had run its course and the industry had briefly boomed and settled down, only about five hundred breweries remained.

Everyone knows that people didn't stop drinking during Prohibition, but the quality of the beer they drank was dramatically affected. Some drank "needle beer" (near beer injected with alcohol) or low-grade homebrew, made with anything they could get their hands on. They used cake yeast and the malt syrup that brewers were making to survive. Other beer generally available during Prohibition was low-quality and relatively weak, made from cheap ingredients with large amounts of corn or rice for fermentation.

Illicit brewers used the high-gravity system, brewing very strong beer, then watering it down. This saved time and money, as did greatly shortened aging times. Federal enforcement agents knew that hops were a commodity really used only for brewing; brewers, therefore, lowered the amount of hops they used to avoid suspicion. For fourteen years, people drank literally anything that was called beer.

These changes brought about some long-term effects. The corn and rice and high-gravity brewing produced a distinctly lighter-bodied beer with an identifiable nonbarley taste. Low hopping rates made for a sweeter beer. Over Prohibition's fourteen years, people got used to lighter lager beer. The process continued over the next three decades as big brewers came to dominate the market.

The rise of big breweries and the decline of small breweries can be tracked to several important developments. World War II brought a need to get lots of beer to troops abroad. Huge contracts went to the brewers that were big enough to fill them. Hops and malt for homefront brewing were considered largely nonessential. Improvements in packaging, such as crimp-top bottlecaps and cans, made buying beer for home consumption easier. Refrigerated transportation enabled brewers to ship beer long distances to reach more customers. These improvements required large capital investments possible only for successful, growing breweries.

Mass-market advertising during broadcast sporting events got the national breweries in front of everyone. The advertising further convinced Americans that light lagers were the only type of beer out there. Advertising was expensive but effective. The big breweries got bigger, and small ones went out of business.

Why did the rise of big national brewers necessarily mean that American beer would become all the same type of light lager? Simple reasons, really: Making it all the same is cheaper and easier. Success breeds imitation. Image is easier to advertise than flavor. A large national brand has to appeal to a broad audience of consumers.

This led to the situation in the 1970s in which one dominant style of beer was made by fewer than forty breweries. People who wanted something else had to seek out the increasingly rare exceptions made by smaller brewers (Stegmaier's and Yuengling's porters kept things going here in Pennsylvania) or buy pricey imports of unknown age and freshness. The varieties of beer styles were unknown to most Americans.

This is the real key to understanding the craft-brewing revolution. These beers are not better made than Budweiser; in fact, Budweiser is more consistent than many American craft-brewed beers. What craft-brewed beers offer is variety.

The American Brewing Revolution

How did microbreweries get started? Fritz Maytag bought the Anchor Brewery in San Francisco on a whim in the mid-1960s. He had heard they were going out of business and knew they brewed his favorite beer.

Fritz was an heir to the Maytag appliance fortune and could afford to indulge his whims. But he got hooked on brewing, and Anchor led the return of beer variety in America. Fritz brewed Anchor's trademark "steam" beer, an ale and lager hybrid; he brewed the mightily hoppy Liberty Ale; and he brewed the strong, malty barleywine he called Old Foghorn. Things were off and . . . well, things were off and walking in the United States.

Next came the microbreweries. Ambitious homebrewers, maverick megabrewers, and military personnel or businesspeople who had been to Europe and wanted to have the same kinds of beer they drank there saw a need for better beer. They started these small breweries, cobbling them together like Frankenstein's monster from whatever pieces of equipment they could find. The beer was anything but uniform—sometimes excellent, sometimes awful—but even so, it found a receptive market.

The revolution started in the West and grew very slowly. New Albion, the first new brewery in America since World War II, opened in 1976 in Sonoma, California. Ten years later, Dock Street and Penn Brewing hired an existing brewery to brew their beers. The first new "brick and mortar" brewery in Pennsylvania, Stoudt's, opened in 1987. Progress was gradual in Pennsylvania until 1995.

By the end of 1994, there were twelve breweries in Pennsylvania, including the six "Old Guard" regional breweries. By the time the champagne popped again at the end of 1995, there were twice that many. In the next two years, the number doubled again. Brewpubs popped up like mushrooms after the rain, microbreweries opened on a loan and a wish. It was an optimistic time, and it seemed like 40 percent growth would last forever.

Then the long-anticipated shakeout hit the industry, and the press has gleefully reported several times since then that microbrewing is dead. Independence and Red Bell crashed in spectacular fashion. Dock Street, the state's oldest brewpub, was ignominiously run into the ground less than six months after changing hands. (The new Dock Street has plenty of "DNA" from the old one.)

Things looked bad for a few years, and the nationwide slump in the hospitality and travel industries after the terrorist attacks on September 11, 2001, didn't do breweries any favors either. In retrospect, though, craft breweries had already started to grow again at that time, and in the years since, they have outgrown every other sector in the beer market.

Craft breweries are part of the landscape now. Brewpubs are established in their communities and more are opening. Victory is booming and developing a national reputation, Tröegs can barely keep up with demand despite constant incremental expansion, and Boston Beer has moved to Pennsylvania and is brewing all their beer in-house for the first time, millions of barrels. Yuengling just keeps powering along.

Maybe more significantly, the process I call "filling in the map" continues. Just look at the arc between Wilkes-Barre and State College. Five years ago, only four breweries were there: Otto's, Bullfrog, Selin's Grove, and The Lion. Today there are eleven, and at least one more will open by the time this sees print. We still have large open spaces on the map, but of the ten biggest cities in the state, only Scranton and Reading are without a brewery (and they've had them—see the Boneyard—and still have exceptional beer bars).

People across the state are discovering the many different ways beer can taste. No one thinks all wine comes in gallon jugs anymore, and everyone knows there are more types than red and white. Beer is well on that same path. Craft beer has become normal.

How I Came to Love All Beer

A growing number of Pennsylvanians look for something a bit more stimulating than a mainstream mug o' suds these days. But even when it comes to those standbys, we have always been remarkably loyal to our local brewers. These were lessons I learned early, in a beer-drinking career reflective of America's beer revolution.

I had my first full beer as a freshman in college. When I was a kid, my father had often let me have sips of his beer with dinner. That was Duke Ale, from Duquesne Brewing of Pittsburgh, one of Pennsylvania's many defunct breweries. But I'd never had a beer of my own until Tim Turecek handed me a Genesee Cream Ale in that 16-ounce, solidly brown and green returnable, dripping with condensation. I drank it, and it was good.

I drank a lot more of them over the next three years. "Genny" Cream, Prior's's Double Dark, Stroh's, and Rolling Rock were my staples, along with Stegmaier, National Bohemian, and National Premium when the money was tight.

Then one night in my senior year at Franklin and Marshall College, I met my medieval history professor for drinks, a special treat for a few legal-age students. The bar was the Lauzus Hotel, in Lancaster, Pennsylvania. Run by old Wilhelm Lauzus, an ex–German Navy man, the bar carried more than 125 different beers in 1981, not too shabby at all in those days. I had no clue and grabbed my usual Stroh's. My professor laughed and slapped it out of my hand. He pulled a German beer, an

Altenmünster, out of the cooler and popped the swingtop. "Try this," he said, and changed my life.

It was big, full in the mouth, and touched by a strange bitterness that I'd never tasted before. That bitterness made another sip the most natural thing in the world, like pepper on potatoes. I've been looking for beers outside the American mainstream ever since that night.

It's increasingly easy to find that kind of beer in Pennsylvania, where our breweries are turning out everything from whopping Imperial stouts to crisp, bitter pilsners to rippingly hoppy India pale ales to bubbly, spicy hefeweizens. Is that all I drink, beers like that? Well, no. When I mow my lawn in hot, humid southeastern Pennsylvania summers, sometimes I want a cold glass of something dashingly refreshing and fizzy. Then I keep it local and reach for one of Pennsylvania's regional brews, or one of our many microbrewed Bavarian-style wheat beers.

Drinking beer has changed a bit in Pennsylvania. There is a smoking ban in bars and restaurants now, which is a pleasant change for nonsmokers (you can taste your beer better, and you don't stink when you get home). After seventy-five years, some supermarkets are finally allowed to sell six-packs, and there is movement in the state legislature to allow distributors to sell them as well, instead of the ridiculous case minimum sale law we are suffering under now.

As I finish up this fourth edition, a couple thoughts occur to me. First, craft-brewed and local beer is showing up all over the state these days. The number of beer specialty bars is growing fast, but what's growing even faster is the corner bars that now have a tap of Victory HopDevil, or Penn Pilsner, or Stoudt's Gold, or Samuel Adams. Craft beer isn't out of the ordinary anymore. Another thing: I'm proud of how well Pennsylvania breweries have done. The largest American-owned brewery is here, Pennsylvania has the fifth-highest number of Great American Beer Festival medals (while having less than a third as many breweries as the most medaled state, California), and we have more pre-Prohibition breweries still open than any other state. Good job, Pennsylvania brewers and beer drinkers!

My family and I have enjoyed traveling to Pennsylvania's breweries and sampling these beers at the source. My son took his first tour of the Yuengling brewery on his first birthday, and my daughter would rather have dinner at a brewpub than at McDonald's. My wife loves a good beer as much as I do and is always happy to see the brim-full growlers I bring home from my research trips. Beer traveling is a lot of fun, and this book will serve as a guide for your travels in Pennsylvania. Hoist one for me!

How to Use This Book

This book is a compendium of information about Pennsylvania's breweries. It also lists some of the interesting attractions and best bars in Pennsylvania. And it offers facts and opinions about brewing, brewing history in the United States and Pennsylvania, and beer-related subjects.

It does not present a comprehensive history of any brewery, nor does it try to rate every single beer produced by every single brewery. It is not a conglomeration of beer jargon—original gravities, International Bittering Unit levels, apparent attenuations, and so on. And it's not about homebrewing. Other people have done a fine job on books like that, but it's not what I wanted to do.

It is a travel guide about breweries and Pennsylvania, home to startling natural beauty and man-made wonders. Sharing information has been a central part of the success of the rise of microbreweries in the United States. I've been sharing what I know for more than twenty years, and this book and its companion volumes, *New York Breweries*, *Virginia, Maryland, and Delaware Breweries*, and the latest, *New Jersey Breweries*, represent my latest efforts to spread the good word.

The book is organized in alternating parts. The meat of the book, the brewery information, is presented in eight sections: one more than the last edition, because we've added so many breweries. The first section begins with a general description of the larger, older breweries that make up the Old Guard. Each of the seven geographic sections—Philadelphia, Philadelphia Suburbs, Pennsylvania Dutch Country, Capital Area, Appalachian Ridge, Northwest Corner, and Pittsburgh—is prefaced with a description of the area for those unfamiliar with it. The "A word about . . ." sections are intended as instructional interludes on topics you may be curious about. There should be something there for almost everyone, whether novice, dabbler, or fanatic.

The history and character, highlights, my observations, and other information about the brewpub or brewery are presented in a narrative section. The annual capacity in barrels, as listed for each brewery, is a function of the fermenting-tank capacity and the average time to mature a beer. Lagers take longer, so on two identical systems with the same fermenter setup, an all-lager brewery would have significantly lower annual capacity than an all-ale brewery.

I have tried, in the past, to list every beer a brewery makes on a regular or seasonal basis, along with all the one-offs and specials. In this edition, I have for the most part given up. It's for a happy reason: There are just so many of them! Victory, for example, now keeps twenty different beers on at their brewpub at all times; Tröegs's ongoing Scratch series

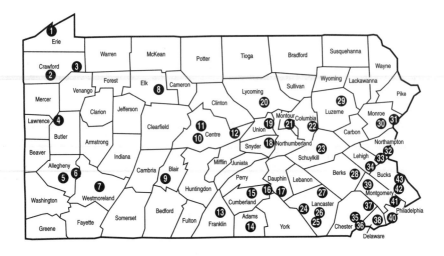

consists of more than twenty beers to date and has spawned a subseries of "Splinter" beers. The lists were getting crazy, so I cut back to year-rounds and seasonals (with the occasional exception, just because that's the way craft brewing is). Similarly, we decided to drop the listings of beers that have won Great American Beer Festival medals, mainly because Pennsylvania breweries have won so many that it just got cluttered.

The other area beer sites I've listed for most breweries may include multitaps, historic bars, or restaurants with good beer selections. Whenever possible, I visited these bars and had at least one beer there. More of these descriptions than in previous editions are based on recommendations from brewers or beer geeks I know personally this time around: Beer bars in Pennsylvania have simply exploded. Another happy reason!

A couple notes on attractions: The Pennsylvania Department of Conservation and Natural Resources has a Web site with a lot of information about the state's great parks, but the URLs are kind of unintuitive, so I didn't list them in the book. You can easily navigate to individual parks from the DCNR main Web site: www.dcnr.state.pa.us.

Where hunting or fishing is mentioned, your best bet is to contact the Pennsylvania Game Commission (717-787-4250, www.pgc.state.pa.us) or Pennsylvania Fish and Boat Commission (717-657-4518, www.fishandboat.com) for license and season information; the Fish and Boat Commission Web site also has great information on fish runs, stream conditions, and stocking.

Finally, I've been biking a lot more lately, and I'd like to recommend the Rails-to-Trails Conservancy's Web site, www.TrailLink.com,

for finding trails in the state. These include trails for walking, biking, ATVs, in-line skating, and horseback riding, all at fairly level grades, usually through great scenery. We've enjoyed them tremendously and support them.

Enjoy yourself!

Author's Note: It just keeps happening! Two more Pennsylvania breweries were set to open just as we did final edits on this edition. I'll tell you about them here, and you can find more at my Web site, www.lew bryson.com. The first is a production brewery, Prism Brewing Company (810-B2 Dickerson Road, North Wales, PA 19454; 888-424-9681, www.prismbeer.com). They were brewing their Bitto Honey IPA and Tea Party Pale Ale at the General Lafayette, but they now have their own 20-barrel DME system: Cheers! The second is the RiverHouse BrewPub (2890 Rt. 405, Milton, PA 17847; 570-523-1900, www.river housebrewpub.com), featuring beers by former Abbey Wright brewer Bart Rieppel. They're right across the river from Lewisburg, smack-dab in the middle of one of the hottest brewing spots in Pennsylvania.

The Old Guard

What a change since 2001! Pennsylvania still has more operating pre-1980s breweries than any other state—five, compared with two each for New York and Minnesota—but we lost two in nine years: Jones, where they brewed the Stoney's brand, and Pittsburgh, which changed its name to that of its iconic Iron City brand just before the end in 2009. Latrobe narrowly dodged closing after its Belgian overlords InBev sold the Rolling Rock brand to Anheuser-Busch (and would get it back when they bought A-B itself a couple years later); Wisconsin-based City Brewing bought the brewery, bringing contracted brewing and jobs.

But the story of the rest of the survivors is a positive one. These brewers survived Prohibition, World War II, and three decades of brewery wars between 1950 and 1980. They made it by working with low debt, a long-tenure workforce that was as dedicated to the success of the brewery as the owners were, a fiercely loyal customer base, and sheer stubborn guts. They did it by adapting to a new beer market or sticking to their guns; they did it through changes in ownership or an amazing longevity of ownership. In short, they did what they had to do to stay open.

These survivors include Yuengling, America's oldest brewery, and Straub, the self-styled "highest brewery in the East." The Lion, in Wilkes-Barre, survived the last twenty years mainly by brewing malt soda for the Hispanic market. Latrobe hangs on by brewing whatever the customer needs, without a house brand at all. I'm also very pleased to welcome the big former Schaefer brewery outside of Allentown to this section of the book for the first time, under its new owners, the Boston Beer Company, brewers of the Samuel Adams beers.

These breweries are like a time capsule of American brewing, keeping alive elements of brewing history. Yuengling and The Lion were the last premicrobreweries in America to brew porter, a dark, rich brew with roots in London. Although porters are traditionally ales, these porters are lager-brewed, easier for these breweries to produce. The Lion even took a traditionalist step backward by once again brewing their porter as an ale; Yuengling, however, still brews their "Pennsylvania porter" as they have for years. Boston Beer uses traditional horizontal lagering tanks—high-maintenance, but they swear by the beer they produce.

While Boston brews with the full variety that defines craft beer and City brews whatever their customers want, Yuengling, The Lion, and Straub largely produce mainstream American lagers, brewed with lightening additions of corn. The beers are not of great interest to a beer geek, but they are all well made and consistent. When I'm in the mood for a sluicing, sloshing, "lawn mower" beer, I always buy local and support Pennsylvania brewers, and so should you!

You should also go visit them. Yuengling and Straub give two of the best industrial brewery tours in the country, taking you right down on the floor. Until recently, you could actually climb the ladders and look into Straub's rare open lager fermenters, practically unheard of in these days of lawyerly precautions. The Lion does tours by appointment, with required hard hats; you know you're going right into the heart of things when you don the one of those! Even if you don't go inside, simply viewing the architecture and the size of these buildings will give you a whole different angle on brewing.

Boston Beer Company

7880 Penn Drive, Breinigsville, PA 18031
www.samueladams.com

Let's have a quick history lesson on this place, just to get up to where we would have been if the previous tenants had been willing to be in the earlier editions.

1972: Brooklyn-based F&M Schaefer opens their new, state-of-the-art brewery outside Allentown. The brewery is a proud statement, with tall windows on the brewhouse facing I-78, and Schaefer makes it theirs by bringing a large statue of Gambrinus, a legendary brew-ing figure, from their Albany brewery, a passing of the torch . . . or flagon.

1981: The name on the sign changes. Schaefer is bought by the Stroh Brewing Company of Detroit. Stroh's, the "fire-brewed beer," brings direct-fire copper kettles to the brewery, heated by huge gas burners right under the kettles. Gambrinus remains.

1992: I tour the brewery with sixteen friends; we are all awestruck by the size. We take a picture with Gambrinus. Meanwhile, Stroh is using the excess capacity of this brewery to do contract work: several malt liquors, some Yuengling Black & Tan at the height of that crazy demand, and some Samuel Adams beers (the Honey Porter was first brewed here).

1999: The name on the sign changes again. Stroh collapses under debt, and Pabst buys the brands and this brewery. It will be the last brewery Pabst owns—for now, at least—and beers brewed here will win more than twenty GABF medals in only three years. Gambri-nus remains.

2001: Pabst closes the brewery, laying off four hundred workers. Diageo, a huge multinational drinks company, buys the facility but does not brew. They use the tanks and bottling lines to mix and package fla-vored malt beverages, like Smirnoff Ice. The sign is taken down. Gambrinus remains . . . but is clearly embarrassed.

2007: Boston Beer buys the brewery from Diageo and spends as much on renovations as it does on the actual purchase, including a new sign. Many of the Pabst and Stroh workers are rehired, most being quite proud of the fact. As Pabst sold the brewery to go all-contract, Boston Beer buys the brewery to bring all brew-ing in-house. Malt cooks again, hops hit hot wort, lagering tanks are cold and full, the bot-tling lines hum. Gambrinus remains . . . and he's smiling.

Forgive me the history lesson, but you should have had that in the previous three editions of *Penn-sylvania Breweries*. Pabst wouldn't play ball and Dia-geo wasn't brewing, and that really bugged me. But when Boston Beer founder Jim Koch announced the company was buying this brewery, I knew that this edition would finally be complete, because Jim defi-nitely gets it.

Beers brewed: The following Samuel Adams beers were brewed at this brewery in 2009: Samuel Adams Boston Lager, White Ale, Noble Pils, Summer Ale, OctoberFest, Winter Lager, Cranberry Lam-bic, Old Fezziwig Ale, Holiday Porter, Boston Ale, Cream Stout, Honey Porter, Cherry Wheat, Pale Ale, Black Lager, Irish Red, Blackberry Wit, Coastal Wheat, Scotch Ale, Dunkelweizen, and Sam Adams Light.

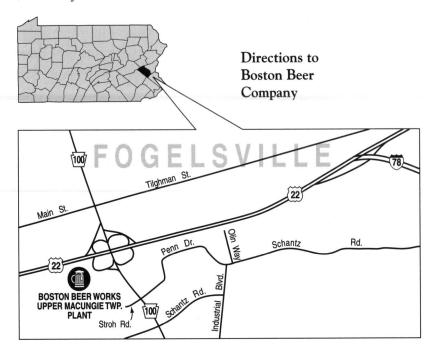

Directions to
Boston Beer
Company

Jim Koch and his Samuel Adams Boston Lager are perfect inheritors for this, what Jim calls "the last of the traditional breweries built in the U.S.," because his beer, unlike other craft beers, has always been brewed in big breweries. When he decided, about twenty-five years ago, to follow in his family tradition—five generations before him were brewers—and make beer, he looked around and considered his options.

"The trade-off was simple," he said. "I could build one of those early 1980s microbreweries with the money I had and sell beer on the local image, 'Made in our tiny little brewery, isn't it cute?' Which is powerful stuff, no doubt. Or I could turn my back on that.

"I thought about something my dad told me," Jim continued, "which is, no matter how good the marketing is, someone's got to drink the beer. You can't put crappy beer out there and expect people to drink it. That led me to put the quality of the beer over the marketing appeal of having a brewery in Boston. Maybe it would have worked the other way. I don't know, and I took a lot of heat for that decision."

But Koch contracted to make his beer in a variety of breweries (including Pittsburgh Brewing and the Lehigh Valley Stroh plant), and it grew quickly, more quickly than any other craft brand. "That was the 'magic' of Samuel Adams: consistently high quality," he said. "I had access to more brewing expertise; I had my dad and [brewing consultant] Joe Owades."

Did Koch decide to take brewing in-house because of a lack of contractors? "No, there's plenty of capacity," he said. "It was a combination of the brewery being available, because Diageo was probably going to close it, and we had the money." The money—about $55 million to Diageo and about that much more in renovations—paled beside projections of building a comparable plant in Massachusetts: $400 million.

That's what it would have cost because, Koch said, this was the brewery he wanted. Brewery technology shifted in the 1970s; brewers went from horizontal fermenters and aging tanks to tall cylindro-conical "unitanks" and switched to high-gravity brewing (see "A word about . . . Brewing Beer" on page 181), mostly to get the volume to feed new high-speed packaging lines.

But those tall tanks put more pressure on the yeast in the tank, Koch pointed out. "Even a micro-brewery's cylindro-conicals are thirty feet tall, and the yeast is at the bottom. The hydrostatic pressure on the yeast has an effect on it; it limits ester production. We want that—we want the full flavors of an all-malt fermentation." The horizontal tanks are more work, harder to clean, but that's what he wanted.

The Pick: Sam Adams—I can call him Sam, we've been friends for years—has made this a better country for lovers of beer. It's just that simple: This beer broke the trail for American craft beer. You youngsters don't know what a relief it was when Boston Lager started showing up in places that previously had only four different taps of the same kind of light lager. The floral aroma of the noble hops, the smooth malt body, the bitter crispness of the finish, all in a whip-fresh glass of cold delight. What a difference it made, and still does. Grab a fresh one and enjoy it. The Noble Pils is a great addition: florally aromatic, an elegant beer. For pure drinking pleasure, though, I'll take the Black Lager, which goes down so smoothly and easily: a relaxing beer.

That's what he got. The brewery is full of them, stretching away in a fermentation hall the size of a train station. There's no high-gravity brewing here, and the bottling lines run only as fast as they have to. "It's not efficient, it's not cheap, but it makes great beer," said Koch.

The upgrades have all come elsewhere. There is an all-new filtering room, with a massive filter and two big centrifuges, all servo-controlled. The brewhouse is all controlled by touchscreens now, and the lab has expanded. Quality director Mike Brennan, who took me through the brewery, looks forward to a day when the lab can expand right out onto the floor and everyone will be doing their own quality monitoring.

That's all part of the difference Jim Koch and Boston Beer have brought to this plant. Brennan has been here since the Stroh days in the mid-1980s. "When you had to throw a switch, you were just told to throw it when you were told," he recalled. "Now they learn what happens when they throw the switch, and why it needs to happen. They're becoming brewers."

A brewery with good bones. That's what Jim told me he was buying back in 2007, the brewery that won the most GABF medals any brewery's ever won in one year. He's staffing it with people who are worthy of its structure, and they're making beer that Gambrinus would be proud of.

Opened: Brewery began operations in 1972; sold to current owners in 2007.

Owner: Boston Beer Company.

Brewers: Jim Koch (founder and brewer), David Grinnell (vice president of brewing), Dan Melideo (director of brewing, Pennsylvania).

System: Two large-barrel Vendome brewkettles, 1.4 million barrels annual capacity.

2009 production: Boston Beer produced approximately 2 million barrels, about 70 percent in Pennsylvania.

Tours: None.

Take-out beer: None available.

Parking: None available.

Lodging in the area, Area attractions, Other area beer sites: See Kutztown Tavern on pages 165–66 and Allentown Brew Works on pages 175–76.

City Brewing Company

119 Jefferson Street, Latrobe, PA 15650
www.citybrewery.com

This used to be a proud spot for Pennsylvanians. Latrobe Brewing was the home of Rolling Rock, a brand that dated from 1939, a crisp, light lager with a hint of corn sweetness that came in silk-screened green bottles bearing the motto: "From the glass-lined tanks of old Latrobe we tender this premium beer for your enjoyment, as a tribute to your good taste. It comes from the mountain springs to you." Following the motto was an enigmatic "33." What did it mean? No one knew for sure, but

Rolling Rock meant a Pennsylvania beer that sold more than a million barrels a year in its heyday.

Then Latrobe was bought by Canadian brewer Labatt, which pumped millions of dollars into the facility: new brewhouse and fermentation hall, both highly automated; new piping; and an automatic cleaning (CIP) system. When Labatt was bought by InBev, the giant Belgian brewing conglomerate that is currently the world's largest brewer, Rolling Rock just kind of chugged along, without much input or expenditure.

Beers brewed: As contractors order.

The Pick: Matt and I tasted some beers City was currently making. The Southampton Double White was a favorite; their brewer Phil Markowski kind of invented the style . . . but I don't even think you can find it in Latrobe.

Things changed rapidly when InBev sold the brand to Anheuser-Busch in 2006. Suddenly, the brewery didn't have a reason to exist, and InBev was actively shopping for a buyer. The county made offers; Governor Rendell got involved; there was talk of possible deals with Boston Beer, Iron City, and even Pabst buying the brewery.

But when the dust settled, the new owner was City Brewing, of LaCrosse, Wisconsin. City was formed in 1999 by a group of investors who bought the old G. Heileman brewery in that town and began making beers under contract for a variety of brands, including flavored malt beverages like Mike's Hard Lemonade. They bought the Latrobe brewery to add capacity and capability; the newer equipment at Latrobe must have been attractive.

After some initial work for Boston Beer, the plant was shut down in 2008, pending more work. That has finally started to happen, and City has been hiring back workers. Iron City is brewed here, since that brewery closed in 2009, under the supervision of former Iron City brewmaster Mike Carota, who's now running brewing operations for City Brewing. They are even brewing beer for Southampton Publick House, a well-respected, very small craft brewery from Long Island, and City does a nice job on beers like their Double White, IPA, and Imperial Porter.

Assistant brewer Matt Falenski met me at the brewery for a walk-through. We met at a backdoor; the small office building from the Rolling Rock days is closed, along with the gift shop, and no tours are given. As I looked around the echoing interior, largely shut down and darkened toward the end of the brewing day, I couldn't help thinking of the old Rolling Rock slogan. When Matt turned with a grin and said it—"Same as it ever was!"—we both had to laugh.

We laughed because it is clearly not the same, of course. Changes were taking place as we walked: men welding new equipment in place here—a new canning line was going in and is now up and running—and disassembling old equipment over there. The tide of green bottles I remember from the old Rock days no longer flows down the bottling line, but the Iron City contract means a large increase in volume. "Production was way down," Matt conceded, "but it's on the way up."

The future of City's operation here is far from certain; the contract brewing business never is. Contracts come and go, brands gain and wane in popularity and sales. But I note that Anheuser-Busch InBev (as the new conglomerate calls itself, for now) is said to be contemplating selling the Rolling Rock brand. If City makes an offer, is there a chance that the Rock might once again be . . . same as it ever was? A guy can dream.

Opened: 1933; sold to current owners in 2006.

Owner: City Brewing, LaCrosse, Wisconsin.

Brewers: Mike Carota, head brewer; Matt Falenski.

System: 500-barrel Acme Brewing brewhouse, 1.2 million barrels potential annual capacity.

2009 production: Brewery was shut down in most of 2009; production has restarted as modifications continue.

Tours: None.

Take-out beer: None available.

Parking: Plenty of free off-street parking . . . if you want to look at the building.

Lodging in the area: Comfort Inn Greensburg, 1129 E. Pittsburgh St., Route 30, Greensburg, 724-832-2600; Mountain View Inn, 1001 Village Dr., Greensburg, 724-834-5300; Knights Inn, 1215 S. Main St., Greensburg, 724-836-7100.

Area attractions: *St. Vincent's College* in Latrobe was the site of one of America's few monastic breweries, and some of the old brewery buildings still stand on the campus. The Steelers hold their training camp at St. Vincent's. The banana split was invented here at Strickler's Drug Store more than a hundred years ago; Strickler's is closed, but you can still get one at the locally owned *Valley Dairy* chain of restaurants. *Keystone State Park* (724-668-2939) north of town offers camping, hiking, boating, fishing, swimming, skating, sledding, and cross-country ski trails. *Idlewild Amusement Park* (724-238-3666, www.idlewild.com) in nearby Ligonier has rides, miniature golf, water rides, and Mister Rogers' Neighborhood with a trolley ride and lifesize puppets; it was recently rated the second-best kids' park in the world. Latrobe is the hometown of Fred Rogers, Arnold Palmer, and professional football.

Other area beer sites: *The Headkeeper* (618 S. Main, Greensburg) has the biggest selection of bottled beer in Greensburg, maybe in southwest Pennsylvania—and they do take-out, too. ***Rick's Sports Bar & Grill*** (5400 William Penn Highway, Murrysville, 724-327-4148) gives them competition on taps; I was shocked to see Chimay White on tap at a sports bar. Locals drink at the *USA Today*–recommended ***Dino's Sports Lounge*** (3883 Route 30 East, 724-539-2566) and ***Sharky's Café*** (201 Route 30 East, 724-532-1620).

Straub Brewery

303 Sorg Street, St. Marys, PA 15857
814-834-2875
www.straubbeer.com

BREWERY, INC.

Straub has a few small claims to fame. It is, by Straub family reckoning, the highest brewery in the East, sitting at an elevation between 1,900 and 2,000 feet above sea level. This puts the brewery just below the Eastern Continental Divide, which means, as Dan Straub laughingly put it, "We get to use the water first!" It is the smallest regional brewery still in operation in Pennsylvania, with an annual capacity of 45,000 barrels. But perhaps most appealingly, it is the home of the Eternal Tap, which I'll explain later. First, let's see where Straub came from and where it's going.

Peter Straub came to the United States from Germany in 1869. He eventually settled in St. Marys in 1872 and first worked at the Windfelder Brewery in town. He was then hired as brewmaster by Francis Sorg at Sorg's brewery up the hill (note the street address of the current brewery). Peter married Sorg's oldest daughter, Sabina, and then bought the brewery in 1878. The copper brewkettle from Sorg's brewery was in continuous use until 1995, when it was finally replaced with a new 160-barrel stainless kettle.

That was one of a number of upgrades in the past twenty years. The rare open lager fermenters were finally replaced with stainless tanks that better

Beers brewed: Straub, Straub Light, Peter Straub Special Dark; a line of specialty lagers is coming out in late 2010.

filled the available space. The bottling line was replaced with a new Krones filler and Krones labeler that do in four days what used to take the old line six. There's an on-site laboratory for the first time. The upgrades were needed to meet a steadily growing demand for this quiet beer, growth that continues today.

Dan Straub, the former CEO who is partially retired these days but still involved, noted that "the joke was that we worked hard so you could take time off to hunt and fish. You can't do that anymore. A beer in your hand, that's so simple. But getting it there is very complex."

The Pick: Straub is a good mainstream lager, and out here in Straub country, it turns over so fast that it's always fresh. If you're on the tour and they offer you a bottle right off the line, take it. This is the freshest beer you may ever get, fresher even than most beer from a brewpub. It's eye-opening.

It wasn't only the equipment that changed. There was a major shakeup in the family-owned brewery's management last year. Bill Brock is the new CEO (Bill's mother is a Straub), and he's the first person to run the company who didn't come up from the brewery floor. He's not even from the beer business. But enough of the family shareholders decided that the brewery needed a new direction.

"When you have a fifth-generation family-owned business," Bill said, "you think of that in every decision. It's not the same kind of decision you'll make in a public company."

"It's not just a job," Dan agreed. "It's who you are."

Maybe more shocking to the company culture is the new brewmaster, Matt Allyn, known better as the craft brewer behind Voodoo Brewery and the Blue Canoe brewpub. Tom Straub, the former brewmaster, has retired. This is the first time the brewmaster is not a family member.

"Matt's already working on the process," Bill said. "The recipe stays the same; the goal's not to change it. But everything we do is being reevaluated. Most of it we'll keep, some of it we'll change. We'll be testing more, looking to increase the shelf life."

"I don't plan to change Straub beer," Matt Allyn confirmed, "just make it more consistent. See, 50 percent of what we do is standard German lager technique. Another 30 percent is proven modern techniques. And about 20 percent is, well, we do it because it works. We need to look at all that."

He's got a good base to work with. Straub has always been free of additives, and the label proudly says that no syrup, sugar, or salt is added. It's all barley malt, shaved corn, and hops. They've also been marking the beer with a bottling date since 1989, one of the very first in the industry to do so.

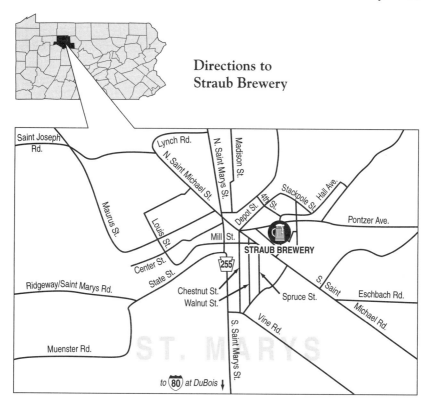

Directions to
Straub Brewery

Straub introduced Peter Straub's Special Dark in 2007, a darker, more flavorful lager, and it was a success. That's given them the impetus to launch a bold new step. "We want to start a line of craft beers," said Bill. "We don't want to reinvent ourselves; more like reintroduce ourselves. So we're not going to do ales. We don't do ales. We're Straub."

"We thought, we've got this modern lager brewery," Allyn said with a big grin. "What would Peter Straub do if he saw it? I think he'd wonder at it for about half an hour, and then he'd roll up his sleeves and say, 'Let's make some beer!' We can make all the family beers now: helles, schwarzbier, bockbier." Look for those in late 2010.

But don't expect a 90-degree turn. That's not the Straub way. "We're financially healthy, because we've never bet the farm," said Dan. "If we just take our time, we can be successful. The strong local loyalty gives us enough buffer that we can stop and think before we react. We want slow growth, not massive growth."

Some things just don't change, which brings us to the Eternal Tap. As long as you're of age, you're welcome to walk into the brewery, up the stairs to the kegging room, and over to the Eternal Tap to pour your choice of Straub, Straub Light, or Special Dark. Free. All the brewery asks is that you limit yourself to two beers (for the ever-present legal reasons) and that you remember to wash your glass. Things like the Eternal Tap make Straub a rare and priceless gem, a brewery with one foot firmly in an older, simpler time.

Opened: 1872.

Owners: The Straub family.

Brewer: Matt Allyn.

System: 160-barrel Vendome brewhouse, 45,000 barrels potential annual capacity.

2009 production: 42,000 barrels.

Tours: Monday through Friday, 9 AM to noon; please call in advance. Gift shop and Eternal Tap open Monday through Friday, 9 AM to 4:30 PM; the Tap is also open Saturday, 9 AM to 1 PM.

Take-out beer: Straub has a brewery store in front where you can get cases (including returnable bottles they had to have specially made) and kegs. They also do home delivery in the local area, including eighthbarrel kegs, which, again, they had to have made. That's what local loyalty costs; the Straub family thinks it's worth it.

Special considerations: The tour does not allow children under twelve and is not handicapped-accessible. Closed-toed shoes are required.

Parking: Small off-street lot.

Lodging in the area: Old Charm B&B, 444 Brusselles St., 814-834-9429; Towne House Inn, 138 Center St., 814-781-1556; Comfort Inn, 195 Comfort Lane, 814-834-2030; Gunners, 33 S. St. Marys St., 814-834-2161.

Area attractions: The biggest attraction in Elk County outside of Straub is Pennsylvania's only elk herd. The free-ranging herd of 350 to 400 animals is most often seen near the St. Marys airport or in the Benezette area. Elk bugling can be heard in September. The other major attraction is the **Allegheny National Forest** (814-723-5150), where you can boat, canoe, camp, cross-country ski, snowmobile, hike, fish, hunt, and picnic. A special part of the national forest is **Hearts Content Scenic Area**, a rare stand of virgin old-growth Pennsylvania forest west of Sheffield; be prepared for miles of well-graded dirt roads to get there. Visit **The Winery at Wilcox** (814-929-5598) if you need a change of pace from beer. Bradford is the home of Zippo lighters and Case knives, two extremely sturdy and attractive pieces of American technology. Visit the museum and family store (814-368-2863).

Other area beer sites: *Gunners* restaurant and bar easily has the best selection of beer in town, good food, and a relaxed and welcoming atmosphere (33 S. St. Marys St., 814-834-2161).

The Lion Brewery

700 North Pennsylvania Avenue
Wilkes-Barre, PA 18705
570-823-8801
www.lionbrewery.com

A relative newcomer among Pennsylvania regional brewers, The Lion Brewery of Wilkes-Barre was founded in 1905 as the Luzerne County Brewing Company. Ted Smulowitz purchased the brewery in 1933, anticipating big bucks in Repeal, and renamed it The Lion Brewery. The Lion outlasted local rival Stegmaier, swallowing up its labels and those of Gibbons and Bartels, two other local brewers. By the early 1980s, The Lion, with its 390-barrel brewhouse, was still brewing its own Liebotschaner Cream Ale and some American premium lagers but was best known among beer geeks for the licorice-hinted, bottom-fermented Stegmaier Porter.

The late Lee Holland, a grand old man who'd been in American brewing for years and did publicity work for The Lion, once told me that Bill Smulowitz, Ted's son, managed to keep the brewery alive by being willing to try anything. "The brewery had to make money to survive," he said, "so whatever new idea came around, Bill gave it a try." Bill said yes to some weird stuff, like cherry-flavored Red Baron (named for the local minor league ball team) and an oat-bran lager for health-obsessed beer drinkers. The brewery pioneered malt-based coolers with the briefly popular Calvin Coolers. They also made the first "clearmalt" years before Zima and Bacardi Silver came along: the bizarre, gin-flavored

Beers brewed: Year-round: Stegmaier Gold, Stegmaier Porter, Stegmaier Amber; Lionshead, Lionshead Light; Liebotschaner Cream Ale; Gibbons, Bartels. Seasonals: the Stegmaier line includes Brewhouse Bock, Midsummer White, Oktoberfest, and Winter Warmer; expect an IPA, Summer Stock, Caramel Porter, Blueberry, and Pumpkin as well. The Lion also makes a very good root beer, the Olde Philadelphia line of sodas, and makes beers under contract for a variety of labels. Leo Orlandini and the brewery were noted as Medium-Sized Brewmaster and Brewery of the Year by the GABF in 1999.

Sting Ray. Such obscure and short-lived beers are the stuff of beer dinner lectures.

Oddest, yet most successful, was malta soda. Dark, sweet, and malt-based, malta is popular in Hispanic and Caribbean markets. It is not fermented but must be made at a facility where it can be brewed, briefly aged, bottled, and pasteurized. The Lion still makes a lot of malta; it is the backbone of the business.

The Lion started contract brewing, too. Familiar names from the past twenty years, like Neuweiler's, Trupert, Hope Lager, Nude Beer, Tun Tavern, Red Bell, and others, came through The Lion, and the brewery continues to take on new brands. They have even brewed some Pabst Blue Ribbon to help that brand, now all contract-brewed, keep up with surging demand.

Between contract brewing, malta and other sodas, and their own brands, The Lion squeaked by. Smulowitz finally got tired and sold the business to an investment consortium, Quincy Partners, which in 1993 pumped new money and spirit into the brewery. Improvements to the plant were made, including the purchase of a new malt mill and a state-of-the-art lagering cellar from the old Val Blatz Brewery. New emphasis on quality control and standard procedures paid off early: The Lion scored a double gold at the Great American Beer Fest in 1994 with Liebotschaner Cream Ale and Stegmaier 1857. Stegmaier Porter became an honest, top-fermenting porter, with a resultant boost in character that is a pleasant surprise to beer snobs.

The brewery also tried a craft-brewed approach. They experimented with a line called Brewery Hill (although the brewery sits in one of the lower points in the area), then tried again under the Pocono name. The Pale Ale was a bargain: bright, aromatic, a fridge-filler. The Lion found more success with seasonals under the old Stegmaier name: bock, Oktoberfest, witbier, and a winter warmer (they actually barrel-aged a small amount recently). I was told that an increased focus on craft-type beers was part of the brewery's strategy.

But the big hit, beerwise, has been Lionshead. Make no mistake about it: Lionshead is aimed at the cost-conscious beer drinker. It initially debuted at $10 a case, though that's gone up a bit since recent increases in malt costs. Still, truckloads of Lionshead leave the brewery every week. "It's just flying out," brewery operations director Leo Orlandini told me. "Even more so since we started doing draft in 2008."

The Pick: I have to go with my heart here: I love the Liebotschaner Cream Ale and hope the plans for it to return succeed. It's a very Pennsylvania kind of beer and so drinkable: smooth, creamy, just a bit sweet, with a nice, clean break at the finish. Look for Lieb!

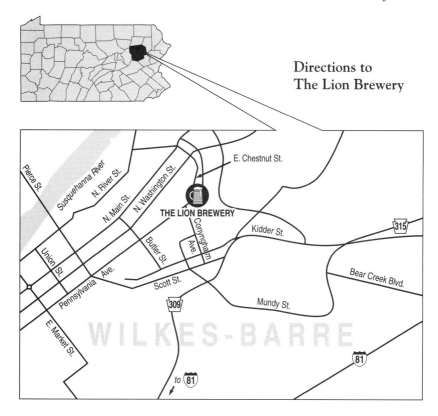

Directions to
The Lion Brewery

More changes are coming. The brewery went private in 1999 in a management buyout, and more money was invested in renovating the physical plant: new grain silos and, more important, a new brewkettle with fully automated controls. That was a big day, as the huge kettle flew through a beautiful blue sky into the open roof of the old brewhouse. It was also the day I first tasted the Stegmaier bock: malty, smooth, and that great mix of sweet and dry.

The owners built up the value of the brewery by quite a bit and sold at a nice profit in November 2007. The new owner, Cliff Risell, has years of experience in the soda business and has continued the physical improvement: a kegging line, a big centrifuge in the filter room, a 10-gallon pilot brewery, new analysis equipment in the lab, and—finally!—a canning line that can handle all kinds of cans for both beer and soft drinks.

Risell has the solid sales and marketing background that is, in my opinion, the missing piece The Lion needs. Why? Walk into any bar in the Wyoming Valley and ask for a Stegmaier; chances are you won't find it. Ask for the local beer and they'll hand you a Yuengling. You have to have the local market on your side; that's one lesson from the Yuengling experience that most people overlook.

"Local sales are going to be a new focus," Cliff told me. We were in the brewery taproom with Leo Orlandini, Bob Klinetob, and most of the brewing staff on a Friday afternoon, sampling some test batches of Stegmaier seasonals, a batch of Liebotschaner Cream Ale (Lieb's supposed to be coming back), and Lionshead. "We changed the sales force, we have a new marketing team."

Great to hear, Cliff. Add that to Leo's news that the brewery's output is a little over 30 percent beer—the highest it's been in years—and all that new equipment, and it's looking like a whole new Lion. If you're in the area, stop in a bar and ask for a Stegmaier.

Opened: 1905 (Stegmaier Brewery, later absorbed by The Lion, opened in 1857).

Owner: Cliff Risell.

Brewers: Leo Orlandini, Bob Klinetob, Darel Matthews.

System: 390-barrel Briggs brewhouse, 500,000 barrels potential annual capacity.

2009 production: 480,000 barrels (including soda).

Tours: Saturday at 1 PM (please call ahead or check Web site for reservations). Not handicapped-accessible.

Take-out beer: None available.

Parking: Free on-site parking available.

Lodging in the area: Best Western East Mountain Inn, 2400 East End Blvd., Wilkes-Barre, 570-822-1011; Frederick Stegmaier Mansion B&B (yes, that Stegmaier, and you can stay in the Brewmaster Room), 304 S. Franklin St., 570-823-9372; Bischwind B&B in Bear Creek, on Route 115, 3 miles south of the Pennsylvania Turnpike, 570-472-3820.

Area attractions: The *River Common* is a park along the Susquehanna in the center of Wilkes-Barre, between the river and the levees that protect the city from flooding. Finally completed, the Common contains an amphitheater, two fishing piers, great views of the river and the city's bridges, and miles of paved trails. It is a gem, and it hosts the city's annual River Fest on the third weekend of June. (More information, including an events calendar, at www.rivercommon.org.) Feeling sporting? The *Wachovia Arena* (255 Highland Park Blvd., 570-970-6700, www.wachoviaarena.com) is the home of the Wilkes-Barre Scranton Penguins (AHL) and the Wilkes-Barre Scranton Pioneers (AFL) and hosts concerts and other events as well. The Scranton/Wilkes-Barre Yankees play at **PNC Field** (235 Montage Mountain Rd., Moosic, 570-969-2255, www.swbyankees .com), and it's a beauty of a ballpark. *Snö Mountain* (formerly Montage; 1000 Montage Mountain Rd., Scranton, 800-GOT-SNOW, www.snomtn.com) is right across the valley, with the ski trails you can see from I-81, and they've got it all: bunny slopes to black diamonds, tube runs, snowboard terrain parks, Snö Cove waterpark in the summer, and a half-mile zipline ride. The big news in the Wyoming Valley, though, is the casino. **Mohegan Sun at Pocono Downs** (1280 Highway 315, Wilkes-Barre, 888-WIN-IN-PA, www .poconodowns.com) has thousands of slot machines and "virtual table games" (video versions of poker, blackjack, and roulette), live harness racing from March to November, restaurants ranging from a Ruth's Chris steakhouse to a Hot Dog Hall of Fame, even shopping. Not much in the way of beer (beer's not for high rollers, I guess), but there is a Crossing Vineyards outlet. Call the Luzerne County Tourist Promotion Agency (888-905-2872) or the Greater Wilkes-Barre Chamber of Commerce (570-823-2101) for more suggestions.

Other area beer sites: We got a great recommendation from Leo one time: **Dukey's Café** (785 N. Pennsylvania Ave., 570-270-6718) is just down the street and has fresh-as-a-daisy Stegmaier and some really good bar food. It's not the dive it once was . . . but we still stop there. A classic, **Elmer Sudds** (475 E. Northampton St., 570-829-SUDD), has reopened under new management and seems to be getting its mojo back. The **Arena Bar and Grill** (380 Coal St., 570-970-8829) is where the Black Rock brewpub was; the parking spots are still tight, but they've got 50 drafts and 250 bottles. I regret not getting to **Dugan's Pub** (385 Main St., Luzerne, 570-283-0153). MyBeerBuzz.com's Bil Corcoran says Charlie Dugan's is a solid Irish place with good craft taps, outstanding bar food, and a great sense of humor. And there's a ton of new places! Beer bars in the Wyoming Valley have simply exploded in the last three years. Sticking to the lower valley, where The Lion and Breaker Brewing are, you'll want to hit these places: **Sabatini's Pizza** (1925 Wyoming Ave., Exeter, 570-693-2270) has good eats, a nice spicy sauce on the pies, and you can drink their big selection of beers with dinner (there's no actual bar), but they also have a tremendous take-out business with beers you don't see many places even in Philly. **AuRants** (941 Main St., Duryea, 570-762-5445) is not that big, tucked in between the tracks and the river, but makes up for it with exceptional beers, boldly planned and executed food, and a great vibe—classy but comfortable. (AuRants is also one of the very few area places still getting kegs in from Bullfrog; worth checking on.) **River Street Ale House** (1575 River Rd., Pittston, 570-602-6374) offers a fat stretch of taps in a sports bar setting: more proof that craft beer is everywhere. The **Anthracite Café** (804 Scott St., Wilkes-Barre, 570-822-4677) is a comfortable neighborhood tappie that keeps things interesting by supporting the locals; look for Breaker and Lion beers here, along with good crafts you won't see every other place. Bil tells me **Madison's** (396 E. Washington St., Nanticoke, 570-735-2654) started as a vodka bar and still is, but they've been upping the beer ante with Breaker taps and some good bottles, and the food's quite nice. **Bart and Urby's** (119 S. Main St., Wilkes-Barre, 570-970-9570) was the only place I've ever been in Wilkes-Barre that made me feel underdressed; kind of refreshing to get good beers in an upscale bar like this. It's bustling on weekends, busy with a good-looking, good-natured crowd of varied ages and styles. Great place to have a craft beer and people-watch. **Krugel's Deli** (720 Wilkes-Barre Township Blvd. [Route 309], Wilkes-Barre, 570-829-BEER) has a whopping cooler of bottles and lip-smacking sandwiches.

D. G. Yuengling & Son

Fifth and Mahantongo Streets, Pottsville, PA 17901
Brewery phone: 570-622-4141
Tour information: 570-628-4890
www.yuengling.com

Andrew Jackson was inviting all his friends to the White House when David Yuengling started brewing at his Eagle Brewery in Pottsville in 1829. The brewery burned later that year, and the new brewery opened up in 1830 on the slope of Sharps Mountain at Fifth and Mahantongo Streets.

Brewing has been going on there ever since, making D. G. Yuengling and Son America's oldest brewery, and one of the country's twenty oldest family-owned companies. The brewery is in its fifth generation of family ownership, and the sixth generation is settling nicely into the harness, even as the brewery continues an amazing three decades of unlikely growth. Let's get a bit more of the history before tackling that.

Beers brewed: Yuengling Traditional Lager, Light Lager, Premium, Lord Chesterfield Ale, Porter, Yuengling Light, Black & Tan.

Why did David Yuengling settle in Pottsville? There was money to be made. Anthracite coal made Pottsville the Houston of the day, and mining was thirsty work. The Phillips Van Heusen shirt company started in Pottsville. Coal mining and textiles made this a prosperous industrial town, and Yuengling's brewery grew along with it.

"America's oldest brewery" should make you wonder: "Did they brew during Prohibition?" Under the leadership of Frank Yuengling, who ran the brewery from 1899 through 1961, Yuengling made it through the Noble Experiment in pretty good shape. They started a dairy (Yuengling ice cream was made in the building across the street until 1986), opened large dance halls in Philadelphia and New York, and yes, they never stopped brewing. While other brewers did things like heating beer to drive off the alcohol, Yuengling invested in an expensive vacuum distillation process that made it possible to brew Juvo, the best-tasting near beer in Schuylkill County. Juvo outsold the competitors by a large margin and kept the brewery staff employed.

When Prohibition was repealed, Yuengling was sitting pretty. The dairy business provided a fleet of refrigerated trucks and a steady cash flow, the successful near-beer business meant they had retained almost all their trained workers, and the dance halls had made them a lot of friends in big markets. On the day of Repeal, Frank turned off the vacuum distillation machine and sent a truckload of Yuengling's new Winner beer to FDR at the White House. Happy days were here again.

They didn't last forever. By the 1970s, anthracite mining was folding and the textile companies had moved in search of cheaper labor. As the area lost jobs, the brewery was in trouble, operating from payroll to payroll some months. The national megabrewers were pushing hard to conquer all markets, and breweries like Yuengling were in the way.

In the end, two things saved the brewery. The dogged loyalty of Schuylkill County beer drinkers made for a steady demand that sustained the brewery on a week-to-week basis, and America's Bicentennial in 1976 raised interest in American history and made the brewery's status as the country's oldest a bankable quality. There was a slow rise in sales from 1976 through the 1980s.

Dick Yuengling Jr., the current owner, didn't start at the brewery. He started driving a beer delivery truck for a local wholesaler in 1973, then took a chance and bought a wholesale-retail beer business in a nearby town, selling Rolling Rock and Pabst. He was in the beer business. "What the hell else could I do?" he recalled. "I didn't know anything but beer!"

By 1985, production at the brewery was down to 137,000 barrels a year, and when Dick went to pick up beer for his business, the workers were telling him he had to come back. His father was getting old and starting to suffer from Alzheimer's, which would eventually claim his life. "They knew it was pretty bleak without a family member taking over," Dick said. So he got the money together and bought the brewery from his father, the traditional Yuengling family way of "inheriting" the business.

The Pick: I prefer a do-it-yourself black and tan mixed from Porter and Lord Chesterfield Ale. The Chet is Yuengling's hoppiest beer and cuts through the Porter more sharply than the Premium. Get a big mug and a few bottles of each beer and find the ratio you prefer.

"When I bought it, a lot of the business was Old German," he said, referring to the bargain-brand beer the brewery made then. "I didn't get into this to sell $4 cases of beer." He decided to buck the trend of the industry—streamlining product lines—and add beers to what was then a varied lineup. Besides the mainstream Yuengling Premium there was the dark, roasty Celebrated Pottsville Porter and the hoppy Lord Chesterfield Ale. Dick and then-brewmaster Ray Norbert added Yuengling Light "because we had to," Dick explained, "and it's a good light beer."

He also pushed the brewery's history and nonnational underdog appeal. A key player, David Casinelli, was hired out of a Philadelphia beer wholesaling family to head sales and marketing efforts. Yuengling started to appear in Philadelphia markets.

At first it was the Yuengling Black & Tan, a premixed blend of Porter and Premium. People in Schuylkill and Berks Counties had been mixing Yuengling Porter with Premium or Lord Chesterfield for years to create a custom-made black and tan. The brewers saw they had a winner. They premixed Porter and Premium, put it in a snazzy 16-ounce can, and released it on the market.

The market was scared. "Everyone cringed," said Casinelli. "A 16-ounce can? Kramer Beverage in South Jersey took two pallets. They were gone in a week, so he ordered six more. He called back the next week and wanted half a trailer load. We didn't have it!" Black & Tan pushed the limits of the brewery's capacity.

But it was Dick's next project that really blew the walls out of the brewery—literally. Yuengling Traditional Lager was a little darker, a little more flavorful, and a lot less national than mainstream beers, and Lager taps cropped up everywhere in southeastern Pennsylvania. When they started on the Philadelphia market, "We were doing maybe 100

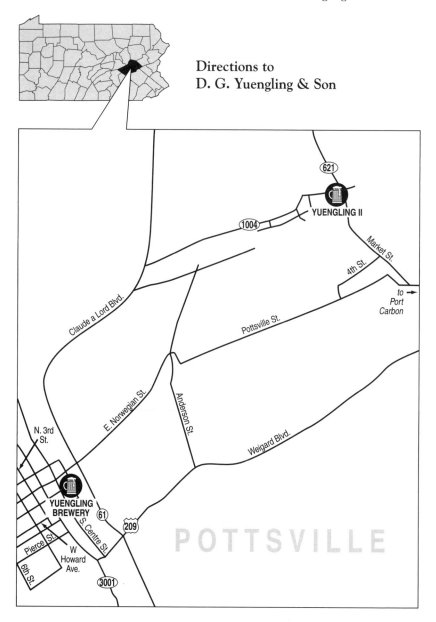

Directions to
D. G. Yuengling & Son

[half-barrel kegs] a month," Dick said. "When we finished, we were doing 10,000."

People in the business told Dick that the premium segment was dead; it was light beer that was the big seller now. "I said, 'Don't bury the segment just yet,'" he told me, grinning a shark's smile. The brewery went to high-gravity brewing for the first time, they put in their first expansion in decades—"By the time we had it in," Dick said with a laugh, "we needed more!" They went to seven days a week and two shifts, they were up to 600,000 barrels capacity . . . and while Budweiser was beginning a slump that continues today, and light beer achieved ascendancy in the greater market, Yuengling couldn't keep up with the demand for their "full-calorie" Lager.

After years of soul searching, in 1998 Dick made the decision to build a second brewery to meet the apparently unending demand for his beer. The new brewery was sited about a mile away in an industrial park by a rail line—something they'd have loved to have at the original brewery—and designed for a capacity of 1.1 million barrels. "Everyone was closing breweries," Casinelli said. "[Industry analyst] Bob Weinberg was the only one who thought it was a smart move."

Shortly after making that decision, Dick took an even bigger plunge. Stroh Brewing, trundling toward dissolution, had shut down a 1.5-million-barrel-capacity brewery in Tampa, Florida. Dick and his staff flew down and looked it over. They weighed the still-growing demand for Yuengling and all the untouched markets on the borders of Pennsylvania against the time until the new Pottsville brewery came online. A big ready-to-run brewery would solve a lot of problems, so in April 1999 they bought it. They hired back most of the laid-off Stroh workers and were brewing Yuengling in a few months, while work on the new brewery in Pennsylvania continued on schedule and under budget.

All three breweries are bustling these days. They have to: Yuengling grew again in 2009, by 11.8 percent, while the beer market as a whole declined by 2.2 percent, the worst year for beer since the 1950s. Today they're neck-and-neck with Boston Beer Company, both just over 2 million barrels in sales. It's an improbable scenario: the hardscrabble brewery that almost closed forty years ago, and the once-tiny craft brewer that started without even owning a brewery, now solidly in place as the two largest American-owned breweries. (Anheuser-Busch, Miller, and Coors are currently foreign-owned; Pabst is American-owned but doesn't own any brewing facilities. Both Yuengling and Boston Beer brew all their beer in-house.) It makes me proud that both of them are making most of their beer in Pennsylvania, only 30 miles apart.

Will success ruin Yuengling? Will the company cheapen the beer, sell out, lose the character that has made them an endearing success story? If you think that, you don't know Dick Yuengling very well. He is committed to running a regional brewery and has no national aspirations. They're moving at a steady pace and taking the opportunity to start doing some fun stuff like the reintroduction of Yuengling Bock, the brewery's first seasonal release in many years.

Success looks good on the oldest brewery in America, and Dick's daughters, the next generation, don't intend to change that. It's going to be their turn to run things at some point. I asked Dick if he was going to hold them to the family tradition and make them buy the business. He said, deadpan, "Yeah, I haven't really saved much." Then he laughed. When the time comes, they're going to have to come up with a lot more money than their dad did!

Opened: 1829.

Owner: Richard L. Yuengling Jr.; chief operating officer, David A. Casinelli.

Brewers: James Buehler, Pottsville brewery; John Callahan, Mill Creek brewery.

System: 450-barrel Enerfab brewhouse, 600,000 barrels annual capacity. (The Tampa brewery has a capacity of 1.5 million barrels; the St. Clair facility, 1.1 million barrels.)

2009 total production (all three breweries): Approximately 2 million barrels.

Tours: Monday through Friday, 10 AM and 1:30 PM; Saturday from April to December, 11 AM, noon, and 1 PM. This is one of the best brewery tours in the country. Others may be more polished or more intimate, but few take you right down onto the floor of a hard-working sizable brewery. Tour includes two complimentary beers in the uniquely handsome brewery taproom. Gift shop open Monday through Friday, 9 AM to 4 PM. You can also tour the Tampa brewery (11111 N. 30th St., Tampa, FL, 813-972-8529).

Take-out beer: None available.

Extras: The only special event at Yuengling is an unofficial one: the First Day of Beer Season. In upstate Pennsylvania, deer hunting is almost a religion, and most public schools have declared the Monday after Thanksgiving—the opening of deer season—a day off, since most of the male students and teachers, and a few females, don't show up anyway. Some nonhunting teachers from Reading began coming out for a brewery tour that Monday, and the event has grown—but not too much. After all, it is deer season!

Special considerations: Kids will enjoy Posty's birch beer in the taproom. This locally made soda is traditional and delicious, a good choice for designated drivers, too. Kids also are allowed on tours; we took my son through on his first birthday. The tour is not handicapped-accessible. Closed-toed shoes are required.

Parking: On-street parking. Don't use the church lot on the far side of the street, or your car will be ticketed or towed.

Lodging in the area: Ramada Inn, 101 S. Progress Ave., Pottsville, 570-622-4600; The Partridge House B&B, 315 S. Centre St., Pottsville, 570-622-8388; Holiday Inn Express, 958 Schuylkill Mall, Frackville, 570-874-1700; The Stone House B&B, 16 Dock St., Schuylkill Haven, 570-385-2115.

Area attractions: The murals you'll see on the brewery tour were done by local artists, and there are more throughout the town. A walking tour of them is available at the Downtown Pottsville Web site (www.downtownpottsville.org). Then hit the road for other attractions. *Jim Thorpe*, Pennsylvania, named for the famous American Indian athlete, has a restored Victorian-era downtown, with shops and taverns, that's great for an afternoon stroll. You'll also find an extensive model train layout (41 Susquehanna St., 570-325-2248) and whitewater rafting expeditions (*Pocono Whitewater Rafting*, 800-944-8392). Tour coal baron *Asa Parker's Victorian mansion* (570-325-3229), which is on the hill overlooking downtown. His son Harry's adjacent mansion is open as a B&B (570-325-8566). For the more outdoorsy types, the *Hawk Mountain Sanctuary* (east of Drehersville on Hawk Mountain Rd., 610-756-6961) is located at the convergence of the autumn migration routes of numerous raptors. The fall months offer unparalleled views of hundreds of hawks, eagles, and other birds of prey.

Other area beer sites: *Maroons* (556 N. Centre St., 570-628-GOAL) is what I've been looking for in the thirty years that I've been going to Pottsville to tour the brewery: a great bar in Pottsville. This classy sports bar, named for Pottsville's NFL football team from the 1920s (really!), has clean-as-a-whistle taps of Yuengling's beers and some PA craft bottles, good bar food, and a full set of plasma screens for sports. Good place to get your Yueng on. The *Porter House Grille* (in the Ramada, see above) claims the county's largest draft selection and sizzling steaks. The *Wooden Keg Tavern* (1 W. Caroline Ave., St. Clair, 570-429-1909) is said to have been a hangout of the Molly Maguires, the Irish coal miners who fought for labor rights. It's a piece of history—with wings and beer! The *Kempton Hotel* (610-756-6588), across from the feed mill in Kempton, is a real find. Three ceiling murals painted by talented local artists depict Kempton history, "the pageant of United States history," and the life of Christ. The snappy bartenders serve brilliantly fresh Yuengling and good regional food.

D. G. Yuengling & Son, Mill Creek Brewery

310 Mill Creek Avenue, Pottsville, PA 17901
570-622-4141
www.yuengling.com

There's not a lot to say here that hasn't already been said in the previous entry. The new brewery isn't open for tours (it took me almost ten years to get in) and probably won't ever be . . . until it's also 150-odd years old, maybe.

I can tell you about the place: it's really big and really modern. Lead brewer John Callahan took me around and showed me anything I wanted to see. It couldn't be less like the old brewery: it's spacious, it's bright, and it's on flat ground!

I asked John how much of the brewery's output was the flagship Lager. "About 90 percent," he said, following it with a fervent "Thank God for Lager!" Lager was what had kept the place open, he told me, the miracle that brought jobs to Pottsville that paid $20 an hour with 100 percent medical coverage. John's probably not the only guy in town who has a special spot in his heart for this beer.

Yuengling Traditional Lager is a phenomenon. "The Light Lager continues to grow," Casinelli said. "The Ale and Porter are doing well. But Lager opens the doors. It's the only brand that can give the majors fits when we enter a new market, and if we don't get some points in the first year, it's a failure."

The best evidence is how people order it in Pennsylvania: "Gimme a lager." Hey, buddy, you want to be more specific: Bud Light, Coors Light, Molson, Heineken, Corona . . . they're *all* lagers! But not here. If you call for "Lager!" you'll get a Yuengling, even in a craft beer bar (and you'd be surprised how many of them have a stash of bottles in the cooler).

I asked how that got started. Casinelli pointed at Dick and said, "Genius." Dick laughed. "I said, 'Just call it Lager,'" he explained. "There were no focus groups. Our name's hard to say, so just say, 'Lager.' At the end of the day, the whole thing, we did it without consultants, or marketers, or public relations. You go in and put a bottle of Lager on the bar. That's it; that's what we have."

Dick's daughter Jennifer works at the new brewery, and her sister Wendy is learning brewing. They're getting a good grounding in beer, and maybe this new brewery is the place to learn about the new Yuengling. Not "new" because the beer's different, or because they use marketing consultants and slick sales software; new because Yuengling is a success, a force to be reckoned with.

This company has faced all kinds of challenges in its 180-plus-year history: fire, untimely deaths, Prohibition, competition from huge national breweries, and managing wildcat growth. Successfully running it from a position of strength is just one more hurdle. The Yuengling family has run the race pretty well so far; that's the way to bet.

Ales and Lagers

If you're going to go to the breweries in this book, you'll have to know how to talk shop with the bartenders and tour guides and not embarrass yourself on the tour. First off, beer is any fermented beverage made from malted barley, usually with an addition of hops. The two main types of beer are ales and lagers.

What's the difference between the two? It's quite simple: two different yeasts. These have a number of small differences, the most important of which is that the optimum temperature for fermentation and aging is higher for ale yeasts (in the 60s F) than for lager yeasts (in the 40s F). That's more than just a thermostat setting. The warmer operating temperature of ale yeast encourages a faster, more vigorous fermentation that creates aromatic compounds known as phenols and esters. These can give ale-fermented beers aromas such as melon, banana, raisin, clove, and vanilla. (I call these aromas "alefruit.")

On the other hand, the cooler lager fermentation produces a very clean aroma and flavor palette. Lagers generally have purer malt and hop characteristics. A lager brewer will tell you that there's nowhere to hide when you make lager beer; the unadorned nature of the beer makes flaws stand out immediately.

I like to think of the two yeasts in terms of jungles and pine forests. Warm ale fermentations are like lush jungles—exotic arrays of flavors, splendid in their diversity. By comparison, cold lager fermentations are more like northern pine forests—intense, focused, and pure.

Among small brewers in America, ale brewers outnumber lager brewers by more than ten to one. Given that lagers are by far the most popular beers in the world, how did this come to be? Tom Pastorius of Penn Brewing put it quite simply: "More ale is being made because it's cheaper, easier, and more flexible." Hard words, perhaps, but the facts bear them out.

After lagers are fermented, they undergo an extended aging period of at least three weeks at low temperatures. The cooling and the tank time required add energy costs and decrease turnover. In the same amount of time, it would be possible to put twice as much ale through those tanks. Add the energy and labor costs of the more complicated decoction brewing process used for some lagers, and you wind up with a product that costs substantially more to brew than ales but has to be priced the same. No wonder there are more ale brewers!

When it comes to lager, Pennsylvania has been blessed with some real pros. The five surviving regional brewers are all about lagers, but we also have one of the greatest concentrations of small lager brewers in the country. Stoudt's was built on lagers, Victory makes excellent classic examples, and Penn founded their business squarely on their Pilsner, Dark, and Gold lagers. Lancaster makes great pilsners and festbier, the Iron Hill brewpubs all make lagers, and even the tiny Bube's and Berwick breweries proudly brew lagers. By any measure, these breweries include some of the very best lager brewers in the country. How did we get so lucky?

In a word, ethnicity. It's no coincidence that the areas of the United States where old brewers survived and new lager brewers sprang up are those that welcomed vast numbers of German, Scandinavian, and Eastern European immigrants. Where those lager lovers settled—Pennsylvania, upstate New York, Wisconsin, and Minnesota—is where lager brewing thrives today.

American beer enthusiasts are slowly coming around to microbrewed lagers. Carol Stoudt attributed their hesitation to a megabrew backlash: "People who have had nothing but bland lagers for years want the extremes: heavy-handed hops, fruit beers, even smoked beers. As their palates become more sophisticated, they'll come around to appreciate the subtleties of a good lager beer." If you haven't had some of Pennsylvania's fine fresh lager beers, be sure to put one or more of these brewers on your list. Put a little sophistication on your palate!

Philadelphia

W. C. Fields wrote his own tongue-in-cheek epitaph: "On the whole, I'd rather be in Philadelphia." Well, me too, W. C. When my wife and I moved to Bucks County in 1991, we mostly stayed out of Philadelphia. What with the city's poor financial condition, the lingering air of disaster from the MOVE battle in which the city bombed one of its own neighborhoods, and the One Meridian Plaza skyscraper fire less than two months after we got there, there didn't seem to be any good reasons to go.

I've learned differently, and I have Ed Rendell to thank. The vibrancy that was missing for years is back, thanks largely to Fast Eddie. When he took office as mayor in 1992, the former district attorney began a whirlwind of action reminiscent of FDR's 100 Days. His landslide reelection gave the city's seal of approval to his work. The *New York Times* called his tenure "the most stunning turnaround in recent urban history." After two terms, the baton was passed to longtime Philly politician John Street just as the last remnants of the long-standing One Meridian Plaza skyscraper fire were finally cleared away; corruption crusader Michael Nutter is currently the man in the mayor's office. Rendell has gone on to become governor of Pennsylvania (the first Philadelphia mayor to do so since 1914), but his stamp remains on the city.

Rendell was well known as an avid fan of Philly's major contribution to American fare, the cheesesteak. Local papers printed plenty of photos showing his big, happy mouth wrapped around these hot, greasy beauties. Check out some classics at Pat's Steaks or Gino's, right across from each other at Ninth and Passayunk. Another well-known politician, Bill Clinton, stood between the two places during a rally, alternately munching one from each—safe politics and not a bad lunch! The city's other staple, the soft pretzel, is available all over and should be eaten with a good squirt of yellow mustard.

Philadelphia is one of the great restaurant centers of the United States. Proprietor-chef Georges Perrier's **Le Bec Fin** (1523 Walnut St.) is one of the best restaurants anywhere in the United States, and the prix fixe lunch is a major bargain. Two celebrity chefs also have restaurants here: "Iron Chef" Masaharu Morimoto's eponymous bastion of Japanese fusion cuisine (723 Chestnut St.), and Jose Garces's string of restaurants: the **Amada** tapas bar (217 Chestnut St.); **Tinto** wine bar (114 S. 20th St.); **Distrito** Mexican café (3945 Chestnut St.); **Chifa**, serving Peruvian-Cantonese fusion cuisine (707 Chestnut St.); and the two newest: **Village Whiskey** (more on that below) and **Garces Trading Company**, an upscale grocery–café with a small state-run wine store (1111 Locust St.). You can also sample the fare of the city's past at **City Tavern** (138 S. Second St.), a restored historic site, where an increasingly (and deservedly) well-known Walter Staib successfully combines eighteenth-century colonial fare with the cuisine of the Black Forest and serves Yards Ales of the Revolution.

But for the beer lover, Philadelphia has three treasures: restaurants devoted to Belgian beer. The oldest, **Bridgid's** (726 N. 24th St., near the art museum), is a small, warmly welcoming bistro. It has an impressive cellar of vintage beers, draft beers, and a very reasonably priced menu of delicious entrées and desserts. **Eulogy** (136 Chestnut St.), a relative newcomer in Old City, caught on fast with a good menu and beer list right out of the gate. Finally, **Monk's Café** (264 S. 16th St.) is one of the very best beer bars in America, with a bunch of Belgian taps (including their own Belgian-brewed Monk's Café Sour Ale) and a ridiculous stack of bottled Belgian beers aging in the cellar. The must-have dishes are mussels steamed in Belgian beers such as Rodenbach or *gueuze* lambic, served with *frites* and delicious French rolls, and steak marinated in Trappist ale. Get on the mailing list for Monk's fabulous, extreme monthly beer dinners; beers make their American debut, sometimes their world debut, at these dinners, usually attended by the brewers in question.

But you didn't come to Philadelphia just to drink beer and eat! This is the heart of American independence, home of the Liberty Bell and Benjamin Franklin and the birthplace of the Declaration of Independence and the Constitution. At **Independence National Historical Park** (215-597-8974, www.nps.gov/inde), visit Carpenter's Hall, Congress Hall, Independence Hall, Franklin Court, and the Liberty Bell Pavilion. The huge new **National Constitution Center** (in the block between Arch and Race Streets and Fifth and Sixth Streets, 866-917-1787, www.constitutioncenter.org) has interactive exhibits; Signers Hall, where lifesize statues of the founding fathers stand for handy photo opportunities; and the emotional, moving "Freedom Rising" live presentation. The **Betsy Ross House** (239 Arch St., www.betsyrosshouse.org) has been restored as a working-class house of the colonial period. **Christ Church** (Second and Church Streets, www.christchurchphila.org) contains William Penn's baptismal font and was the church of fifteen Declaration signers. Benjamin Franklin and four other signers are buried in the Christ Church burial ground at Fifth and Arch Streets.

Other famous people lived in Philadelphia as well. The peripatetic Edgar Allan Poe lived at 532 N. Seventh St. for a year. You can tour the house, and a library and audiovisual program are next door (www.nps .gov/edal). Louisa May Alcott was born in Germantown; visit the **Germantown Historical Society**'s museum (5501 Germantown Ave., www.germantownhistory.org). At the **National Shrine of St. John Neumann** (1019 N. Fifth St., www.stjohnneumann.org), the first American male saint's remains can be viewed in a glass casket under the main altar.

Philadelphia also has a number of fine museums. The **Philadelphia Museum of Art** (at the end of the Benjamin Franklin Parkway, 215-763-8100, www.philamuseum.org) houses one of the world's best collections. And yes, that's where Sylvester Stallone did his dance in *Rocky*. Just down the parkway is the **Franklin Institute Science Museum** (222 N. 20th St., www.fi.edu), an extensive display of hands-on science exhibits. You could easily spend a day in these two museums, but I would also send you down to the river to see the **Independence Seaport Museum** (Penn's Landing, 215-925-5439, www.phillyseaport.org). You can visit this museum of Philadelphia's maritime heritage and crawl around the USS *Becuna*, a World War II–era submarine, and the USS *Olympia*, Admiral Dewey's flagship from the Spanish-American War (sadly, the *Olympia* may be too badly damaged to continue as an exhibit; check the Web site for the latest updates).

Philadelphia hosts a number of annual events, starting on January 1 with the **Mummers Parade**, a unique folk-art festival put on by associations much like the "crews" of New Orleans's Mardi Gras. The elaborate feathered outfits and string bands (mostly banjos and saxophones) are impossible to describe concisely. Go, freeze, enjoy. The **Philadelphia Flower Show** draws flower fanciers to the Convention Center in early March. May brings the **Dad Vail Regatta** on the Schuylkill, a happy, exciting mob scene. (Philly almost lost this event in 2009, but it's solidly placed here again.) June now brings **Philly Beer Week** (see A word about . . . Beer Festivals on page 298).

You might also have heard that we're no longer a town of losers: the Phightin' Phils brought home a World Series championship in 2008, and it was sweet. The family and I watched the victory parade from City Hall (after I ducked into McGillin's for a pre-parade Yuengling on my way to meet them—hoping to start a new tradition of my own), along with more than a million other proud Pennsylvanians. The new *Citizen's Bank Park* must have been part of the reason, not to mention the best-in-MLB beer selection: We've got a ton of local beers, and not just hiding in one specialty section either! Catch a Phils game (www.phillies.com) and see what it's like to actually get a beer you like at the game. If you want to try Philadelphia's new sport, the *Philadelphia Union Major League Soccer Team* (www.philadelphiaunion.com) kicked off its first season in June 2010 at the new PPL Park in Chester; can't say anything about the beer, but the support's been huge.

There's so much more. Go to www.visitphilly.com and get the full package of travel information. You'll have a great time. And don't forget the cheesesteaks!

Back in the third edition, I decided that it made more sense to throw everything together in this section for Philadelphia, as more and more great beer bars have spread across the city, and you wouldn't want to miss any of them, plus it's easier to have all the city's attractions and lodging suggestions together in one list. So the **Lodging**, **Area attractions**, and **Other area beer sites** for Philadelphia are all consolidated here.

Lodging in the area: Crown Plaza Philadelphia West, 4100 Presidential Blvd., 215-477-0200; Comfort Inn, 100 N. Christopher Columbus Blvd., 215-627-7900; Holiday Inn Independence Mall, 400 Arch St., 215-923-8660; Penn's View Inn, a historic hotel in a building dating from 1828, 14 N. Front St., 215-922-7600; Radisson Plaza Warwick Hotel, 1701 Locust St., 215-735-6000; Chestnut Hill Hotel, 8229 Germantown Ave., 215-242-5905.

Area attractions: Independence Mall and all the historic buildings and exhibits are described in the introduction to this section. If you're looking for some "real Philly," head down to the open-air *Ninth Street Market* (www.9thstreetitalianmarket.com), also called the Italian Market, which runs south from the 700 block of Ninth Street. The market is open Monday through Saturday mornings, starting around 8 AM. You can find meat, great cheeses, cookware, olives, pastries, fresh fish, and produce—but don't touch the produce; it's a market tradition that the seller picks it for you. *South Street* is Philly's answer to Greenwich Village. Take some time to walk around and shop, then maybe stop over at the *Dark Horse*

(421 S. Second St., 215-928-9307) for its great single malt and tap beer selection, or **Bridget Foy's** (200 South St., 215-922-1813), an excellent place to sip a cool beer and people-watch. Both are on Headhouse Square at Second and South.

If you're at the big, beautiful fountain at Logan Circle on the Benjamin Franklin Parkway, it's only a ten-minute walk to the **Philadelphia Museum of Art** (26th St. on the Parkway, 215-763-8100, www.philamuseum.org; Renoir, Monet, Cezanne, Van Gogh, Rubens—they're right here in Philadelphia); the **Franklin Institute Science Museum** (20th St. and Benjamin Franklin Parkway, 215-448-1200, www.fi.edu), the **Please Touch Museum** (in its new location at 4231 Avenue of the Republic, 215-581-3181), a very popular children's science museum; and the **Rodin Museum** (Benjamin Franklin Parkway and 22nd St., 215-763-8100, www.rodin museum.org), with the largest collection of Rodin originals outside of Paris. You're also not far from one of Philadelphia's odder museums, the **Mütter Museum** (19 S. 22nd St., 215-563-3737, www.collphy phil.org) of the College of Physicians of Philadelphia, with its displays of disease, genetic oddities, and medical grotesqueries. It's as unsettling as it sounds; use your judgment on visiting! Following the Benjamin Franklin Parkway past the art museum will lead you into **Fairmount Park**, Philly's immense greenway. There you'll find **Boathouse Row**, the Victorian boathouses of the city's sculling teams, decorated with strung lights that sparkle across the Schuylkill. Also in the park are the restored Fairmount homes (215-684-7922, www .fairmountpark.org), including **Strawberry Mansion**, the largest of the homes, and Cedar Grove, an eighteenth-century Quaker farmhouse. If you go straight across the Schuylkill on Girard Avenue, you will see the signs for the **Philadelphia Zoo** (3400 Girard Ave., 215-243-1100, www.philadelphiazoo.org), which features a children's zoo, a primate house, and a captive balloon for sightseeing.

In the heart of the city stands **City Hall**, a "hollow square" French Second Empire style building, unmistakable with its 37-foot statue of William Penn on the top, and gleaming now after a sandblasting facelift. It is the largest city hall in America. Walk down to the **Reading Terminal Market** (12th and Filbert Streets, www .readingterminalmarket.org), the other of Philadelphia's great markets, a bit touristy but no less real for that, with stands selling fish, flowers, meat, cheese, produce, spices, and Bassett's ice cream (one of the city's great secrets), and studded with great little restaurants cooking with fresh food from the market. If you want something a bit more exotic, Philly's **Chinatown** wraps around the Convention Center north of the market.

Main Street of Manayunk is a very happening strip of shops, bars, and restaurants, pleasant to stop in or stroll along, and **Manayunk Brewing** is right on it. Just wander on down Main Street, shopping, eating, and drinking as you go. A **Rails to Trails** rail-trail goes past the back of the brewpub on its way from the Art Museum all the way out to Valley Forge National Historical Park. Punch up www.TrailLink.com for an excellent guide to all of the state's rail-trails.

Other area beer sites:

Northeast Philadelphia. The **Grey Lodge Pub** (6235 Frankford Ave., 215-624-2969) is still the only real beer bar in Northeast Philly. Its pleasantly eccentric owner, Scoats, has taken the Lodge from a somewhat run-down boozer to a destination bar that was an *Esquire* "Best Bars in America" pick. The G-Lodge has a constantly changing tap menu, cask ale every day, and a bottle collection that ranges from 40s of Old Milwaukee to 750s of high-end lambics, as well as an excellent whiskey selection. But what put the Grey Lodge on the map is Friday the Firkinteenth, a cask ale festival that occurs every Friday the thirteenth, when Scoats puts as many as two dozen casks of locally brewed real ale up on the bar, and the place just goes mad for a day. It's all about great beer in a comfortable, completely unpretentious neighborhood bar setting. Ray Swerdlow's **Six Pack Store** (conveniently located at 7015 Roosevelt Blvd., 215-338-6384) is one of the few bottle shops in town and has a great selection of the big East European lagers I love.

Northern Liberties. You can easily walk to six good bars in this hot neighborhood. Start in the southwest corner at **Abbaye** (Third and Fairmount Sts., 215-940-1222), which is kind of a combination of Bridgid's, Monk's Café, and Standard Tap. The taps are quite good, and usually have something out of the ordinary, and the food is outstanding. Walk north one block on North Third to . . . **North Third** (801 N. Third St., 215-413-3666). If the weather's pleasant, you'll want to eat out on the sidewalk, with the trees and the torches and all. Inside, it's very arty, and the beer's well chosen, with good taps and a solid Belgian bottle selection. If you're looking for another of Philly's best, take a right on Poplar and walk down to **Standard Tap** (at the corner of Poplar and N. Second Streets, 215-238-0630); there's also a branch of **The Foodery** bottle shop and deli across Poplar. If you look down American Street as you walk down Poplar, you'll see the sign marking what is thought to be the site of the first lager brewery in America. You'll find only local and regional draft beers at Standard Tap (plus a full bar), and this is probably the best draft system in the city. The food is fully up to the quality of the beer; try the fried smelts with a glass of Sly Fox O'Reilly's Stout while you're sitting out on the upstairs deck on a cool evening. From here you can walk down to Brown and take a left to the **Druid's Keep** (149 Brown St., 215-413-0455), a secluded, rough gem of a corner neighborhood taproom with good beers on tap and in bottle, and a small bar where you can settle in to enjoy them. Walk back to Second, turn left, and **700** (700 N. Second St., 215-413-3181) is only a block away, with a very select assortment of great bottled beers and usually at least one rare beer on tap as well. This is not your usual geek bar, anyone might be drinking good beer here, and there's a good selection of off-beat liquor as well. If you want one last quick one, head north on Second to the swell new Piazza at Schmidt's (yes, another former brewery site), and you'll find **Swift Half** (1001 N. Second St., 215-923-1600), with a view out onto the piazza and a sharp set of taps and bottles, and just the thing you need for a quick one: half-pint glasses of any draft.

Old City. **The Plough and the Stars** (123 Chestnut St., 215-733-0300) is an upscale Irish pub with delicious food and just the beers you'd expect, plus a nice assortment of Irish whiskeys. **Eulogy** (136 Chestnut St., 215-413-1918) was described earlier (see page 30). The **Khyber Pass** (56 S. Second St., 215-238-5888) is one of the city's oldest bars and a longtime friend of good beer, with a backbar that dates from the 1876 Centennial Exposition in Philadelphia. The **Race Street Café** (208 Race St., 215-574-0296) is walkable from here, and it's bustling, friendly, and quite hip to beer. **Brownie's Pub** (48. S. Second St., 215-238-1222) is in Old City, but it's not fancy, it's not a hipster joint, and it's not expensive. They know their beer, too; a good oasis of normal in this area. Lots of taps at the **Irish Pol** (45 S. Third St., 267-761-9532); forty at last count. Like Brownie's around the block, the Irish Pol is not really part of the Old City "scene," just a good bar. **Society Hill Hotel** (301 Chestnut St., 215-925-9570) has a classy bar on the first floor, a nice change from the sometimes crazy Old City bar scene.

Fairmount/Art Museum. Park once (likely in the big lot at 23rd Street and Fairmount Avenue) and visit all these places: **Bridgid's** (726 N. 24th St.) was described earlier (see page 30). **London Grill** (2301 Fairmount Ave., 215-978-4545) is famous for its bar menu; it's a bit more upscale but still quite beer-friendly. The **Belgian Café** (2047 Green St., 215-235-5000) is an offshoot of Monk's that brings outstanding food and beer to a larger, arty space. **Bishop's Collar** (2349 Fairmount Ave., 215-765-1616) is laid-back and well-beered, with an old marble floor and a rotating tap selection. **Aspen** (747 N. 25th St., 215-232-7736) is pretty, comfortable, and stepping up their beer; it reminds me of the small neighborhood restaurants in the Fan in Richmond. Okay, **Kite and Key** (1836 Callowhill St., 215-568-1818) might be a little far from your parking spot, but it's worth moving—good eats and a good vibe, and a real good set of American craft bottles. Walk a bit more, and you'll find **St. Stephen's Green** (1701 Green St., 215-769-5000). Nice place for a beer, even better if you can get the outdoor seating; it's a magical spot when the trees are in bloom.

Center City. **McGillin's Old Ale House** (1310 Drury Lane, 215-735-4515) is Philly's oldest bar, open and owned by the same family since 1861, a great place to have a beer with a buddy or your spouse, and they have some really good stuff on tap. **Time** (1315 Sansom St., 215-985-4800) is where excellent Ludwig's Garten used to be . . . but Time marches on. The beer's great, as is the whisky and absinthe. There is frequently a cover charge for live music. **Varga Bar** (941 Spruce St., 215-627-5200) has an excellent set of taps (and they do growlers!), a great small spirits selection, and bartenders who can tell you all about them. **McGlinchey's** (259 S. 15th St, 215-735-1259) may not look like much—one big room dominated by a big U-shaped bar, and with pretty plain hand-lettered signs—but the people are real, and you'll find the cheapest prices for good beers in town. **Moriarty's** (1116 Walnut St., 215-627-7676) is probably the opposite end of the spectrum, with nicely dressed folks looking for fun, but the beer's still great, and the wings are honking huge! When you stop to visit Nodding Head, make a little left at the foot of the stairs and get some fresh shellfish and stout at the **Oyster House** (1516 Sansom St., 215-567-7683), the new incarnation of this revered seafood house. And don't miss the bars belonging to the godfathers of Nodding Head. **Fergie's** (1214 Sansom St., 215-928-8118) is the bar where Fergus Carey himself runs a square house and pulls one of the finest jars of Guinness in the city (and an excellent Yards ESA as well). Fergie is partnered in **Monk's Café** (264 S. 16th St., 215-545-7005) with the beer genius and Burgundian bon vivant Tom Peters, a man who has brought much incredibly good beer to Philadelphia. Go see what Monk's has on tap today, and eat some mussels! It's one of America's foremost beer bars. Before Tom got Monk's, he managed a bar at 263 S. 15th St., which is now the address of **Jose Pistolas** (215-545-4101), where you'll find bar food with a Mexican flair that will do you right and beer that will do you righter, a place the cool beer kids go. **Good Dog** (224 S. 15th St., 215-985-9600) is not far away, and as anyone can tell you, they have the best burger around. Howling good beer, too. One of the better Irish pubs in the city, a favorite of my *Malt Advocate* publisher, **The Black Sheep** (247 S. 17th St., 215-545-9473), is just around the block; stop in for a jar of Guinness. **Misconduct Tavern** (1511 Locust St., 215-732-5797) is a sports-loving place with a nautical theme that knows good beer and serves great mac and cheese; rare, if not unique. Probably the best bottle shop in the area is **The Foodery** (10th and Pine Streets, 215-928-1111), with hundreds of different bottles, including some fairly rare and vintage stuff. That's "vintage," not "old"; these beers are aged on purpose, like wines. Bring your wallet and go crazy.

Rittenhouse Square Area. *Tria Café* (123 S. 18th St., 215-972-8742), is centered around three "fermentables": beer, wine, and cheese. Neat idea, and beer definitely does not take a backseat to either of the other two. (There's another Tria now open at Washington Square West, on the corner of 12th and Spruce, and another one coming in University City.) **Village Whiskey** (118 S. 20th St., 215-665-1088) is a Jose Garces project, so you know the food's phenomenal and innovative, but there are also some good beers and more than 80 different whiskies. That's right: eighty-plus, and they're as good as you can get in Pennsylvania, too. It's right beside his wine bar, **Tinto**, so whatever you want to drink, there you are. There are two Irish pubs, the **Irish Bards** (215-569-9585) and the **Irish Pub** (215-568-5603), practically side by side at 20th and Walnut Streets. Take your pick: The Bards probably has a better jar of Guinness, but the Pub's food seems better to me. **Pietro's Coal Oven Pizzeria** (two locations: 1714 Walnut St., 215-753-8090; and 121 South St., 215-733-0675) serves up a broad range of beers and superb pizza; often overlooked by the beer cognoscenti. **Devil's Alley** (1907 Chestnut St., 215-751-0707) has all the standard wonderfulness—dead-on tap selection, yummy comfort food, crazy devil décor—then nails it down with the great second-floor window room. Good cocktails, too. **Doobie's** (2201 Lombard St., 215-546-0316) is another of Philly's divey gems; you gotta love a place that's so unassuming, cranks good bar food out of a tiny kitchen, and serves up craft beer with unassuming aplomb. A favorite of area brewers. Follow the prabbit to **Pub and Kitchen** (1946 Lombard St., 215-545-0350); the pig/rabbit logo will lead you to good beers and exceptional food. Gastropubs are hot in Philly.

Manayunk. ***Dawson Street Pub*** (100 Dawson St., 215-482-5677) is tucked way back along the tracks and is one of the city's great unknown bars, but it's definitely worth hunting for, with cask ale on every day and a deep bottle selection; try the vegetarian chili. The **Flat Rock Saloon** (4301 Main St., 215-483-3722) has Manayunk's biggest bottled beer selection. **Old Eagle Tavern** (3938 Terrace St., 215-483-5535) is a solid, unpretentious Manayunk mainstay that has seriously upped their beer game. Squeeze into **Union Jack's** (4801 Umbria St., 215-482-8980)—it's not real big, and it's a narrow street, too—for a good selection of craft taps and bar food in a truly unpretentious atmosphere. Well-worth getting off the beaten Manayunk track to find.

South Philly. I'm using a broad definition of South Philly here . . . ***Brauhaus Schmitz*** (718 South St., 267-909-8814) brings German beerhall simplicity and camaraderie (and beer!) to South Street, and it looks like it's touching off a host of imitators . . . great! **Chick's Café** (614 S. Seventh St., 215-625-3700) keeps saying they're a wine bar, but all I see is delicious food, some well-kept taps of craft, and Phoebe Esmon's drop-dead cocktails. There are two bars known by four-letter acronyms down here: **South Philly Tap Room** (1509 Mifflin St., 215-271-7787) is a tight and cozy joint that pulls in the rare beers and pioneered good beer in this part of town. The **Pub On Passyunk East** (1501 E. Passyunk Ave., 215-755-5125) has a hip crowd, cool arched bays to hide in, and a beer selection chosen to be different from everyone else; we like that. No lemming bars, please, even when it's craft. **Hawthornes** (738 S. 11th St., 215-627-3012) had to fight The Man to get open, but now they're serving more than a thousand bottled beers, growlers off sixteen great taps, and doing one heck of a take-out business. Open the door at **Ultimo** (1900 S. Fifteenth St., 215-339-5177) and you'll see a java fanatic-grade coffee shop—fresh-ground Counter Culture coffees done in Chemex pots (or brewed to order in pour-over "one-hitters"), espresso, macchiatos, all that jazz—but look a bit further and you'll find **Brew**, the bottleshop section run by the good folks at South Philly Tap Room. Awesome combo. **Devil's Den** (1148 S. Eleventh St., 215-339-0855) is another of the hot newcomers in this craft-crazy city. The adventurous taps make it a must-stop; the menu is still settling down. Don't let the unassuming, somewhat shopworn look fool you: the **Royal Tavern** (937 E. Passyunk Ave., 215-389-6694) serves an exceptionally great burger and cutting-edge beers. **The Headhouse** (122 Lombard St.) was not quite open yet when I wrote this. It's a project of Bruce Nichols, one of the original movers behind Philly Beer Week. I'll see you there. **New Wave Café** (784 S. Third St., 215-922-8484) has that corner neighborhood bar feel with better beer; try to grab a sidewalk table in good weather. Need a break from beer? Drop in at **Southwark** (701 S. Fourth St., 215-238-1888) and ask the bartender to make you something nice with rye whiskey. One of the city's very best cocktail bars.

Other Neighborhoods. Brendan Hartranft has been tending bar in Philly for years; I first met him in the mid-nineties, when he was working tables at the age of sixteen. He sussed out that I knew beer and started grilling me. I kept running into him other places, and finally he and his wife, Leigh Maida, opened one of their own, and then another, and then another—three instant successes. **Memphis Taproom** (2331 E. Cumberland St., 215-425-4460) has great taps, well-selected bottles, cask all the time (I had a cask Norman cider there last time that was awesome), and outstanding food; try the King Rarebit. **Local 44** (4333 Spruce St., 215-222-BEER) serves twenty top-notch draft beers and only one bottle: Orval. Just because. Again, great food. **Resurrection Alehouse** (2425 Grays Ferry Ave., 215-735-3533) is small but has that Hartranft–Maida combo of great beer and food. Brendan likes to get the underhyped beers others may have overlooked. **Grace Tavern** (2229 Grays Ferry Ave., 215-893-9580) is an easy walk from Resurrection Alehouse and has a divier feel, but serves a decadently delicious burger and has a great beer menu (look for the lambics). Despite the name, **Sidebar Bar & Grille** (2201 Christian St., 215-732-3429) isn't a cocktailist hangout; the main focus is the acclaimed food, followed closely by American craft drafts. Things get big on the other side of the Schuylkill at **City Tap House** (3925 Walnut St., 215-662-0105): two huge rooms, expansive outdoor terrace (with sexy-cool firepits), and sixty taps; the most I've ever seen in Philly. Try the Tartufo pizza with truffle oil and a delicious fried egg. **Mad Mex** (3401 Walnut St., 215-382-2221), the popular Pittsburgh chain of big-burrito-margarita-craft beer restaurants, has an outpost by the UPenn campus. Good vegetarian options here, too. The **White Dog Café** (3420 Sansom St., 215-386-9224) was one of the city's first bars to serve good beer, and it still has good beer, well-made food, and a commitment to liberal causes and education that is admirable in a restaurant and bar.

If you want live music and good beer, you've got two excellent choices. Rougher around the edges and a bit more intimate: that's the **North Star Bar** (2639 Poplar St., 215-787-0488). For a more polished concert space, head to **World Café Live** (3025 Walnut St., 215-222-1400), a music/restaurant venue run by popular indie radio station WXPN; you can catch a "Free at Noon" show (check the Web site for schedules; www.worldcafelive.com) with a top-notch craft beer.

I'm putting in **The Institute** (549 N. 12th St., 215-765-8515) because, like Scoats in the Northeast, they had the guts to open a beer bar with no other ones around—and it's a good one. Closest beer bar to Temple University! **Prohibition Taproom** (501 N. 13th St. 215-238-1818) is kind of on the borderlands, too, but they have one of the best small tap selections in the city, along with good food (and this was the very first place I took notes on for this edition). **Cherry Street Tavern** (129 N. 22nd St., 215-561-5683) has that "you're welcome here" vibe, loud and clear, and a nice enough set of taps to keep you in your seat. Beautiful backbar, too. **McMenamin's Tavern** (7170 Germantown Ave., Mt. Airy, 215-247-9920) is a great neighborhood bar with a beer selection that doesn't mimic every other beer bar in town, surprisingly adventurous food (and dynamite wings), and P. J. McMenamin, one terrific guy. **The Mermaid Inn** (7673 Winston Rd., 215-247-9797) is a neat little tucked-away gem, a small bar in an old building with some good taps and a great small-group live music scene. You could be on your way to the Italian Market when you stop at **For Pete's Sake** (900 S. Front St., 215-462-2230), a friendly corner bar with an Irish feel and a full array of Irish whiskeys, all the way up to the phenomenal Redbreast, but also with plenty of beer surprises, like draft Chimay White. **Kraftwork** (541 E. Girard Ave., 215-739-1700) is brand-new and awesome, following the Philly trend of pairing craft beer with a toothsome, adventurous menu; gotta love a place that has both a charcuterie board and eggplant-squash terrine. William Reed and Paul Kimport's second project is **Johnny Brenda's** (1201 Frankford Ave., 215-739-9684), a real dive bar that has been turned into . . . a great dive bar, with clean floors and great beer and a Mediterranean menu that has proved incredibly popular.

The first and last pub you'll see if you travel to Philly by train might be **Bridgewaters** (in 30th Street Station, 215-387-4787). Don't overlook it, and don't rush off to your train: The beer alone is too good to rush, and the food's double-take good for a train station eatery. This is a hidden gem I've been telling folks about for years.

Nodding Head Brewery and Restaurant

1516 Sansom Street, upstairs, Philadelphia, 19102
215-569-9525

The buzz was on in Philly's beer culture for months after the Samuel Adams Brew House quietly closed in May 1999. Tom Peters and Fergus Carey, owners of Monk's Café, were going to buy it and open a brewpub, but it didn't happen, Tom and Fergie didn't say a word, and the buzz chased itself till it wore out. Then suddenly the word was out: Nodding Head.

Owners Curt Decker and Barbara Thomas (Tom Peters's wife) ripped out the old extract brewhouse and put in a specially designed, very compact JV Northwest brewhouse. Large parts of the engineering were done by Nodding Head's first brewer, Brandon Greenwood.

One very traditional part on the mash tun was the Steele's masher, an auger-centered grist hydration device, which current brewer Gordon Grubb was proud to show me. "I don't think there's more than one or two other ones in the country," he said, "and there should be. I can dial in the hot and cold water going in and hit my exact mash temperature every time." Okay, kind of jargonish. What this thing does is actively mix the cracked malt and hot water going into the mash tun, and it gets the grist at the exact temperature and with the correct proportion of water from the first instant of mashing. Believe Gordon: That's a very good thing for consistency and quality.

That's just one example of how they do things at Nodding Head— they're very serious about the beer, and they don't do things the way other brewers do them. "We don't take ourselves seriously," Curt stipulated. "We're very serious about the beer, but you've got to have fun."

They've gotten more serious about the beer in the past five years. "We're stepping out a bit more on beer now," Curt said. "We have the core beers— Grog, BPA, and 60 Shilling—to let us do the fun stuff." As evidence, he pointed out the limited bottling they're doing of sour and wild beers (replacing "outside" beers in those categories; all the beer

Beers brewed: Year-round: Grog, 700 Level Ale. Seasonals: Ich Bin Ein Berliner Weisse, BPA, 3C Double IPA, Monkey Knife Fight, 60 Shilling, Chocolate Stout, Sledwrecker Winter Ale, Pilsner, Abbey Normal.

at Nodding Head is Nodding Head beer now), barrel-aged beers, and much bigger beers than they used to do.

"Which leaves me wondering . . ." Curt mused, "do we get more respect now from the local beer geeks? Or are we too much to handle for the core drinkers?" That's the kind of thing brewpub owners struggle with: Who are you satisfying, and what's best for the business?

For now, Nodding Head's walking that line down the middle, balancing those very nice core beers—with core seasonals like 700 Level (blonde ale), Doc (a very dry German hopped blonde), and the tart Ich Bin Ein Berliner Weisse in the summer—against some adventurous stuff like Grog d'Oer (a stronger, Belgian-yeast version of Grog), George's Fault (an award-winning honey-spiked strong ale), and the 10th Anniversary 4C I tasted when I talked to Curt and Gordon. The 4C is a "bigger and better" version of the 3C double IPA (the 3 Cs are Cascade, Chinook, and Centennial hops; 4C adds Columbus) that was like licking the inside of a hops bale wrapper—in a good, fresh way.

For Gordon and Curt, hops are not about bitterness; they're about flavor and aroma. "You don't need huge BUs [Bittering Units] with American hops," Gordon said. "It's about aroma and flavor. We're generally less bitter than other brewers' beers, but we use more hops."

You'll get a chance to try that when you stop in and climb the steps beside the entrance to the Oyster House. You'll emerge in the main barroom, with the small bar and the brewery to your left, booths and tables to your right, and the bulk of the bobblehead collection in front of you. There's another room behind the bar, but I rarely get very far from the bar.

If you're hungry, let's start with two important words: crab cake. Can't go wrong, and if you want to stay shellfishy, get some mussels to follow. If you're of the vegetarian persuasion, you're in luck: Nodding Head has big carnivore plates (ribs, rack of lamb, and the excellent burger among them), but they take vegetarian preparations as seriously as the beer: imaginative and well executed.

If you were wondering, Nodding Head, which sounds so very British-pub-like, is actually very American; it's a reference to the bobblehead dolls that you see everywhere these days. When they were just getting started on planning and were throwing around names over lunch, nothing sounded good. Then Tom Peters said he'd been having a recurring

The Pick: Ich Bin Ein Berliner Weisse. "If we never do anything else," Curt Decker said, "we saved Berliner Weisse. I'm most proud of that." Nodding Head's dead-on version of this low-alcohol, tart German wheat beer is piercingly puckery: perfect summertime refreshment.

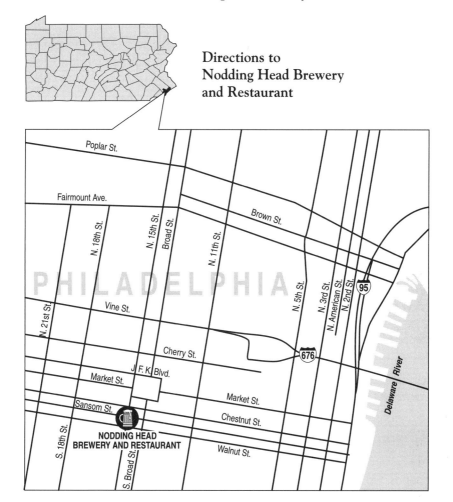

**Directions to
Nodding Head Brewery
and Restaurant**

dream that he was following a car that had a rear window full of bobble-heads, all nodding. "Well, I didn't have anything," Curt said with a laugh, "and how are you going to argue with a dream?!"

Stay very serious about the beer, but have fun: How are you going to argue with a dream?

Opened: December 1999.
Owners: Curt Decker, Barbara Thomas.
Brewers: Gordon Grubb, Mike Fava.
System: 7-barrel JV Northwest brewhouse, 850 barrels potential annual capacity.
2009 production: 750 barrels.
Brewpub hours: 11 AM to 2 AM daily.

Tours: By appointment.
Take-out beer: None available.
Food: Expect anything from game dishes to a full vegan section in the menu. The selections range all the way from salads and sandwiches to full-bore entrées. Call about the weekend brunch.
Extras: Full liquor license. Live music for special occasions (call for schedule). Dartboards.
Special considerations: Kids welcome. Vegetarian meals available.
Parking: On-street parking is dicey at best. There is a parking garage across the street (Fifteenth and Sansom Streets); expect to pay center city rates.

Yards Brewing Company

901 North Delaware Avenue, Philadelphia, PA 191123
215-634-2600
www.yardsbrewing.com

Yards Brewing Company is a classic microbrewery story . . . mostly. Two friends, Tom Kehoe and Jon Bovit, started homebrewing together at Western Maryland University and discovered a knack and a love for it. They thought about brewing, then they considered what they were in college for . . . and the next thing you know they're working in a tiny brewhouse tucked into a tiny, back-alley space, and going to beer festivals to get their name out there.

That is when I met Jon and Tom, back in 1995, when I was starting out as a beer writer. I was wandering through a fest, writing notes, when a cloud of East Kent Goldings hops aroma enveloped my head and drew me into the Yards booth. WOW! How did they do that? Turns out, they put a little cloth bag full of Goldings—a hop pocket—into each keg. A lot of work, but a traditional way of doing things, and it sure worked.

Beers brewed: Year-round: Yards ESA (Extra Special Ale), Philadelphia Pale Ale, IPA, Brawler, George Washington Tavern Porter, Thomas Jefferson Tavern Ale, Poor Richard's Tavern Spruce. Seasonals: Saison, Trubbel de Yards. Draft only: Old Ale, Old Bartholomew Barleywine, Cape of Good Hope Imperial IPA.

Beer geeks caught on to Yards first and spread the word. Customers found the ESA (Extra Special Ale) surprisingly approachable, and many had their first beer from a handpump because of it. Yards quickly maxed out the brewing capacity of its site and moved to a larger spot in Manayunk.

Time passed, and Bovit left the company. Tom took on new partners, Bill Barton and his wife, Nancy, who supplied a badly needed infusion of capital. After adding a bottling line and new beers, they needed space again, and they moved to a former brewery in the Kensington neighborhood, the old

The Pick: The Brawler has become my go-to beer when I'm driving or I feel like "going a few rounds"; it's tasty and drinkable. I also find myself drinking a lot of the brightly hoppy Philly Pale Ale. It's a great answer to the local bartender who told me, "I don't think pale ale has anything to say." Listen up, fella.

Weisbrod and Hess Brewery—"The Oriental Brewery" as it was known. The beer was selling well, the neighborhood improved (as they almost always do when a brewery moves in), but things weren't good at Yards.

The partnership wasn't working out, and the direction of the company wavered. After a lot of negotiations, sometimes acrimonious, the partners decided to split: Tom took the Yards name and the brands, the Bartons kept the building and the equipment and opened shop as Philadelphia Brewing (see the next listing).

Yards needed a brewery, and fast. Tom found a place on Delaware Avenue, not all that far from the Kensington brewery: "A much more visible address," he said. It was a big building, with plenty of room to grow . . . once fifty-four "screw piles" had been drilled down as much as 55 feet into the ground below to support the weight of the brewhouse, which cost four months and more money than Tom likes to think about.

The brewhouse was a showpiece JV Northwest system that was formerly at the Ybor City brewery in Florida. "That's the one I wanted," Tom said. "I'd seen it, I wanted it, and we got it. The guys at Deschutes had one and told me that with enough tanks, you can get 110,000 barrels a year out of it."

Tom picked up brewer Tim Roberts, who was coming off a truly underappreciated stint at the defunct Independence brewpub, and Frank Winslow, who came with some serious food-processing experience and who handles quality control. Add in operations manager Steve Mashington, and they were ready to roll. The first brew—ESA, of course—was on Labor Day 2008.

ESA is still the brewery's signature beer, the one they hang their hats on, but Philadelphia Pale Ale is the big seller that you'll see most places in town. Philly Pale went through some tweaking, and the last one—lightened up by substituting some pilsner malt for their usual English

**Directions to
Yards Brewing Company**

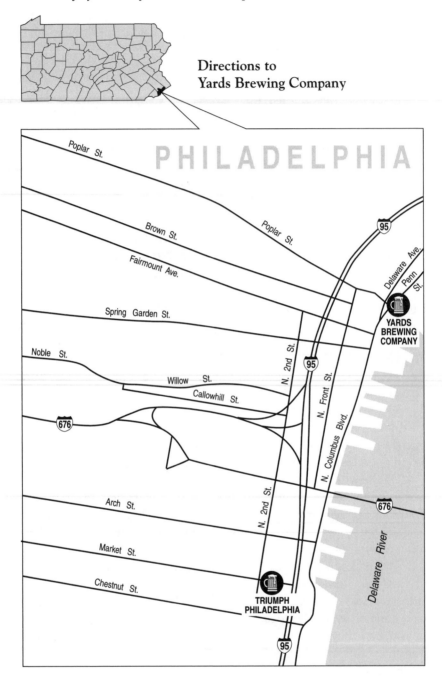

malt, and adding some zingy Amarillo hops—just blew things up. I remember the first pint I had, at the Standard Tap. There were five beers on tap I'd been waiting to try, but I had the Philly Pale first and just stuck with it. I didn't want to drink anything else

Until Brawler came out, that is. Brawler, "a pugilist-style ale," represents something near and dear to my heart: a tasty, drinkable beer at low alcohol levels. Brawler, a dark ale with a delicious malt twist, is only 4.2 percent, and I can drink it all afternoon if I pace myself. Other folks must feel the same way, because it's a popular tap in town as well.

It's a popular tap in Yards's own tasting room, which just opened early in 2010. It's not a brewpub, Kehoe and Mashington both insisted, because they don't want to stay open till 2 AM (or upset their bar accounts by competing with them). But you will be able to buy a pint if you want, or a flight of four different beers. The menu's small for now, but it's enough to have something to nosh on while you're looking around and having superbly fresh Yards.

Their plans are ambitious. "We want to be a midsize regional brewer in five years," said Mashington. "We shouldn't have to sell outside the region; there's still a lot of beer to sell in Philly. We can still sell a lot of cask in Philly, too; that's part of our tradition, and we'll always do that."

Yards has rebooted. But like a computer restarting, it's not a completely new thing. It's the same as before, only fresh, quicker, ready for a whole new job of work. Stop by and see how it happens.

Opened: October 1994; current facility opened September 2008.
Owners: Tom Kehoe, with family and friends.
Brewers: Tim Roberts, Frank Winslow, Mitch Albach.
System: 50-barrel JV Northwest brewhouse, 16,000 barrels potential annual capacity.
2009 production: 10,500 barrels.
Tours: Saturday, 11 AM to 4 PM.
Take-out beer: Growlers, six-packs, and cases; sixtels and half kegs (call for availability).
Special considerations: Kids with parents welcome. Closed-toed shoes required. Handicapped-accessible.
Parking: Off-street parking . . . which may be a lot tighter now that the Sugarhouse Casino is open.

Philadelphia Brewing Company

2423-39 Amber Street, Philadelphia, PA 19125
215-427-BREW (2739)
www.philadelphiabrewing.com

"This is not a new company!"

Nancy Barton was emphatic about that. "We have a new name and new beers . . ."

"We got new T-shirts and letterhead, too," her husband, Bill, threw in, grinning.

". . . but it's the same building, the same equipment, and the same employees," she continued. "It's the same company!"

The Bartons have a clear reason for wanting to get that message out: Philadelphia Brewing is in the building that this area thought of as the Yards Brewery. They were partners in Yards, working here, until they split with partner Tom Kehoe. Kehoe took the Yards names and beers, the Bartons got the building and equipment, and as Nancy said, the employees stayed with them.

Let's back up just a bit to see how they got to this point. Bill and Nancy bought into Yards because they were looking for their own business and liked craft beer. Nancy started selling Yards in the area, and they decided to take the plunge. The brewery was in Manayunk at the time, and when the lease was coming up on that building, Bill started looking for a new place.

One day when he and Nancy were going to a tasting at Philadelphia Beer Company, a distributor in the Kensington neighborhood, they saw a sign that said, "W&H Bottle Dept." They called brewery historian Rich Wagner, and he told them it was the old Weisbrod and Hess brewery, also known as "The Oriental Brewery." The building dates from the 1880s; the actual brewhouse area was built in 1906.

"It was really trashed," Nancy said. "Lots of graffiti, trash, dead animals. But structurally it was perfect." (You can see what it was like: Rich Wagner has a video of a 1987 visit to the site on YouTube—

Beers brewed: Year-round: Kenzinger, Walt Wit, Newbold IPA, Rowhouse Red. Select Brews: Fleur de Lehigh, Phila-Buster, Philly'z Navidad, Joe Coffee Porter, Shackamaxi-mum Stout, Biberry, Harvest From the Hood, Winter Wunder, Kilty Pleasure.

search "rich wagner weisbrod" and you'll find it.) The neighborhood was no prize, either; there was one really bad day when they found a body across the street.

Still, it was a solid place, built for brewing with drains in place, and given the state of Kensington at the time, the price was right. They bought the building in May 2001, and after some back-and-forth between the two sites, started brewing in March 2002. The building was a hit with the beers' fans, the big tasting room was the site of a series of events that became legendary, and the beer sold well in Philadelphia.

The partnership was not working out, though, and eventually the split took place. Bill and Nancy found themselves with an established building and workforce, good relationships in the area (they'd worked hard at becoming involved in the neighborhood, and it was paying off in a better overall atmosphere for blocks around), a great chance to start fresh.

All they needed was a name. They threw around a few but settled on the simple and instantly iconic Philadelphia Brewing. It fit with their desire to stay local and self-distribute, and as Matt Nienhuis, who's currently selling and distributing the beers in Pittsburgh, said, "We'd hate it if someone else got that name." They went with it.

Then they had to decide on beers. "Dan Weirback told us, 'I envy you. You get to start over,'" Bill said. "We wanted to keep it simple, just use two yeasts. I had 'Kenzinger' in my head as a brand name for years. I thought, we have to have an IPA, but we need something lighter, too."

That paid off: Kenzinger, with its floridly retro label, is the brewery's main seller, and a summertime favorite of mine. The other three main brands, Walt Wit (Belgian white), Rowhouse Red (farmhouse ale), and Newbold IPA, fill out a spectrum of Philly favorites and Philly references: Walt Whitman, the familiar rowhouses of the city, and the New-bold neighborhood.

Three parts to the puzzle: community involvement, a familiar name for a brand new brewery, and new beers. The final piece that makes Philadelphia Brewing what it is: self-distribution, which fits right in with the others.

"How am I going to get a wholesaler's rep to sell me over a brand like Corona?" Bill asked. "When we went to self-distribution, there was no one in front of us, we had control of it, and we make more money.

People call *us*, and we sell them beer. Our salespeople know the beer, and they can take orders directly; our drivers know the beer and the brewery, and they can take orders. This is old-school stuff; every brewery used to do it this way."

It worked. With the relationships everyone at the brewery had in the local beer business, the excitement over a new local brewery, and the great taste of Kenzinger, the brewery was a hit. "We sold more every week," Bill said of the first year. So much so that they had to add four new 60-barrel tanks in 2009, and another four in 2010.

What's ahead for this not-a-new-brewery? "There are a lot more bars we could be in, right here in the city," Nancy said. "There's plenty of market here. We've got a warehouse in Pittsburgh now, and we're self-distributing there. It's in the old Duquesne brewery; I guess we have a thing for old breweries."

If you've got a thing for old breweries, go see what one looks like when it's all spiffed up. Don't be afraid of the neighborhood; like so many others, it's really benefited from having a brewery move in—or move back in, in this case. Take the tour, see The Pig (the big, pink horizontal aging tank used for the brewery's special beers), and relax in the big tasting room. After that you can walk down the corner to Atlantis ("The Lost Bar"; 2442 Frankford Ave., 215-739-4929), the bar Nancy calls "our East office"; they have four Philly Brewing taps, and the brewers often drop in after work. Grab a stool and a Kenzinger; you'll feel like a part of the Philadelphia Brewing community.

Opened: Company established August 2007; brewing in January 2008.
Owners: Bill and Nancy Barton.
Brewers: Josh Ervine, John Rehm, Ben Shamberg, Dean Browne.
System: 30-barrel custom-fabricated brewhouse, 15,000 barrels potential annual capacity.
2009 production: 9,500 barrels.
Tours: Saturday, noon to 3 PM.
Take-out beer: Kegs (call for availability), cases.
Special considerations: Kids welcome. Closed-toed shoes required. Handicapped-accessible.
Parking: Small off-street lot and usually plenty of free street parking available.

Manayunk Brewing Company

4120 Main Street, Philadelphia, PA 19127
215-482-8220
www.manayunkbrewery.com

Manayunk has lost a bit of its gleam to neighborhoods like Northern Liberties, but it is still one of Philadelphia's hot areas. Fashionable beaneries and trendy boutiques line Main Street, drinking decks overhang the canal, and parking is almost unavailable. Manayunk is a Lenape Indian word meaning "The Place Where We Go to Drink," so it practically screams for a brewpub called Manayunk Brewing Company. That's what developer Harry Renner thought, and he had just the spot for it.

The space—originally a water-powered woolen mill, the Krook's Mill of the house beer by that name—works beautifully, with its original brick walls, seating for over four hundred, and an operating in-floor scale that has become a favorite conversation spot. But this isn't just a brewpub, it's a complex. There's a patio with a tiki bar and an upper deck—with another bar—overlooking the Schuylkill and the canal, expanding seating to almost eight hundred in good weather. The bar, in classic brewpub style, is backed with glass to expose the good-looking 15-barrel Bohemian Brewing brewhouse. Back at the far end of the dining room are stone pizza ovens and another, quieter dining room, with yet another bar. There is a sushi bar, and a banquet room upstairs, also with its own bar—there are six bars altogether, with more than fifty taps. They've got it all, baby.

Manayunk's been through some tough times and endured trials that might have closed other breweries. The brewery was slammed by Hurricane Floyd in 1999, with the tanks in the brewhouse floating loose, ripping glycol cooling systems out of the wall; it took five weeks of nonstop work to get the brewery back online. Harry's father was murdered at the brewpub two years later, in a robbery gone bad. Then Harry himself died after complications from surgery in 2004. His family, however,

Beers brewed: Year-round: Bohemian Blonde, Manayunk Lager, Schuylkill Punch, Krook's Mill Pale Ale, California Dreamin' Imperial IPA, and a rotating Belgian-type beer. Seasonals: I had St. Alpha IPA, Quaker City Stout, and Yunkers' Nocturnem . . . but anything can happen. Don't expect anything to be on regularly—change has always been the style at Manayunk.

decided that the brewpub should stay open, which is probably exactly what Harry would have wanted.

Doug Marchakitus just started as the head brewer in late 2009, and he's tweaking and creating and adding beers as he goes. "It's a continuously evolving brewery," he told me. "Schuylkill Punch is a good example. It's been around since the beginning, when it was a fairly light raspberry beer. Then it got stronger, and then it went Belgian in character. Now it's a lager and pretty strong, 7.0 percent. I might tone that back."

The Pick: You should know that the California Dreamin' weighs in at 8.4 percent . . . because you'd never guess it. It is not sticky sweet, nor is it crazy bitter; it is simply way too enjoyable and drinkable for a beer this size. Be warned, but don't be scared.

If you look at the menu and the beer list, you'll see evidence of that evolution, because bits and pieces of beer history are scattered throughout. More than any other brewpub I know, Manayunk has retained something from every head brewer who's ever worked there. The popular California Dreamin' Imperial IPA was Chris Firey's thumbprint: big, hoppy, bold, a bit brash. Jim Brennan rebuilt the brewery after Floyd and lavished love on the lagers that survive despite the time they take to brew right. The first brewer, Tom Cizauskas, named Schuylkill Punch and Krook's Mill, and it was he who instituted the beer pairings with every menu item, which continues today.

And Larry Horwitz, who brewed between Brennan and Firey? His legacy walks the brewery floor: Doug Marchakitus was his assistant at Iron Hill, North Wales, where Larry went after Manayunk. "I learned a lot from Larry, particularly on the technical side," Doug said. It shows in how well attenuated his beers are; none of the beers I tasted were overly sweet, and all finished clean as a whistle.

Manayunk has been through a lot—a lot of water over the dam. And it is *still* a good place to spend an evening, to end an evening, or to while away a weekend afternoon. Come on down—it's The Place Where We Go to Drink!

Opened: October 1996.
Owners: The Renner family.
Brewers: Doug Marchakitus, head brewer; Bill Young, Jeff McCracken.
System: 15-barrel Bohemian Breweries brewhouse, 2,800 barrels potential annual capacity.
2009 production: 1,500 barrels.
Brewpub hours: Monday through Thursday, 11 AM to midnight; Friday and Saturday, 11 AM to 2 AM; Sunday, 10:30 AM to 11 PM.
Tours: By appointment.

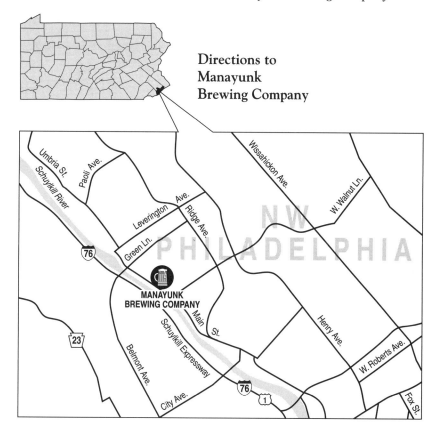

Directions to Manayunk Brewing Company

Take-out beer: Growlers, six-packs.

Food: The menu at Manayunk varies as months pass, and it maintains a high level of quality and innovation . . . but the grilled meatloaf and mahogany wings have righteously stayed on there since opening day. Find them and love them.

Extras: Live music (call for schedule). Happy hour Monday through Friday, 5 PM to 7 PM. Sunday, jazz brunch from 10:30 AM to 2:30 PM. Extensive outdoor seating in good weather.

Special considerations: Kids welcome. Vegetarian meals available.

Parking: On the street and at some small lots, but can be a bear on weekends. The brewpub has valet parking service during evening hours Wednesday through Sunday. In the summer months, there is a boardwalk from the Lock Street parking lot down to the outside bar.

Earth Bread + Brewery

EARTH

Bread + Brewery

7136 Germantown Avenue
Philadelphia, PA 19119
215-242-MOON (6666)
www.earthbreadbrewery.com

If you ever wondered how Tom Baker and Peggy Zwerver's Earth Bread + Brewery ("We really do prefer the + sign," Peggy told me) happened to wind up at this corner of Germantown Avenue in Mt. Airy, in the building with the mural on the wall (it's *Walking the Wissahickon*, by local artist Brian Ames), all too conveniently close to McMenamin's Tavern, it's simple. "We found it on craigslist," Peggy said. Simple as that!

Not really. "Bill and Nancy Barton [of Philadelphia Brewing] mentioned that Mt. Airy would be perfect for our kind of business," Tom added. "It's a simple, inexpensive menu, which is great, but you need a lot of seats. This place had affordable space, and the neighborhood is green, progressive, and has a lot of kids. The menu's perfect for families, and the more places there are in the neighborhood, the more people come to the neighborhood."

What goes on at Earth Bread + Brewery? It may not be unique, but it's unusual. The Earth part is about sustainability and reuse: composting the scraps, using wood for fuel, reducing the carbon footprint by using local food as much as possible. "We've been trying to eliminate bottles as much as possible," Tom said.

Bread is the simple menu Tom mentioned, made in the brick-and-stone, wood-fired oven you see on the lower level. It's all about flatbreads. And a flatbread is . . . ? Tom opened his hands in a gesture of small surrender and grinned.

"It's a pizza," he said, "but if you call it a pizza, people have an expectation about pizza—it's covered in tomato sauce and cheese and lots of toppings, which this isn't. We put so much work into the dough: It's twenty-four hours in the making. We're fermenting it slowly, creating flavor. We don't put a lot of toppings on; it's about the bread."

Beers brewed: Every one is different; the house selection changes every time Tom brews. There are four house beers and seven guest beers.

It's much more like pizza I've had in Italy, especially their Traditional Bread: house-made tomato sauce, house-made mozzarella, dressed with fresh basil, but nothing in excess. The Seed Bread, on the other hand, is much less traditional—and delicious. It's my favorite, with roasted garlic, pine nuts, pumpkin and sesame seeds, and just a bit of mozzarella. I never thought I'd like that, but it's great. Tom and Peggy are both vegetarians, but that didn't stop them from putting meat—sausage, chicken, turkey—on the menu. There are also salads, some simple and tasty appetizers and desserts, and soups.

The Pick: I could just say, "What's the point" here . . . you'll never see any beer I pick again! But instead, I'll say that Tom's been brewing some great lower-alcohol beers, beers you can have several of, and I love to see that.

The Brewery part, of course, is why you're reading this, because Tom Baker is the guy who was behind Heavyweight Brewing, a brewery that dared much and feared little while it was open. Tom brewed big beers, small beers, funky beers, spiced beers, smoked beers, beers brewed from bread, whatever he wanted.

When he closed Heavyweight and announced that he and Peggy would be opening a brewpub, people waited anxiously to see where (some more than others; plenty of suggestions were made, mostly along the lines of "How about in my town?"). They settled in Mt. Airy, moving from New Jersey to live in the neighborhood, and moved in the brewhouse from Heavyweight.

That's when things got a bit unusual, as I mentioned. "I brew once a week," Tom said. "I just made the forty-eighth beer since we opened [in October 2008], and none were the same." Tom got tired of brewing the same beers over and over at Heavyweight and had said he wouldn't do that at the brewpub. We mostly thought he would wind up making some things regularly . . . but we were wrong, and Philadelphia's beer scene is richer for it. You beer geeks want new beers? There's new beer here all the time!

Obviously, brewing once a week isn't going to keep enough taps full to keep people interested, so Earth features guest taps, mostly from local brewers, but not all. "We have twelve taps," Tom said, "and we're making one soda, so that leaves four taps for house beers and seven for guests. I'm not scared of the competition, I'm okay in my skin. I've got a lot of friends brewing in the area, so I don't have to make everything!"

They even invite the brewers in. "We like hosting events with other brewers," Tom said. "We're doing one every Thursday night; at least, we'd like to. They're very busy nights."

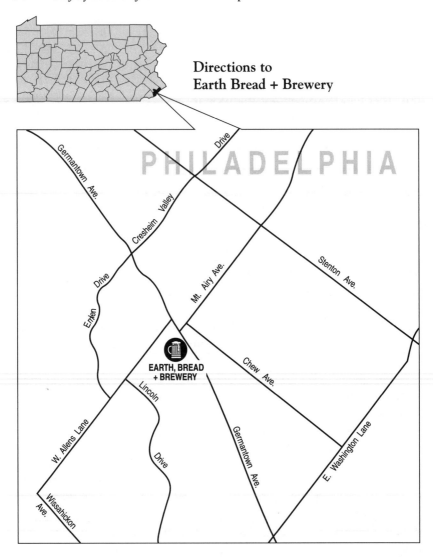

**Directions to
Earth Bread + Brewery**

Earth has become part of the neighborhood, which was an initial shock. "We spent a year planning, nine months building," said Tom. "It was our space . . . and now it's theirs. It was weird at first. But we made it the kind of place we'd like to go, and the regulars made it their place." They were right about the greenness; most of the regulars walk to Earth.

Tom and Peggy are doing a lot of things here that I love. The menu's simple but varied, and it changes, just like the beer selection. Tom does low-alcohol beers frequently, and there's nothing I like better than having two great-tasting beers and not having to worry about getting behind the wheel. They're slowly adding good spirits that are here for sipping, not sloshing with cheap mixers.

When Tom shut down Heavyweight, I wrote this as a eulogy for the place: "For seven years you reminded us what microbrewing—true microbrewing—is about. It's about someone with a vision and some stainless, making beers like no one else, beers that you make because you think they might be really good, or very interesting, or something completely different." Tom's doing that every week now, and after you've had a flatbread in the warm glow of the oven and a couple beers that no one's ever made before—or will again—you'll know just what I mean.

Opened: October 2008.

Owners: Tom Baker, Peggy Zwerver.

Brewers: Tom Baker, Jon DeFibaugh.

System: "A Frankenstein system," according to Tom: a 7-barrel DME mash tun with a Specific Mechanical kettle, brewing into two 10-barrel Century fermenters (named Lynne and Leslie), 350 barrels annual capacity.

2009 production: 300 barrels.

Brewpub hours: Tuesday, through Thursday, and Sunday, 4:30 PM to midnight; Friday and Saturday, 4:30 PM to 1 AM. Closed Monday.

Tours: Take a look at the brewhouse; it's right there at the end of the main bar.

Take-out beer: Growlers.

Food: Centered on flatbreads made in a wood-burning oven, salads, and simple appetizers and desserts. You really should try the seed flatbread and the warm olives.

Extras: Earth has added a small but choice spirits selection. Table Tennis Tuesday brings out the paddles and balls, and it's very popular. There is also a dartboard. Lots of local art is on display, and no TVs are to be seen.

Special considerations: Kids welcome; you'll see a lot of families here. Tom and Peggy are vegetarians, and solid vegetarian options are always available.

Parking: There's a free municipal lot just a few doors down, as well as metered street parking, which is free after 6 PM. Earth is just a few blocks from the SEPTA R7 Sedgwick station and R8 Allen Lane station.

Dock Street Brewery

701 South 50th Street, Philadelphia, 19143
215-726-2337
www.dockstreetbeer.com

I remember the original Dock Street brewpub, at 18th and Cherry. It was stylish, with a great address, frosted design on the glass door, and big mural-size original art on the walls. Waitstaff and bartenders wore sharp black and white, and their shoes tapped echoingly on the floor as they brought food from the open kitchen or beers from the splendidly long bar.

I've been going to the new Dock Street brewpub, at 50th and Baltimore, since before it opened (more on that shortly). It is not stylish; it's in an old firehouse—a neat-looking old firehouse, but still a firehouse—in a reviving neighborhood, with concrete floors and an echoing hard ceiling overhead. The staff wear what they wear, and the kitchen—an oven and a prep area—is right behind the bar, and the beer is on taps behind a bar that does run the length of the room.

What a difference! But it seems like one that is standing on its head. Shouldn't the rough place that looks a little shoestring have been in the old days of craft brewing and the fine temple of beer be from today? If you think that, you don't know Rosemarie Certo, Dock Street's owner, manager, and muse.

"Why do it that way then and do it this way now?" she asked, and she has the right to answer. Rosemarie was there in the original Dock Street, married to founder Jeff Ware. "We were elevating the status of beer, letting people know it's not all about sawdust on the floor. Now beer has that cachet. So let's take it back to its roots!"

Rosemarie laughed. "I'm an old hippie," she confided. "My mother said I never did anything the easy way, I never look for the straight road." The firehouse at 50th and Baltimore certainly qualifies.

As little as five years ago, this was a neighborhood I generally avoided. Vacant businesses, dam-

Beers brewed: Year-round: Rye IPA, Bohemian Pilsner, American Pale Ale. Seasonals: Summer Session, Man Full of Trouble Porter, Prince Myshkin Russian Imperial Stout, Sudan Grass Ale, American Saison, Hop Garden. Specialties: Born Again Tripple, Sexual Chocolate, Illuminator Bock, Prisoner of Hell, Satellite Espresso Stout, Bubbly Wit, Barley Wine, Flemish Sour.

aged houses . . . the only thing that drew me at all was a corner place called The Wurst House, which had a good selection of bottled beer at stupidly low prices. It's symbolic of what's happened here that new owners have renamed the place The Best House (but unfortunately, they cut the beer selection).

Dock Street came in just as things were turning. "No way I wanted to go to 50th and Baltimore," Rosemarie confided. "But the first time I came here, the building connected. It's from another time. I started talking to people in the area, and they're artists, musicians, anarchists, professors . . . families. It's a thinking neighborhood, eclectically counter-culture."

The Pick: I'd be lying if I said it was anything but the Rye IPA. I've enjoyed this beer since the first time I put lip to it, and I continue to enjoy it every time I see it. Dry, crisp, bitter, aromatic—it cuts like a knife cast in superchilled ice, clean and brisk as an Antarctic wind.

She went ahead with the site. Some of the folks in the neighborhood didn't want a brewery in their backyard, especially one church group who thought it would bring drunks and bad influences. Somewhat predictably, this brought supporters out of the woodwork in this neighborhood! That's when I went to the preopening opening I mentioned above and heard local community leaders say things like "Dock Street will jump-start the revival of the Baltimore Avenue Corridor." Going on what I've seen with brewpubs elsewhere, they're likely right on that.

Dock Street's been open since August 2007 now, and going there is like brewpubbing was in the late 1980s. The menu's simple and innovative, with some returning faves from the old Dock Street days: Flammenkuche Pizza with caramelized onion, smoky bacon, and crème fraiche, and Trio Fries, hand-cut ribbons of potato, sweet potato, and leek. The room has deliberately been left largely unchanged from the firehall days, the main differences being the addition of the bar and oven and that big brewery looming behind the glass.

The big difference from the 1980s, of course, is the beer. Drinking brewpub beer in the 1980s was a crapshoot; drinking at Dock Street is a sure thing. Despite a number of changes in brewers already (including an opening stint by beloved former McKenzie's star Scott "The Dude" Morrison), the beer has been quite good. I tasted four during the interview, and they were uniformly excellent, especially the throwback Dock Street favorite Bohemian Pils and the new Rye IPA (that one's getting some good traction in local bars, too). There's an ongoing and expanding barrel-aging program that's great to see; the original Dock Street was a pioneer in barrel aging.

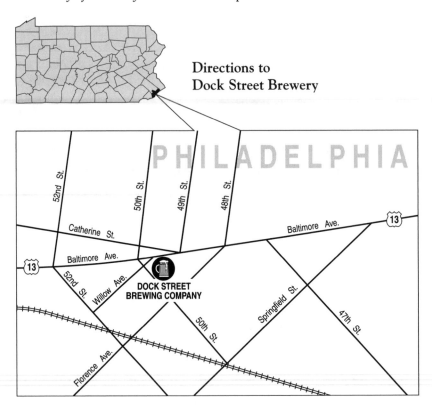

Directions to Dock Street Brewery

Go on out to Dock Street and see what's going on in the firehouse. I guarantee at least something will strike you as counter to the popular trends of brewpub beer and service and look. "I love blowing people's minds," said the old hippie. "I love the craft beer business, and I have a keen sense of what's good. And I really love it when people ask, 'Why is she still here?' I've been in this a long time, and I just can't stop."

Dock Street. What once was new . . . is new again.

Opened: The original Dock Street opened in October 1985; present location opened August 2007.

Owner: Rosemarie Certo.

Brewers: Ben Potts, brewer; Justin Quinlan, assistant brewer.

System: 15-barrel Pub Brewing system, 1,300 barrels annual capacity.

2009 production: 1,150 barrels.

Brewpub hours: Monday through Wednesday, 3 PM to 11 PM; Thursday, 3 PM to midnight; Friday, 11:30 AM to 1 AM; Saturday, noon to 1 AM. Closed Sunday.

Tours: On request, subject to brewer availability.

Take-out beer: Specialty bottles, growlers, and kegs (call for availability).

Food: At the heart of the Dock Street menu is a wood-fired oven, which produces great thin-crust pizza. Try the rotisserie chicken, raised with no hormones or antibiotics, or the burgers made from cattle locally raised the same way and fed with brewery spent grain. Full vegan entrées are also on the menu.

Extras: Occasional live music; check the Dock Street Web site. The biggest attraction is the area, a bohemian, upscale, counterculture neighborhood and all that goes with that. It is, as Rosemarie said, "eclectic." Visit www.ucityphila.org for ideas.

Special considerations: Kids welcome. Vegetarian foods always available.

Parking: On-street parking.

Triumph Old City

117-121 Chestnut Street, Philadelphia, PA 19106
215-625-0855
www.triumphbrewing.com

It is hard for me to enter any of Triumph's three brewpubs without running into Jay Misson's ghost, but this one is where his influence lies heaviest. Jay was the head brewer for the company, a larger-than-life guy. He put an indelible stamp on these three breweries—after having left his mark on modern craft lager brewing across the country—before a tragically young death in June 2008. This was the one he helped design and build and had full influence on, and I think of him every time I walk upstairs or drink one of Patrick Jones's fine lagers.

Triumph owner Adam Rechnitz remembered meeting Jay twenty years ago, when he wanted to learn to brew and Jay was making crazily authentic lagers at the old Vernon Valley brewery in northern New Jersey. They'd grown up only a few miles from each other near the Jersey Shore but met for the first time at the brewery. It was momentous . . . at

Beers brewed: Regulars: Honey Blonde, Amber Ale, IPA, German Pilsner, a rotating set of stouts. Specials: Oktoberfest, Kinder Pils, Pumpkin Ale, Glass Hammer barleywine, Hefeweizen, Maibock, Saison, Jewish Rye, Dunkel Lager, Kellerbier, Love Potion (tripel), Scotch Ale.

least, it was for Adam. "Here was this huge guy, and we shook hands," Adam said, "and I thought, 'This is a brewer? I'm not big enough to be a brewer!'"

Adam was, though, and after just a weekend brewing and hanging around with Jay at Vernon Valley, he knew it was what he wanted to do. "I packed up my car and drove to UCal–Davis," he said. "I took a few brewing courses with Dr. Michael Lewis, drove to Seattle, and got a job washing kegs at Hale's Ales. I eventually moved up to brewing." But in the early 1990s, it seemed like everyone wanted to open a brewery, so Adam started doing a lot of consulting.

That's how he met Ray Disch, at a seminar at Anchor Brewing put on by famed brewing chemist Joe Owades. Disch had an idea for a brewpub in New Jersey. "As a consultant, you're paid to be behind the scenes," Adam said. "Set things up and walk away when it's done. But I thought that this brewpub–micro thing was going to hit the East Coast with a vengeance, and I wanted a piece of the action."

He laughed. "It was a terrible mistake, and that's how it started."

What's all that have to do with Triumph Old City? It's all about influences. Ask Patrick Jones why he keeps at least six beers on, with a couple lagers always in the mix. "We always have six on—always," he said. "Jay insisted." It doesn't matter to Patrick that Jay's been gone for almost two years . . . and it shouldn't. Jay insisted because it was a good thing to do.

Patrick has put his own influence on the place, to be sure. The Kinder Pils says it clearly, if not loudly. Kinder Pils was the gold medal winner at the 2009 Great American Beer Festival in the new Session Beer category for lower-alcohol beers. "It was a lark," Patrick admitted. "Random ideas win!" It's also a great beer for big glasses and long conversations.

"I'm keeping consistency with the recipes," Patrick said. "But the Glass Hammer is our first barleywine, the Brunch Stout is new. We don't want all the pubs to be the same, so we do our own beers." The Brunch Stout, by the way, is an imperial oatmeal coffee-and-cream chocolate stout; *two* meals in a glass, as Patrick said with a grin.

There's one more thing that Jay instituted that Patrick definitely goes along with, and you should, too. On the first Thursday of the month, they tap a 32-liter wooden barrel of fresh beer, a new beer for the month. The barrels are like the ones used in Düsseldorf's altbier breweries; Jay showed them to me in a top-to-bottom tour of the place before they opened, and he was jazzed to have gotten hold of real ones. If he'd had time, he probably would have put in the keg elevator the Germans use to bring new barrels up from the cellar.

So go down to Triumph, in this oldest section of Philadelphia with its cobblestones. Step into the foyer and look at that second-story soar that all three Triumph pubs have. Climb the stairs to the upper bar (and check out those screaming steel monkeys midway between floors) or stay down below at the long split-level bar. Get a pilsner and enjoy the crisp aroma. Try some of the beautifully simple plates of charcuterie or vegetables, or dive right into a pot of mussels. Have another pilsner. And say hi to Jay. I'm sure he's there.

Opened: April 2007.
Owner: Adam Rechnitz.
Brewer: Patrick Jones.
System: 15-barrel Newlands system, 2,300 barrels annual capacity.
2009 production: 1,000 barrels.
Brewpub hours: Seven days a week, 11:30 AM to 2 AM.
Tours: Saturday, 1 and 3 PM.
Take-out beer: None available.
Food: The menu has gone through a lot of changes here and is only now settling down. Look for the influences of the city: a variety of cuisines, solid vegetarian offerings, and smart use of the increasing number of artisan cheeses and cured meats available in Philadelphia. Look for Jay's influence, too: big, juicy chunks of meat. He loved that.
Extras: Live music, karaoke, or open mike four nights a week; see the Web site for schedules.
Special considerations: This is a more adult-friendly atmosphere; I'd take my teenagers here, but probably not younger kids. Vegetarians will find a good assortment of choices.
Parking: There are pay lots in the area (I use the one off Letitia Street) and metered parking with the ticket system. If you're willing to walk, the meters get a lot cheaper and easier to find about four blocks north.

A word about . . .

Micros, Brewpubs, and Craft Brewers

My kids, much to my delight, are quite good writers and have developed large vocabularies; they're interested in words and what they mean and how people use them. I've explained to them that oftentimes what people say is said because they don't want to say something more blunt or honest. Code words, euphemisms, and evasions are part of our everyday speech. Here's a little secret of the beer world: "Microbrewery" is just another code word.

When the new brewing movement started in America in the 1970s, no one knew what to call these little breweries. "Brewery pub," "boutique brewery," and "microbrewery" were all used. By the early 1980s, two words had settled into general use: "microbrewery" and "brewpub." Anchor Brewing's Fritz Maytag once told me that he thought "microbrewery" caught on because the Apple II microcomputer was very hot at the time.

At the time, the industry's pundits defined a brewpub as a brewery that sold most of its beer in an in-house taproom. They defined a microbrewery as a brewery that produced less than 15,000 barrels a year. These terms gained legal recognition in some states, as deals were struck to allow the new businesses to start up and tax rates were determined. The federal government acknowledged the special nature of small breweries in the early 1990s, granting a substantial tax break to those with an annual production under 50,000 barrels.

Eventually the industry itself came up with a whole set of labels. The Brewers Association's definitions boil down to this: A "brewpub" is a brewery that sells 25 percent or more of its output on premises by the glass; a "microbrewery" is a packaging brewery making less than 15,000 barrels. A "regional" brewery makes between 15,000 and 2 million barrels a year. Brewers larger than that are called "large brewers." Beer geeks continue to call large brewers by the somewhat derogatory term "macrobrewer."

But the growth of some successful micobreweries has made these definitions an uncomfortable fit. Boston Beer Company sells around 2 million barrels a year, and Sierra Nevada Brewing Company is pushing 800,000 barrels. Clearly these are no longer *micro*breweries, yet their beer is exactly the same as it was. "Microbrewery" has a cachet that most microbrewers don't want to surrender. What to call them?

Some propose the blanket term "craft brewery." This implies that the beer is somehow crafted rather than produced in a factory. Again, the Brewers Association has a definition: "An American craft brewer is small, independent and traditional." Break that apart: "Small" means less than 2 million barrels annual production. "Independent" means that no more than 25 percent of the brewery is owned by a noncraft brewer. "Traditional" essentially means that the brewery makes all-malt beers, though they make some exceptions for wheat and the like (what I call "politically correct" adjuncts, as opposed to corn and rice).

I feel this is more about membership in a trade association than it is about what kind of brewery they are. Yuengling is not a craft brewery, Boston Beer soon won't be, even longtime craft breweries like Widmer, Redhook, and Goose Island aren't craft breweries under this definition.

We also have a new term, "nanobrewery," which is still being defined. It's a very, very small brewery, one like Breaker Brewing or Copper Kettle, although it's hard to tell where to draw that line. No more than 500 barrels in a year? Batches under 3 barrels in size? A really, *really* small brewhouse?

Putting a label on a brewery these days is not as easy as putting a label on a bottle. What do you call a place like The Lion, a regional brewery that not only brews mainstream lagers with corn, but also has a line of all-malt specialty beers, not to mention a huge output of all-malt sodas? What about Porterhouse, where they have their own four beers and four other beers from Philadelphia Brewing (which supplies their brewer, too)? What about Berwick Brewing, where the reality—a brewpub—didn't match the plan of a packaging brewery? These breweries aren't readily pigeonholed.

The fact is, "microbrewery" has always been a code word, and so is "craft brewery." They both mean the same thing. They describe a brewery that makes beer in an authentic manner—using ingredients and techniques appropriate to a given style of beer or brewing—and that brews beers other than mainstream American-style lager. What do I think such places should be called? How about *breweries*?

The distinctions are really all nonsense. Brewery size has nothing to do with the quality of a beer. Guinness Stout, the beer to which most microbrewers hopefully compare their own dry stouts, is brewed by a globe-girdling gargantuan of a company. Blending batches, once a touchstone of noncraftiness, is likewise a nonissue. It goes on at microbreweries across the country.

In this book, I have bowed to convention and called Pennsylvania's Old Guard breweries "regionals" and used the words "brewpub," "microbrewery," and "craft brewery." Brewpub is the best of these terms. A brewery where beer is taken directly from the conditioning tanks to serving tanks and sold from a tap on-premises truly deserves a unique name. But if I had my way, the others would all be called simply breweries. To differentiate a brewery based on the kind of beer it makes seems to be missing the point. Categorizing them by size penalizes the ones that succeed and outgrow the class. Call them breweries, and then let the beer do the talking.

FROM HORSE COUNTRY
TO THE DELAWARE
Philadelphia Suburbs

Southeastern Pennsylvania is often called "the five-county area." This includes Philadelphia, Bucks, Montgomery, Chester, and Delaware Counties. If you take out Philadelphia County, the remaining counties are considered the suburbs of Philadelphia, even though they reach almost to Bethlehem in the north and well into Amish farm country in the west.

Of course, there are suburbs and there are suburbs. Bucks County has cookie-cuttered Levittown and Montgomery County has the gritty streets of Norristown. The tightly packed streets of Upper Darby blend Delaware County right into Philadelphia, and Chester County's Coatesville is like a little bit of Rust Belt. These are border counties, where farmers and financiers coexist in the gently rolling countryside.

The well-known Main Line area stretches out through Montgomery, Delaware, and Chester Counties. This is a wealthy strip of beautiful old homes, boutiques, and Mercedes-Benz dealerships along what used to be the Main Line of the Pennsylvania Railroad, now the SEPTA commuter rail line. Out here, tucked away among the big homes, you'll find the controversial Barnes Foundation, one of the world's great art collections . . . for now. The Barnes Foundation, with its huge collection of French Impressionist, Postimpressionist, and Early Modern artwork and unique approach to art education, is finally leaving Merion for a new home in Philadelphia (scheduled for 2012), but there is still a substantial presence of the arts in the suburbs.

Chadds Ford on Brandywine Creek is home to the Wyeths and the Brandywine River Museum. On the northeast edge of the five-county area is New Hope, a well-known artists' colony and haven for alternative lifestyles on the Delaware River. (Chadds Ford and New Hope used to be BYOB territory for the beer traveler, but McKenzie Brew House and Triumph have changed that.)

Not far from New Hope is Doylestown, where James Michener lived and endowed an excellent art museum. You'll also find the Mercer Museum and the Moravian Pottery and Tile Works, the lifework of Dr. Henry Mercer, an enthusiast of American folk art and craftsmanship. His mansion, Fonthill—a concrete castle—is a unique example of free-form architecture filled with artwork and memorabilia that Mercer collected.

Valley Forge National Historical Park is here in the suburbs, with miles of trails and reconstructions of the cramped huts where the Continental Army spent the harsh winter of 1777. In Bucks County, at Washington Crossing Historic Park, there's an annual reenactment of General Washington's famous Christmas crossing of the Delaware. You can get a dramatic overview of the area from Bowman's Hill Tower, a 110-foot tower atop the hill used by Continental Army lookouts.

The area is dotted with Revolutionary War battle sites. Brandywine Battlefield near Chadds Ford is where Washington was defeated by the British in 1777. Historical markers note little skirmishes like the battle of the Crooked Billet Inn in Warminster and a Loyalist raid that occurred in the alleys of my own little town of Newtown.

Chester County is horse country. The area's biggest equestrian event, the annual Devon Horse Show, is where the cream of the county show off their horses—and themselves.

If all this sounds a bit upper-crust, it can be. Although the suburbs have plenty of working stiffs and average joes and janes, you can't help noticing that much of it is a very wealthy area. Big $500,000 homes are commonplace (even after the recession knocked prices down a peg), luxury cars clog the narrow roads, and you can't throw a rock without clocking a doctor or lawyer. So don't throw any rocks around. Just relax, see the sights, and stop someplace nice for a beer.

There are a lot more places to stop for a beer out here these days, too. The Philadelphia suburbs still have the thickest concentration of brewing in Pennsylvania, with more breweries crowded into the area than any other. Three have closed since the last edition, replaced by three new ones, including another Iron Hill and a second McKenzie. Philly continues to rule on beer bars, but even there the suburbs are catching on. It's a good time for a beer lover to live in the counties.

McKenzie Brew House, Glen Mills

451 Wilmington Pike, Glen Mills, PA 19342
610-361-9800
www.mckenziebrewhouse.com

Ryan Michaels had it tough his first couple years at the McKenzie Brew House. He was brewing in the shadow of "The Dude," Scott Morrison, an experienced and adept brewer who'd quickly become a luminary in Philadelphia beer circles. When Morrison was abruptly shown the door in 2006, Ryan, as his assistant, stepped into his shoes. The beer geeks were still huffing and puffing over Morrison's dismissal (a dismissal he has privately admitted was not unjustified) and didn't even notice what Ryan was doing: quietly building on Morrison's philosophy and success. They finally noticed when he won a gold medal at the GABF in 2007 for his Saison Vautour; that kind of thing's hard to ignore.

It's not hard to see the origins of Ryan's direction. "I never home-brewed," he said, a rarity among craft brewers. He was tending bar at the now-closed Valley Forge Brewing Company when it started its decline. As the owner-brewer lost interest, Ryan started brewing. He went directly from Valley Forge to McKenzie and started learning about saison.

Saison is a Franco-Belgian kind of beer, brewed with spices, spritzy, sometimes tart, sometimes dry, but always refreshing. It's become a signature beer at McKenzie, and one that Ryan champions.

"Scott was brewing saisons that were blowing people's minds when I started," he said. "Saison Dupont is a desert island beer for Gerald and me, so it's a thing we kept up, a legacy." Ryan's very proud and pleased that saison has joined the year-round ranks at the two McKenzie brewpubs.

"The saison's on all the time because it's our favorite and other people are drinking it and they're asking for it," he said. "And, well, after the gold medal, Bill [Mangan, the owner] was a lot more receptive. That's cool, and having people asking for a saison is like a dream come true." I'm not sure which GABF gold medal Ryan's talking about; Saison Vautour won it again in 2009.

Beers brewed: Year-round: McKenzie Light, Wit, Saison Vautour, American Pale Ale, English Brown Ale, Oatmeal Stout. Specialties: Grisette, Fantine, Chateau McKenzie, and a lot more.

Take saison bigger and you get something like a biere de garde, a French "farmhouse" beer. What is biere de garde? "It's marketing," Ryan said, with a quick grin, "old, farm-style marketing. You made the beer bigger so it wouldn't go bad, and you gave it a name: biere de garde."

Take it smaller, though, and you have what Ryan calls Grisette, and he laughs when he says it. "A grisette is one of two things," he explained. "It's a low-alcohol beer that's tart and refreshing, or it's a high alcohol beer of no particular distinction. Ours is the first one."

The Pick: I'm no dummy: Saison Vautour keeps winning medals, and there's a reason—it's excellent beer. The flavor's great, the spiciness is dead-on, and the body is very close to the Saison Dupont model. Beautiful, for a kind of beer that's getting more and more popular around here . . . and who would have ever thought that would happen?

It certainly is. The first time I had the Grisette was at the 2009 connoisseur tasting at the Kennett Square beer festival; the connoisseur tasting was all session beers that year. Ryan filled my glass with Grisette, and I took a swig. It wasn't just spicy, it was peppery, a good dose of black pepper that put some real zing in a beer that was under 4 percent; definitely not a beer of no particular distinction.

"We're lucky to be able to brew saison so often," Ryan said. "It's a chance to change things. But with the Grisette, it's a balancing act: keeping it light, keeping it interesting, not letting the spices overwhelm it. It's fun, but it's like a white whale we keep chasing: a 3 percent saison that's great to drink and sells well."

Making beer that sells isn't a problem. Ryan and Gerald are changing the light lager to a light ale. ("We like to call it a light mild when no one's listening," Gerald said.) "It's still selling and we like it," Ryan told me. "It's easy to get excited about the saisons, but if we can brew the light and it sells and we like it, that's great."

A lot of that attitude comes from being able to brew what they want, with top-notch ingredients. "Bill is big on good ingredients in the food, and we get to do that, too," Ryan said. "We get Maris Otter malts for the British ales, French malt for the Belgians. Bill and Scott both believe in keeping it simple—use the best ingredients, because it's all about process."

It shows in the beer, it shows in the food: The menu at McKenzie has always been well prepared and delicious, coming out of the big, open kitchen. The downstairs lounge has evolved from a game room into a more comfortable, relaxing area with couches and chairs.

The beer is good and dependable and continues to change. Not the beers you'll see on the list; that doesn't change much. Ryan picked that up from Scott as well. "So many brewpubs get caught up in making as

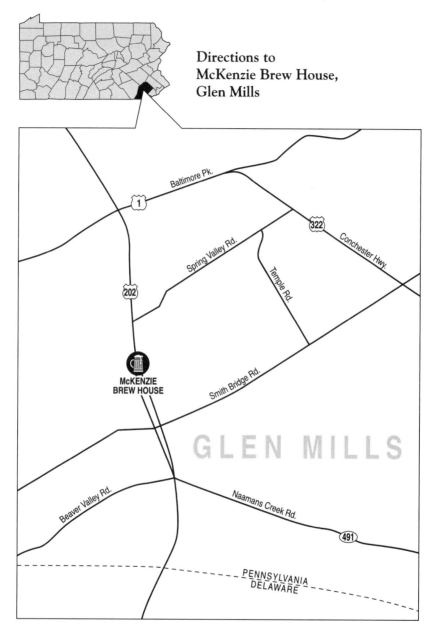

**Directions to
McKenzie Brew House,
Glen Mills**

many styles as they can," he said. "I'd rather really dial in the beers I want to make, the ones people like. I believe in five different sessionable beers . . . but then I can make saison. That's freedom to brew."

Saison has landed at McKenzie. They've made the beer, and the drinkers have caught up. Who knows what will happen next?

Opened: December 2001.

Owners: Bill Mangan.

Brewers: Ryan Michaels, head brewer; Gerald Olson, brewer.

System: 10-barrel Specific Mechanical brewhouse, 1,400 barrels potential annual capacity.

2009 production: 1,200 barrels.

Brewpub hours: Seven days a week, 11:30 AM to 2 AM.

Tours: On request, subject to brewer's availability.

Take-out beer: Growlers, some 750-milliliter specialty bottles available.

Food: Great small dishes with a Mediterranean flair. Key things here: hummus plates; the Santorini Sampler, featuring tzatziki and tapenade with warm pitas; and a great selection of Italian pickables. Move on to the delicious fresh grilled fish, grilled meatloaf, lump crab cakes, and the great daily soups (Maryland crab and brie bisque every day), or stay simple with a burger or a Baja Mahi taco with lime aioli.

Extras: Downstairs is Metro, with a granite bar serving big killer martinis, plenty of comfy couches, and DJs Thursday through Saturday.

Special considerations: Kids welcome. You won't find vegetarian entrées, per se, but there are substantial vegetarian sides—stir-fried vegetables, grilled asparagus—as well as a range of salads and the reliable pizzas.

Parking: Large free on-site lot.

Lodging in the area: Brandywine River Hotel, 1609 Baltimore Pike, Chadds Ford, 800-274-9644; Holiday Inn Express, 1110 Baltimore Pike, Glen Mills, 610-358-1700; Best Western, Routes 1 and 322, Concordville, 610-358-9400.

Area attractions: See the listing for Iron Hill, West Chester (page 76).

Other area beer sites: The *Half Moon Restaurant and Saloon* (108 W. State St., Kennett Square. 610-444-7232) has a worthy selection of crafts, plus good food that goes well beyond pub grub. *Firewaters* (1110 Baltimore Pike, Concord, 610-459-9959) has fifty taps and more than a hundred bottles, another like the highly successful and geek-beloved Firewaters in Atlantic City.

Iron Hill Brewery, West Chester

High and Gay Streets, West Chester, PA 19380
610-738-9600
www.ironhillbrewery.com

This is a big place. There's a good-size bar, a big dining room, and more dining nooks tucked in here and there. But big as it is, Iron Hill manages to fill it. Iron Hill was the "Brewpub of Dreams" in West Chester—the partners built it and people came, in droves. The biggest problem the West Chester store had in its first six months of business was making enough beer to meet demand. I remember stopping by in December 1998 and finding mostly "guest beers" from area craft brewers and only one Iron Hill beer on tap. People drank them right out of beer.

What a problem to have! That's all taken care of now, with new tanks in place, and everyone's happy. Even with the experience partners Mark Edelson, Kevin Finn, and Kevin Davies had from operating their first Iron Hill brewpub in Newark, Delaware, they just weren't ready for the terrific thirst they found in West Chester.

That first Iron Hill has been a smashing success, winning popular opinion polls for best restaurant, best brewpub, and best place to look at women (and they say geeks are only interested in beer!). Though the West Chester pub isn't an exact copy of it, most of the good bits have been carried over. The dark wood decor is in place, looking elegant and established. The menu is similar, with well-executed pub food and adventurous yet solid dinner entrées. The service is attentive and friendly, just as it always is in Newark.

"We spend a lot of time and money on server training," West Chester head brewer Larry Horwitz told me. "There's two hours of beer training for each new server."

Beers brewed: Iron Hill's house beers include Iron Hill Light Lager, Raspberry Wheat, Vienna Red Lager, Ironbound Ale, Pig Iron Porter, and a rotating Belgian style. Seasonals and specials: Highland Flame 60-Shilling Scotch Ale, Kryptonite Imperial IPA, Malthra the Destroyer Barleywine, Hefeweizen, Dunkelweizen, Wild Boar, Belgian Pale Ale, Dry Stout, Abbey Dubbel, Russian Imperial Stout, Hopfvenweiss, Cherry Dubbel, Farmer Chuck Saison, Framboise, India Black Ale, Tripel, Cannibal, Hopzilla, Lambic de Hill . . . does Larry make a new beer every day? The Iron Hill bottled reserves are available; ask your server what's current.

He called a relatively new server over and asked her to run a sampler for me. She not only tapped and arranged the beers expertly and without pause, but also gave me brief, accurate descriptions of each one that went well beyond the "this is our pale ale, it's hoppy; this is our stout, it's black" you'll get many places. Best of all, she did it without an air of imposition or recitation; there was a real feeling that she not only knew what she was saying, but understood it as well. "Every one of our servers can do that," Larry said proudly.

What about servers that don't like beer? I asked. It drives me crazy when I run into servers trying to sell me beer who have no idea what it tastes like because they don't drink it. What are they doing working at a brewpub? "They don't work here," Larry said. "That was one of the first questions Mark asked me: 'Do you like beer?' Is this an interview? He was serious!" Larry laughed out loud. Then he dragged me back into the cold room and tapped up a sample of barleywine. Larry likes beer.

He likes working at Iron Hill, too. "These guys are great—they're really serious about beer, and they let me make anything I want as long as I make the regulars," Larry said. "And it's always brand new equipment, always top-of-the-line malts and hops, and never cutting any corners on the process." Larry beamed with pleasure. "I *love* this place!"

Larry was formerly the brewer at Iron Hill, North Wales, where I worked on a writing project with him that involved some seriously technical brewing issues. I gained a lot of respect for his scientific brewing savvy. "Larry's always the one asking nerdy questions at Master Brewers Association meetings," another Iron Hill brewer told me. That's the kind of brewer Iron Hill hires.

Although the partners have always said that Iron Hill is a restaurant first and a brewpub second, you'd never know it from the quality of the brewing. When you're as concerned about the total quality of your establishment as these guys are, nothing really comes second. The beer is not just good, it's outstanding. They do ales that are superb and regularly put some in cask to serve as "real ale" to the connoisseurs. They also have made a commitment to brewing lagers; the Light Lager is well made, the Vienna Red is malty and clean, and crisp, hoppy pilsners make regular appearances.

I like drinking at a place with a happy brewer. I like drinking at a place where I know everyone really likes beer. I like drinking at a place where the staff know their beers well enough to explain them to my

The Pick: Larry makes a Belgian Pale Ale that packs great flavor into a beer with under 5 percent ABV: malt, spun candy, spice. My hat's off to a brewer who can thrill me without throwing a ton of stuff in the kettle (or slamming my forebrain).

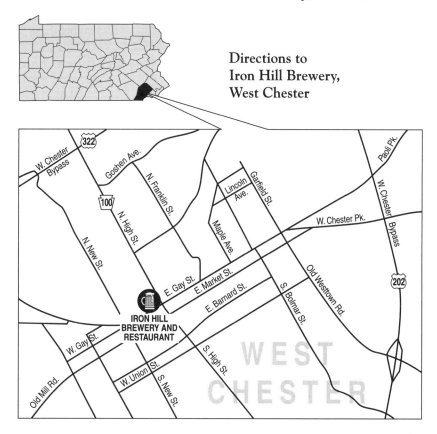

Directions to
Iron Hill Brewery,
West Chester

mother. I like drinking at Iron Hill, West Chester, because Larry Horwitz—like Edelson, Finn, and Davies—likes beer. It makes a difference.

Opened: September 1998.

Owners: Mark Edelson, Kevin Finn, Kevin Davies.

Brewer: Larry Horwitz, head brewer; Jean Broillet, assistant.

System: 8.5-barrel Specific Mechanical Systems, 1,600 barrels potential annual capacity.

2009 production: 1,250 barrels.

Brewpub hours: Sunday and Monday, 11 AM to 11 PM; Tuesday through Thursday, 11 AM to midnight; Friday and Saturday, 11 AM to 1 AM.

Tours: On request.

Take-out beer: Growlers and bottled reserve.

Food: "Regional American fare" doesn't do justice to this toothsome menu, ranging from well-executed pub fare to the saffron-infused Brewmaster's Mussels and daily salmon specials. Sundays are special, with a popular, laid-back brunch and a prime rib special for dinner. Save room: Iron Hill's desserts are phenomenal.

Extras: Pool tables. Outdoor dining in season. Mug club. Frequent special dinner deals: check Web site for details.

Special considerations: Kids welcome. Vegetarian meals available.

Parking: On-street metered parking can be tight, but there is a garage at Chestnut and Walnut Streets.

Lodging in the area: Abbey Green Motor Lodge, 1036 Wilmington Pike, 610-692-3310; Microtel Inn, 500 Willowbrook Ln., 610-738-9111; Holiday Inn–West Chester, 943 S. High St., 610-692-1900.

Area attractions: Fly over to the *American Helicopter Museum* (1220 American Blvd., 610-436-9600, www.helicoptermuseum.org) and check out the vintage rotary-wing aircraft and museum exhibits. Nearby is *Longwood Gardens* (800-737-5500, www.longwood gardens.org), the former country estate of Pierre Du Pont and one of the most impressive horticultural displays in the United States. The conservatory building and 3.5 acres of greenhouses allow year-round displays of bounteous flowering plants. The gardens have three sets of impressive fountains. Reservations are suggested for seasonal shows. This is also mushroom country; growers in Kennett Square and Avondale supply most of the country's mushrooms. There is an annual *Mushroom Festival* (888-440-9920, www.mushroomfestival .org) in Kennett Square in September. Not far away are the Brandywine-area attractions, including *Brandywine Battlefield Park* (Routes 1 and 100) and the *Brandywine River Museum* (610-388-2700, www.brandywinemuseum.org), which houses artwork by the Wyeths. The *Brandywine River* offers a beautiful, serene canoe trip; paddle your own or check into the canoe rental services in the area.

Other area beer sites: This used to be a pretty barren area, but things have picked up since Iron Hill came to town. The *Spence Café* (29 E. Gay St., 610-738-8844) is a great seafood restaurant, a good place for live music (jazz, blues, and alternative), and one of the area's best bottled beer collection. Want Irish? One of the local chain of *Kildare's Pubs* (18–22 W. Gay St., 610-431-0770) is in town, and it's a nice rendition of the theme. A bit out into the country is *Four Dogs Tavern* (1300 W. Strasburg Rd. [Route 162], 610-692-4367), a comfortable place in an old building, with great food and a smart selection of taps at a cozy bar. Also see the Victory listing on page 86.

Boxcar Brewing

306 Westtown Road, Unit C, West Chester, PA 19382
484-887-0538

Boxcar Brewing coupled onto the *Pennsylvania Breweries* train just as it was leaving the station: I found out about this new brewery only a week before I sent in the manuscript. Patrick Mullen, once the celebrity beer manager at the Drafting Room in Exton and now a rep for Sierra Nevada, sent this e-mail to a couple beer writers: "Anyone ever heard of Boxcar Brewing in West Chester? I ran into the owner this week at Goshen Beverage." Half an hour later, I had Jamie Robinson on the line.

"We're making ales," he said in response to my first blurted question, what are you doing? "We're starting with Boxcar Original Ale. It's a pale ale, not overly hopped, about 5 percent. It's definitely a craft beer, but it's not going to knock people's socks off. We look to appeal to micro-brew lovers and other people as well. People that are into the extravagant stuff, people who are into Rolling Rock and Miller Lite, they can all enjoy this."

Don't look for more beers any time soon. Jamie and partner Jason Kohser (Jamie's wife's cousin) are pulling out of the station nice and slow. "Once we've got this one dialed in and we feel comfortable about it, we'll try something else," he said. "We'll look into IPAs, we're going to do a stout down the road."

Before you start thinking this is something in a basement somewhere, Boxcar is no nanobrewery. They're brewing in 10-barrel batches, although they are hand-bottling for now. "We're using old dairy tanks we got in Lancaster," Jamie told me. That's old school!

Why Boxcar? "There is a long history of railroad workers in my partner's and my wife's families," Jamie said. "They have at least two family members that are still conductors. Boxcar was just something we came up with, and it stuck. It all follows our simplistic branding. The cases look like train cars or cargo with a stamped logo." They're packaging the beer in 12-ounce bottles and kegs.

Both Jamie and Jason were working in the wine business before they knew each other, Jason out in California. When he came east, he realized he couldn't make that kind of wine here. He gravitated

Beers brewed: Boxcar Original Ale.

The Pick: Haven't even had a chance to see this beer, let alone taste it. It's literally out this week.

to beer and started homebrewing. After he and Jamie had met through Jamie's wife, they started homebrewing together. "After about three years, we got more serious about that," Jamie said.

And here they are, starting up a brewery. All aboard, beer train's leaving!

Opened: February 2010.
Owners: Jamie Robinson, Jason Kohser.
Brewers: Jamie Robinson, Jason Kohser.
System: 12-barrel custom-made system, 800 barrels annual capacity.
2009 production: Not available.
Tours: By appointment.
Take-out beer: Cases and kegs.
Parking: Plenty of off-street parking.
Lodging in the area, Area attractions, Other area beer sites: See Iron Hill, West Chester, on page 76 and Victory on pages 85–86.

Iron Hill Brewery, Media

30 East State Street, Media, PA 19063
610-627-9000
www.ironhillbrewery.com

I gave you some of the Iron Hill story in West Chester, and I'll give you more in North Wales. Here in Media, let's just talk Iron Hill, Media, and brewer Bob Barrar.

The first time I went to the Media Iron Hill was for one of Iron Hill's Brewer's Reserve nights. They do these less regularly than they used to, but they're a lot of fun, and you should come out for them if you get a chance (check the Web site for scheduled events). They invite an outside brewer or two or more—or in this case, a distiller, Anchor—to come in and share their finest beer, and all the Iron Hill brewers bring a keg or cask of their finest, and those beers go on special that night. You can tour the brewery, hang out with all the brewers, get a free pint glass, and have a rare chance to taste a bunch of GABF medal–level beers all at once. Okay, you actually get that chance at Iron Hill pretty often, but this is more so!

Anyway, it was a cold December night, and Cathy and I went over to Iron Hill Media. Mark Edelson had told me that the brewery was built in an old supermarket, and I wasn't really expecting much. Cleanup on aisle six, I guess. But I was stunned. Iron Hill doesn't spare expense on interior architecture in any of its restaurants, but this one was beautiful, easily my favorite in the group. High ceilings give a huge feeling of space that the warm tones of the wood and paint keep from being intimidating. The lighting is subdued and indirect.

"Supermarket?" I asked Mark. "There was a suspended ceiling," he said. "They removed it, and there was all this space up there. The architect loved it and talked us into using it." He shook his head with a painful grin. "It's gorgeous, but it was expensive, and it's a bear to heat it in the winter." Suffering for the art builds character, Mark. (Besides, he's since told me that they've significantly minimized the problem; smart guys!)

Bob Barrar is the brewer here—"Bob the Brewer," as he's known. I drank his imperial stout that night, and it was a deep, dark, rich beauty of a beer. "I love wintertime," Bob confided to me. "I like big Belgians, I like Russian imperial stouts, the big beers you can make in wintertime." With Bob's bushy black beard, the Russian imperial stouts are a natural, but I have to question how much a man who consistently wears a pair of cargo shorts regardless of the temperature really *likes* winter!

It does show in his beers. Bob's regular beers are well-made, competent brews, but his passion and craft are lavished on the bigger beers. Even his Pig Iron Porter shows evidence of that love. His West Coast Gold is a light golden ale with a bargeload of hops in it—completely unbalanced, and that's the point. Bob loves the Belgian types: His Dubbel was deep and sweet, yet complex and structured—much nicer than most other American-brewed dubbels I've had—and his Tripel was similarly deep, spiked with bright spice and yeast notes, a beautiful masterwork of a beer. At Iron Hill, they call Bob "The Medal Machine" for all the honors his beers have won at the Great American Beer Festival.

This is probably a good place to tell you about the Iron Hill Bottled Reserve project, since it's mostly big beers. Iron Hill doesn't do beers for

Beers brewed: Iron Hill's house beers include Iron Hill Light Lager, Raspberry Wheat, Vienna Red Lager, Ironbound Ale, Pig Iron Porter, and a rotating Belgian style. Seasonals: Altbier, Barleywine, Belgian White, Bohemian Pils, Dry Stout, ESB, Hefeweizen, Imperial IPA, India Pale Ale, Lambic de Hill, Maibock, Munich Dunkel, Nut Brown Ale, Oatmeal Stout, Oktoberfest, Old Ale, Russian Imperial Stout, Saison, Tripel, Vienna, Wee Heavy, Oud Bruin, Doppelbock, Weizenbock . . . and a lot more. The Iron Hill bottled reserves are available; ask your server what's current.

the take-home market, at least, not the greater market. But at Iron Hill, you can get big bottles (and sometimes *huge* 3-liter bottles) of special beers, like the Russian Imperial Stout, The Cannibal, strong Belgian, aged vintages of Old Ale (very nice), Wee Heavy, Quadrupel . . . you get the idea. There aren't a lot of these bottles, and they're not cheap, but they are special. Not every Iron Hill has the same ones; ask what they have. You can take them home, or you can share them at your table or the bar.

The Pick: Not every Iron Hill house beer is exactly alike. Bob's Pig Iron Porter is righteous, a wild boar of a Pig Iron Porter, heavy, gutsy, and maybe even a little threatening, beer with a bite to it. Hops, chocolate, fruit, weight, alcohol—take a sip, it's all in there, waiting. Take one on.

I've been to Media in the summer, and Bob's big, hoppy beers are great in the heat. But I think I'm going to make a habit of going to Media in the winter, to see what big, deep beers Bob has to sip on while I look out the front windows at the cold, cold weather that can't touch me in that extravagantly heated beauty of a brewpub.

Opened: June 2000.
Owners: Mark Edelson, Kevin Finn, Kevin Davies.
Brewer: Bob Barrar.
System: 8.5-barrel Specific Mechanical brewhouse, 1,000 barrels potential annual capacity.
2009 production: 820 barrels (est.).
Brewpub hours: Sunday and Monday, 11 AM to 11 PM; Tuesday through Thursday, 11 AM to midnight, Friday and Saturday, 11 AM to 1 AM.
Tours: On request.
Take-out beer: Growlers and bottled reserve.
Food: See the listing for Iron Hill, West Chester, on page 75.
Extras: Mug club. Frequent special dinner deals: check Web site for details. Iron Hill also hosts a local beer festival in the parking lot beside this site in May; watch the Iron Hill Web site for details.
Special considerations: Kids welcome. Vegetarian meals available.
Parking: Street parking, plus public lots on both sides of the restaurant.
Lodging in the area: Alpenhof B&B, 2001 N. Ridley Creek Rd., Media, 610-891-8222; Howard Johnson–Springfield, 650 Baltimore Pike, Springfield, 610-544-4700.
Area attractions: The shopping in Media is good: boutiques and antiques abound. **Ridley Creek State Park** (1023 Sycamore Mills Rd., 610-892-3900) has fishing and trails for biking, walking, cross-country skiing, and horseback riding . . . if you have a horse with you.

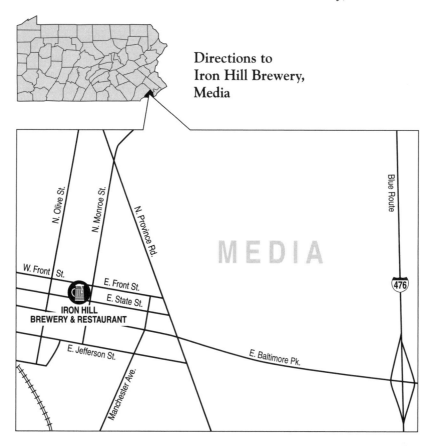

Directions to
Iron Hill Brewery,
Media

Other area beer sites: ***Quotations*** (37 E. State St., 610-627-2515) is right across the street and always has something hot on tap; quite a few somethings, actually. ***Pinocchio's Restaurant*** (131 E. Baltimore Pike, Media, 610-566-7767) looks like just another pizza place, but they've got some great beers pouring and hundreds of bottles for take-out. Definitely worth a look.

Victory Brewing Company

420 Acorn Lane, Downingtown, PA 19335
610-873-0881
www.victorybeer.com

Victory is aptly named. It is a victory of the beer geek over the marketer. The two principals, Ron Barchet and Bill Covaleski, are childhood friends who homebrewed together for years. Then, through an odd set of circumstances they wound up brewing at the same microbrewery. One thing led to another, and they decided to open their own. After years of plans, salesmanship, and sweat, Victory was born.

Victory has grown tremendously but still doesn't compromise for the market. Ron and Bill believe that there is a market for uncompromising beer. "Everyone else is brewing what they think the market wants," said Ron. "We're brewing what we want, and we're beer geeks."

They're uncommon beer geeks, at that. Victory brews lager as well as ales—*great* lagers—bucking the national trend in microbrewing. Pennsylvania does have the greatest concentration of lager microbrewers in the country, but I suspect that Ron and Bill are brewing lagers not just because they want them, but because they know that the best chance for a craft brewer at catching a truly large part of the American beer market lies with good lager beer.

"Festbier is the number-two beer in our pub," Ron said, noting that out in the wider market, Festbier lags quite a bit back in the pack. "The people coming in those doors keep us grounded in what we can pull off with beer without sitting on old kegs."

Some kind of strategy is working, because Victory has become Pennsylvania's largest craft brewer. The brewery just expanded their capacity with a new fermentation tank farm that planted four 440-barrel tanks—huge tanks by "microbrew" standards—in the back of the brewery buildings, where an eye-popping automated grain handling system

Beers brewed: Year-round: HopDevil Ale, Golden Monkey, Victory Lager, Prima Pils, Storm King Stout, Hop Wallop, Baltic Thunder, Helios Ale, V Twelve, Donnybrook Stout, WildDevil, Mad King's Weiss, Braumeister Pils (of some sort), Uncle Teddy's Bitter (mostly at the pub). Seasonals: St. Victorious Doppelbock, St. Boisterous Hellerbock, Whirlwind Wit, Sunrise Weissbier, Old Horizontal Barleywine, Festbier, Moonglow Weizenbock. Always more new beers at the pub.

was already installed. The tank farm is already prepped with room for eight more of the big tanks, which would give them the capacity to pump out 100,000 barrels a year; that's confidence—and planning. It's not unwarranted, given that 18 percent growth (almost all in established Victory markets) brought them within an eyelash of 50,000 barrels in 2009.

The Pick: Too many great beers! Drink the St. Boisterous Hellerbock, one of the best examples of this beer brewed anywhere. Helios is broad-shouldered yet refreshing. Grab some cask-conditioned Uncle Teddy's at the pub. Finally, in their Lager, Victory has mastered the malt character of the Munich helles, a beer that evaporates from your glass. This is my dad's Pick, too, one of the few craft beers he truly enjoys. It's part of the greatness of this beer that he and I can both love it.

"We use them to brew HopDevil, Golden Monkey, Prima Pils, and the big seasonals," Bill said of the new tanks. With their highly automated and efficient 50-barrel brewhouse, they can fill one of them in a day. "We could have had a 100-barrel brewery that did four brews in one day, but our 50-barrel kettle does over eight, and we have more flexibility to do smaller one-offs."

Those one-offs are filling the twenty-plus taps in Victory's revamped taproom. "We spent a lot of evenings watching families being told it would be an hour wait for a table," Bill said. "Everything was twelve years old and starting to fall apart anyway, and a run-down restaurant isn't a good face. The pub's a very important marketing tool for the beer. It's also the highest-volume restaurant in Chester County, which is absurd—it's a pizza and beer place!"

The renovation cost $2.7 million in all and took three months, but they opened on time . . . even though workmen were still finishing off decorative touches and TV installation over the bar as we drank to the occasion. We drank broadly, too, because the taps were full of a great variety of beer that has not let up in the two years since then.

"Those pub-only onetime beers benefit the Victory drinker who never even gets here," Ron said. "Filling twenty taps leads to experimentation, which may lead to new regular beers, like Yakima Twilight or WildDevil." I like that math, almost as much as I like the dark, stingingly hoppy Yakima Twilight. Always having the choice of two or three cask-conditioned ales, a new single-hop pilsner, a smoked beer, and the latest Belgian tweak works for me.

The centerpiece of the bar might be the dramatic new growler filler. The bartender takes your flip-top 2-liter growler and puts it in the filler, which looks something like the "food replicator" in cheesy science fiction: a glass door with buttons spaced on either side of it, one for each beer on tap. The bartender closes the door, presses the button corresponding to the beer you want, and walks away. A light comes on so you

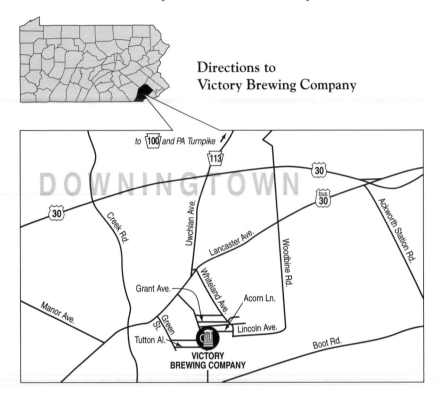

Directions to
Victory Brewing Company

can see your growler being automatically cleaned, rinsed, preevacuated of air, and filled under counterpressure (no foam-over). The bartender opens the door, flips the cap closed, and hands you the growler.

"It is an attraction," Bill admitted. "We're no geniuses; we just wanted to offer as high a quality growler fill as you get in our bottled beers. It was $12,000 and it's already paid for itself. The waste is much less, the bartenders have more time, and our growler sales quadrupled."

That's what I like about these guys: They always have a good reason for the cool stuff they do. If they're making a great variety of beers, it's because they like them, and if other people do, that's good, too. If they're putting new toys in the brewhouse, it's because it makes the beer taste better or stay fresher longer. If they're expanding the barroom, it's because it's a marketing tool.

Come on! They're doing it because they're having fun, because they want to make the best beer they can. They're doing this so they have great beer to drink and a great place to do it. That's why they're Pennsylvania's biggest micro: They're brewing like nobody's watching. I hope they get away with that for years.

Opened: February 1996.

Owners: Victory Brewing Company.

Brewers: Ron Barchet, Bill Covaleski, and a staff of eight.

System: 50-barrel Rolec brewhouse, 67,000 barrels annual capacity.

2009 production: 49,000 barrels.

Brewpub hours: Monday through Saturday, 11:30 AM to midnight; Sunday, 11:30 AM to 10 PM.

Tours: Friday 4 PM; Saturday noon. No high heels or open-toed shoes allowed.

Take-out beer: Growlers, single 22-ounce and 750-milliliter bottles, six-packs, cases, kegs.

Food: Victory's wood-fired oven bakes great pizzas, and the in-house smoker uses American hickory. All the chicken and pork on the menu are Pennsylvania-raised. You can get fresh salads, hearty sandwiches (do yourself a favor: get the Dietrich. You're welcome), and some of the best fries around. Before you make a decision, be sure to check the seasonal specials; some old favorites are there from years gone by. If you just want a snack, try the homemade, hand-rolled soft pretzels. Victory also brews a great root beer.

Extras: Screens for sports over the bar. Monday is open mike night, the Victory Jazz Quintet plays monthly, and there are frequent special dinners and events; check the Web site for schedules. Visit the well-stocked gift shop for a huge range of V-gear.

Special considerations: Kids welcome. Vegetarian meals available.

Parking: Lots of free off-street parking; please stick to the lined spaces!

Lodging in the area: Hampton Inn, 600 W. Uwchlan Ave., Exton, 610-363-5555; Faunbrook B&B, 699 W. Rosedale Ave., West Chester, 610-436-5788; Holiday Inn Express, 120 N. Pottstown Pike, Exton, 610-524-9000.

Area attractions: If it's apple-picking time, go to **Highland Orchards** (610-269-3494, www.highlandorchards.net) to pick your own. They do have already picked apples for sale, too. The **Stargazer's Stone** (Route 162 and Stargazer Road) was an observation point for the surveying of the Mason-Dixon line. The **Brandywine River Museum** (1 Hoffman's Mill Rd., Chadds Ford, 610-388-2700, www.brandywine-museum.org) presents the Brandywine Valley's influence on American art, including landscapes, still lifes, and the incredible Wyeth family. If you have younger kids, you'll want to visit **Springton Manor Farm** (860 Springton Rd., Glenmoore, 610-942-2450), a demonstration farm with pigs and poultry in a petting area. Admission is free. If you want to see how things used to be done on the farm, back in the days of steam, you'll want to hit the Old Thresherman's Reunion at the **Rough and Tumble Engineers Historical Association** (on the eastern edge of Kinzers, on the north side of Route 30; full schedule at www.roughandtumble.org). They have a number of events during the year, but the Old Thresherman's Reunion, in mid-August, features one of the biggest collections of steam tractors, steam shovels, early gas and diesel tractors, stationary steam engines, and "hit and miss" engines that you'll find anywhere—everything from a huge stationary Corliss engine to a tiny Sterling cycle engine you could hold in the palm of your hand.

Other area beer sites: *Station Taproom* (207 W. Lancaster Ave., across from the SEPTA station, Downingtown, 484-593-0560), with twelve solidly craft taps, is the westernmost stop of an excellent train-based pubcrawl on the SEPTA R5 line that beings at 30th Street Statoin with Bridgewaters and includes Teresa's Next Door (Wayne), TJ's (Paoli), and the Flying Pig (Malvern). All aboard for beer! *Ron's Original Bar and Grille* (74 E. Uwchlan Ave., Exton, 610-594-9900) has upped the craft game immensely, and the stone and tile décor make this place a cut above the ordinary. Get a glass of great beer at the *Drafting Room* (635 N. Route 113, Exton, 610-363-0521), where they've had some of the best beer events in the 'burbs. The *Whip Tavern* (1383 N. Chatham Rd., Coatesville, 610-383-0600, www.thewhiptavern.com) is right out in the country south of Coatesville, and that's part of its charm; the other part is the excellent English pub food and great selection of tap and bottle beers, with—of course—an emphasis on English ales. See the listing for Iron Hill, West Chester, on page 76 for more suggestions.

McKenzie Brew House, Malvern

240 Lancaster Avenue, Malvern, PA 19355
610-296-2222
www.mckenziebrewhouse.com

"Stainless never dies" is a favorite brewing aphorism of mine, and this brewery's Canadian-built heart came out of Brü, a brewpub I used to frequent and love in Rochester, New York. I'm happy to report that Ryan Michaels and Gerard Olson are putting it to good use here at the McKenzie Brew House's second operation in Malvern.

It is both brewers, too. During the interview, I noticed that while Ryan is the head brewer, Gerard's included in every conversation. "We both brew at both places," Gerard said. "We try to keep it as collaborative as possible." It's worked well, given that the two pubs have similar designs and identical menus.

Still, you can't call it too corporate, too "chain," when the beers they're making are so adventurous, almost avant-garde. There's a serious barrel-aging and souring program going on—we like that kind of thing around Philly—and the specialty bottlings are top-notch.

You'll find the same kind of atmosphere and good times at both places; the only real differences are the addresses and the design of the underground bar area. Glen Mills is more upscale, Malvern is more active and publike. The beer is great both places.

Opened: April 2006.
Owner: Bill Mangan.
Brewers: Ryan Michaels, head brewer; Gerard Olson, brewer.
System: 15-barrel Criveller brewhouse, 2,500 barrels potential annual capacity.
2009 production: 1500 barrels.
Brewpub hours: Seven days a week, 11:30 AM to 2 AM.

Beers brewed: Year-round: McKenzie Light, Wit, Saison Vautour, American Pale Ale, English Brown Ale, Oatmeal Stout. Specialties: Grisette, Fantine, Chateau McKenzie, and a lot more.

The Pick: I love multisite breweries: more Picks! I have to tip my hat to the Grisette: low alcohol, high flavor, and that unexpected peppery spice is great with shellfish. But the bottled Chateau McKenzie is awesome: Mellows as it warms and breathes, broadening into one of the maltiest oak-aged beers I've had. Enticing and delicious.

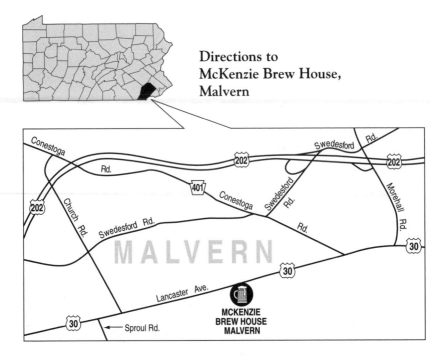

Directions to
McKenzie Brew House,
Malvern

Tours: On request, subject to brewer's availability.

Take-out beer: Growlers, some 750-milliliter specialty bottles available.

Food: Same as at McKenzie's Glen Mills location (see page 72).

Extras: The Underground pub is more informal, with pool tables, foosball, video golf, air hockey, darts, and my favorite: authentic shuffleboard. A deck is also available in warm weather.

Special considerations: Kids welcome. You won't find vegetarian entrées, per se, but there are substantial vegetarian sides—stir-fried vegetables, grilled asparagus—as well as a range of salads and the reliable pizzas.

Parking: Large free on-site lot.

Lodging in the area, Area attractions: See Victory on pages 85–86 and Iron Hill, West Chester, on page 76.

Other area beer sites: The *Flying Pig Saloon* (121 E. King St., Malvern, 610-578-9208) is as comfortable as broken-in jeans, with a bottle collection that's definitely worth your time and ten rotating taps of the good stuff. Just up Lancaster Avenue is *TJ's Restaurant and Drinkery* (a right turn out of the McKenzie lot right into Paoli: 35 Paoli Plaza, 610-725-0100), a joint so good, with such a great array of beers that I've used them in stories for national magazines. Cool place, too. The multitap *Boat House* (16 Great Valley Parkway, Great

Valley Corporate Center, Malvern, 610-251-0207) has good food to go with the beer selection. See the listings for Victory on page 86 and Iron Hill, West Chester, on page 76 for more suggestions.

Sly Fox Brewhouse and Eatery

520 Kimberton Road (Route 113)
Phoenixville, PA 19460
610-935-4540
www.slyfoxbeer.com

Last edition, I wrote how things had changed completely at Sly Fox: "A new logo, a new menu from a new chef, new beers, a great new tap system, a new outdoor dining area, new events, new attitude—and much of it is thanks to their new brewer."

How about this for change: They're moving the whole brewpub. You don't get much more changed than that. Actually, brewpubs don't move that often. Breweries, sure, there's less disruption, less need to make people aware of where you are. But a brewpub depends on folks knowing where to drop in, have a pint, have dinner, catch a band, watch a game.

It's not really that big a deal: They're moving across Route 113, from one plaza to another. It was a matter of space. The original spot, much as it felt—how'd I put it? ". . . as if Grandma decided to build a brewery in her home," that's it—anyway, homey as it was, it was cramped. You felt it in the bar, you felt it in the dining room, and they felt it in the brewery and the kitchen, too.

When the space came open across the street, the decision was made to move. It hasn't happened yet, but as I write this, they're finishing up painting; by the time you have this book in your hands, they'll be in and settled.

I haven't seen the actual place yet, but brewer Brian O'Reilly—the "new brewer" mentioned above, who now seems like a fixture, impossible to imagine the place without him—walked me around the space. It's in a plaza, all on one level, and the brewery is still visible from the barroom.

There's outdoor seating, which is important, and lots of parking; also important.

As we stood outside the place, though, and Brian was talking about how things were going to look, I was nervous about something. Finally, while he was nattering on about some brewer thing, steam fittings or drains or something, I blurted out, "But what about the goat races? Will they let you have the Goat Races?" Now *that's* important!

Brian got a huge grin on his face and said, "That's the best part! The new landlords are Austrians—they think the goat races are *great!*"

So I'll have to explain. When O'Reilly first moved to the area, he brewed at a now-defunct brewpub up the road in Collegeville. He had a head for events even then, and he organized—now there's an overstatement—goat races for May Day. I remember that first one (yes, I went: I'm a sucker for anything that involves beer and farm animals): four goats, standing in the rain, and maybe eighty people. There were, however, good bock beers, wursts, and a German band inside. When O'Reilly moved to Sly Fox, he quickly persuaded the Giannopoulos family to pick up the tradition.

It's been an incredible success. In 2008, almost two thousand people showed up on a perfect spring afternoon to watch goats race. Oh, and drink O'Reilly's great beer, and there's the excitement in waiting for the Maibock to be named for the winning goat (really!), but . . . two thousand? For a goat race? Then 2009 rolled around, and it was raining again. O'Reilly admitted to me that he was not optimistic. "I was thinking, 'If it pours, we're screwed,'" he said. "It poured . . . and people thought it was even better!" Lots of people—fifteen hundred people showed up in pouring rain to watch goats race, which, I will submit to you, is even more amazing (or weird, okay) than two thousand showing up in sunny weather.

What's it all mean? It means that Sly Fox makes really good beer, good enough to get people to a rainy goat race. But also, and I think more importantly, it means that Sly Fox has grown a community around this pub. This was no drunken mosh. It was a family event; there were kids

Beers brewed: Year-round: Phoenix Pale Ale, Pikeland Pils, Royal Weisse, Rt. 113 IPA, Black Raspberry Reserve, O'Reilly's Stout. Helles Golden Lager, Saison Vos, O'Reilly's Stout, Chester County Bitter (cask only), Ichor, Incubus. Seasonals: Christmas Ale, Dunkel Lager, Gang Aft Agley, Helles Bock, Helles Eisbock, Instigator Doppel Eisbock, Instigator Doppelbock, Odyssey Imperial IPA, Octoberfest, Seamus' Irish Red Ale, Slacker Bock, Slacker Eisbock, TBD Maibock (may be the fastest goat win!), Whitehorse Wit. Occasionals: Abbey Xtra, Blob Ale, Burns' Scottish Export, Charles Bridge Pilsner, Dale's 10K, Foxy Lady Kolsch, Grisette, Keller Pils, Panacea, Pete's Peerless Ale, Pughtown Porter, Rauch Bier, Renard D'or, Schwarz Bier, Standard Ale, TeRYEdactALE . . . and more to come, undoubtedly.

everywhere, grandparents. That's wonderful, and Sly Fox is very, very good at it.

And as O'Reilly said, "Thank God for the 4-H Goat Club." Really? "Yeah, I always know we'll have at least ten goats!" The new location will have plenty of room for goat racing, although it may not be as challenging a course; it's flatter. You work with what you have.

About that great beer . . . As you can see from the list, O'Reilly and his right-hand man, Tim Ohst, aren't afraid to tackle anything (although we haven't seen much in the way of sour beers, the new darling of the geekerie). They nail the lagers, they make some of the best Belgian styles in this Flemish-happy area, and the cask ales just keep getting better. Anything you try will be at least good, and some of them are phenomenal.

The Pick: Gang Aft Agley makes me do just that, and it's great tonsil oil for getting limbered up for declaiming on Burns Night. It's multilayered, malt-heavy, and luscious. I'd also advise you to get the Keller Pils if it's available; too few brewpubs offer an unfiltered pilsner, and I think it's just the best way to drink this style—it's alive, vibrant, and charged with hop spirit.

Take the O'Reilly's Stout, for instance. I once complained to Brian that it was too dry; astringent, almost. He nodded, listened, then told me I was crazy. Strangely, I found myself looking for the taps, at first to see if he was right, then because I liked it, and now I'm drinking O'Reilly's Stout as my go-to beer in Philly. I hate it when he's right.

I can be at Sly Fox in less than an hour by slipping through the beautifully winding roads of Valley Forge National Historical Park. I do it often, and the new place will be just about a minute closer, I think. But it's not just the great beer, good food, or energized service that brings me back. It's that Goat Race vibe: the sociable feel, the "never a stranger" vibe that folds you in. Hope to see you there soon.

Opened: December 1995.

Owners: The Giannopoulos family.

Brewers: Brian O'Reilly, brewmaster; Tim Ohst, head of brewing operations; Steve Jacoby, Ricky Yerkers, Dave Braunstein, brewers.

System: 15-barrel Pub Brewing Systems brewhouse, 1,200 barrels annual capacity.

2009 production: 305 barrels.

Brewpub hours: Monday through Thursday, 11:30 AM to midnight; Friday and Saturday, 11:30 AM to 1 AM; Sunday noon to 10 PM.

Tours: On request; brewhouse is right behind the bar, behind glass.

Take-out beer: Six-packs, 22s, 750s, cases, growlers. Sly Fox is getting a growler filler like Victory's; line up and watch it work!

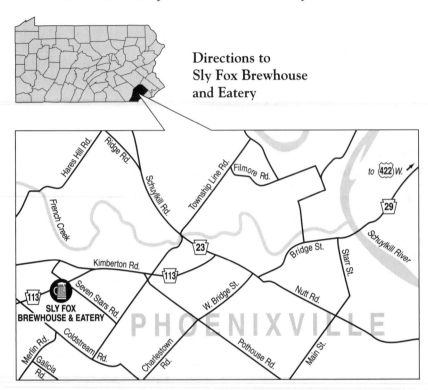

Directions to
Sly Fox Brewhouse
and Eatery

Food: Sly Fox's menu not only has all the standards—wings, steamed clams, tacos, burgers, bratwurst, fish and chips, chicken parmesan—they've got more: stuffed grape leaves, a classic Cuban sandwich (my constant choice), gyros, and Black & Blue Raspberry Salad. There are some real choices on this menu.

Extras: Sly Fox has no liquor license, but you'll find an excellent selection of Pennsylvania wines.

Special considerations: Kids welcome. Limited vegetarian meals available.

Parking: Plenty of free parking in off-street lot.

Lodging in the area: Morning Star B&B, 610 Valley Forge Rd., Phoenixville, 610-935-7473; Mainstay Inn, 184 Bridge St., Phoenixville, 610-933-7998; French Creek Inn, 2 Ridge Rd., Phoenixville, 610-935-3838.

Area attractions: You're not far from *Valley Forge National Historical Park* (described in the introduction to this section), down Route 422. *French Creek State Park* (west on Route 23, then north on Route 345) has camping, swimming, boating, fishing, 32 miles of hiking trails and 15 miles of cross-country skiing trails. The park is also the location of the *Hopewell Furnace National Historic Site*

(215-582-8773, www.nps.gov/hofu), a reconstructed anthracite iron furnace and ironmaking village.

Other area beer sites: *The Epicurean* (Route 113 and Township Line Rd., Phoenixville (610-933-1336), a very nice restaurant with six good taps and a wide bottle selection, also has a six-pack store that sells bottles to go. *The Pickering Creek Inn* (37 Bridge St., Phoenixville, 610-933-9962) is the bar everyone told me to hit in town, and they were right. The taps were eye-popping in their geek-itude, and they were good, too! Food's tasty, service was friendly and knowledgeable, and the setting by the creek is pleasing.

Iron Hill Brewery, Phoenixville

130 East Bridge Street, Phoenixville, PA 19460
610-983-9333
www.ironhillbrewery.com

Phoenixville is the smallest of the eight Iron Hills, smaller even than the first one in Newark, Delaware. This was an opportunity to get into a town that looked ready to turn around—the ill-fated Destiny brewpub (has a ring to it, doesn't it?) jumped in but couldn't make it work—and Iron Hill grabbed the brass ring.

It's worked out well for them. "When we moved into Phoenixville," Mark Edelson said, "it was dead in the day, no street traffic. Now it's great." I couldn't argue. I remember going to Phoenixville back in the early 1990s, when the Royal Scot was one of the better bars in the area for beer (sadly gone under), and the place was deserted then. But I'd just been bar-hopping in Phoenixville the night before talking to Mark: It was freezing, and windy, but people were going to dinner at Bridge Street restaurants, walking along the sidewalks, talking and having a good time. It's a different place these days.

Tim Stumpf works the smallest brewery in the chain but keeps the beers rolling. It's a tight fit, but the space works. The reward for you in all this smallness is that this is the most intimate of the Iron Hills. I like

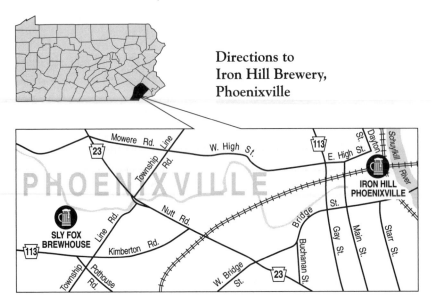

**Directions to
Iron Hill Brewery,
Phoenixville**

slipping in there nice and quiet on an afternoon, popping open my laptop at the bar, and getting some work done while having a pint of something like Tim's Schwarzbier. I saw Iron Hill partner Kevin Finn doing the same thing one day. Of course he was; it's quiet, it's not echoing-huge, and you get very personal service from the bartenders. Actually, I guess he gets good service at every Iron Hill.

Come to Phoenixville, walk around town, and slip into Iron Hill. Don't make much noise; we'll have a quiet beer together.

Opened: October 2006.

Owners: Mark Edelson, Kevin Finn, Kevin Davies.

Brewers: Tim Stumpf, head brewer; Matthew Gundrum, assistant.

System: 5-barrel specific mechanical brewhouse, 700 barrels potential annual capacity.

2009 production: 620 barrels.

Brewpub hours: Sunday and Monday, 11 AM to 11 PM; Tuesday through Thursday, 11 AM to midnight, Friday and Saturday, 11 AM to 1 AM.

Beers brewed: Iron Hill's house beers include Iron Hill Light Lager, Raspberry Wheat, Vienna Red Lager, Ironbound Ale, Pig Iron Porter, and a rotating Belgian-style. Seasonals: Hefeweizen, Irish Dry Stout, American IPA, Schwarzbier, Roggenbier, ESB, Berliner Weisse, Tripel, Russian Imperial Stout, Bourbon Barrel-Aged RIS, Wit, Abbey Dubbel, Munich Dunkel, Oktoberfest, Saison . . . and more. The Iron Hill bottled reserves are available; ask your server what's current.

The Pick: Simple, satisfying: Irish Dry Stout. It was an Irish kind of day, gentle rain and no breeze as fall was shutting down the trees for the year, and this beer suited it to a T: not too big, proper bitter bite, a hint of graham cracker.

Tours: On request.

Take-out beer: Growlers and bottled reserve.

Food: See the listing for Iron Hill, West Chester, on page 75.

Extras: Mug club. Frequent special dinner deals; check Web site for details.

Special considerations: Kids welcome. Vegetarian meals available.

Parking: On-street metered parking; town lot across the street.

Lodging in the area, Area attractions, Other area beer sites: See Sly Fox, Phoenixville, on pages 92–93.

Sly Fox Brewery and Pub

314 Lewis Road, Royersford Plaza
Royersford, PA 19468
610-948-8088
www.slyfoxbeer.com

The Sly Fox pub in Royersford looks big: a good-size bar, nice booths, the fireplace snuggery, and the dining room, plus a banquet room and a game room. It's big, but believe me: the real action is in the back. Walk back the hall past the banquet room and bathrooms, turn right, go through the door to your left, and you come into O'Reilly's Kingdom: the big Sly Fox brewery. It may not have the size or the impressive German hardware of a Victory or Tröegs, it may not have been around as long as Stoudt's, but Sly Fox has something those breweries don't: cans.

"When we opened Royersford," Sly Fox brewmaster Brian O'Reilly explained, "we were going to sell draft beer in Philly and big bottles of Ichor and Saison Vos: 750-milliliter bottle with the corks. Dogfish Head was selling their old corking-caging machine, and it was too cheap to pass up. But while we were doing the research, the supply of 750-milliliter beer bottles dried up. We decided to do 22-ounce bottles, but then we realized we didn't have enough outlets. We needed a 12-ounce package to open doors. I saw what Oskar Blues was doing and thought about cans."

Oskar Blues, a Colorado brewery, was the first American craft brewer to successfully do their own canning. They had learned about a deal from Ball for smaller runs of cans and a small canning machine. Once they stopped laughing—craft beer in cans!—they realized it made sense. The key to their success was that they didn't screw around: They put big, gutsy beers in their cans, like a heartily hopped pale ale and a big fat Scottish ale. They were a huge hit with craft beer drinkers looking for a lightweight, nonbreakable package: boaters, hikers, sports fans.

Beers brewed: Same as the Sly Fox Brewhouse and Eatery list, minus the Chester County Bitter.

The Pick: One of the cans seems right here, and the one I reach for most often is Pikeland Pils. It's crisp, it's hoppy, it's well made, it's delicious. And I can drink it from a can just like the guy with a Miller Lite. O'Reilly said so.

"Cans made sense," O'Reilly concurred. "They were economical; it was the same investment as glass. There are green reasons, but at our size, that's not a big consideration. But they're *cool*, they're different, and there wasn't a local brewer doing them. We got a lot of local press and attention [I know I wrote about it; it was *cool*], but we really just wanted to be able to pull a can of our beer out of the cooler!"

Think about that: how the craft beer drinker has been denied that simple pleasure, the dense, cold feel of a can in the hand, popping the top, and pouring cold beer right into the mouth. "The guy who likes good beer but doesn't want to drink it out of a wine glass," O'Reilly said, laughing, "that's the guy who wants the can. It's okay to drink it right out of the can, too. You have my permission!" Sorry to shock my geeky friends: Of all the Sly Fox cans I've put away, probably five out of six involved no glassware. It's just too fun!

It's easy, too. When I take beer somewhere remote, where good beer can't be found, or where I want to take it camping or biking, Sly Fox cans beat bottles hands-down. They take up less room, they weigh less, they don't break (at least not into razor-sharp shards), and when you're done with them, they crush down and pack out quite nicely. There's even choice: Sly Fox is doing pale ale, pilsner, dunkel, and weiss, and just added IPA in 2010. That's three of the major beer food groups right there!

"The cans are our bread and butter," O'Reilly said. "We're canning the Rt. 113 IPA now. I can see us buying a bigger rotary filler. The pubs are doing well, but production is on a different curve now. We actually tried to slow down growth last year and become more profitable, and it worked very well. We had a great year."

It's not all about Brian O'Reilly, of course. The Giannopoulos family keeps the brewery on track and has always been very smart about

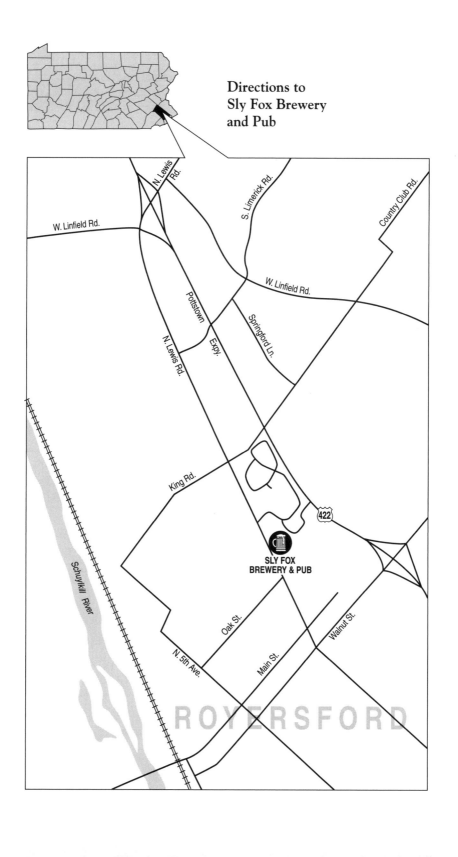

Directions to
Sly Fox Brewery
and Pub

N. Lewis Rd.

S. Limerick Rd.

Country Club Rd.

W. Linfield Rd.

Pottstown Expy.

N. Lewis Rd.

W. Linfield Rd.

Springford Ln.

King Rd.

422

SLY FOX
BREWERY & PUB

Schuylkill River

Oak St.

N. 5th Ave.

Main St.

Walnut St.

ROYERSFORD

reinvesting in the pubs and the brewery. John Giannopoulos has worked his business connections to line up new sources of kegs for the brewery, and his brother Pete—who came up with the whole Sly Fox idea to begin with; both brothers brewed at one time or another—continues to be a daily presence on the spot at the pubs.

Bigger things are ahead for Sly Fox. They'd been selling beer to promote their brewpubs; then they moved into promoting a brand. Now they're riding a tiger of strong growth. Can they do it? Yes, I think they can.

Opened: October 2004.

Owners: The Giannopoulos family.

Brewers: Brian O'Reilly, brewmaster; Tim Ohst, head of brewing operations; Steve Jacoby, Ricky Yerkers, Dave Braunstein, brewers.

System: 20-barrel Beraplan brewhouse, 10,000 barrels potential annual capacity.

2009 production: 6,423 barrels.

Brewpub hours: Sunday through Wednesday, 11:30 AM to 1 AM; Thursday through Saturday, 11:30 AM to 2 AM.

Tours: On request, subject to brewer availability.

Take-out beer: Six-packs, 22s, 750s, cases, growlers, kegs.

Food: Similar to the menu at the Phoenixville Sly Fox (see page 92), but with some different items. Stop by both places, you won't be bored.

Extras: Full liquor license. Private dining room. Large game room with pool tables, darts, video games, and a full-size shuffleboard table.

Special considerations: Kids welcome. Vegetarian meals available.

Parking: Large on-site lot

Lodging in the area: Shearer Elegance B&B, 154 Main St., Linfield, 610-495-7429; Staybridge Suites, 88 Anchor Parkway, Royersford, 610-792-9300.

Area attractions: *Pottsgrove Manor* (100 W. King St., Pottstown, 610-326-4014) is the restored 1752 home of John Potts, ironmaster, merchant, and founder of Pottstown. The house is built of sandstone in the Georgian style, a typical eighteenth-century Philadelphia merchant's home. See the listing for Sly Fox, Phoenixville, on page 92 for more suggestions.

Other area beer sites: The *Craft Ale House* (708 W. Ridge Pike, Limerick, 484-932-8180) hit the ground running and has changed the whole game in this area. It's not just the excellent beers they run through here; the food and the service match the quality of the beer. Cool place. *Ortino's* (800 Main St., Schwenksville, 610-287-8333) and **Northside** (1355 N. Gravel Pike, Zieglersville, 610-287-7272), both owned by the Ortino family, really get the whole good beer idea. Northside is bigger and more like a bar.

Rock Bottom, King of Prussia

160 North Gulph Road
The Plaza at King of Prussia (beside Sears)
King of Prussia, PA 19406
610-230-2739
www.rockbottom.com

Serious About Our Food. Crazy About Our Beer.

There's something that irks me a bit about beer geeks: Rock Bottom often gets very little credit from the geekerie, usually something about "It's a chain," or "The beers are all bland brewpub beers," or "The people there might start drinking craft beer someday." All I can figure is that these guys haven't actually spent much time in a Rock Bottom.

When I think of Rock Bottom, I think of Van Hafig, who used to be at the Arlington, Virginia, Rock Bottom and is now wowing the beer-savvy people of Portland, Oregon, or Geoff Lively, a genius with cask ales who I hope is chained to a long-term contract at the Bethesda Rock Bottom. In my experience, Rock Bottom brewpubs are places with bright, technically skilled brewers who like to stretch things as much as they can.

Clearly Rock Bottom thinks of Brian McConnell, the brewer at Rock Bottom, King of Prussia, in that same way. They have him overseeing—"auditing"—brewing at their brewpubs from Boston to DC, including the Homestead Rock Bottom near Pittsburgh and the District Chop House in DC. "It's a loose oversight," Brian said. For what it's worth, I definitely put Brian in that same category as well. I've been following him around for years, and not just because he's a great guy with a big sense of humor: Brian McConnell brews good beer, and he's still doing it here in King of Prussia.

Beers brewed: Regulars: Lumpy Dog Light, Munich Gold, Prussia's Pride IPA, Penn's Curse Amber, a rotating wheat, and a rotating dark beer (stout, porter, or schwarzbier). Specials: Grand Cru, Sub-Zero IPA, Nightmare on Bourbon Street, Mocha Stout, Liquid Sun Hefeweizen, Goat Toppler Maibock, King's Wit, Czech Mate Pilsner, Rocktoberfest, Fire Chief Ale . . . and more all the time.

He's got pretty clear views on brewing his own beers, too, and Rock Bottom backs him up. "A chain will get that 'It's all the same beer!' thing," he said, "but it's not; it wouldn't make sense to hire guys like us to do that. You could put some twenty-three-year-old kid in there, just following a book. If you're going to have a brewer on the premises, let 'em brew. With the food, go for consistency; with the beer, go for stand-out quality. Any brewpub chain should be doing it that way."

The Pick: Prussia's Pride has never failed me, with a sharply hoppy nose that is downright enlivening and a burst in the mouth that follows through exactly on what the nose promises. I love that in a beer. If the Czech Mate Pilsner's on, don't hesitate—it's a great soft-bodied pils.

Brian knows about brewpub chains. He came to this Rock Bottom from the John Harvard's chain of brewpubs, starting part-time at the DC John Harvard's back in 1997, then brewing at the Wilmington outpost. For a short time, he was holding down brewmaster duties at three area John Harvard's, but then the chain started to contract back to its New England roots and the pubs closed right out from under him, so he wound up at King of Prussia.

This Rock Bottom is a little bit different from the rest, but only a little. Like Brian, it used to be part of a New England brewpub chain: the Boston-based brew moon company. I remember it when it was brew moon; the décor has changed completely, but the brewhouse is just the same, and the pub's still conveniently located inside the mall, right beside a large parking lot.

While we're busting stereotypes about chain brewpubs, let's bust some about "mall brewpubs" as well. Rock Bottom is in the big King of Prussia mall complex, one of the biggest malls on the East Coast. But I hear the same damning, faint praise all the time about brewpubs in malls: "Well, it's not bad, for a mall brewpub." Eh? Check this scenario: I'm in the mall. It looks like a mall. Now . . . I walk into the brewpub. It looks like a brewpub. What makes it a "mall brewpub," *except for its location?* The mall part is all outside! If I took you in blindfolded and sat you down at the bar, how would you know you were in a mall?

Rock Bottom does a great job of providing good beer and good food with great service in a setting that's easy to get to: I can be at the bar ordering a cold Prussia's Pride IPA within seven minutes of getting off Route 202. They have the Rock Bottom Mug Club, which is a ridiculously good deal—because it's *free.* You're going to raise a fuss because it's in a mall?

I used to commiserate with Brian that his beers were being overlooked because of this prejudice, but he's built a solid core of regulars—not robots, he said: "This is their place, but they go to other places"—that

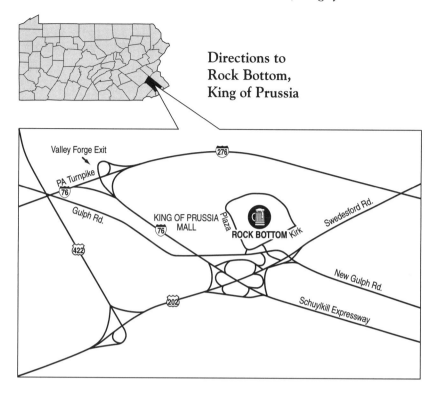

Directions to Rock Bottom, King of Prussia

are experienced and beer-savvy. They've helped spread the word, and Rock Bottom is now mentioned in the same conversations as Victory and Sly Fox: well deserved. More to the point, perhaps, beer sales are up 39 percent since Brian started in 2006. I told you he was good.

If you turn up your nose at Rock Bottom, King of Prussia, because it's a chain or because it's in a mall, you're missing a good brewpub, one that's well worth going out of your way to enjoy. Think about it a bit, then stop in and have one of Brian's excellent beers. You can e-mail me to thank me.

Opened: January 2001.
Owner: Rock Bottom Restaurants.
Brewer: Brian McConnell, Pete Raffetta (part-time).
System: 15-barrel Pub Brewing System, 1,500 barrels potential annual capacity.
2009 production: 1,200 barrels.
Brewpub hours: Monday through Thursday, 11:30 AM to midnight; Friday and Saturday, 11:30 AM to 2 AM; Sunday, 11:30 AM to 11 PM.
Tours: By appointment.

Take-out beer: Growlers.

Food: Rock Bottom's menu really has a bit of everything, and everything I've ever had has been delicious. I particularly like their home-style favorites, like chicken-fried chicken, alder-smoked salmon, jambalaya, and barbecue ribs. Don't miss the white cheddar potatoes, a Rock Bottom signature side.

Extras: Full liquor license.

Special considerations: Kids welcome. Vegetarian meals available.

Parking: Lots of free mall parking.

Lodging in the area: McIntosh Inn, 260 N. Gulph Rd., 610-768-9500; Holiday Inn, 260 Mall Blvd., 610-265-7500; Fairfield by Marriott, 258 Mall Blvd., 610-337-0700.

Area attractions: Hey, the *Plaza and Court at King of Prussia* together constitute one of the biggest malls in the country, what more do you want? If "shop till you drop" doesn't thrill you, *Valley Forge National Historical Park* is just across the road; check out the Valley Forge Visitors Bureau Web site (www.valleyforge.org) to get all the stuff to do there and in the surrounding area. And all the excitement of Philadelphia is just a hop, skip, and a half-hour traffic jam away down the Schuylkill Expressway.

Other area beer sites: *Capone's Restaurant* (224 W. Germantown Pike, Norristown, 610-279-4748) has become justly famous for the wide selection of taps Matt Capone brings in; the man's obsessed, in the best kind of way. Great bottle shop in the back, too; don't miss it. *Teresa's Next Door* (126 N. Wayne Ave., Wayne, 610-293-0119) launched directly into the top tier of area beer bars a couple years ago with a consistently fantastic set of taps, backed up with a deep bottle collection, proper glassware, great food, and a beautiful look. They've never looked back and continue to set the standard in the western suburbs. Some of their success is due to the beer advice of Matt Guyer at *The Beer Yard* (behind Starbucks at 218 E. Lancaster Ave., Wayne, 610-688-3431, www.beeryard.com). Matt has built up a great selection of case beer and the best selection of micro kegs you'll find in the state; he also knows one heck of a lot about beer. Check out their Web site regularly for fresh Philly-area beer news.

General Lafayette Inn

646 Germantown Pike
Lafayette Hill, PA 19444
610-941-0600
www.generallafayetteinn.com

Brittingham's Irish Pub, just two doors down Germantown Pike from the General Lafayette Inn, is a great place to go for a good jar of Guinness. Brittingham's is in a building that predates the American Revolution, built in 1744.

Big deal, 1744. The Brittingham is the new kid on the block. The General Lafayette was built in 1732 and has been a tavern, hotel, or restaurant nearly the whole time. The age of the building is evident in the small rooms and low doorways in the older parts, as well as the uneven, originally hand-dug basement that makes life interesting for brewer Christopher Leonard.

Make that brewer-*owner* Chris Leonard. After founder Mike Mc-Glynn died in 2003, Chris put together the finances and in 2004 became the owner of the General Lafayette. He once told me the reason he brewed: "I thought I'd do something for a living that I'd really do for free: play guitar, play ice hockey, or brew." I asked him then, would you run the place for free?

"No," was his quick response. "For a while I would, but then I'd hire someone and I'd be brewing. It's a matter of getting good people you can trust. Get the system in place and train them up. Hopefully I can manage people well enough. The rewards are so much greater."

It turns out the risks are great, too. Chris is in the process of reinventing the General Lafayette after almost losing it. A lot of money went into a project to open a second location in Philadelphia, The Tiedhouse. "It seemed like a good opportunity," Chris said. "We had staff problems, beer serving problems." The Tiedhouse closed, after draining cash out of the General.

Beers brewed: Year-round: Raspberry Mead-Ale, Germantown Blonde, Sunset Red Ale, Pacific Pale Ale, Chocolate Thunder Porter. Specials: Loch Ness Monster Scotch Ale, Copper Crow IPA, Blackhop, Mirage, The Phantom, The Grim Reaper Imperial Stout, Alt Who Goes There? and more to come.

There were a number of issues, but he takes the blame. "There were lots of changes that should have happened," he told me recently. "Tougher management, for one thing. I'm the boss." He's also cooking, running the kitchen, and changing how the General does business. Food costs, for instance, are down. "We're making everything now," he said. "We were paying a lot for convenience: no-bid purchases, prepped foods, deliveries we could have picked up ourselves." He's been cutting costs in other areas, too, like employment. "I've made cuts we should have made months ago," he said. "I've honed the staff down to some really great people."

What's the aim? "I want this place to run as well as it can. I can't close, I just can't do that." He recently invited people to invest in the General and had a great response, giving him some breathing room.

What he's planning on doing with that breathing room is basic: sell beer. Chris told me he was talking to Matt Guyer, the owner of the Beer Yard in Wayne and one of the more beer-savvy guys in the area. "I was telling him about the problems we were having and the beer," Chris said. "And he picked up a bottle of Bear Republic Racer 5 and said, 'Just make this. That's what people want.'"

These days, Guyer's not far off: A blazing IPA is a good bet. Chris Leonard is planning on playing it. "I want to get out of the kitchen and back in the brewery," he said, "focusing on the beer. Possibly a new brand." He poured me a glass of what might be that new brand: Copper Crow IPA, named for the street Chris grew up on. It was hoppy but not killer bitter up front; it had a hoppiness in the back that built like slow heat.

This isn't easy for Chris. "I love malt," he said. "It's much more interesting and complex than just hopping something. When I hop a beer, I'm looking for hop flavor, not just bitterness." But he can see what sells, and there are more hoppy beers on the lineup these days.

The beer at this underrated brewpub is still excellent, still interesting, still top-notch and innovative. "The beer's a draw," Chris affirmed. "More people come just for the beer than for any other single thing. You've got to compete with the beer bars. Your beer's got to be *good*, and you've got to have variety . . . or they'll go to the beer bar." It's great to hear a brewpub owner talk so positively about beer, as a draw rather than as a gimmick or a waste of floor space.

The Pick: I stuck Mirage in the list in hopes that Chris will continue to make it, a 3.2ish percent Belgian pale ale that manages to squeeze a pleasant pint's worth of flavor into your glass without spiking your brain. Two-pint lunch, anyone? Otherwise, the way to go here is Chocolate Thunder, a rich, delicious porter that tickles me in a righteous way.

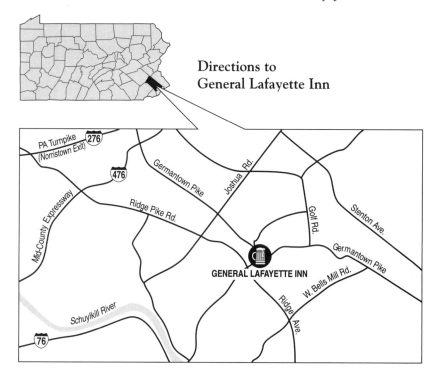

**Directions to
General Lafayette Inn**

GENERAL LAFAYETTE INN

But then, Chris Leonard isn't just an owner. He's an owner-*brewer*. "You're going to see a lot more of our beer," he promised. "I've got a four-head Maheen [bottler] in the basement. We're going to be bottling 10 to 15 barrels a month."

Then he'll be hitting the streets, selling the beer he's made in the brewpub he manages. Chris Leonard is juggling everything: cooking, brewing, sales, booking musical talent, and still managing his staff. He's even redoing the Web site. "I wake up running," he admitted.

I hope he can slow down sometime soon, when things start running well on their own at the General. You can't close, Chris: It's only twenty-two years to the General's 300th anniversary!

Opened: January 1997.
Owners: Christopher Leonard, William Leonard.
Brewer: Christopher Leonard, brewmaster; Russ Czajka, brewer.
System: 7-barrel DME brewhouse, 900 barrels potential annual capacity.
2009 production: 500 barrels (est.).
Brewpub hours: Monday through Saturday, 11:30 AM to 2 AM; Sunday, 10 AM (for brunch) to 2 AM.

Tours: By appointment or by request as possible.

Take-out beer: Growlers, half kegs, 5.2-gallon minikegs.

Food: A new, simpler menu that still offers tasty choices. The appetizers range from standards like fried mozzarella and soft pretzels to white bean hummus and cheesesteak spring rolls. The mussels and flat-breads are a good value, but my favorite is the steak frites.

Extras: The live music has expanded. Tuesday is open mike night; Wednesday is an invitation-only open mike (the step before "making it"); and there are live acts Thursday through Saturday nights. Check the Web site for schedule and accompanying drink specials.

Special considerations: Kids welcome (special menu). Vegetarian meals available.

Parking: Large off-street lot.

Lodging in the area: You can stay right at the inn—a separate building in the rear is a quiet, secluded five-bedroom, four-bath guest house; call the inn for details. Other lodging includes Chestnut Hill Hotel, 8229 Germantown Pike, 215-242-5905; The Inn at King of Prussia, 127 Gulph Rd., King of Prussia, 800-528-1234.

Area attractions: One of the best attractions when you're at the General Lafayette is Germantown Avenue itself. Drive toward Philadelphia and watch the neighborhoods change. The shopping in Chestnut Hill is great; I blow way too much at **Penzey's Spices** (8528 Germantown Ave.), but the cooking inspiration is worth it. Less than a mile away is the **Morris Arboretum** (100 E. Northwestern Ave., Philadelphia, 215-247-5777, www.business-services.upenn.edu/arboretum), where gardens and whimsy combine with horticulture classes and other education (I did a beer tasting there).

Other area beer sites: **Brittingham's Irish Pub** (next door, 610-828-7351) is actually a pretty good place on its own, with an excellent jar of Guinness and a great Irish breakfast on weekends. One of the area's original multitaps, **Flanigan's Boathouse** (113 Fayette St., Conshohocken, 215-828-BOAT), goes through a lot of beer, so you can count on the freshness. **Baggataway Tavern** (31 N. Front St., West Conshohocken, 610-834-8085) is something you may not see anywhere else: a lacrosse-focused sports bar ("baggataway" was a Native American game like lacrosse). The good beer and savvy bartenders are a universal language. **Lucky Dog Saloon** (417 Germantown Pike, Lafayette Hill, 610-941-4652) gets the nod from Chris.

Iron Hill Brewery, North Wales

1460 Bethlehem Pike
Shoppes at English Village
North Wales, PA 19454
267-708-BREW
www.ironhillbrewery.com

Iron Hill is one of the most successful small brewpub chains in the country. I have nothing to back up that statement: no numbers, no comparisons, no spreadsheets, nothing. I don't care, I'm sticking with it, because I know what I see. I see eight busy brewpubs that all look terrific. They're all filled with bright, energetic staff that show more energy and customer-service savvy than you find most places these days—not just among brewpubs, but among restaurants. The food is excellent, fresh, and innovative without being outlandish. The brewers are proud, happy, technically proficient, and imbued with an honest camaraderie. And the beer, my friends, is just fantastic. That is success. You can't be doing that well, with so many happy people, and not be making it.

How many happy people? I was talking to Mark Edelson about that on a chilly January morning in 2004. I remember it was chilly because we were at this Iron Hill, in North Wales, watching the Iron Hill brewing staff man- (and woman-) handle the new brewhouse, kettle, mash tun, and tanks into the uncompleted building, with then North Wales brewer Larry Horwitz (now at Iron Hill, West Chester), a man of many talents, running the forklift.

"You know," Mark confided to me, "I have to think to remember everyone's name now. We're working with a payroll of almost five hundred people these days." But I looked at that team of brewers, every one of whom had honestly volunteered to come out and shove a couple tons of steel around in

Beers brewed: Iron Hill's house beers include Iron Hill Light Lager, Raspberry Wheat, Vienna Red Lager, Ironbound Ale, Pig Iron Porter, and a rotating Belgian style. Seasonals: Altbier, Barleywine, Belgian White, Bohemian Pils, Dry Stout, ESB, Hefeweizen, Imperial IPA, India Pale Ale, Lambic de Hill, Maibock, Munich Dunkel, Nut Brown Ale, Oatmeal Stout, Oktoberfest, Old Ale, Russian Imperial Stout, Saison, Tripel, Vienna, Wee Heavy, Oud Bruin, Doppelbock, Weizenbock.

the freezing cold, and saw people who were happy with their work. The same crew shows up at events like Friday the Firkinteenth and parties together.

I had a conversation with Mark about the Iron Hill business again recently, this time sitting inside an established, busy, and best of all, warm Iron Hill, North Wales. They had just opened their eighth brewpub, in Maple Shade, New Jersey (the first new brewpub in the Garden State in years), and had enough money in the bank to build a couple more. Mark was telling me how they plant new Iron Hills.

The Pick: A very nice iteration of Iron Hill's Ironbound Ale. It's hoppy, it's clean, it's fresh as a daisy, it's poundable: what more do you want from a beer like this?

"We look at the demographics of places we'd like to be," he said. "The Lehigh Valley would be great, Harrisburg, and we're not done with the Philly suburbs. We're at the point where real estate people are coming to us, towns are coming to us, but they don't get it. It's all about what's within 5 to 7 miles. No one comes farther than that for dinner, not really, not often. We look at parking, costs, what kind of employees we can find there. And we've gotten a lot better on negotiations."

How big is the company? "We just hired a human resources person," Mark replied. "Why did we wait till we had 800 employees! We can still get all the brewers together once a month, and we do. They all bring a sample of the same house beer, and we taste them blind. That's incentive . . . to not come in last!"

We talked about growth. "This is not a business where you want to take your foot off the pedal," he said. "You take your foot off, you'll lose control, and you'll crash. But as a growing company, the owners have to deal less with the day-to-day stuff. We're still too hands-on. The company should be less dependent on the three of us and more on the organization.

"You have to figure out what business you're in and work with that," he continued. Iron Hill used to have a lot more bar business. "We used to have a huge bar business, and it's good money, really good money, but you have to decide if the noise, and the puking, and the broken bathroom fixtures are good for a restaurant. And it's not. So that's okay, that was business we could lose. We're not in that business anymore."

That's about the time brewer Vince Desrosiers came over with some of his new Belgian pale ale for us to try, and, well, we kind of got sidetracked. So let me tell you about North Wales. The pub has familiar Iron Hill elements: dark red-brown wood interior, an open kitchen, hollow square bar, and the cast-iron "barley bird" decoration. It's divided into four bays—two high-ceilinged dining rooms, the bar, and the brewery—with connecting passages at each end. The menu is identical to the other Iron Hills, with all items prepared from scratch ingredients. Every location has a chef, not just cooks, and all the chefs get together to set the menu.

Vince is working his first shift as an Iron Hill head brewer, and he's doing great. I've stopped in a couple times (this is the closest Iron Hill to my home), and his house beers are dead-on.

Not really a surprise. Iron Hill's got this down to an art.

Opened: March 2004.
Owners: Mark Edelson, Kevin Finn, Kevin Davies.
Brewer: Vince Desrosiers.
System: 8.5-barrel Specific Mechanical brewhouse, 1,000 barrels potential annual capacity.
2009 production: 700 barrels (est.)
Brewpub hours: Sunday and Monday, 11 AM to 11 PM; Tuesday through Thursday, 11 AM to midnight; Friday and Saturday, 11 AM to 1 AM.
Tours: On request.
Take-out beer: Growlers and bottled reserves.
Food: See the listing for Iron Hill, West Chester, on page 75.
Extras: Mug club. Frequent special dinner deals; check Web site for details.
Special considerations: Kids welcome. Vegetarian meals available.
Parking: Large on-site free lot.
Lodging in the area: Joseph Ambler Inn, 1005 Horsham Rd., North Wales, 215-362-7500; Comfort Inn, 678 Bethlehem Pike, Montgomeryville, 215-361-3600; Residence Inn, 1110 Bethlehem Pike, North Wales, 267-468-0111.
Area attractions: There are a lot of malls in the area, and **English Village** itself is an upscale plaza. See the listings for Porterhouse on page 120 and Crabby Larry's on page 113 for more suggestions.
Other area beer sites: The **Iron Abbey** (680 Easton Rd., Horsham, 215-956-9600) is new, impressively well beered, and has a good menu to boot. I've been going to **Otto's** (233 Easton Rd., Horsham, 215-675-1864) since I moved here in 1991, and we love the German food and well-kept German beers.

Crabby Larry's Brewpub, Steak, & Crab House

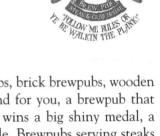

237 West Butler Avenue, Chalfont, PA 18914
215-822-8788
www.crabbylarrys.com

I like brewpubs. Big brewpubs, little brewpubs, brick brewpubs, wooden brewpubs. A brewpub with beers for me and for you, a brewpub that smokes a mean barbecue. A brewpub that wins a big shiny medal, a brewpub that throws funky stuff in the kettle. Brewpubs serving steaks on a white tablecloth, brewpubs serving soups of fresh veggies and broth. A brewpub for pizza, served on a big dish; or a fine brewpub market, stuffed full of fresh fish! I like brewpubs.

It seems like only yesterday that I was reading Margaret Wise Brown's *The Friendly Book* to my children. I always liked how many different kinds of things there were to like. Brewpub owners seem largely to have forgotten that. They tend to fall into a rut, with the same general "concept," the same general menu: artichoke and spinach dip, some kind of encrusted salmon, and wings, quesadillas, and burgers on a bar menu . . . There are exceptions, to be sure, but I've never seen one quite as out of the ordinary as Crabby Larry's.

Crabby Larry's is a seafood market and operated for ten years under the name of Jones Family Seafood. Then Larry Jones took over, added a restaurant to serve up the fish and seafood in dinners, and renamed it Crabby Larry's. Larry seemed pleasant enough to me, so I'm assuming it's a nickname that refers to the big steamed "beautiful swimmers" he serves up . . . but you never know.

Next, Larry got the idea to stick a little brewery in his seafood market, which in Pennsylvania meant that he could then offer his house-brewed beers and Pennsylvania wines by the glass—not a bad deal for a lot less than the price of a liquor license. So he got himself a little 2.5-barrel electrically heated brewkettle from North American Brew Systems, a bunch of malt extract, and hooked up with a local homebrewer to run the system.

Beers brewed: Year-round: Golden Treasure, Calico Jack Amber, Dead Man Walkin' IPA, Whiskey Vanilla Smoked Porter, Anne Bonny Irish Stout. Seasonals: Saison, Hefeweisen, Octoberfest, Chocolate Raspberry Stout, My Wild Oat Winter Warmer, The Great Pumpkin Ale, Irish Red Ale, Raspberry Wit.

The beer wasn't that great at first, but it got better as improvements were made: some new equipment, a new water filter, and a lot of help from the guys at Keystone Homebrew in Montgomeryville. One of the Keystone Homebrew guys did the brewing for a while after the first brewer moved on. The beer got better, noticeably better (the new water filter helped a lot), and more interesting.

The Pick: I could eat oysters and drink the Anne Bonny Irish Stout all day long here. Smooth, creamy, and clean, with just a hint of graham cracker.

It got so much more interesting, in fact, that Larry got interested himself. "My wife, Dani, and I are doing most of the brewing now," he told me at my latest visit, when I was surprised to see that Larry had picked up some new, much smaller tanks.

"I got them at a scrapyard," he said, clearly proud of them, and there's certainly plenty of precedent for small brewers recycling tanks! "They're stainless steel, came with the fittings already in place. I didn't like the 7-barrel tanks we had. They were too big. If I put one batch in, there was all that space in the top, and that's not good for freshness."

The tank closest to the brewing equipment is wood-clad. "That's got a glycol jacket I put on it," Larry said. "I can cool it to do lagers." Sounds like someone really caught the bug.

It's paid off for the drinkers who know about Crabby Larry's. The beer selection has increased, and they're doing some interesting seasonals; a chocolate-cherry stout was coming up for Valentine's Day. But it's still just house beer and Pennsylvania wine. "Some people come in, they want a martini or a Coors Light," Larry said. "Sorry, don't have that!"

Don't forget the fish, because this is undisputedly, unabashedly a seafood restaurant. There are some serious steaks on there, sure, but there's a whole separate section just for the different grilled fish offered. Seafood appetizers, seafood soups, seafood casseroles, steamed crabs, seafood pasta—the backdoor of this place must be the favorite hangout for every cat within 3 miles. I got the Crab Bread, a *boulle* sliced open, stuffed with lump crabmeat, and doused with melted cheese and a rich, garlic-laced crab broth, and broiled. It was sloppy but delicious. I recently made a trip up to Chalfont just to get another one. And you can always pick up some fresh seafood to take home; it is still a seafood market.

Do you like brewpubs? All kinds of brewpubs? If you like fish, too, I've got just the place for you, tucked away in a little shopping plaza in Chalfont . . .

Opened: November 2001.
Owners: "Crabby" Larry and Dani Jones.

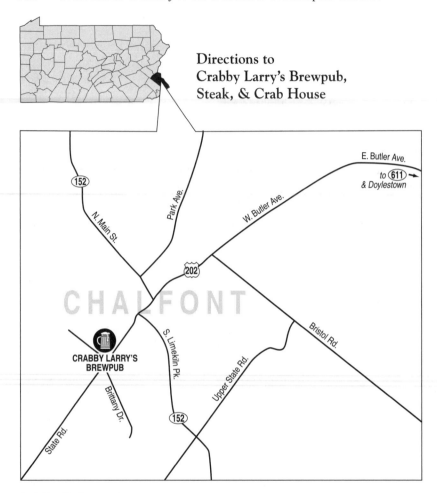

Directions to
**Crabby Larry's Brewpub,
Steak, & Crab House**

Brewers: Larry and Dani Jones.

System: 2.5-barrel North American Brewing Systems extract brewhouse, 250 barrels potential annual capacity.

2009 production: 50 barrels

Brewpub hours: Closed Sunday through Tuesday. The market opens Wednesday and Thursday at noon, Friday at 11 AM, and Saturday at 10 AM, and it closes at 9 PM each night. Dinner starts at 4:30 PM on Wednesday through Friday, 3:30 PM on Saturday. There is no lunch service.

Tours: The brewery's right there in the front of place; if Larry's there, ask him a question.

Take-out beer: Growlers.

Food: Fish, shellfish, and combination platters of both, in plain and fancy dishes. Steamed hardshell crabs and jumbo lump crab cakes are a specialty. Some great beef, too, with steaks, ribs, and prime rib. Kids' menu. A selection of Pennsylvania wines is available.

Extras: Seafood market has fresh fish, salads, and sauces for take-out.

Special considerations: Kids welcome. Vegetarian requests happily accommodated.

Parking: Large, free, on-site lot.

Lodging in the area: Joseph Ambler Inn, 1005 Horsham Rd., North Wales, 215-362-7500; Chalfont Motor Inn, 413 W. Butler Avenue, Chalfont, 215-822-2532; Comfort Inn, 678 Bethlehem Pike, Montgomeryville, 215-361-3600.

Area attractions: Doylestown has a cluster of interesting and different museums, all related to Henry Chapman Mercer, a local Renaissance man. The **Mercer Museum** is a five-floor wander through the implements of a variety of preindustrial trades, from tinsmithing to whaling, whole parts of our culture that no longer exist. Mercer's home, **Fonthill**, a castle of concrete and tile, is also open for touring (Pine and Ashland Sts., 215-345-0210, www.mercermuseum.org). Mercer put his ideas to work at the **Moravian Pottery and Tile Works** (130 W. Swamp Rd., 215-345-6722, www.buckscounty.org under Government/Departments/Parks and Recreation; you'll find many more interesting sites here as well—it's worth the dig), where a group of artisans created decorative tiles and mosaics, which adorn many area homes. The Tile Works offers tours, an internship program, and a serious gift shop. Visit the **Peace Valley Winery** (159 Beaver Valley Rd., Chalfont, 215-249-9058, www.peacevalleywinery.com) if you feel like a change of palate. **Delaware Valley College** (700 E. Butler Ave., Doylestown, 215-345-1500, www.delval.edu/themarket) has a strong program in agricultural studies, food science, dairy science, and agribusiness, and proves it with a farm market where students sell produce, eggs, cheese, milk, honey, and salad dressings. You can also visit **Tabora Farm and Orchard** (1104 Upper Stump Rd., Chalfont, 215-249-3016 www.taborafarmandorchard.com) for a wide variety of fresh baked goods, deli sandwiches, and farm-fresh produce.

Other area beer sites: **Blue Dog Family Tavern** (4275 County Line Rd., Chalfont, 215-997-9988) and **Blue Dog Pub** (850 S. Valley Forge Rd., Lansdale, 215-368-6620) are both aimed at folks that want the best choice of craft beer in town with their burgers. See also the listing for Porterhouse Restaurant and Brew Pub on page 120.

GG Brewers

282 N. Keswick Ave., Glenside 19038
215-887-0809
www.ggbrewers.com

I like a small brewpub. There's just something about it, something cozy, the feel that someone decided to do this just for you and a few friends. I don't think there are enough small brewpubs, though I'll admit that the economics of the thing may not work that well. Who knows? Not me; I'm a writer and a beer drinker, not a businessman.

GG Brewers is *really* small, the smallest brewpub I remember seeing in twenty-three years of visiting them. There are production breweries with smaller tasting rooms, but for straight-up brewpubs with no outside sales, GG wins the small race. They're not much bigger than the barroom alone at Selin's Grove: room for thirty people, tops.

Yet they keep chugging along. GG makes it, I think, on the sheer energy of owner-brewer Gerry Martin. The last time I was in, Gerry never stopped moving. The entertaining thing is that he wasn't always just working. He talked to another customer about his beer choice (telling him that if he really wanted a hoppy beer, the current batch of pale ale actually had more hops character than the Hop Attack IPA); he explained to the whole room—easy enough to do—the trouble they'd been having with their cable company; and he not only noticed Cathy and me looking at the wine list, but also took time to explain that he'd chosen those wines from that vineyard (Pennsylvania's Galen Glen) because they make wines in the German style, noting that their sweet wines weren't really all that sweet . . . and then poured us a short sample. He was right, too; it was easily the best Concord wine I've ever had.

I'll be honest: I can't tell you much about GG or about Gerry Martin. I've only been there three times (Glenside just isn't on my normal routes), and because of Gerry's busy schedule I never got to interview him. It's not even easy to do the usual incognito thing I like to do: Gerry has instituted a "no note taking" policy at the brewpub as the result of a sadly ugly incident with one rude patron.

Beers brewed: Keswick Light, Hop Attack, Amberly Eyes, Naughty Boy Stout. Occasionals: Smoke Gets in Your Rye, Never Go Back Porter, Apricot Stout, Bachelor Party Ale, Brown Eyed Girl, Franklin Pale Ale, Grandma's Cookies Porter, IPA, Keswick Light, Oatmeal Cream Stout, Red Light Ale, What's Up Weizenbock.

Odd, perhaps, but quirks are what make this industry interesting.

What I can tell you is that any brewpub this small that has stayed open this long in such a beer-savvy area has to be doing something right. Part of that's the menu. There's a little something for everyone—meat, pasta, seafood, veggies—and it's all reasonably priced. Be sure to check the specials; we had some tasty pot stickers when we dropped in.

But part of it's the beer, too. I'll be honest, I wasn't overly impressed when I first visited. I thought the porter I had needed to be better integrated; flavors were sticking out all over. But the other two times I was in, the beers were notably better. The last pale ale I had was clean, hop-flavorful, really drinkable, and not overly bitter, the kind of beer a geek might not give a second glance but most other craft drinkers would happily neck all afternoon. If Gerry isn't reaching for the stars with the "extreme" beers that are popular now, neither is he falling on his face. He's making good beers that people enjoy drinking—a sure recipe for brewpub success.

If you catch a concert at the Keswick, don't fight the crowds at the Keswick Tavern. Slip into this little place across the street. Gerry's keeping it open just for you and a few friends.

The Pick: Naughty Boy Stout—how can you not like that! Think of an export stout, only not quite as heavy or sweet; or a heavier, sweeter Irish stout, if you prefer. Naughty Boy meets them in the middle. Drink up, you naughty boy.

Opened: March 2006.

Owner: Gerry Martin.

Brewer: Gerry Martin.

System: 4-barrel custom system, 350 barrels annual capacity.

2009 production: 120 barrels (est.).

Hours: Tuesday through Sunday, 4 PM to 2 AM. Closed Mondays.

Tours: No tours, but Gerry is usually willing to talk beer with patrons.

Take-out beer: None available (beer runs out too quickly!).

Food: A broad menu includes pasta, steaks, ribs, and seafood dishes; pub grub and sandwiches; several solid vegetarian options. Very reasonable prices.

Extras: Da Mug Club. Live music, usually once or twice a month; check Web site for schedule. Dartboard, checkers, and chess on hand, too.

Special considerations: Kid-friendly in early evening hours. Vegetarian selections available.

Parking: On-street metered parking; can get tight when there's an event at the Keswick, but it's a very safe neighborhood for walking.

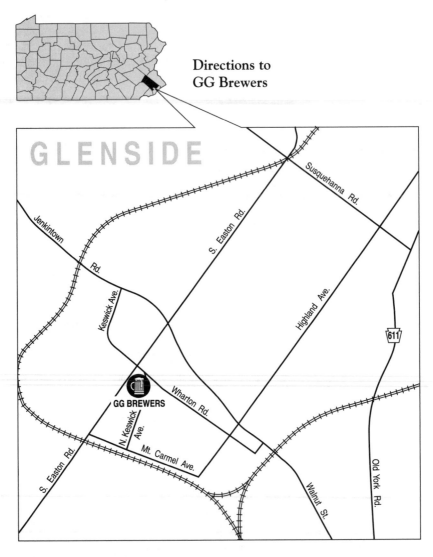

**Directions to
GG Brewers**

Lodging in the area: See the listings for Philadelphia on page 32 and General Lafayette on page 106.

Area attractions: The **Keswick Theatre**, right across the street (291 N. Keswick Ave., 215-572-7650, www.keswicktheatre.com), is one of the Philadelphia area's best spots for live music and presents national acts in a surprisingly intimate 1,300-seat setting. We've seen Little Feat, Dr. John, the subdudes, and David Bromberg (and they have beer, but did I mention it was *right across the street* from GG?). See the listing for Philadelphia on pages 32–34 for more suggestions.

Other area beer sites: ***Union Jack's Pub*** (2750 Limekiln Pike, 215-886-6014) is one of several widely scattered Union Jack's. They're all different, but they all have great beer. The ***Austrian Village*** (321 Huntingdon Pike, Rockledge, 215-663-9902) has become a new favorite of mine. Old-school German food from an authentic Austrian chef, small bar, classic look, and solid tap selections. Not hip by any means . . . which is great, no?

Porterhouse Restaurant and Brew Pub

5775 Lower York Road, Lahaska, PA 18931
215-794-9373
www.porterhousepub.com

The Porterhouse Restaurant and Brew Pub is not the only brewpub to have been at this location. Like a couple other places in this book—Nodding Head, Blue Canoe—Porterhouse moved in after another brewpub had failed or moved on. The first brewpub tenant was the Buckingham Mountain brewpub. But different owners and a different approach to brewing have completely changed the place.

"We had a lot of work to do," said partner Lisa Fricke, who manages the brewpub. "It was filthy, and there was no equipment at the bar, not even shelves for glasses. We tore up the carpet and cleaned before laying new carpet. We did major renovations." They removed the four serving tanks behind the bar, opening up an intimate dining area and expanding the bar, redoing the surface in a distinctive quarry tile. The upstairs was converted to an upscale dining room. The only thing left from the old regime is the brewhouse and the fermenters.

Fricke and her two partners, chefs Clay Hull and Chris McDonald, had years of experience in the restaurant business. They bought a brewpub only because the timing and the price were a great match.

Beers brewed: North Lager, Peace Keeper Porter, and the House Brown Porter are on most of the year. The rest of the time, Dean just brews whatever strikes his fancy, with an emphasis on Belgian and English styles, though he does throw in a pilsner occasionally.

"We had few options on the brewery," Fricke said. "It was too difficult to remove, and we didn't know enough about brewing to know if we were hiring a good brewer."

That's why they originally approached River Horse Brewing in Lambertville, New Jersey, just across the Delaware River. River Horse supplied a brewer to make house beers and sold Porterhouse four of their regular beers. That program worked for a while, then Porterhouse switched their "affiliation" to the newly formed Philadelphia Brewing Company, and Dean Browne started brewing at the pub.

The Pick: House Brown Porter must be my Pick—it's what I drink the most of. It's a great all-rounder with the menu, thanks to the mellowing influence of that brown malt, and it's a perfect beer for the bar, thanks to the lower alcohol. I do love a good porter.

Dean's a tall, affable Canadian with whom I share a great fondness for bourbon; I've run into him in Bardstown, Kentucky, during the Kentucky Bourbon Festival. He's been with Philadelphia Brewing since the beginning, and loves the chance Porterhouse gives him to brew.

"My course for the brews at Porterhouse has been an outlet for myself," Dean told me, "but I do like to brew beers that bring along the wine and cocktail drinkers up there. To that end, I tend to brew up beers like my North Lager—kind of a hoppy dunkel lager—a lot like the old, pre-Molson Creemore Springs Lager from Ontario." That's not the only Canadian connection he makes. There's a beefy Baltic porter in the regular rotation called Peace Keeper, Dean's tribute to the Canadian armed forces and their prominent role in UN peacekeeping missions.

The third beer that's in regular rotation at Porterhouse is . . . another porter! The House Brown Porter (or "Brown(e) Porter" as Dean jokingly put it) is my go-to at Porterhouse. "I brew that using old-style English brown malt," Dean said. "The brown malt gives it a nice, round, roasty flavor without much bitterness.

"For the rest of the brews," he added, "I've been playing with farmhouse-style ales fermented with Belgian yeasts. It's all done using top-quality malts and hops. I use a lot of floor-malted barley from the UK. All the beers fall in between 4 and 7 percent ABV, with a preference for the lighter side. I'm really pretty much on my own when it comes to deciding what to brew up here."

Given the backgrounds of Fricke and her two partners (who are excellent chefs and nice guys, by the way), it's not surprising that the business concentrates mostly on the menu. See the list of entrées, the pastas with salmon or pan-flashed vegetables, the bronzed grouper, crispy duckling with Brie and pears, and an 18-ounce. Delmonico steak. Even the pub menu gets the treatment, with a praline chicken salad sandwich,

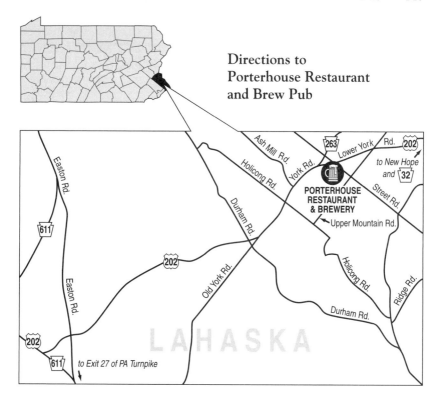

mussels "brewshetta," and a steak queso wrap (no cheesesteaks here). This is a restaurant cleverly disguised as a brewpub.

The upstairs dining room gives a view across a conservancy-protected farm to the southern ridge, a beautiful slice of rural Bucks County. But you can walk to the shops of Peddler's Village, and the famous Rice's Flea Market is only 2 miles away, if you need to persuade some companions to come out for a visit. Once they get here and see the menu and taste the beer, it may be hard to get them to leave!

Opened: April 2002.

Owners: Lisa Fricke, Clay Hull, Chris McDonald.

Brewer: Dean Browne.

System: 10-barrel Pub Brewing Systems brewhouse, 700 barrels potential annual capacity.

2008 production: 200 barrels (boiler malfunction crippled brewing in 2009).

Brewpub hours: Tuesday through Thursday, 11:30 AM to 9 PM; Friday and Saturday, 11:30 AM to 9:30 PM; Sunday, 11:30 AM to 8 PM.

Tours: None available.

Take-out beer: Growlers. Six-packs of beers from Philadelphia Brewing and other craft breweries also available.

Food: A carefully prepared high-end set of alluring appetizers (the smoked Maine trout is a favorite) and innovative entrées with an emphasis on serious steaks and seafood parallels a more pubby menu of award-winning burgers and chili.

Special considerations: Kids welcome. Vegetarian meals available; the lunch menu is your best bet.

Extras: Full liquor license. Mug club.

Parking: Plenty of off-street parking available.

Lodging in the area: Golden Plough Inn, Route 202 and Street Road, 215-794-4004; Red Roof Oxford Valley, I-95 and Oxford Valley Road, 215-750-6200.

Area attractions: Next-door *Peddler's Village* (www.peddlersvillage .com) is a 42-acre complex of shops and boutiques, a favorite shopping destination for the area. It also has Giggleberry Farm, a great place for young kids, and includes the Grand Carousel, a lavishly restored Philadelphia Toboggan Company carousel from 1922, a treat for carousel fans of all ages. Another favorite, about 2 miles from the brewery, is *Rice's Market* (215-297-5993, www.ricesmarket.com), a long-running (since the 1920s) flea market open year-round on Tuesdays, rain, snow, or shine, and on Saturdays from March to December. *Buckingham Valley Vineyards* (215-794-7188, www.pawine .com) is just 3 miles south of Buckingham on Route 413 (the intersection is west of the brewpub on Route 202) and has a self-guided tour and a tasting room.

Other area beer sites: Head west 3 miles on Route 202 to the Route 413 intersection and you'll find two good beer places. The *Heart of Oak* taproom (215-794-7784) is tucked under Baci's restaurant, and you'll find a very English menu (chicken and leek pie, bangers and mash, Scotch eggs) with some very English taps. Right across the street is the *Candlewyck Lounge* (215-794-8233), a beef and ale restaurant that also has a good deli with a bottle shop. The bottle shop has an excellent selection of Belgian, German, and local beers at pretty good prices. In nearby Doylestown, there are enough places for a pubcrawl. If you start at *Stephanie's Lounge* (29 Main St., 215-489-1644), you may not want to leave. They've got the best tap selection in town, backed by a deep bottle selection and a solid menu with local touches, plus a bottle shop around the corner where you can buy anything they have in bottles. The *Mesquito Grill* (128 W. State St., Doylestown, 215-230-RIBS) is a neat little trio of bars connected by a larger dining space. They have a great set of taps, but these are almost secondary to the knockout bottle selection, an absolutely uncompromising list that's available for take-out. The third and final stop on your crawl is **Muggs on Main** (211 S. Main St., 215-489-7795), which is simply a divey kind of bar—low ceiling, still determinedly smoky because there's no food—with good craft beer, friendly bartenders, and a great jukebox. My local bar, **Isaac Newton's** (off the town parking lot in the middle of Newtown, 215-860-5100), has seventeen outstanding taps, including at least two Belgians, and a deep, well-chosen bottle selection. While I'm putting in my locals, I wouldn't want to miss the **Hulmeville Inn** (4 Trenton Rd., Hulmeville, 215-750-6893), where owner Jeff Lavin has been pulling in some great limited-release drafts and the members of the local homebrew club (the ALEiens) are my homeboys (and girls). Word of warning: The Hulmeville is still a smoking bar.

Triumph Brewing Company, New Hope

400 Union Square Drive, New Hope, PA 18938
215-862-8300
www.triumphbrew.com

I've lost one of my best lines. "The best place to go for a beer in New Hope," I'd tell people when they'd ask where to find a good beer in this artsy little town on the Delaware, "is Lambertville." New Hope has lots of good restaurants and a number of popular bars, but the beer selections they offer generally range from predictable to pathetic. You were best off to walk across the bridge to Lambertville, New Jersey, to someplace like the Inn of the Hawke.

Triumph has made a liar out of me, and I couldn't be happier. Well, actually, I could. The brewpub up by the New Hope and Ivyland Railroad station was *supposed* to be where I live, in Newtown, and having a brewpub within biking distance would have made me deliriously happy. But a coalition of Quakers and bar owners browbeat the town council into putting so many restrictions on the proposed site that Triumph decided against locating here and went off to New Hope.

It's worked out well for them. The pub's really caught on in this tourist town. "It just keeps chugging along and growing in the middle of a global recession," brewer Brendan Anderson told me. "I don't know why, but we're doing well."

It might be the beer. Brendan was trained by John Eccles, who in turn was trained by the late Jay Misson, both lager-philes. Misson was the head brewer for Triumph before his death, and he'd have been proud of the way Eccles trained Brendan.

"I won a medal at the GABF for my hefeweizen," Brendan said, not to brag, but to deliver the punchline: "It was the only ale I knew how to make! I've been making them since then, and I'm having fun. Adam's a brewer, so he lets us push boundaries. I've got more freedom than most brewers; at least, I feel like I do."

He still does plenty of lagers, and usually has one on, one in reserve, and one in production. But the big seller is the Bengal Gold IPA. "The IPA commands the tank space," he said. "It sells, it gets all it needs."

If you've been to Triumph in Princeton, the New Hope pub is similar in design (they had the same architect), though not as strikingly narrow or high. It has lots of exposed brick; high ceilings straight up to a second level; a raised, exposed brewhouse; and a distinctly uncluttered look that the warm brick and wood keep from being stark.

The menu is a bit exotic and delicious, with real vegetarian choices and innovative appetizers. But the bar menu will be familiar to any brewpub regular, and they've kept their trademark house-cut fresh potato chips, served in a big paper cone, great greasy beer food.

You don't have to go to Lambertville to get a good beer in New Hope anymore—though it's still a gorgeous walk across the bridge right down the hill from Triumph. You could even take a growler along and bring New Hope's good beer to Lambertville.

Beers brewed: Year-round: Honey Wheat, Amber Ale, Bengal Gold IPA, German Pilsner, Imperial Stout, Raspberry Wheat. Seasonals: Octoberfest, Kellerbier, Helles, Dunkles, Blonde Doppelbock, Bock, Roggenbock, Rauchbier, Imperial Stout, Double Amber, Jewish Rye, Oatmeal Cookie Stout, Coffee & Cream Stout . . . and a lot more. Current taps for all three Triumph brewpubs are on the Web site.

Opened: April 2003.
Owner: Adam Rechnitz.
Brewer: Brendan Anderson.
System: 10-barrel Newlands brewhouse, 2,000 barrels potential annual capacity.

2009 production: 910 barrels.

Brewpub hours: Monday through Wednesday, 11:30 AM to midnight; Thursday through Saturday, 11:30 AM to 2 AM; Sunday, noon to midnight.

Tours: Saturdays at 1 and 3 PM.

Take-out beer: Growlers; call ahead for kegs.

Food: Triumph has simplified the menu, and they're working more with local producers, but they still offer adventurous appetizers, like a country terrine with truffled egg salad and a goat cheese tart, and main dishes of shrimp brochette and braised lamb shank. They also have their trademark fresh-cut and house-made "cone o' chips," cheesesteak sliders, and a variety of sandwiches on the bar menu. You'll also find a variety of vegetarian dishes: a black bean burger, root vegetable shepherd's pie, pumpkin gnocchi, and more. Brendan suggests the Cookie Pie with a glass of stout or the Buffalo spring rolls with an IPA.

Extras: The entertainment at Triumph has been upgraded, with a larger stage and bigger acts. Live music or a DJ every Friday and Saturday, karaoke Thursday; call or check the Web site for schedule. Pool tables, dartboard, and increased number of TVs.

Special considerations: Kids welcome, and there's a kids' menu. Vegetarian meals available.

Parking: Triumph's reasonably priced lot is a steal in New Hope; it's a ticket system, so don't forget to buy and display your ticket.

Lodging in the area: 1870 Wedgwood Inn, 111 W. Bridge St., just down the hill, 215-862-2520; Mansion Inn, 9 S. Main St., 215-862-1231; Inn at Lambertville Station, 11 Bridge St., Lambertville, NJ, 609-397-4400.

Area attractions: You can see (and hear) the **New Hope and Ivyland Railroad** (32 W. Bridge St., 215-862-2332, www.newhoperailroad .com) right out back. Steam and antique diesel engines will take you on a ride on this historic short-line railroad; the dinner trains and fall foliage runs are very popular. The town of **New Hope** is one of the most popular strolling and shopping towns in southeastern Pennsylvania, with shops galore, restaurants from deli to haute cuisine, and some of the best people-watching around. If you're feeling dramatic, it's also the home of the **Bucks County Playhouse** (215-862-2041, www.buckscountyplayhouse.com). A warning: Parking can be tough, and the police are active. **Lambertville**, just across the Delaware

The Pick: I should pick a lager, but I really love what Brendan does with stouts. The Coffee & Cream Stout, an invention of Triumph, Princeton, brewer Tom Stevenson, is like creamy coffee, just the way I like it, with bubbles and booze in it. The Oatmeal Cookie Stout is spot-on, right down to the hint of cinnamon. The IPA is always a winner.

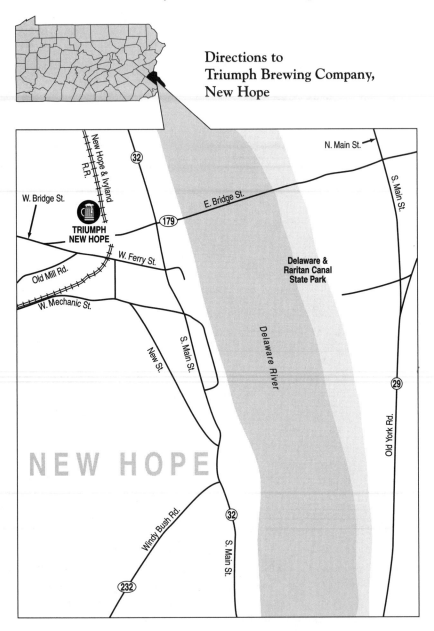

**Directions to
Triumph Brewing Company,
New Hope**

River (the bridge has a pedestrian walkway and offers great views), is noted for its large number of antique shops; you can't go two blocks without hitting one. Tubing on the river in summer is a great way to cool off and see the sights; **Bucks County River Country** (2 Walters Lane, Point Pleasant, upriver from New Hope; 215-

297-5000, www.rivercountry.net) rents tubes, kayaks, canoes, and rafts, and they'll bus you upriver so you can float down. They do have a strict no-alcohol policy, so tube in the morning! **Washington Crossing Historic Park** (215-493-4076, www.ushistory.org/washingtoncrossing) is downstream from New Hope by way of a pleasant drive along the river. The Visitors Center is temporarily closed due to budget constraints, but the park is open and events are still taking place. You'll find trails for biking and hiking on both sides of the river, accessible at the parks (there's a New Jersey state park on the other side of the narrow metal bridge at Washington Crossing); we prefer the one on the New Jersey side, as it's better maintained and more complete, and you can even ride it the whole way to the Ship Inn brewpub in Milford! In warm weather, **Sesame Place** (Oxford Valley, 215-752-7070) is a ton of fun for young children. Big Bird's theme park was recently rated the fourth-best kids' park in the world. See the listing for Porterhouse Restaurant and Brewery on page 120 for still more suggestions.

Other area beer sites: There is finally a bar with a bit more than the usual beer selection in New Hope: **Michael Kelly's Irish Pub** (26 W. Bridge St., under Villa Vito, 215-862-9936) has a small set of craft drafts and the good Irish whiskey you'd expect. Why not walk across the bridge into New Jersey and take a tour of the **River Horse Brewery** (80 Lambert Lane, Lambertville, 609-397-7776)? While you're there, try to slip into **The Boat House** (8 Coryell St., 609- 397-2244). The beer selection is not great, but it's a cool bar, a locals' spot, tucked away down an alley; be cool. Also in Lambertville is the **Inn of the Hawke** (74 S. Union St., 609-397-9555), where they've been serving craft beer for almost twenty years. Go in warm weather and sit out back under the tall, leafy trees. **Mitchell's Café** (11$^{1}/_{2}$ Church St., 609-387-9853) is a Lambertville institution, open since 1868 and run by the same family since 1969. It's not the beer that's the draw—it's Guinness, mostly—but the top-notch live music: first and third Wednesday of every month is Irish traditional music, the second is a Cajun jam, and the fourth is "old-timey music." If you see my friend Mark Stewart playing the bouzouki, buy him a beer! **Triumph's** other brewpub (138 Nassau St., Princeton, NJ, 609-924-7855) is in Princeton, New Jersey, not too far away, where brewer Tom Stevenson takes a more ale-brewed slant on things and the architecture is, if anything, even more striking than in New Hope. See the listing for Porterhouse Restaurant and Brewery on page 120 for more suggestions.

A word about . . .

Pennsylvania Hotel Bars

The pint is not always the point. That's something you should keep in mind as you are beer traveling. While great beer is a goal in itself, I have found that there is equal pleasure to be found in the hunt for great bars. Some of them may serve nothing more lofty than Yuengling Lager, and offer simple fare of hot dogs and cheese plates. Yet there is for me a sheer joy to walking into a place where you feel instantly at home, or where you find neons for beer brands long passed away, or an ornately carved wooden backbar with a hunting scene painted 50 years ago.

I love these great Pennsylvania bars as much as the great Pennsylvania beers. There are some beauties in the cities. The Northeast Taproom in Reading pulls off being a great bar with great beer, something that is all too rare. McGlinchey's, in Philadelphia, will serve you good cheap beer and good cheap food and you might meet anyone there. But my real love is reserved for the great bars out in the hills and forests of Penn's Woods.

I tended bar outside of Strasburg, Pennsylvania back in the 1980s. I banked some money for graduate school and learned a lot about people and drinking. I always suspected that a lot of the reason the owner built the bar was so that his friends could come by and have a beer with him. As I served these guys, most of them World War II and Korea vets, I kept hearing about drinking "down at the hotel."

The hotel (which they pronounced "HO-tel," as opposed to a Hilton or Ritz-Carlton "ho-TEL") they were talking about was a hotel bar, in this case the Strasburg Hotel or sometimes the Rawlinsville Hotel. These were not hotels in the normal sense; I don't know of anyone ever staying overnight in one . . . at least, not intentionally. They were simply bars, watering holes, although they used to be much more.

The Pennsylvania hotel bar is a holdover from colonial and stagecoach days. Colonial travel was appallingly difficult and expensive because of the hills, ridges, and waterways that began just outside of Philadelphia. Philadelphians considered a voyage to England easier than a journey to Reading, and they were right. Taverns, inns, and hotels opened through the southeastern part of the Commonwealth—at the various "stages" the coach traveled between—to sustain the traveler with a bed, hearty road-worthy fare, and a pot of restorative cider, ale, or whiskey.

As roads were built and railroads replaced stagecoach lines, the hotel evolved into a restaurant and saloon. The hotel became more a place for the local worker than for the traveler. European immigrants provided the workforce that carried America into the industrial age, and they also provided the thirsty throats that propelled us into the lager age. The hotel bar, complete with cuspidor and "free lunch," kept the beer cold and flowing.

After Prohibition's gloomy days, when drinking went undercover in the speakeasies, the poolhalls, and the so-called "seafood houses," the hotel bar was back, at least in upstate Pennsylvania. But soon after World War II Americans started to cocoon themselves in living rooms lit by the blue glow of a television and cooled by central air and readily available packaged beer. The hotel's appeal slipped. It was no longer the center of socializing, that role being usurped by firehalls, American Legion and VFW clubs, and bingo halls.

The upshot of these trends is that genuine hotel bars are a vanishing breed, and unchanged examples are a little harder to find every year. Almost as many have been ruined by ham-handed "restorations" as have been turned into homes, shops, and hardware stores. But there are still some beauties to be found out in the ridge country of Berks, Schuylkill, and Lehigh Counties. We'll take a quick tour through some of the best.

High on the list is the Kempton Hotel. Located at the intersection of PA Rts. 737 and 143, east of Hawk Mountain (610-756-6588), the Kempton has managed to renew itself without losing its 'real deal' appeal. It was built in 1874 to house and feed the men building the Berks-Lehigh railroad, and it survives as the local bar, restaurant, and meeting place for a large, thinly populated area. The kitchen serves up regional fare like chicken and waffles, pig stomach stew, and hickorynut pie. Look up to admire one of the unique attractions of the Kempton. Two local artists have painted three murals on the hotel ceiling: Kempton History in the bar, the Pageant of American History in the dining room, and the Life of Christ in the back banquet room. It's worth the trip.

If you head south on Route 737 about three miles or so you will come to the little village of Stony Run. The Stony Run Hotel sits on the corner, a big white building with green trim (2409 Route 737, Kempton, 610-756-4433). New owners Jerry and Marie Boltz took over in 1998, intending to restore the hotel. I honestly worried, but what they have done should be a model for such restoration. The bar is almost untouched, including the backbar, an imposing beauty with two massive wooden pillars, hand-carved in nearby Topton over 100 years ago. If you order a bottle, it may be opened with a Stegmaier promotional bottle opener from the 1940s; Marie said they found a box of them in a back room. The major change was a spotless new modern kitchen, a welcome addition to any bar. They've even left the outhouse in the backyard, although indoor plumbing has been added.

If you want to try some of the hearty and filling Pennsylvania Dutch hotel food, you can't do better than Haag's Hotel in Shartlesville (just off Exit 8 of I-78 west of Allentown, 610-488-6692). The family-style tables at Haag's are authentically laden, brimming over with ham, chicken, sausage, beef, gravy, potato filling, sweet potatoes, green beans, chicken pot-pie, dried corn, pickled beets, pepper cabbage, pickles, applesauce, large-pearl tapioca, stewed apricots, sugar cookies, shoo-fly pie, cherry pie, apple pie, and ice cream, with plentiful dishes of bread and butter, cottage cheese, and apple butter on the side. This is solid food that lines the belly like bricks and mortar.

One of my favorite spots in upstate Pennsylvania is the town of Jim Thorpe. There's lots to do here, but the must-see for the beer traveler is the Hotel Switzerland, right at the square under the hill. The bar and steakhouse underneath is now The Molly Maguires (not too imaginative in Jim Thorpe . . .); it's still the Switzerland to me. Belly up to the dark wooden bar and imagine yourself a coal magnate, surveying the world over a cold mug of lager. Come hungry; they do serve a fine steak dinner and usually have some good beer to go with it (5 Hazard Square, 570-325-4563).

You can get the best of both worlds at the Douglassville Hotel. The big porch outside and the big menu inside will tell you it's a real hotel, and the beer list, sporting imports and micros from all over, will make you a happy geek. The bar gets a little loud at night, so I usually stay in the dining room. Hog into the salad bar, where you'll find things like chow-chow (pickled vegetables) and Froot Loops, then get a big plate of the house special, Veal Gruyère (U.S. Route 422 East, Douglassville, 610-385-2585).

They're not all in the Pennsylvania Dutch country, either. I found a real gem while poking around Altoona after visiting Marzoni's, the U.S. Hotel, dating from 1835, in Hollidaysburg (401 S. Juniata St., 814-695-9924). There's a solid twin-pillar back bar lit by original glass marble "bunch o' grapes" lights, tile walls, a footrail, and even a tiled trough with intact plumbing at the foot of the bar, so "gentlemen" wouldn't have to search for a spittoon. Belly up to this one, and you'll really know what it was like, back when.

There are more fine old hotel bars out there. If you can find an out-of-print book called *Bars of Reading and Berks* by "Suds" Kroge and

"Dregs" Donnigan, buy it. It's a somewhat dated but invaluable guide to these old bars and a hilarious read to boot.

But you can try any small town along the Appalachian front, and chances are you'll find a hotel. You'll know the thrill of discovery, whether it's an original pressed-tin ceiling, an ornately carved or painted backbar, or just a fresh clean squirt of Yuengling. It's out there, waiting. Go and find it.

Pennsylvania Dutch Country

M ost people think of Lancaster County alone as Pennsylvania Dutch country, thanks to the county's busy tourist bureau. There are indeed a lot of Amish farms and "Dutchie" accents in Lancaster, but you'll find them up through Lebanon and Berks counties as well, and on into the Lehigh Valley. This is my home territory. I was born and raised in Lancaster County, like all my family before me since 1741, so I'm a bit nuts about the place.

The small cities of the area—Lancaster, Reading, Allentown, Bethlehem, and Easton—were at first market towns. They became industrial towns, and now they are finding their own way in the shifting economy of the twenty-first century. All of them have come to realize that their heritage is bankable, so you will find them eager to please tourists. Lancaster has been this way for years, but Reading and the towns of the Lehigh Valley also have learned the art of promotion and the value of tourism.

This is Pennsylvania's breadbasket. Watered by rivers like the Schuylkill, Conestoga, and Lehigh, small farms cover the landscape, producing milk, fruit, vegetables, soybeans, and even cigar tobacco. There are some fine restaurants here, serving everything from nouvelle cuisine to massive, multicourse "Pennsylvania hotel" dinners. The regional fare is hearty and simple, with farmboy's delights such as chicken pot pie, dripping with gravy and freighted with great raftlike noodles, and molasses-and-cake-filled shoofly pies.

You'll also find good beer here, thanks to some great little breweries. Carol and Ed Stoudt started things in northern Lancaster County back in 1987, with Pennsylvania's first microbrewery in modern times. They have since been joined by a bevy of brewers, all making fine products. True to their heritage, some of them brew German-style lager beers, and the local population laps it up.

Visiting these breweries will give you an opportunity to take a leisurely drive through gently rolling hills and past beautifully kept farms. One of my favorite drives is to head east from New Holland on Route 23, along the ridge through the Twin Valley area to Morgantown. You can also take a shopping trip from the factory outlets along Route 30 in Lancaster up Route 222 to the factory outlets in Reading. And if you get thirsty on the way, Stoudt's is just off Route 222.

There is also the attraction of the Amish themselves. They live among us "English," as the Amish call all people outside the faith, but they strive to keep themselves separate. Please respect their privacy. Although the Amish of Lancaster County are more worldly than some of their brethren in upstate New York or Indiana, they still try to live in accordance with their beliefs. There are plenty of Amish attractions, some better than others. The Amish Farm and House is one of the more accurate ones, on Route 30 east of Lancaster (717-394-6185, www.amish farmandhouse.com).

There are two other areas in Pennsylvania Dutch Country that you should visit. The high bluffs on the lower Susquehanna near Holtwood Dam are breathtakingly beautiful in spring and fall. Trails there range from easy strolls by Pequea Creek along old trolley beds to soaring climbs that challenge the experienced day hiker. Far to the east is the Delaware River, curving quietly with gentle splendor through some of the prettiest countryside in Pennsylvania. Taking a drive along the Delaware is a wonderful way to spend the afternoon.

Wherever you go in Pennsylvania Dutch Country, take your time; the pace is wonderfully slow here. You'll find plenty to see, lots of shops to visit, and countless backroads to explore. You may come for the Amish, but be sure to take a look around. You'll be back for the beauty.

Lancaster Brewing Company and Walnut Street Grille

Plum and Walnut Streets
Lancaster, PA 17603
717-391-6258
www.lancasterbrewing.com

I grew up in Lancaster County. Our line of Brysons has lived there since 1741. My mother's side of the family has farmed in the county for more than two centuries, and her father and my father ran a general store outside Strasburg. My father and I both went to Franklin and Marshall College in Lancaster, where I met my wife. My parents still live there, in the little town of Paradise, and my children have played in the fields where I played.

I want you to understand how much this land means to me. I don't live there now—which is not to say that I don't live there anymore. But I know and love the farm-dotted valleys and ridges of Lancaster, the woods of the southern end, the river hills and the tiny roads of the northern reaches. It's my home, and it always will be, no matter where I move.

I tell you all this because I want you to understand how deep-down glad and proud I am that Lancaster Brewing survives. I've always felt a connection to the brewery. Back when it was Lancaster Malt Brewing, we shared initials; buying LMB gear was like getting free monogramming. I was at the brewery's opening; I signed books there.

Brewing in Lancaster is a natural. The county once had fourteen breweries and was known nationwide as a brewing center. H. L. Mencken favored beer from the city's Rieker Star Brewery (a brewery that would become the bar where I had my first nonmainstream beer, which launched me on the path that put these words in front of you). Lancaster beers sold in Boston in the 1940s for $10 a keg, a princely sum for beer. But the last brewery went silent in 1956, and local folks drank other people's beer for thirty-nine years. Locally made beer finally made a comeback when Lancaster Brewing opened in 1995.

Beers brewed: Year-round: Hop Hog IPA, Gold Star Pilsner, Amish Four Grain Pale Ale, Milk Stout, Litening Lager, Strawberry Wheat, Celtic Rose, Shoo-Fly Porter. Seasonals: Hefeweizen, Baltic Porter, Oktoberfest, Winter Warmer, Rare Rooster Rye, Doppelbock, and others. (Bottles are currently all done at The Lion.)

It hasn't been the easiest of rides for the brewery. There have been problems with ownership; there was a bankruptcy in 1998; and at the end of 2009, longtime brewer Christian Heim and sales director John Frantz (both of whom were minority owners of the company) were abruptly let go. Majority owners Irene Keares and Jim Weber are running the business.

The Pick: The Milk Stout is a sweet stout that is still somewhat roasty, a drink refreshing yet rich. My wife would walk over my back to get this beer. It's embarrassing to admit, but the combination of Milk Stout and Strawberry Wheat is truly delicious. And it is *not* a "girly beer!" Get some Gold Star, too: It's smooth and creamy, then comes through with a hoppy middle and a long bitter finish.

The beer is the responsibility of a man who has been a fixture in southeast Pennsylvania's craft brewing community for almost twenty years: Bill Moore. When I asked Bill how he was handling the recent changes in brewery management, his response could have come from the building and the business itself: "Hey, I'm still standing!"

That's no small statement. Bill had been working in nuclear power plant construction and got into the beer business because he just loved the idea. It was a love that took him down quite a few steps: His first job was separating returnable bottles at a wholesaler. "The first day," he recalled, "I was at that for eight hours in the backroom, and it was smelly and hot, but they had to come get me to stop. I was happy—I was in the beer business!"

From there, he moved on to selling beer for Stoudt's, which turned into brewing. Well, not just brewing. Like at any other brewery back in the early 1990s, people at Stoudt's wore multiple hats. "I brewed, I kegged, I delivered it, too. I even cooked in the kitchen!" Bill said with a laugh. He also got out and spread the word. I remember Bill hosting a beer dinner I went to back in 1992. "All part of the job," he said when I reminded him of that event. "I met all the retailers, all the bar accounts. I loved it."

Bill took the reputation he'd built at Stoudt's and became head brewer at Independence (where he would win medals with his beloved festbier recipe), then jumped to Sly Fox when Independence faltered, then moved down the road to Sunnybrook (a short-lived brewpub in an old-school ballroom; "I loved that brewery," Bill said), and finally wound up at Lancaster, which let him do what he wanted to: "I just want to brew lager beer," he said, tossing his hands up in the air and grinning the wry, sideways grin that's almost as much a Bill Moore trademark as his bushy full beard.

"I've been in the same house in Douglassville for twenty years," he said. "I've been a bunch of places, brewed a lot of beer, and met some great people. I love this business."

The brewery's been through almost as much as Bill and is wearing its age as gracefully. The historic brick building is a renovated tobacco warehouse dating back to the 1880s, which was also used to house prisoners of war during World War II. The dark wood floors, massive wooden beams, high, intricate brick ceilings, and copper accents make for a comfortable space, lived-in and solid. The bar and the casual dining area wrap around an open drop to the attractive 15-barrel JV Northwest brewhouse below, an interesting change from the usual behind-the-bar setup.

The beer is solid and delicious. The fest beer is great, and it ought to be; Bill's been honing it to perfection for almost eighteen years. But his ales work, too. The best-selling Hop Hog IPA has a great hop flavor; beware the scarily well-hidden 7.9 percent ABV. The new Shoo-Fly Porter really does remind you of its namesake molasses-based pie, rich but not sticky, and quite drinkable. Old favorites like the Milk Stout and Strawberry Wheat are still good and still popular.

By my count, this is the third major change for Lancaster Brewing. I don't know if it's going to last as long as my family has in Lancaster, but I intend to retire here, and I'm hoping Lancaster Brewing will be around when I do.

Opened: April 1995.

Owner: Privately held corporation; major shareholders include Irene Keares and Jim Weber.

Brewers: Bill Moore, brewmaster; Dale Tomel and Troy Kreider, brewers.

System: 15-barrel JV Northwest brewhouse, 8,000 barrels potential annual capacity.

2009 production: 5,000 barrels (est.).

Brewpub hours: Open Sunday through Thursday, 11:30 AM to midnight; Friday and Saturday, 11:30 AM to 2 AM.

Tours: By appointment.

Take-out beer: Growlers, six-packs, "barn box" twelve-packs, cases, kegs.

Food: The Walnut Street Grille is a busy restaurant and a popular spot for private parties. It features a full menu with ale-simmered mussels, a brewery-special meatloaf, white chili, and a delicious lamb burger with feta and tzatziki sauce. Vegetarians will enjoy the falafel platter.

Extras: Dartboard; backgammon and chess–checkers boards built into the bar tables.

Special considerations: Kids welcome (special menu). Vegetarian and specially prepared meals available.

Parking: Small lot on Plum Street. Street parking can get tight at times. Weekends and evenings, you can park across the street.

Lodging in the area: Lancaster Arts Hotel is very beer-friendly and offers a Brewmaster Package with Lancaster Brewing, 300 Harrisburg Ave., Lancaster, 866-720-ARTS; Days Inn, 1492 Lititz Pike, Lancaster, 717-293-8400; Fulton Steamboat Inn, Routes 30 and 896, Lancaster, 717-299-9999 (we laughed when this big steamboat-shaped place went up, but friends have raved about their stays here); Gardens of Eden B&B, 1894 Eden Rd., 717-393-5179; The King's Cottage B&B, 1049 E. King St., 717-397-1017 or 800-747-8717.

Area attractions: Call or visit the Web site of the Pennsylvania Dutch Visitor's Bureau (717-299-8901, www.padutchcountry.com) to get information about the many attractions in the city and county. Lancaster's selection of factory outlets rivals Reading's these days; you'll find most of them on Route 30 east of Lancaster. **Reading China and Glass** in Rockvale Outlets (717-393-9747, www.rockvalesquare outlets.com) has cheap pint glasses and sometimes sells "yards of ale" glasses. **Dutch Wonderland** (2249 Lincoln Highway East, 866-386-2839, www.dutchwonderland.com), recently rated the fifth-best kids' amusement park in the world, is a park just for the little ones, with scaled-back flumes, roller coasters, and bumper cars ideal for kids under ten. **Wheatland** (1120 Marietta Avenue, 717-392-8721, www.wheatland.org), the home of James Buchanan, Pennsylvania's admittedly not-very-notable contribution to the presidency, is a beautifully restored Federal-era mansion with original furniture and the Tangier Arborerum; hours are reduced in the winter. The **Lancaster Science Factory** (454 New Holland Ave., 717-509-6363, www.lancastersciencefactory.org) is right around the bend from Lancaster Brewing on New Holland Avenue. It offers a new interactive science experience that will keep your kids amused and amazed, and hey, blowing giant bubbles can be fun at any age! For tubers, a float down the Pequea Creek is a great way to cool off in the sticky heat of a Lancaster summer. You can rent tubes at **Sickman's Mill** (717-872-5951, www.sickmansmill.net) in Conestoga (you can camp there, too). Take old sneakers and don't wear a white suit; the river's muddy sometimes. Just north of Ephrata, the **Green Dragon Farmers Market and Auction** (www.greendragonmarket.com) is open every Friday, with a livestock auction, food stands, and more interesting people than you can shake a shoofly pie at; it's the farm-life equivalent of a mall. Don't forget to stop by the **Julius Sturgis Pretzel House** (219 E. Main St., Lititz, 717-626-4354, www.juliussturgis.com) for their tour; you can take a twist at making your own pretzel. Then walk over to the **Wilbur Chocolate Company** (48 North Broad St., 717-626-3249, www.wilburchocolate.com) and get dessert.

Other area beer sites: You won't find a lot of taps at **John J. Jeffries** (in the Lancaster Arts Hotel, 300 Harrisburg Ave., 717-431-3307), but what's there is prime stuff, and they're really up to speed on it. The **Lancaster Dispensing Company** (33–35 N. Market St., 717-299-4602) has been one of Lancaster's best watering holes for years and is slowly catching up to the better-beer idea. **Annie Bailey's** (28 E. King St., 717-393-4000) kicks the Irish theme right in downtown; the pleasant surprise is a broader selection of beer than you'd expect, including a dedicated Spring House tap. **The Pressroom** (26 W. King St., 717-399-5400) is quite stylish, with a more "big city" feel . . . but the pretzels on the bar are locally made Hammonds. If you want someplace very nice to eat with a couple good beers *or* a wine list with over fourteen hundred selections . . . **Strawberry Hill** (128 W. Strawberry St., 717-393-5544) fits the bill. You'll find a small but select draft and bottle selection; they love wine, but they've had good beer for more than years (good whisky and cognac, too). **Bulls Head Public House** (14 E. Main St., Lititz, 717-626-2115) brings you real ale on two handpumps every day from Paul Pendyck, the man most responsible for bringing cask ale to America. This is great cask ale!

Iron Hill Brewery, Lancaster

781 Harrisburg Avenue, Lancaster, PA 17603
717-291-9800
www.ironhillbrewery.com

Oh, I was born too late. I entered Franklin and Marshall College a full thirty years before Iron Hill opened just across Harrisburg Avenue. I drank Rolling Rock at the Town Tavern, $2.50 pitchers of Stroh's at the Shamrock Café, and whatever it was that was 50 cents a glass at Hildy's Tavern ("Where Frederick meets Mary" was their slogan and their address). The same thing happened to me with grad school: I lived only two blocks from where the Sharp Edge would one day open in Pittsburgh.

Lucky seniors: Paul Rutherford is brewing great stuff for them. "I keep a good lager on all the time," he said. "I've got a helles, a pilsner,

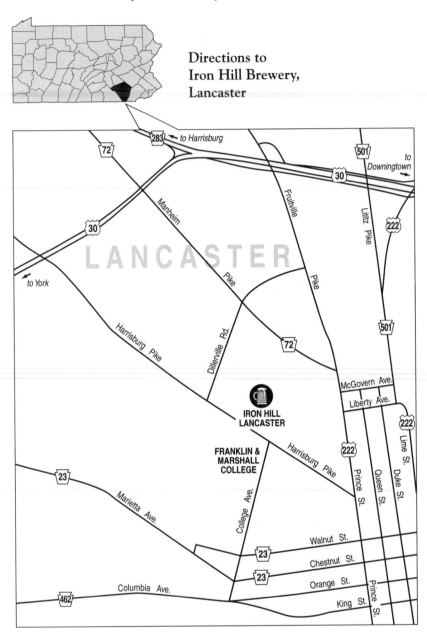

**Directions to
Iron Hill Brewery,
Lancaster**

and a Dortmunder; the Dort's my recipe. Lagers go very well here." I know they do. I've been hearing from my mother about Paul's Vienna lager. My mother and her sisters and aunts go out for lunch at various places in Lancaster County, and Iron Hill's become a favorite.

"Lancaster bars like local beers," Paul said. "That's why Spring House is doing so well. They like hoppy beers, too. They've been loving the Kryptonite Double IPA and the Imperial Coffee Porter. Actually, they like the 'out there' stuff too: Berliner weisse, rauchbier, sour beers, whatever."

I think there's a lot of pent-up craft demand in Lancaster. As you can see under the Lancaster Brewing entry, there's not a lot of beer bar talent in the town—not a single dedicated beer bar, but bars with some beers that happen to be there. That's probably why Iron Hill was totally slammed when they opened.

It's just as well I was born too late. I'd rather be born too late than not graduate because I spent all my time at Iron Hill.

Opened: November 2007.

Owners: Mark Edelson, Kevin Finn, Kevin Davies.

Brewers: Paul Rutherford, head brewer; Colin Farrell, assistant.

System: 8.5-barrel Specific Mechanical system, 1,200 barrels annual capacity.

2009 production: 1,000 barrels.

Brewpub hours: Sunday and Monday, 11 AM to 11 PM; Tuesday through Thursday, 11 AM to midnight; Friday and Saturday, 11 AM to 1 AM.

Tours: On request.

Take-out beer: Growlers, bottled reserves.

Food: See the listing for Iron Hill, West Chester, on page 75.

Extras: Mug club. Frequent special dinner deals; check Web site for details.

Special considerations: Kids welcome. Vegetarian meals available.

Parking: Large free lot in back.

Beers brewed: Iron Hill's house beers include Iron Hill Light Lager, Raspberry Wheat, Vienna Red Lager, Ironbound Ale, Pig Iron Porter, and a rotating Belgian style. Seasonals: Pilsner, Dortmunder, Helles, The Costanza Rye, Biere de Mars, Maibock, Braveheart, Abbey's Fault, Tripel, Black Double Wit, Oompa Loompa Chocolate Stout, Rye IPA, Irish Red, and more. Bottled reserves also available.

The Pick: Abbey's Fault, a triple with a lot of hops, is a sick idea but great. The Costanza was a fluffy rye with caraway, nicely done. But it was Paul's simple Helles— bright, bread-fresh, and dryly malty—that took me away, centered me in the beer moment. Brilliant.

Spring House Brewery

2519 Main Street, Conestoga, PA 17516
717-872-0925
www.springhousebeer.com

The first time I visited Spring House Brewery was in August 2007. I was with my father and Uncle Don, spinning down the narrow winding roads of southern Lancaster County, the River Hills area. For them, it was memory lane as they pointed out where the trolley used to run from Lancaster all the way down to Pequea, on the banks of the lower Susquehanna; where my father swam across the river; and where a surprising number of heretofore unmentioned old girlfriends lived.

For me, it was a hunt with my beer senses tuned to high gain: I didn't know where Matt Keasey was setting up Spring House, and I didn't have a GPS. All I had was a road and the knowledge that it was near the small town of Conestoga. Looking, looking, looking—hey! There's foam insulation poking out through the cracks in that barn: Gotta be a brewery!

Sure enough, as we pulled in, there was a stainless steel tank peeking out through a door. This was the place, and there was Matt, standing by his new brewkettle. New to him, of course; stainless never dies, and this system was out of a place called Via Maria in Holland, Michigan.

We talked for a bit, and Matt showed us around the converted tobacco barn. The brewery was on the main floor; the tasting room would go up above. We looked out back at fields stretching up the hill and went into Matt's house, right beside the barn, where there was an actual springhouse, and a spring pool right there in the house, with water lilies and goldfish.

The house dates back to 1794, and Matt said it had only been electrified in 1970. He'd bought the house and barn in 2005, as part of a developing plan to get into brewing. That started when he began homebrewing and wound up talking to Mike McDonald, the excellent brewer at Whitemarsh Brewing outside of Baltimore. Whitemarsh was looking at opening a second brewpub at the time, and Lancaster was a possibility.

Beers brewed: Year-round: Seven Gates Pale Ale. Seasonals and specials: Goofy Foot Summer Wheat, Belgian Wit, Atomic Raygun Imperial Red, Planet Bean Coffee Stout, Beyond the Gates Double IPA, Kerplunk! Imperial Chocolate Stout, Two Front Teeth Holiday Ale, Robot Bastard! Belgian IPA, Smoked Porter.

The plan fell through, though, and Matt started talking to Artie Tafoya at Appalachian. Matt was doing quality control screening at Appalachian one night a week, a sideline to his lab job at Lancaster Laboratories. When that plan got put on the far back burner as well, Matt was determined to go ahead with it on his own, but not as a brewpub. He would do a production brewery.

The plans were for draft only, with bottling of the flagship beer, Seven Gates Pale Ale, to be done at The Lion. Matt wanted to be open by November 2007, and he just made it. I heard good things, and when I finally got some draft Seven Gates (at the Pressroom, in Lancaster), it was deliciously clean and bright.

The Pick: Two Front Teeth was like Christmas candy, those colorful assortments of hard candies you used to see that were spiked with spices and bold flavors. There's a big saison spicy-sweet character right out front, a candy-malt middle with spice shot through it, and then a nice cherry note on the end, finishing with just a bit of that spicy candy thing. Nicely done; do it again, please!

The plans for bottling at The Lion fell through, as did alternate plans for brewing at Yards. "I couldn't keep up with the sales of Seven Gates," Matt told me, "so I went to Appalachian; they're doing the 12-ounce bottles. It's a crazy industry."

He's bottling some very limited editions of the big beers, which have been popular. "That's what sells," he said. "They're taking off and I can't keep up. That's the business. I need to get a 22-ounce bottle filler. I could be selling more of them in bottles."

That's just one problem about doing well. The other is bigger: When's he going to have to move? He knew the day was coming; I remember him telling me when we first talked in 2006 that he didn't want to call the business Conestoga Brewing because he knew he'd be starting small and then moving.

"The five-year plan is to move," he said. "We're limited in space here, and I have to have the chemical wastes hauled away. But the well water's really good; it's coming up from 650 feet. We just have to soften it a little. So when do you move?"

Take my advice: Go see Spring House now. Let me tell you why.

The last time I visited Spring House was in January 2010. A light snow was falling on a gray, cold day, and I was alone on the road south from Lancaster. But when I got to Spring House, the parking lot was full. ("The BeerAdvocate and ratebeer Web sites have been great at getting the news out," Matt said. "People come in from all over.") The inside of the brewery glowed with reflected light from the white insulation, and people were talking and laughing in the upstairs tasting room. Matt opened a couple big bottles and shared them around, and there was a

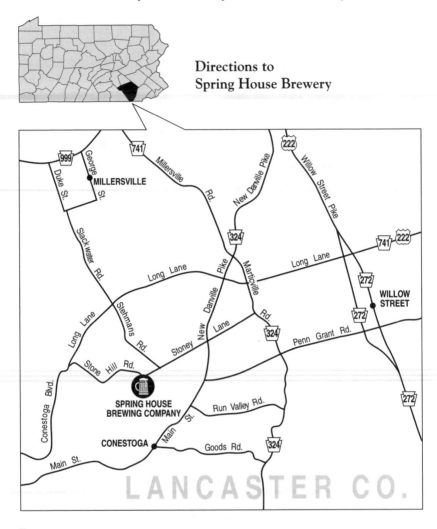

Directions to
Spring House Brewery

lively business in growlers going on. This time I was on memory lane, back to the old days of craft brewing: the vibe, the friendliness, the size . . . only the beer was much more adventurous. Catch that moment and get to Conestoga as soon as you can.

Opened: Nov. 2007.
Owner: Matthew Keasey.
Brewer: Matthew Keasey.
System: 12-barrel JV Northwest system, 2,100 barrels annual capacity.
2009 production: 900 barrels.

Tours: Wednesdays and Fridays, 7 PM.

Take-out beer: Growlers available Wednesday and Friday, 6:00 PM to 9:00 PM; Saturday noon to 5:00 PM.

Special considerations: Kids allowed but must be supervised.

Parking: Small off-road lot. Do not park on the road; there's not really enough room.

Lodging in the area, Area attractions, Other area beer sites: See Lancaster Brewing on pages 136–137.

Bube's Brewery

102 North Market Street, Mount Joy, PA 17552
717-653-2056
www.bubesbrewery.com

Six blind wise men went to Bube's to find out what it was like. When they returned, the people asked them, "What is Bube's like?"

The first man said, "Bube's is a brewpub, with well-made and tasty beers, friendly bartenders, and comfortable surroundings."

The second man said, "No, Bube's is a museum of brewing history, telling the tale of a young man who brought his love and knowledge of lager brewing from Germany to America."

The third man said, "Fool! Bube's is an ornate and intimate setting for amusing murder mystery theatricals, accompanied by artfully created cocktails."

The fourth man said, "Where did you go, dotard? Bube's is a beer garden, an exceptionally lovely green oasis in the middle of town where people enjoy beer in relaxed informality and good cheer."

The fifth man said, "Verily, you're all nuts. Bube's is a deep set of catacombs, antique lagering cellars where people dine and celebrate, often entertained by mummery and music."

The sixth man said, "Mummery, flummery! Bube's is a nightclub, a warm, friendly bar with good beer and spirits, that turns into an intimate venue for live music as the night lengthens."

Beers brewed: Always five of the following on tap at any time, but all beers rotate: Red Ale, Kölsch, Heffweizen, IPA, Nut Brown Ale, Bavarian Lager, Imperial Stout, Honey Cream Ale, Scotch Ale, Porter, Belgian Tripel. "We will always be adding to the list," Sam Allen said.

And the people said, "How can this be? Bube's is a brewpub, a nightclub, a museum, a theater? Are these not wise men? How could they all find Bube's so different?"

And Lew said, relax, they are all correct, for Bube's is a big place, a fun place, a place that sizzles with imagination and drama and the never-ending energy that keeps it evolving for the pleasure of its guests. And besides, the blind guys missed the homebrew shop, the brewery tour, the art gallery, the banquet room upstairs, and the local craft shop. You need some new wise men, folks.

The Pick: I've enjoyed a whole afternoon of Porter in the beer garden (which has been expanded and is feeling really German these days), but the Nut Brown Ale is really a stand-out: rich but drinkable, tasty and friendly. That's a pretty authentic kölsch, too: I've had my share in Köln as well.

I probably missed a couple things myself, because Bube's (it really is pronounced "boobies"; it's German) at the Central Hotel in Mount Joy is a rambling complex that is always expanding at the behest of proprietor Sam Allen. Allen is a former actor who has found his niche and his calling creating a series of wonders and comforts here at this old brewery and hotel complex.

It really is a historic brewery, founded and run by Alois Bube in the 1800s. The full history is in the small museum upstairs from the lobby (the lobby was the location of the original brewery). Bube made lager beer, beer that the brewery was well-known for. "We called it Bube's Brewery when we opened," Allen said. "But people kept calling and coming to visit and asking, "Where's the brewery? We did a study with the business department at Lebanon Valley College, and after we did all the work, they told us we had an image problem: People expected a brewery and there was none." He grinned and chuckled. "No kidding!"

Allen wanted to brew, wanted to add a brewery, but how to do it in the room he had? I first reported on their intent to add a brewery in the mid-1990s, and a few more times in the late 1990s. "We spent the first four years doing all the legal paperwork," said Allen. It finally came through, and on November 28, 2001, the brewery served its first legal, house-brewed beer since 1917. It was a great day.

The beers are brewed in a tiny room by two guys named Bryan Teets and Rick Kunkle—Pennsylvania Dutch names are always a little risky—and they rotate through a number of styles. But there's almost always a kölsch on, for two reasons. "I wanted something that the first-time visitor to a brewpub could drink," said Allen of the easygoing style. "That's doing the beer world a service. I also spent a semester at the University of Köln [where kölsch was born and is still the beer of

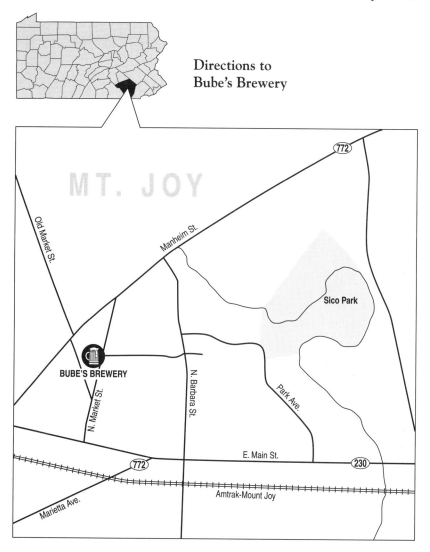

**Directions to
Bube's Brewery**

MT. JOY

Old Market St.

Manheim St.

772

Sico Park

BUBE'S BREWERY

N. Market St.

N. Barbara St.

Park Ave.

E. Main St.

772

230

Amtrak-Mount Joy

Marietta Ave.

choice] and drank my share, so please keep that in mind when you're critiquing the kölsch!"

Bube's is an experience, run like few other places in the East. What it really reminded me of was the McMenamin's brewpubs and bars in Oregon and Washington, inspired reusers of solid old buildings and patrons of incidental art. We could use a few more Bube's around these parts. Stop in and see what I mean, and be sure to explore. I've been going to Bube's for years (I started dating my wife there), and I never knew they had a beer garden till my visit for the third edition. Huh. Blind man!

Opened: Brewery reopened November 2001.

Owners: Sam Allen, Tobin Garber.

Brewers: Bryan Teets, Rick Kunkle.

System: 3.5-barrel Specific Mechanical brewhouse, 350 barrels potential annual capacity.

2009 production: 200 barrels (est.).

Brewpub hours: Monday through Saturday, 11:30 AM to midnight; Sunday, noon to 10 PM.

Tours: 5 PM to 10 PM. Tours of the historic brewery area available seven days a week.

Take-out beer: Growlers.

Food: Depending on where you dine, there are a number of menus, with items ranging from sausage en croute to a daily sorbet to start, followed by entrées that feature both vegetarian dishes and honking big cuts of meat and fish. There really is something for everyone here . . . as long as you're hungry.

Extras: Live music on weekends, murder mysteries, ghost tours, feasts of a variety of types, and an unpredictable series of special events in the Bottling Works. Bube's is almost a theme park: there's the brewing museum, great cocktails in the Alois Bar, art gallery, gift shop with locally made crafts, beer garden (with outdoor pool table), the Catacombs for private parties and banquets, and unusually decorated lodging upstairs.

Special considerations: Accommodations for kids, vegetarian meals, and the handicapped vary by restaurant; please call with specific concerns.

Parking: Good free street parking and small lot.

Lodging in the area: The Olde Fogie Farm B&B (106 Stackstown Rd., Marietta, 877-653-3644) is a working farm and a rare B&B that's perfect for small children; Olde Square Inn, 127 E. Main St., Mount Joy, 800-742-3533; Holiday Inn Express, 147 Merts Dr., Elizabethtown, 717-367-4000.

Area attractions: Hershey is not far away, and I think we all know what that means; if you don't, roll down the window and sniff. This is the home of **Hershey's Chocolate World** (Hersheypark Drive, 717-534-4900, www.hersheyschocolateworld.com), a ride through the making of chocolate, chocolate-themed cafés, and a huge chocolate gift shop. **Hersheypark** amusement park (100 W. Hersheypark Drive, 800-HERSHEY, www.hersheypark.com) has *eleven* roller coasters (including the classic wooden Comet) and a water park, or you can just walk around and feed the carp in the stream; the **ZooAmerica Wildlife Park** (Hersheypark Drive, 717-534-3860) is included in admission to Hersheypark and focuses on the animals of North America. Or you can just stop alongside the street and breathe deeply, till you gain a pound or two. The **Cornwall Iron Furnace** (off Route 322, follow signs on Route 419 to Rexmont Street, 717-272-9711, www.cornwallfurnace.org) is a restored iron mine and furnace; these are actual, original restored buildings, not re-creations. This was an important source of iron during the colonial period and operated as a furnace through 1883.

Other area beer sites: *Shank's Tavern* (36 S. Waterford Ave., Marietta, 717-426-1205; limited hours, call ahead) is a longtime spot for better beer that's holding up well; it opened in 1814 and has been run by the Shank family since 1930. It's an easy walk from there to *McCleary's Public House* (130 W. Front St., 717 426-2225), where you can sit at the small bar, or enjoy live music on weekends . . . or finish up research for a brewery guidebook: McCleary's was my very last stop this time around. See the listings for Harrisburg (page 191) and Lancaster (page 137) as well.

Swashbuckler Brewing Company

83 Mansion House Road (on the Renaissance Faire grounds)
Manheim, PA 17545
717-665-7021
www.parenfaire.com

The first time we saw Scott Bowser was in the first edition of *Pennsylvania Breweries*, brewing so-so beers (and a pretty darned good cider) at the Summy House in Manheim. Then, in a plot twist reminiscent of *A Connecticut Yankee in King Arthur's Court*, Scott left Summy House, took a right turn on Route 72, and disappeared into the Renaissance.

What really happened is that Bowser got a call from Chuck Romito at the Mount Hope Vineyards, home of the Pennsylvania Renaissance Faire. "How can we get your beer up here?" Romito asked. "We've got no beer here, but we get 150,000 people a year."

Scott Bowser maybe didn't make the best beer, but nobody ever accused him of being slow on the uptake when there was a buck to be made. "A hundred fifty thousand people in the summer and no beer?" he said to me with a big grin and a snort of laughter. "How can you go wrong!"

Beers brewed: Seasonal (all beers brewed from May through October): Swashbuckler's Gold, Red Sea Amber, Plank Walker's IPA, Captain Rude's Blackwater Stout, Bootie Barleywine, Lil' Dickens Cider, Sharkbait Saison, Oktoberfest, Marly's Mirth Gruit, Pyrate Wild Ale, Wetlands Wit, and others.

He almost did, but only by aiming too low. He took his little 3-barrel brewkettle and a couple of 7-barrel tanks up the road, and quickly found he was in over his head. "We got behind after a week," Scott said. Time to get serious. He scanned the boneyard section of brewers' forums and found a system. "We went out to Las Vegas and bought Holy Cow's 12-barrel system. We had to; we sell more beer in fifteen weeks than some restaurants do in two years."

When I stopped in for a visit for the third edition, Scott had created a small fiefdom inside the Renaissance Faire walls: three bars, a turkey leg and seafood stand, and big plans. He also had much better beer—eye-openingly better beer—and he was running flat out to get it ready for the season opening the next day. He was also doing carpentry work as the Faire's general contractor. Busy man.

Little did I know how busy. By the time I saw Scott again a couple years later, he owned the Renaissance Faire. King Bowser the First! Pretty impressive for a guy who was running a little brewery in a restaurant in Manheim.

Scott delegated the brewing duties to Mark Braunwarth, an experienced brewer who'd brewed at the noted Natty Greene's in Greensboro, North Carolina, and in the Rock Bottom system. Good as Scott's beers had been, Mark took things up a level, or maybe two. I talked to him in the winter, when things were more relaxed, and he seemed almost nervous, wanting to be back to work.

"When the Faire's on," Mark said, "it's like a small city. There's about five hundred employees and thousands of guests. It's eighty-hour weeks and mad brewing schedules right up to the last day—and then it almost completely shuts down. And you miss both seasons of the year when you're in the other one."

The fact that there is another season shows how much the beer has improved. There's enough demand for it that the pub stays open through the winter, Thursday through Saturday, though it does close in April so the preparation for the Faire can begin: construction, repair, and those eighty-hour brewing weeks.

Once the Faire opens, you'll now find the beer everywhere, not just in Swashbuckler Square. "The entire premises are now licensed," Scott said. "We merged the brewing and winery companies, and now we can do more drink stations, set up temporary stations during the jousting, really anything we want on the grounds. The PLCB was a lot of help; they had a real pro-business attitude."

As you might guess, he's not standing still. Mark told me about possibilities for a production brewery that he and Scott were looking at. "Maybe in 2012, 2013," he said. "We're looking to go as green as possible with it: water recovery, energy efficiencies, repurposed materials. That would allow us to go all specialty beers on this system." If you're wondering what that means, well, Mark's experimented with some wild and sour beers already, and they'd be perfect for an authentic Renaissance feel.

But on a sunny afternoon in late May, drinking beers with Scott out on the deck in front of the pub, looking over at the bright red pirate ship—fully rigged, with cannons—that all seems far off in the mists of the future. We're living in the past here, a past that never was, with beer better than any pirate ever knew (in cleaner glasses, too). It was a lucky day when Scott left the Summy House and headed up the road to the Renaissance.

The Pick: Be sure to get some Lil' Dickens Cider if they have it: It's a beer-cider hybrid, made with local Kauffman's cider (my hometown favorite), and it's dry and not too fizzy. But the main Pick is the Gold. This might be the best kölsch being made in Pennsylvania, which I think would surprise some folks. It surprised me! Kölsch is traditionally served in little 200-ml glasses, but I'd like this in a mug.

Opened: March 2000.

Owner: Scott Bowser.

Brewer: Mark Braunwarth.

System: 12-barrel Century Manufacturing brewhouse, 2,000 barrels potential annual capacity.

2009 production: 700 barrels.

Brewpub hours: The hours vary with the operation of the Faire, a schedule that changes every year. Best to check www.parenfaire.com for times and dates. In general, the pub is open Thursday through Saturday during the Faire (mid-August to Halloween) with a Faire ticket, and Thursdays and Fridays (4:30 to 10:30 PM) and Saturdays (11:30 AM to 11:30 PM) for straight pub traffic from November through the end of April . . . but that might change. Check the Web site.

Tours: Subject to brewer availability . . . and that's pretty slim while the Faire's on. Call ahead.

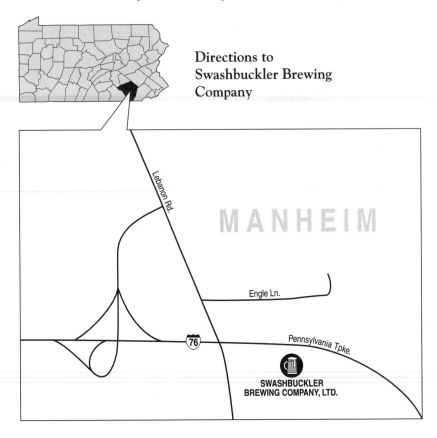

Directions to
Swashbuckler Brewing
Company

Take-out beer: Growlers.

Food: Brick-oven pizza, rotisserie beef and chicken, broiled seafood, and a lot of other "fare" are available throughout the grounds; in the off-season, the pub serves a good variety of sandwiches and a limited menu of appetizers and full dinners.

Extras: You've got the whole Renaissance Faire: 25 acres of medieval theater! In addition to the beer, the brewery also offers Mount Hope wines.

Special considerations: Kids welcome. Vegetarian food available (limited menu in off-season).

Parking: Large free lots.

Lodging in the area: Hampton Inn, 2764 S. Lebanon Rd (Route 72), 717-665-6600; Country Inn and Suites, 1475 Lancaster Rd., Manheim, 717-665-5440; Rose Manor B&B, 124 S. Linden St., 717-664-4932.

Area attractions: To get to the brewery during the season, you're going to have to go to the *Pennsylvania Renaissance Faire* (717-665-

7021, www.parenaissancefaire.com), which features jousting, balladeers, wizards, shops, artisans, and (of course) pirates! But the Faire's more than just the Faire. Events continue past mid-October, with "Edgar Allan Poe Evermore" through mid-November followed by a Victorian Christmas through New Year's. And Scott sells beer the whole time. Besides the Faire, the **Mount Hope Estate Winery** is right there on the grounds. Also see the listings for Bube's (page 146), Appalachian (page 189), and Lancaster Brewing (page 136) for more suggestions on the attractions that surround Swashbuckler.

Other area beer sites: *Quentin Tavern* (81 W. Main St., Quentin, 272-4700), about 5 miles north of the Faire, has good food and usually carries Swashbuckler beer to boot. See the listings for Bube's (page 147), Appalachian (page 191), and Lancaster Brewing (page 137) for more suggestions.

JoBoy's Brew Pub

31 South Main Street, Manheim, PA 17545
717-664-5402
www.joboysbrewpub.com

I'm afraid I may have gotten off on the wrong foot with Jeff "Boy" Harless. Jeff and his wife, Jo, opened their brewpub in Manheim in the Summy House, the historic home along Main Street where Scott Bowser had his brewpub before he moved up the road to the Renaissance Faire and went Swashbuckling. I got there on a quick trip just after I'd finished writing the rest of this edition, figuring to write it up and get it in during the editing process.

So . . . I might not have taken enough time to frame my first question clearly. "You're an award-winning barbeque cook, and you've got a barbeque restaurant," I said. "Why the beer?"

What I meant was, why are you *brewing* beer, but that's not what Jeff heard. He looked at me with a mixture of pity, confusion, and pain and tried to explain the obvious. "It's *barbeque*," he said. "You know, barbeque and *beer*? What else would you serve with it?" You have to like the way he thinks!

I quickly explained that he could have easily bought beer like so many other places do; why did he want to make his own? He gave me a very practical answer: "It's a lot more profitable this way," he said, with a slow grin. "Even with all the time I spend brewing, we still make a lot more than we would buying beer." He admitted that wasn't necessarily taking his labor into account, but that's a common fudge factor in a new business.

It's a lot of labor, too. Jeff's working on a half-barrel SABCO Brewmagic system, essentially a couple of converted kegs—professionally finished and hooked up to computerized controls and log keeping—and the beer has turned out to be more popular than he anticipated.

"It's hard to keep up," he said. "I've been brewing all the time, but our biggest problem is running out of beer. I've got a good supply of paper bags on hand, though." He pointed to the brown lunch bag hiding his fourth tap.

The long-term solution is a bigger brewery, and he's already got those plans in motion. He has a building in town lined up: Jeff is an Air Force veteran, and another vet in town wanted to help him out, so they've got a deal worked out for the space. He'd like to get a 10-barrel brewhouse put in to cool down his brewing cycle.

Jeff's beer is good—it's clean, it's tasty, and it's definitely not wimpy—but he made it clear that it's not the main focus. "This is a barbeque restaurant first," he said. "We also make beer, but this is about North Carolina–style barbeque. We cook low and slow over hardwood; the pork butts are in there about twelve to fourteen hours." They make their own sauces (a North Carolina–style vinegar-based sauce and a rich Memphis-style), spice rubs, salsa, and guacamole, which is made fresh to order.

He's got two smokers in the small kitchen, Ole Hickory units made in Cape Girardeau, Missouri. Jeff proudly told me that they're very efficient with wood, and looking at the thick, insulated walls of the smokers, I could believe it. It's a versatile way of cooking, and they use it for a lot of things at JoBoy's: Besides the usual ribs, pork shoulder, chicken, and brisket, they also smoke the kids' menu hot dogs, a delicious cabbage side dish, the meat for their award-winning tacos, and the bacon-wrapped, cream-cheese-stuffed, fresh jalapeños Jeff calls Atomic Buffalo Turds. As a barbeque fan, I found the smell in the kitchen enough to get me drooling.

You'll find another touch of the South at JoBoy's: NASCAR. If there's a race going on, the televisions are showing it, but that's just the start. There are also photos of NASCAR greats, autographed and framed, hanging on the walls—from Jeff Gordon to Richard Petty. The memorabilia is all authentic, and the pit crew coveralls behind the bar are loaned by a Manheim resident who worked the NASCAR pits for years.

One more thing about JoBoy's. I haven't said much about Jo, Jeff's wife. While Jeff took the time to talk to me, she was busy keeping things running. She was making friends with customers, something that's already a signature at JoBoy's. She and Jeff are a team and a loving couple. Take a look at the framed collections of love notes on the walls: Jo saved all of Jeff's notes to her, with the little stick figures he would draw on them. That's the origin of their logo—two line-drawn people clinking glasses, toasting their success.

"This is my dream," Jeff said, and Jo nodded. "I wanted to do barbeque right." Barbeque first . . . but the beer's worth a stop as well.

Opened: April 1, 2010.

Owners: Jo and Jeff "Boy" Harless.

Brewers: Jeff Harless.

System: 1/2-barrel SABCO Brewmagic system, 130 barrels annual capacity.

2009 production: N/A

Brewpub hours: Tuesday through Saturday, 11 AM to 10 PM.

Tours: Jeff will show you the brewery, if the kitchen is not too busy.

Take-out beer: Growlers are planned but not yet available.

Food: Jeff and Jo will be happy to show you why they won barbeque awards on the competitive circuit. They're cooking low and slow: pulled pork, pork ribs, beef brisket, and chicken, and it is authentically hardwood smoked, using hickory, apple, and cherry wood. But they're innovative, too, with BBQ tacos, smoked cabbage with barbeque sauce and bacon (amazing!), and the soon-to-be-famous Atomic Buffalo Turds. Try the made-to-order guacamole and salsa, enjoy the fresh-cut fries. There are even smoked hot dogs for the kids.

Extras: Growler club planned. NASCAR on two TVs twenty-four/seven.

Special considerations: Kids always welcome. No vegetarian meals.

Parking: Limited on-street parking.

Lodging in the area, Area attractions, Other area beer sites: See Swashbuckler on pages 150–151 and Lancaster Brewing on pages 136–137.

Stoudt's Brewing Company

Route 272, Adamstown, PA 19501
717-484-4386
www.stoudtsbeer.com

Carol Stoudt is a pioneer. When she founded Pennsylvania's first micro-brewery in 1987, she was one of the country's few female brewers. She followed her own course, brewing the German-style lagers she and her husband, Ed, adored. She set high standards and met them. Stoudt's is one of the winningest breweries in the history of the Great American Beer Festival, with a total of more than twenty medals. Carol was suc-cessful, and every time a story was done on brewers, she was part of it, proving women could make it in the field.

"The gender issue?" she responded when I asked how that had played out. "It's over. It's not an issue anymore. It's because of the success of craft brewing. When I started, we had to brew for the beer geeks; they were the only ones interested in flavorful beers. Now the Gold's selling well, we're brewing for the broader market. It's everyone, so everyone is getting involved."

The success has allowed Carol and Ed to do things they've wanted to do, follow courses that are natural to them. They brought all produc-tion in-house in 2004 after years of contracted brewing to do their 12-ounce bottles. They've built a bakery, and a creamery is getting up to speed. "We're planning to make cheese and bringing in local produce," Carol said. "We're trying to be as local as possible, and focus sales closer to home."

That's a major change. Back when she started, sales calls were tough. Local bars, faced with their first sales call by a microbrewed beer representative, would just say, "That doesn't sell." Carol recalls that it took a long time to get the bars in Adamstown and Denver to carry the local beer. "You had to go to Reading to get a Stoudt's," she said. "That's changed, and part of it is that other brewers in the

Beers brewed: Year-round: American Pale Ale, Scarlet Lady ESB, Pils, Gold. Big beers: Double IPA, Fat Dog Stout, Triple. Seasonal: Okto-ber Fest, Maibock, Heifer-in-Wheat, Smooth Hoperator, Karnival Kölsch, Winter Ale. Brewer's reserve: Old Abom-inable Barleywine, Double Abbey, Barrel-Aged Imperial Oatmeal Stout, Saison Percheron, Retro Bock, Baltic Porter, Scrawny Dog Stout, and more.

area do great lagers. It's like better restaurants in an area: If there are more, they all do well. It's like a community."

Yet some things haven't changed. "Ed still cuts every piece of meat that gets sold in the restaurant by hand and grinds fresh hamburger every day," Carol said. "He shucks oysters, I do hostess duty. You have to."

The solid core of Stoudt's appeal is still there: the brewery hall, a spacious roofed area with a small open courtyard. When you enter it, two things are clear. First, signs of the Stoudts' German heritage are proudly displayed. Coats of arms from German cities and provinces adorn the walls. Trestle tables enhance the "permanent tent" beerhall aura of the place.

The Pick: Stoudt's Pils is roaringly great beer with a teetering balance of hops and malt that seems born to drink with red meat. Reacquaint yourself with this one. If you want to go big, the Fat Dog is irresistible, big, rich, heavy, luscious . . . *fat.*

Second, the Stoudts have willingly embraced the idea that the beer-hall can be a place for the whole family. Families and children are welcome at the Oktoberfest celebrations on Sundays in October. These are not sloppy, beat-the-clock swill fests, but rather a time for people to enjoy good company in the warm glow of a few mugs of festbier and the comfort of a plate of wurst and potato salad. As the accordion plays and feet stamp the dance floor, you can forget the world outside in the happy whirl of skirts, a beer, and a cigar out in the courtyard.

Stoudt's doesn't brew a huge amount of beer; it is definitely still a micro. The effect that Carol and her brewery have always had on the industry, however, is macro. She makes good beer. The three annual Microbrewery Festivals they do live up to this standard. They are not the biggest; each session is limited to twelve hundred people. But they are some of the best on the East Coast. The brewers are well taken care of, and they are easily accessible to visitors. Carol and Ed try to make it fun for everyone.

The beer side of the business is strong, Carol said. "The Gold's picking up, after years," she noted. "The German styles are our roots, and there's a 'palate taste' for them in this area, even if people don't realize it. We've entered New England, and it's doing very well with the Gold and the Pils. That's extremely gratifying."

Then Carol laughed, a laugh that turns heads and reminds me why it gets so loud so quickly whenever the two of us get together. "Everyone wants big bottles now," she said. "And of course, after all those years when big bottles were all we did here, we sold our big bottle filler! So we're back to bottling by hand. We're doing more one-offs, barrel aging, fun stuff. We did a Kölsch last year that did so well we added it to the regular lineup."

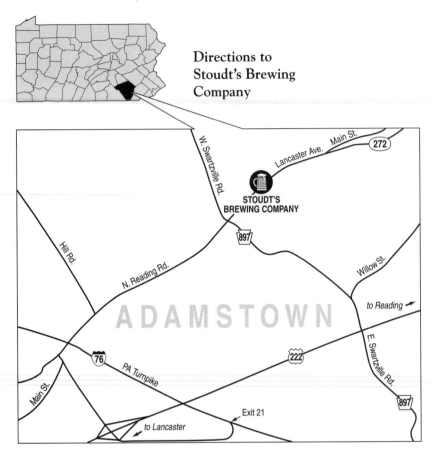

Directions to Stoudt's Brewing Company

These days, Carol is a relaxed business owner, focusing on what's important to more than just the bottom line. She's comfortable with her brewery's place in the beer world, from beer choice ("It's okay to drink a Gold if you like that; twenty years ago, it wasn't dark or even amber, it wasn't different. Now people just like the beer, not the difference") to the competition ("I hate that word; you can't survive if you're the only kid on the block—it's too lonely"). "The quality is there," she said of the brewery's production, "the diversity is there. If you're making good beer and you're profitable, that's good." Bull's-eye, Carol. I don't know if anyone could say it better.

Opened: May 1987.
Owner: Carol and Ed Stoudt.
Brewer: Brett Kintzer, Gary Gagliardi, Justin Lee, Matt Krafft.

System: 30-barrel Mueller/Criveller brewhouse, 15,000 barrels annual capacity.

2009 production: 11,000 barrels.

Brewpub hours: Monday through Thursday, 4:30 PM to 11 PM; Friday and Saturday, noon to 11 PM; Sunday, noon to 9 PM.

Tours: Saturday at 3 PM; Sunday at 1 PM.

Take-out beer: Cases or six-packs of all varieties.

Food: Light fare at the pub—soup, sandwiches, and munchies. The bock-wurst is exceptional! Fine dining can be had at the adjacent Black Angus restaurant, which is owned by Carol's husband, Ed Stoudt, with renowned top-choice steaks, hand-cut by Ed, "fresh-catch" fish, a raw bar, and big salads. You can also begin or end your meal with an artisanal cheese plate, which should include Stoudt's own cheese soon. There also are vegetarian choices, even in "The House That Beef Built."

Extras: Wednesday is open mike night in the pub; Friday sees live acoustic music. Check the Web site for bands and schedules. There's an on-site bakery and creamery, and fresh bread and artisanal cheeses are on sale at the Wonderful Good Market, Friday through Sunday, 8 AM to 4 PM. The brewery hosts three great Microbrewery Festivals in June, August, and October, with lots of brewers, good German food, and great music. It also hosts a Battle of the Brewery Bands in July, one of the most fun brewery events I've ever attended, and it's all a charity benefit (check the Web site for schedule and tickets for all events). On the five Sundays before Christmas, the beer hall becomes a traditional German Christkindlsmarkt, selling antique toys and Christmas items and serving German holiday specialty foods.

Special considerations: Kids welcome in the brewery hall. Special children's menu. Vegetarian meals available.

Parking: Plenty of parking in the big side lot.

Lodging in the area: Holiday Inn Lancaster County, Route 272, Denver, 717-336-7541; Black Forest Inn, Route 272, Adamstown, 717-484-4801; Adamstown Inn, 144 W. Main St., Adamstown, 800-594-4808. Camping is available at Shady Grove Campground, Route 897, just north on Route 272, Denver, 717-484-4225.

Area attractions: The antiques markets in Adamstown, including one in the same compound as the brewery, are regionally renowned. *Stoudtburg*, a planned European-style community started by the Stoudts, is an experimental shopping and living area behind the

Black Angus complex. The Stoudts have constructed and sold buildings to artisans, who set up shops on the first floor and live on the second floor, much like in European towns. Down the hill in Adamstown is the outlet shop of the **Bollman Hat Company** (3017 N. Reading Rd., 717-484-4615): cowboy hats, Stetsons, fedoras, berets, and orange hats with the pull-down flaps—if it's a hat, they sell it. A guided tour of the restored buildings at the **Ephrata Cloister** (632 Main St., Ephrata, 717-733-6600, www.ephratacloister.org) gives tourists insight into a communal religious society founded in the 1730s. Just up Route 222, **Reading** is known for its outlets—VF Outlet Village, Reading Outlet Center, Reading Station, and others. Just follow the signs. For a great view of the city, make your way up to the **Pagoda** (www.readingpagoda.com), a Japanese-style tower (albeit one trimmed in pink neon) that sits on Mount Penn. It's eye-catching at night. The route to the Pagoda defies written description; check the Web site for directions. The **Daniel Boone Homestead** (400 Daniel Boone Rd., Birdsboro, 610-582-4900, www.danielboonehomestead.org) is about 9 miles east of town on Route 422 and includes the restored birthplace of Boone, a blacksmith shop, sawmill, and barn. The **Mid-Atlantic Air Museum** (at the Reading Airport, 610-372-7333, www.maam.org) displays restored military and commercial aircraft and puts on an annual air show—the first place I ever saw a B-17 in the air.

Other area beer sites: The **Adamstown Transfer Company** (26 Willow St., Adamstown, 717-484-9304) is . . . well, it's what we in the trade call a *bar* bar. The beer's not fancy, and neither is the place, but if you're looking for a drinker's bar, this is it. Sit down and relax. **Zia Maria's** (2350 Reading Rd., Denver, 717-336-1333) is an Italian restaurant with a pub, serving local beers (like Stoudt's, Victory, and Sam Adams—hey, Sam Adams is a local beer around here!). The **Alpenhof** (2 miles south of Shillington on Route 10, 610-373-1624) is a traditional German *gasthaus* type restaurant with a good stock of German beers. Meanwhile, up the road in Reading . . . the **North-East Taproom** (12th and Robeson Streets, 610-372-5284) was Reading's best beer bar for years, and this corner joint still has it. Go see what a neighborhood bar can be. **Canal Street Pub and Restaurant** (535 Canal St., 610-376-4009) sat right over a brewery, but no one seemed able to make it work. The pub keeps on chugging, and it's a good place for craft beer; always has been. **Bixler's Lodge** (1456 Friedensburg Rd., 610-779-9936) has been a Reading staple for years, and they've got good beer, too. The **Speckled Hen Cottage**

and Alehouse (30 S. Fourth St., 610-685-8511) is right in front of what used to be Pretzel City Brewing, in a restored eighteenth-century log house, and boasts good British imports and great food. The *Ugly Oyster* (21 S. Fifth St., 215-373-6791) has plenty of beer in an actual transplanted Yorkshire pub . . . look, ordinarily I hate this kind of thing. But unlike most of these "pub in a box" deals, the beer's too good to ignore. There are also a number of excellent old hotel bars in the small towns north of Reading: Fleetwood, Krumsville, Bowers, Virginville, and Kempton are the homes of some of my favorites.

Union Barrel Works

6 North Reamstown Road, Reamstown, PA 17567
717-335-SUDS
www.unionbarrelworks.com
Union Barrel Works declined to participate in this entry.

What's the story behind that name? "We just brainstormed a list of names," Tom Rupp told me. "We liked Barrel House and worked with that. It's just a name."

That's the kind of no-nonsense guy Tom Rupp is. No flummery about historical significance, nothing made up; there's no story, there's just a name, and that's what he tells you. That's how he declined to cooperate with me on this entry. I blogged about a short visit to Union Barrel Works in 2008 and made a mild criticism of the bartender. When I called about setting up an interview for the book a year later, Tom told me directly that was why he had nothing more to say to me, and I grudgingly respect that.

My respect for his stand at Union Barrel Works is nonetheless more than grudging; it's as honest as Tom is himself. Tom bought this building and worked for six years on restoring it—more on that shortly—reportedly spending $750,000 and putting up with months of bureaucratic delay on things as trifling as a meter for the sprinkler system. ("If we

Beers brewed: Year-round: Kolsch, Lager, Mindblock Mai-Bock, Pale Ale, Round Boy Stout, Wobbly Bob Dopplebock. Seasonals and specials: Blond Bock, Uncle Fester, Hefeweizen, Double Barrel, Hop Knockers IPA, Pilsner.

have a fire, they want to get paid for their water," he told me at the time, "but they've already metered it when it goes in the tank!")

But the real reason that I respect Tom Rupp, despite our current disagreement, is that he steadfastly stuck to his guns on the beers at Union Barrel Works. "Lagers," was his one-word answer when I asked him back in 2007 what the beers would be, and he's stuck to that. He's never been a fan of hoppy beers at all, though he does brew ales (Round Boy Stout is a great one), including a 36 IBU pale ale for Union Barrel. I remember Tom telling me he was making an IPA when he brewed at Neversink, and telling me he used more hops in that beer than he did in all the rest put together.

The trend today in craft beer is hops, hops, and more hops, and lagers in general get very little love. But since Union Barrel Works came to town, Reamstown is like Brigadoon—what the rest of the world's doing doesn't really matter here. The beers here are not heavily hopped; four out of six regulars are lagers, and it's working. Reviews are good and business is steady . . . though I have heard that Tom's making some IPAs these days.

That's no surprise, really: Tom Rupp makes good beer. I remember his kölsch at Neversink, a pale gold beauty with just the right firmness to it. Like Bill Moore, he brewed at Stoudt's before that, and all that experience—over fifteen years—has culminated here.

"Here" is a beautifully restored 1911 brick building right in the middle of this little town. It was originally a hardware store, then a garment factory, and the original maple floors and tin ceilings have been restored to glowing beauty. The bar and backbar came out of the old Showboat hotel bar in Reading, and they're beauties. The bar serves only house beer and Pennsylvania wines (featuring Kog Hill and Glades Pike wines), having no liquor license.

Interesting story on those tin ceilings: You'll notice the distinctive two-toned paint on them, dark brown borders on cream centers. That was the idea of Dave "Suds" Wardrop, one of America's earliest beer writers and a local graphic arts teacher. He cowrote *Bars of Reading and Berks*, long out of print, but still a wonderful read; he could sum up the entire character of a bar in less than twenty-five words. Wardrop asked Tom if he could help with the place and Tom painted part of the ceiling.

This is a brew*pub*, so there's food here, and it's good. It had better be: Tom's son David is manning the kitchen. The delicious smoked trout

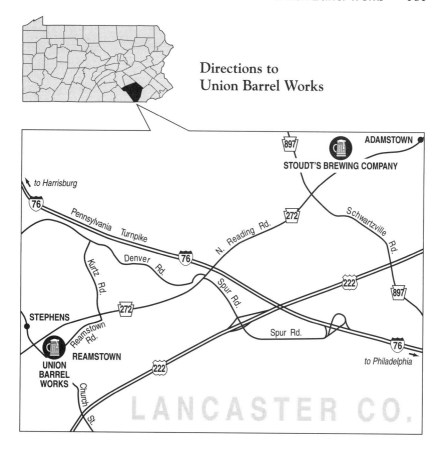

Directions to
Union Barrel Works

chowder is his own creation, first served to thousands at the Pennsylvania Farm Show; it's a can't-miss when you visit. He's got a deft hand with seafood, but the rest of the menu's up to snuff as well.

I hope Tom and I can settle our differences. Even if we don't, Union Barrel Works is a great place for you to visit. I don't know if I'd show Tom your copy of this book, though.

Opened: April 2007.
Owners: Tom and Amy Rupp.
Brewer: Tom Rupp.
System: 15-barrel JV Northwest system, 1,300 barrels annual capacity (est.).
2009 production: Not available.
Brewpub hours: Tuesday through Sunday, open at 11 AM. Closed Monday.
Tours: Contact Tom for tours.

Take-out beer: Growlers.

Food: David Rupp is a well-trained and innovative chef, and the broad menu reflects that; the smoked trout chowder is just a beginning. This is solid food; enjoy.

Extras: UBW has live music almost every weekend and has frequent beer or wine dinners; check the Web site for schedules.

Special considerations: Kids welcome; this is a favorite spot for family dining. Vegetarian meals available.

Parking: On-street parking and large lot in back; observe the signs and don't park in the wrong lot.

Lodging in the area, Area attractions, Other area beer sites: See Stoudt's on pages 157–159.

Kutztown Tavern/ Golden Avalanche Brewing Company

272 West Main Street, Kutztown, PA 19530
610-683-9600
www.kutztowntavern.com

Kutztown, no matter what anyone from Lancaster will tell you, is in the very heart of Pennsylvania Dutch country. I say this as a Lancaster native who grew up in a home with a backyard bordered by an Amish farm. But there are more real Pennsylvania Dutch people in Kutztown and nearby towns than there are Amish in Lancaster. Almost everyone talks with a "Dutchie" accent up here, whether they're discussing the relative merits of different butchers' ring bologna or the computer needs of their law firm. They're big eaters, frugal with their money, and loyal to a fault.

Kutztown Tavern is aimed right between their eyes. The food is solid, with an in-house bakery for pies and cakes, and it comes in bountiful portions.

Beers brewed: Year-round: Blonde Lager, Youngallen's Lager, Olde Brick Alt, Onyx Cream Stout, Donner Weiss. Seasonals: Winter Bock, Oktoberfest, Spring Bock, Moosalicious Brown Ale, Anniversary Barleywine, India Pale Ale, Munich Dunkel, White Ale, and a variety of fruit wheat beers.

Allen Young, the pub's first brewer, who set up the Beraplan brewhouse, was shocked by that. "The dinners are huge," he told me, "and they expect to get more than they can eat." If they're the Dutchmen I know, they probably tucked in and finished it anyway.

The Pick: The Olde Brick Alt is tasty, aromatic, and solid as its namesake. I'd like to see a few more beers like this under the "alt" handle in American brewpubs.

Bob Sica, the current brewer, confirmed that the portions are still hefty. "These people come to *eat*," he said. "While they're here, I sell some beers to them." He's a transplant from New Jersey who graduated from Kutztown University, but he admitted that the big portions were something he enjoyed, too.

Bob graduated in the 1990s as a musician, and he was looking for a job to do during the day. "I saw this guy moving a couch and asked him if he needed help," Bob said. The guy was Allen Young, and Bob wound up with the assistant brewer job. Bob got married and had two kids, and when Allen moved on, the "job to do during the day" turned serious. "I had to move up to head brewer," he said.

The brewpub started out focused on German styles; understandable, with a German-built brewhouse in a Pennsylvania Dutch community. "There was no hopback, no carbonation stone," said Bob. "Everything was naturally carbonated. We're doing more ales now, more styles, and it's a lot more fun. They still like the Germans, though; I took the Donner Weiss off and caught a ration for it. It's on year-round now.

"We've found our niche," he said. "We hustled for outside accounts for a while, but I couldn't do eleven taps here if I was still doing that. I work the bottle shop Monday and Friday, ordering ungodly amounts of Coors Light for the college crowd. They drink on the weekends, but the rest of the week we're doing well with the families. We have a great business with the professors; they're here every Friday afternoon, and they like beer!"

It all started with Shorty's, the nightclub downstairs. Shorty's was a bar in town before the current Kutztown Tavern owners, Don and Matt Grider, came along. Seeing a big cash flow and a liquor license, the Griders invited Shorty's owner, Harry Bieber, in as a partner and set up Shorty's in the basement. The wide-open main room is superb for mad dancing when the DJs kick in. The backroom, with its brick walls and low ceiling, manages to make pool tables and video games almost cozy, a good place to retreat from dance fever.

Up above is where things are about dinner, and conversation, and beer. Here the long bar, spacious dining room, and glass-enclosed brewhouse set the tone, and the tone is cool. The atmosphere is sophisticated,

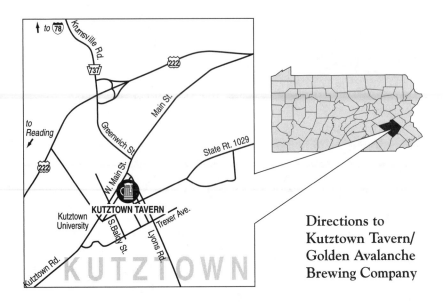

**Directions to
Kutztown Tavern/
Golden Avalanche
Brewing Company**

with an artfully designed new-construction backbar and attractive place-
ment of bottles, yet they have managed to retain the familiar air of the
Pennsylvania hotel bar. Those hearty meals and fresh baked pies, cakes,
and muffins help that a lot.

The tavern does a good business in that bottle shop, too. Bob took
me out for a look around. There's some great craft beers in the coolers,
and yes, plenty of Coors Light, but I can't remember the last time I saw
such an assortment of malt liquor. College drinking is alive and well
in Kutztown.

By the way, the Golden Avalanche of the brewing company name is
the former Kutztown University team name. No one's quite sure what a
"golden avalanche" is, which is probably why these days the teams are
known as the Golden Bears.

Bob didn't even look wistful when he admitted he was no longer a
musician that brewed, but a brewer who played music on Saturday
nights. "I'm not going anywhere," he said. "I've got a good gig here." If
the Beraplan brewhouse could talk, I think it would say the same thing.

Opened: August 1999.
Owners: Don and Matthew Grider.
Brewers: Bob Sica, head brewer; Christian Mosebach, brewer.
System: 8.5-barrel Beraplan system, 500 barrels potential annual capac-
ity.
2009 production: 500 barrels.

Brewpub hours: Seven days a week, 11 AM to 11 PM. Shorty's is open till 2 AM.

Tours: By appointment.

Take-out beer: Growlers, and a large selection of other beers in take-out shop (for off-premises consumption only).

Food: Full menu is offered: seafood, chicken, steaks, pizza, sandwiches, daily lunch and dinner specials; pies, cakes, and muffins baked on-premises.

Extras: Bob Sica plays live acoustic music every Saturday. The action is downstairs at Shorty's. DJ on weekends, no cover, large dance floor. Pool tables, video arcade, eleven TVs, and thirty-six taps of house and guest beers.

Special considerations: Kids welcome. Vegetarian meals available.

Parking: Plenty of free parking in community lot behind the brewpub.

Lodging in the area: Die Bauerei B&B, Route 222, Kutztown, 610-894-4854; New Smithville Country Inn, 10425 Old Route 222, Kutztown (610-285-2987); Main Street Inn, 401 W. Main St., Kutztown, 610-683-0401.

Area attractions: *Crystal Cave* (610-683-6765, www.crystalcavepa.com) is north of town; follow the plentiful signs. The cave has a large formation of delicate crystalline growths, as well as the usual "this formation looks like an ear of corn" stuff, although the Jack Frost formation at the end of the tour is striking. The *Kutztown Folk Festival* (888-674-6136, www.kutztownfestival.com) in July celebrates fine craftworks, including quilts, folk art, toys, and furniture, as well as antiques, music, storytelling, and hearty Pennsylvania Dutch food. Antiques are big in the area. *Renninger's Antique and Farmers Market* (740 Noble St., 610-683-6848, www.renningers.com) has many different dealers in one spot on weekends. *Antique Complexes I and II* (610-944-0707 or 610-944-9661, www.antiquecomplex.com) are two large antique markets a bit south along Route 222, near Fleetwood. Up Route 737 north of town, you'll find the *Wanamaker, Kempton and Southern Railroad* (610-756-6469, www.kemptontrain.com), one of the oldest steam excursion lines operating in the United States. Ride the steam train 3 miles from Kempton to Wanamaker, and get some of the fresh Yuengling and gut-tickling Pennsylvania Dutch eats at the *Kempton Hotel* (9910 Kistler Valley Rd., Kempton, 610-756-6588).

Other area beer sites: *Kutztown Bottling Works* (78 S. Whiteoak St., 610-683-7377) makes their own birch beer, cream soda, and sarsaparilla. They are also a beer distributor and sell a good selection of micros and imports. The **Bowers Hotel** (call for directions, 610-682-2900) is a preserved gem, south of Kutztown in Bowers, a town too small to be on most roadmaps. The original hotel was built around 1822; the large addition that remains was built in the late 1800s to serve the Reading Railroad stop. The bar has been carefully restored without losing its personality.

Bethlehem Brew Works

569 Main Street, Bethlehem, PA 18018
610-882-1300
www.thebrewworks.com

The Bethlehem Brew Works is a classic example of a phenomenon you could call "brewpub anchoring," when a brewpub establishes the core for a neighborhood revitalization. The initial idea is often met with a degree of skepticism, because a substantial part of the population believes that letting a brewery into the neighborhood will lead to public drunkenness, wanton and willful destruction of property, a decline in social values and school test scores, human sacrifice . . . But a brewery is foremost a production business with good wages and local responsibilities, something most communities encourage. A brew*pub* offers all that and more: It has a vested interest in developing and maintaining a good neighborhood that will attract customers to walk by and walk in.

Brewpubs make very good neighbors, and that's what has happened in Bethlehem. "There wasn't anywhere to go for a nice evening out in downtown Bethlehem," co-owner Jeff Fegley told me. "We took the chance. We came to downtown Bethlehem, and we made it. We gave people someplace to go. There's a cluster of good restaurants around here now. Sometimes I worry that we showed the corpo-

Beers brewed: Year-round: Valley Golden, Fegley's ESB, Steelgaarden Wit, Steelworker's Stout, Hop'solutely Triple IPA, Belgian Kriekbier. Seasonals: Alleviator Tripelbock, Hefeweizen, Framboise, Zomerbier, Weizenbock, Rude Elf's Reserve, CH-47 American Pale Ale, Insidious Imperial Stout, Smoke and Oak IPA, Dubbel, PrePro Pils, Maibock, Oktoberfest, Pumpkin Ale, Apricot Coriander . . . and more all the time.

rate restaurants the way, but we're different from them. We'll always be different."

They are that. The menu's different, with adventurous appetizers like the Meze Hummus assortment (which includes the popular garlic ale hummus and a black olive tapenade), spicy fish tacos with red cabbage slaw, "brewschetta," and an ever-changing selection of fabulous house-made soups "that aren't really low-fat at all," said Peg Fegley with a laugh. (She's got to be talking about the beer and cheddar soup, and I urge you to put your diet aside and have some; it's delicious.)

The decor is different, tied to the image of Bethlehem as the home of Bethlehem Steel. The trim is skid-proof diamond plate, the booths are topped with steel pipe dividers, and the walls are studded with old hand-carved casting patterns. It could be an industrial look, but the warmth of dark wood and the street-side windows make it a sheltered gathering place.

The Pick: Last time around, I said, "I'll take a walk on the wild side and pick the Belgian Kriekbier. I thought it would be a somewhat tart cherry beer, but this one has some real funk and sour cherry flavor. It's not over the top at all, but I've had less assertive Belgian imports. Not for the beginner, but the geek will find this rewarding." I'm going to stick with that and note that it ages really well, too.

Then there's the beer. Bethlehem has turned out to be a malt-loving kind of town, and the Fegley's ESB and Bagpiper's Brew Scotch Ale are very popular taps. Don't worry, geeks: They know what to do with hops, too—the new and immediately popular Hop'solutely Triple IPA (that's right: triple, at 11.5 percent) is always on tap, and you can get it to go in growlers or the new cork-and-cage 750-milliliter bottles. Brewer Lewis Thomas has returned; he was always unafraid of the less conventional beers and brews a rewardingly funky and sour Framboise, along with a number of other Belgian styles.

Lewis isn't the only part of the Brew Works that's returned and renewed. In early December 2008, a kitchen fire closed the Brew Works for a couple weeks. When we stopped in just before Christmas, though, they were gamely back at it with a limited menu, and by January they were in full swing. According to Jeff, it was a blessing in disguise . . . kind of. "It was tough, like starting over," he said. "But it was an opportunity to be shut down and move in new equipment, new floors. In the end, it was a big overall improvement in quality."

The brewpub is located in the heart of downtown and so is a popular site during Musikfest, the hot nine days in August when more than three hundred musical acts of all types come to Bethlehem. It's New Orleans on the Lehigh as beers hit the streets in plastic cups, and cops (mostly) look the other way. Four of the free-music "platzes" are within easy walking distance of the brewpub. You'll find more music in the Brew Works at

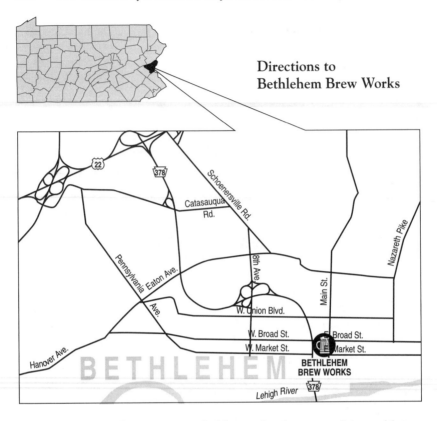

Directions to Bethlehem Brew Works

that time, too—folk, country, rock, blues, what have you. It's a wild time and a lot of fun (and really busy; have a beer while you wait).

The rest of the year, this is a family-friendly place for lunch and dinner. "At six o'clock, every high chair in the place is full," Peg said. I've been taking my kids there for years and never had a problem with inappropriate behavior (from other guests *or* my kids, thank you!).

What do you do if you do want a more adult, singles-scene experience with the Brew Works feel? Go downstairs to the Steelgaarden Lounge, a Belgian beer bar that has become one of the most popular spots in Bethlehem, a spot that outdraws the brewpub at times. More than a hundred Belgian bottled beers (and the Brew Works' own quite respectable Belgian types on draft), comfy couches and armchairs, three pool tables, and a cutting-edge sound and lighting system make this one cool place for the sophisticated beer lover.

Speaking of sophisticated beer lovers . . . the Brew Works got some national exposure during the crucial 2008 presidential primaries. The future commander-in-chief dropped in, and there's a great picture of him clinking glasses with a very happy Peg Fegley. Obama's tipple? A Fegley's

ESB, and his reaction was solid: "Now, that's a good beer. I like that. That's good stuff." He should know; he and his wife, Michelle, were frequent guests at Chicago brewpub Piece when he was just another Illinois legislator. (He also had a Yuengling during the campaign; this is definitely a beer-drinking president.)

Things have changed significantly in Bethlehem. Sometimes all it takes is a couple beers among friends to make everything look a bit more cheerful, a bit more settled. Stop by the bar at the Steelgaarden, and you'll find out just what I'm talking about.

Opened: April 15, 1998.

Owners: Peg, Dick, Rich, Nicole, Jeff, and Mike Fegley.

Brewers: Lewis Thomas, brewer; Nick Micio, assistant.

System: 15-barrel Pub Brewing system, 1,500 barrels annual capacity.

2009 production: 1,130 barrels.

Brewpub hours: Sunday through Wednesday, 11 AM to midnight; Thursday through Saturday, 11 AM to 2 AM.

Tours: By request, subject to brewer availability (all parts of the brewery are open to view).

Take-out beer: Growlers and large specialty bottles.

Food: The popular garlic ale hummus has become part of a tapas-like assortment of hummus, tapenade, and beer-soaked tomatoes, served with warm pita wedges. The beer and cheese soup still rocks, and you can pig out on Slag Pot Meatloaf or wienerschnitzel. It's a full menu, folks, and one with real vegetarian choices: out-of-the-ordinary salads, pierogie casserole, Pomodoro pasta, and the house-made veggie burger. Both Brew Works have committed to using free-range, organic, local, and sustainable foods as much as possible: meats, seafood, and produce.

Extras: Firkins tap at 5 PM on Thursday nights, with one-cask special batches like whiskey stout or chocolate ESB, and once a month 100 percent of firkin sales are donated to a local charity. The Mug Club is very popular but limited in membership; ask your server for details. Full liquor license, with a good selection of single malts. Monthly Pints and Policy discussion of local issues has been very popular; topics and dates are on the Web site. A private, glass-enclosed dining room, The Fishbowl, is available for private parties and business functions. The Steelgaarden Lounge downstairs has more than a hundred Belgian beers available (plus BBW Belgian-types), three pool tables, no TVs, a top-of-the-line sound system, lounge furniture, and a funky lighting system that slowly changes colors. A private bar, The Annex, also is available for private parties.

Special considerations: Kids welcome. Cigars allowed at the bar. Vegetarian meals available.

Parking: Free and pay lots nearby; validation stamps available.

Lodging in the area: Radisson Hotel Bethlehem is just down the hill from the brewpub, 437 Main St., 610-867-2200; Comfort Suites, 120 W. Third St., 610-882-9700; Courtyard by Marriott, 2160 Motel Dr., 610-317-6200.

Area attractions: First, there's some fun shopping in the **Main Street Commons** anchored by the Brew Works. The kids and I have been Christmas shopping for years there—for Cathy, at the Foo Foo Shoppe (610-814-2656), and for our dogs, at the Bone Appetit Bakery (610-332-2663)—and Keystone Homebrew (610-997-0911) has a shop in the basement, with a nice selection of breweriana, too. We've made a Christmas tradition of lunch at the Brew Works, shopping in the Commons, and then about an hour of browsing and buying at the **Moravian Book Shop** (428 Main St., 888-661-2888), a bookstore since 1745 and still a great one, yet it's so much more: gift shop, gourmet candies and kitchen gadgets, a large assortment of Christmas decorations (including Moravian stars), a coffeeshop. We usually pick up a little something for the ride home at the **Chocolate Lab** (446 Main St., 610-865-5781), where the chocolate is so good you don't know whether to nibble and make it last or just scarf it and pass out from joy. That's just a start on the shopping; you'll also find jewelry, Irish goods, artwork, clothing—a great array. There are three big annual events in Bethlehem. The nine days of **Musikfest** (www.musikfest.org) draw approximately 1 million people every August to hear performances by more than three hundred musical acts. It's a big, big deal, and the Brew Works is right in the middle of it. Christmas is also huge in Bethlehem, as you might guess from the permanent electric star on the hill over town. Two hundred thousand visitors enjoy candlelight walks and a traditional **Christkindlsmarkt** (www.christmascity.org) featuring Christmas handicrafts. The **Celtic Classic Games** (www.celticfest.org) in September, featuring traditional Highland games and Irish, Scottish, and Welsh music, is not as well known as the other two events but is getting big; ESPN covers it these days. **The Smithy** (425 Main St., 610-332-6247, www.historicbethlehem.org) is a restored, working 1750s-era blacksmith shop right next to the Hotel Bethlehem. It's open on weekends from April to December; check the Web site for details. The big question in Bethlehem for years was what was going to become of the huge shuttered Bethlehem Steel works. The answer: a **Sands Casino** (www.pasands.com). Maybe not the first thing you'd think of, but that's innovation! The Sands has 3,000 slot machines and recently expanded its offerings to include more than a dozen types of table games. There's the parade of entertainment you'd expect at a casino, plus multiple restaurants, two of them Emeril franchises. The funny thing is, the St. James Gate Pub at the casino is doing monthly beer dinners; check the Web site for schedules. One more thing: Just up the road in Nazareth is the **Martin Guitar Company** (510 Sycamore St., Nazareth, 610-759-2837, www.martinguitar.com), which displays a collection of vintage Martin guitars, acknowledged as some of the best in the world, and gives free tours on weekdays between 11 AM and 2:30 PM. Get more information on area attractions from the **Lehigh Valley Convention and Visitors Bureau** (800-747-0561, www.lehighvalleypa.org).

Other area beer sites: **Starfish Brasserie** (51 W. Broad St., 610-332-8888) serves great seafood and has a few well-chosen taps, along with an award-winning wine list and sharply shaped cocktails. **Ripper's Pub** (77 W. Broad St., 610-866-6646) is a friendly, relaxed, below-street-level place to grab a nice jar of Guinness. The **Tally Ho** (205 W. Fourth St., 610-865-2591) is a Lehigh University hangout, and the kids are drinking better beer these days (they're still smoking, though; be forewarned). My friends keep raving about the **Bookstore Speakeasy** (336 Adams St., Bethlehem, 610-867-1100) on the south side of Bethlehem. It sounds great—jazz, adventurous menu, rare beers, classic cocktails—let's discover it together.

Allentown Brew Works

812 West Hamilton Street, Allentown, PA 18101
610-433-7777
www.thebrewworks.com

The Allentown Brew Works was a long time coming. I remember sitting down with Jeff Fegley and looking at blueprints way back in . . . 2004, I think. The place looked great on paper, but there were issues with the city, and finances, and I didn't know when things would ever get going. It wasn't in the same cloud-cuckoo-land as Red Bell's imaginary State College brewpub (see the note in The Boneyard), but it wasn't happening, either.

It finally did open in June 2007, and it was worth the wait. There are three floors to this place, and none of them are small. How big are they? There's 30,000 square feet of serving space, room for about seven hundred people, but that doesn't really give you the idea, so try this: in the first two years they were open, they ran a bicycle race *through* the first floor and did a couple laps inside. It was crazy—probably why they don't do the Tour de Brew anymore—but it wasn't because there wasn't enough room!

That's the first floor, where the main bar, the kitchen, and the brewery are located. There's also a sweet Biergarten out the backdoor that's great on summer evenings. Up on the second floor is another bar, what they call the High Gravity Lounge. It's the aboveground alter ego of the Steelgaarden at the Bethlehem Brew Works, only the focus here is on "high-gravity" beers (see *gravity* in the Glossary): Everything is 7 percent and up, the big bad boys of beer, including Belgian, British, French, German, and again, the Brew Works' own big beers, like Hop'solutely, Insidious, and Alleviator.

Below ground is the Silk Lounge, a thoroughgoing nightclub. Brew Works beers, yes, and a wide selection of "world beers" (not just "world light lagers," either), but also bottle service with high-end champagne and club-popular spirits like Grey Goose and Patron. There is a dress code; check it on the Web site.

Beers brewed: Year-round: Valley Golden, Fegley's ESB, Steelgaarden Wit, Steelworker's Stout, Hop'solutely Triple IPA. Seasonals: Double IPA, Pawn Shop Porter, Pig Pen Pilsener, Espresso Stout, Epiphany, Honey Cream Ale, Saison, Hop Explosion, Pigtail Ale, Loco Lime, Oktoberfest, Farmhouse Ale, Neuweiler Ale, Bail Bond Bock, Stop, Hop, and Roll, and more.

The brewpub is right in the center of town, and things bustle a bit around it, but as time has passed, the Brew Works has become a large part of that bustle. "Allentown is a different cat," said brewmaster Beau Baden, comparing the two sites. "It's actually a slower downtown than Bethlehem. They want to rev that up."

The brewpub's doing their part, and Beau's certainly doing his. Beau has a charismatic presence; he's a big guy who crackles with good-natured energy. He's definitely taken the Brew Works beers up a step—in intensity, in quality, and in profile. These are not the overlooked beers they used to be; people are talking about them. With names like Hop'solutely, Insidious, and Hop Explosion—and beers that back them up—it's hard to miss them.

The Pick: Hop'solutely is 11.5 percent and doesn't really feel like it—more like about 8 percent, but there you are. It's sweet and bitter, light and solid. The bitterness is intense but enhanced by equally intense fizz. My only issue here is that it's maybe too *too* much . . . but that's the West Coast IPA thing. West Coasters would not like how sweet it is, but that's how it goes: *Vive la différence*!! I'm also pretty partial to that Espresso Stout: I do like a coffee beer, and this is a good one.

Production is revving up. They've got the Criveller bottler out of the defunct Old Lehigh brewery to fill the specialty bottles, and they're brewing more beer to fill up new taps. The Brew Works on the Green has opened at the Allentown Municipal Golf Course, a great opportunity to build awareness of the name, and they're selling a lot of beer. They're selling Brew Works beer at the local minor league baseball park, too (the Iron Pigs!), so Beau's got his work cut out for him.

There's plenty going on inside the Brew Works, thanks to an old friend of mine, Wendie Lazansky, who's working there as the events manager. I'm on their e-letter, and there are events every week: trivia contests, martini nights, Lenten dialogues (really, preachers in brewpubs), fashion shows, political discussions, ladies' Texas Hold 'Em lessons and tournaments, cask ale charity events, comedy nights . . . there's even a story hour at 11:30 AM on the first Saturday of every month, presented by the Allentown Public Library's Children Services. My favorite: Yappy Hour, dog-friendly Monday evenings in the Biergarten in warmer weather. My boy Penderyn and I will be there this summer!

Whew. It takes a lot to get through everything at a place this big, this busy, and we've barely even touched the beer. That's kind of how I felt when Beau sat me down after an hour's worth of tour and started pouring samples: fourteen of them! I am at your service, though, no matter how tough the job, and I tasted them all. To be honest, it was hard to stop, because these were really good beers. Pig Pen Pilsener, dry and soft; Hop Explosion, wicked sticky with hops; Pawn Shop Porter, a nice estery dark ale; Bagpiper's Scotch Ale (two GABF medals so far), rich

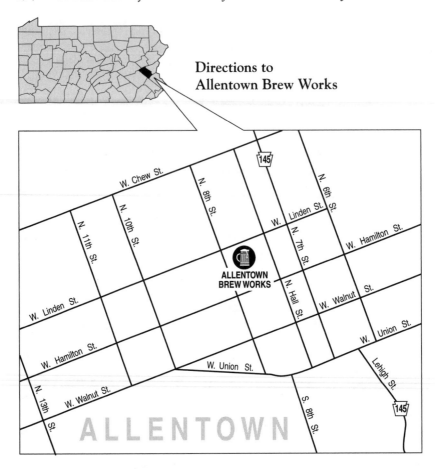

Directions to
Allentown Brew Works

and malty with a touch of smoke; Hop Monster, a big, big beer on a racy light frame; and the lambics they do, different ages and intensities. It was a tour de force, very impressive.

Allentown better get revved up soon. The Brew Works is moving so fast they might leave the town behind!

Opened: June 2007.
Owners: Peg, Dick, Rich, Nicole, Jeff, and Mike Fegley.
Brewers: Beau Baden, brewmaster; Nick Micio, assistant.
System: 15-barrel Pub Brewing system, 2,700 barrels annual capacity.
2009 production: 1,180 barrels.
Tours: Saturday at noon.
Take-out beer: Growlers, specialty bottles, kegs (call for availability).
Food: The menu is much like that at the Bethlehem Brew Works, but there are differences. Try the onion porter dip—it's pretty cheesy—or

the apricot chipotle mustard wings. The beer and cheese soup is here, of course, but you can also try a Mediterranean sourdough turkey sandwich or the Monument Pasta. Vegetarians get more choices, too: baked manicotti bechamel, Mayfair Garden pasta, and a California veggie wrap. Both Brew Works have committed to using free-range, organic, local, and sustainable foods as much as possible: meats, seafood, and produce.

Hours: Sunday through Thursday, 11 AM to midnight; Friday and Saturday, 11 AM to 2 AM.

Extras: Mug club is very popular but limited in membership; call for details. Full liquor license, with a good selection of single malts. DJ in the Silk Lounge on Friday nights. Private dining room available for private parties and business functions, and private lounge in the Silk Lounge; call to reserve. There's something going on almost every night at the Allentown Brew Works, some every week, some one time only; check the Web site for schedules.

Special considerations: Kids welcome. Dogs welcome in the Biergarten on Monday nights (check Web site). Many vegetarian choices.

Parking: Metered parking on the street can be tight; there's a municipal lot around the corner.

Lodging in the area: Allentown Comfort Suites, 3712 Hamilton Blvd., 610-437-9100; Glasbern Country Inn, 2141 Pack House Rd., Fogelsville, 610-285-4723; Scottish Inn and Suites, 1701 Catasauqua Rd., 610-264-7531.

Area attractions: Allentown is dominated by the PPL Building at Ninth and Hamilton. Head for that and you'll be able to find the **Liberty Bell Shrine** (622 W. Hamilton St., in the lower level of Zion's UCC Church, 610-435-4232, www.libertybellmuseum.org). This was where the Libery Bell and the bells of Philadelphia's Christ Church were hidden from the British when they occupied Philadelphia in 1777. The **Allentown Art Museum** (610-432-4333, www.allentownartmuseum.org) has exhibits of European and American art, textiles, the Fuller Gem Collection, and a collection of Indian and Tibetan art. Allentown's minor league baseball team, the **Iron Pigs** (610-841-PIGS, www.ironpigsbaseball.com), plays at **Coca-Cola Park** (555 Union Blvd.). You'll find Brew Works beer there. For hootin', hollerin' fun, get out to **Dorney Park and Wildwater Kingdom** (on Hamilton Boulevard west of Allentown, 800-386-8463, www.dorneypark.com). You'll find five roller coasters, including Steel Force coaster and the new Possessed; the Peanuts playland for the kids; and an extensive water park.

Other area beer sites: The ***Tavern on Liberty*** (2246 Liberty St., 484-221-8765) has a huge selection of bottles and a solid tap selection. There is smoking (how many exceptions to the rule *are* there?), so be warned. The ***Tap and Table*** (4226 Chestnut St., 610-965-1009) has brought Belgian food to Emmaus (the beer was there already); it's a gastropub with a growing reputation. The ***Farmhouse Restaurant*** (1449 Chestnut St., 610-967-6225) brought Belgian and craft beer to Emmaus almost twenty years ago, way ahead of the curve, and puts icing on the cake by being a superb restaurant. A great splurge for the beer and food lover. Also see the suggestions for Bethlehem Brew Works on page 171 and Weyerbacher on page 180; it's not far between towns.

Weyerbacher Brewing Company

905 Line Street, Easton, PA 18042
610-559-5561
www.weyerbacher.com

Weyerbacher
Brewing Company, Inc.

Dan Weirback used to service swimming pools and deliver potato chips. But when he got bitten by the brewing bug, he just had to go with it. His choice of brewery name reflects his German ancestry. "The family name was Weyerbacher before the immigration officers got hold of it," Dan explained.

Weyerbacher started in an old livery stable on Sixth Street. After running it for a few years as a production brewery, Dan opened a tiny pub right next to the brewery. It was a huge success, at least in the eyes of the people who loved hanging out there. You'll still hear people talking about it; it's still missed. I know I miss it. I was there for the last night at the pub, and it was insane: an upside-down Christmas tree hanging from the ceiling, wall-to-wall mug-clubbers, frenzied waitresses, busy bartenders.

But the pub and livery stable are long gone, as are the struggling days that went with them. Weyerbacher almost went under back then, and it took the act of an Idiot to save them. They'd always done well with their Raspberry Imperial Stout, a big raspberry chocolate truffle of a beer. But the pale ale and ESB they were counting on to be the mainstays just weren't doing it.

"We expected to be selling in multiple states," Dan told me recently. "But everyone was making the same beers, and we were handicapped by poor packaging and our equipment. It was clear after a year that it wasn't working. When we opened the pub, we started trying new stuff."

Blithering Idiot barleywine was the stuff that worked. "The Idiot, more than anything, showed us that you could charge more for an esoteric beer," Dan said. They told their wholesalers about the beer, and the reaction caught them all by surprise: It sold out in two weeks. Retail sales once the beer hit the floors were just as immediate. People loved the Idiot. I've seen lines twenty deep at beer festivals, waiting for Dan to hook up a keg of it.

"It was market testing," Dan said. "We let the customers decide. As their tastes developed, we went into more experimental beers." Beers like Riserva and Muse are the direct result of a talk they had with Allagash brewer Rob Tod about using *brettanomyces* yeasts; there are beers aging in Chaddsford Winery barrels at the brewery now, a variety of oaks and previous wines.

Weyerbacher learned the Dogfish Head lesson: If you do it right, and do it often enough, big beers can get you to the point where you can start making regular-strength beers. The solid market impact of beers like the Idiot, Double Simcoe IPA, and Merry Monks Ale has established the Weyerbacher name and reputation to the point that people are looking at their wholly drinkable Blanche, House Ale, and Hops Infusion.

They've been doing it without the pub, too. The big facility out on Line Street is slowly filling up with tanks and barrel-aging projects, and the pub has been replaced by online feedback and Saturday visitors center hours.

The changes continue, only in a more directed way. The main beers—Merry Monks, Hops Infusion, and Blithering Idiot—underwent some major changes over the past three years. Merry Monks and the Idiot had drifted a bit and were brought back closer to their original formula; Hops Infusion became more balanced and drinkable.

Beers brewed: Year-round: Merry Monks Ale, Hops Infusion, Blithering Idiot, Double Simcoe IPA, House Ale (Pennsylvania only), Old Heathen. Seasonals and specials: Autumnfest, Black Hole, Blanche, Blasphemy, Anniversary beers, beginning with Decadence, Fireside Ale, Harvest Ale, Heresy, Muse Farmhouse Ale, Prophecy, QUAD, Raspberry Imperial Stout, Riserva, Scotch Ale, Slam Dunkel, Tiny, Verboten, Winter Ale. Cork-and-cage bottles are released on an irregular schedule; check the Web site. The Brewers Select series continues, from Alpha through to India, so far . . .

"It's not a medal beer," Dan said of Hops Infusion. "The IPA paradigm has changed. But you can drink it, and you'll want to drink it. That's a medal."

Around 2003, they made a hard decision—no more new beers. "They were too expensive," Dan said. "It was a really depressing time for the brewers. Brewers Select was the answer." This line of one-offs, named for the letters in the NATO phonetic alphabet—Alpha, Bravo, Charlie, and so on—was, as Dan put it, a way to do what they used to do at the pub.

It's working: Alpha has become Verboten (initially Zotten, but that turned out to be the trademarked name of a Belgian beer), Charlie is now Fireside. Verboten is an excellent Belgian pale ale, and some of us are pushing Dan to make it year-round. They're learning about brewing, too: Echo, for instance, was a rye IPA that was good but "just too hard to make," said Chris Wilson, shaking his head.

Weyerbacher, like many of the Pennsylvania brewers that started up in the mid-1990s, is at a point where their equipment has gotten a lot more serious. "We have a new whirlpool, a new kettle, a new bottling line, and a lot of new efficiencies," Dan said. "It's made a huge difference: lower costs, better quality, less waste. We grew production just through efficiencies. Our lives are better."

That's a lot of change. "It's painful," Chris admitted, "but it's worth it."

Dan Weirback and his brewery are finally at the point where they don't have to worry about survival every other week. "We've never had this kind of intensity of interest before," Dan said. "That's the big change." If you make interesting beers, people get interested.

The Pick: It's not just the label, though it's one of the best around. I've always loved Dan's imperial stout, and Old Heathen carries on almost unchanged: big, bitter, lean, almost austere. I don't like a sweet imperial stout; as I heard one geek say, "No thanks, I like my beer fermented." But when they take it that one vanilla- and oak-laced, boozy step further and make Heresy . . . it brings to mind a quote from *Patton*: "God help me, I do love it so."

Opened: August 1995.
Owners: Dan Weirback and private investors.
Brewers: Chris Wilson, head brewer; Chris Lampe, Geoff Michalski, Dan Hitchcock, Sean Anderson, Chris Reilly.
System: 25-barrel Century Manufacturing brewhouse, 9,000 barrels annual capacity.
2009 production: 6,000 barrels.
Tours: Saturday only, at 12:30, 1:15, and 2:15 PM. Brewery visitors center open Saturdays from noon to 3 PM.

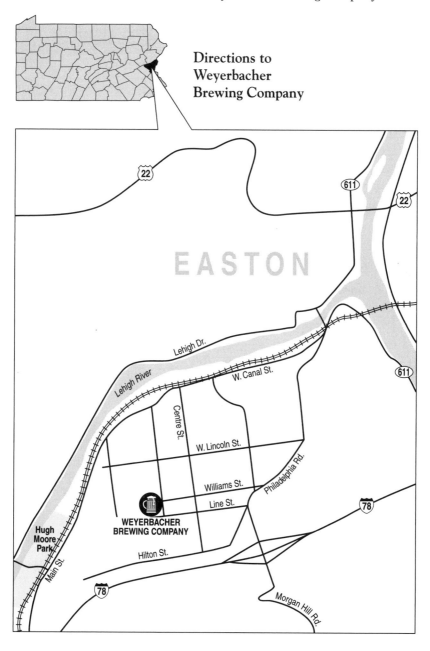

Directions to
Weyerbacher
Brewing Company

Take-out beer: Bottles, growlers (Weyerbacher label only, please), and kegs on Saturdays only.

Special considerations: Kids welcome.

Parking: Off-street lot

Lodging in the area: Lafayette Inn, 525 W. Monroe St. (610-253-4500); Best Western Easton Inn, 185 S. Third St. (610-253-9131); Days Inn, Route 22 and 25th St. (610-253-0546, 800-329-7466).

Area attractions: Easton is home to Binney and Smith, makers of Crayola crayons. The **Crayola Factory** at Two Rivers Landing (30 Centre Square, 610-515-8000, www.crayola.com/factory) is the company's public face. Kids can draw on the walls, make crayons, and do other colorful stuff. In the same building is the **National Canal Museum** (610-559-6613, www.canals.org), celebrating the history of America's canals. You can get a canal boat ride during the summer. In April and early May, Easton holds its **Forks of the Delaware Shad Fishing Tournament and Festival** (610-258-1439, www.shadtournament.com for precise dates), which ends with a big celebration of planked shad, lots of other good eats, and the Doo Dah Parade. You'll find good canoeing opportunities on both the Delaware and Lehigh rivers and other activities in the **Delaware and Lehigh National Heritage Corridor** (610-923-0537, www.delawareandlehigh.org).

Other area beer sites: **Pearly Baker's** (southeast corner of Centre Square, 610-253-9949) is a somewhat fancy but never snooty multi-tap with first-class dining. **Mother's Bar and Grill** (3 Lehns Court, 610-559-1700) is tucked in the alley behind Pearly's and is a much more . . . earthy place—a bar for sure, and the beer's not quite as exotic, but sometimes that's just what I want. **Porter's Pub** (Seventh and Northampton Streets, 610-250-6561) is a neighborhood bar that boasts twelve taps and a good selection of Belgian bottles. Across the Delaware, about 15 miles downriver in Milford, New Jersey, is the **Ship Inn** (61 Bridge St., 908-995-7007), a brewpub with good British-style ales. There's one other place I want to tell you about: the **Interstate Market** (480 Industrial Dr., Easton, 610-559-1962). You may have read that the Altoona-based Sheetz markets are not being allowed to sell beer because they're gas stations, and that's illegal in Pennsylvania. Tell me why it is, then, that not only does the Interstate Market sell Exxon gas and beer, but you can even get growlers of draft beer to go? Good beer, too, and the sandwiches are tasty. Sometimes I just can't believe this state.

Brewing Beer

You don't need to know much about beer to enjoy it. I don't understand how this new BlueTEC diesel in my car really works, but I know that when I stomp on the accelerator, the car's gonna go!

Knowing about the brewing process can help you understand how and why beer tastes the way it does. It's like seeing the ingredients used in cooking a dish and realizing where the flavors came from. Once you understand the recipe for beer, other things become more clear.

Beer is made from four basic ingredients: water, hops, yeast, and grain, generally barley malt. Other ingredients may be added, such as sugars, spices, fruit, and vegetables, but they are extras. In fact, the oft-quoted Bavarian Reinheitsgebot (purity law), first promulgated in 1516, limited brewers to using only water, hops, and barley malt; yeast had not yet been discovered.

In the beginning, the malt is cracked in a mill to make a grist. The grist is mixed with water and heated (or "mashed") to convert the starches in the grain to sugars (see *decoction* and *infusion* in the Glossary). Then the hot, sugary water—now called wort—is strained out of the mash. It is boiled in the brewkettle, where hops are added to balance the sweetness with their characteristic bitterness and sprightly aroma. The wort is strained, cooled, and pumped to a fermenter, where yeast is added.

A lager beer ferments slow and cool, whereas an ale ferments warmer and faster. After fermentation, the beer will be either force-carbonated or naturally carbonated and aged. When it is properly mature for its style, the beer is bottled, canned, kegged, or, in a brewpub, sent to a large serving tank. And then we drink it. Happy ending!

Naturally, it isn't quite that simple. The process varies somewhat from brewery to brewery. That's what makes beers unique. There are also major differences in the ways microbrewers and mainstream brewers brew beer. One well-known distinction has to do with the use of non-barley grains, specifically corn and rice, in the brewing process. Some microbrewers have made a big deal of their Reinheitsgebot, proudly displaying slogans like "Barley, hops, water, and yeast—and that's all!" Mainstream brewers like Anheuser-Busch and Pennsylvania's regional brewers all add significant portions of corn, rice, or both. Beer geeks howl about how these adjuncts make the beer inferior. Of course, the same geeks often rave about Belgian ales, which have a regular farrago of ingredients forbidden by the Reinheitsgebot.

Mainstream brewers boast about the quality of the corn grits and brewer's rice they use, while microbrewers chide them for using "cheap" adjunct grains and "inferior" six-row barley. Truth is, they're both right . . . and they're both wrong.

Barley, like beer, comes in two main types: two-row and six-row. The names refer to the rows of kernels on the heads of the grain. Six-row grain gives a greater yield per acre but has more husks on smaller kernels, which can give beer an unpleasant astringency. Two-row gives a plumper kernel with less husk but costs significantly more. Each has its place and adherents.

When brewing began in America, farmers and brewers discovered that six-row barley did much better than two-row in our climate and soil types. Two-row barley grown the same way as it had been in Europe produced a distinctly different malt. This became especially troublesome when the craze for pale lagers swept America in the mid-nineteenth century. The hearty ales they replaced had broad flavors from hops and yeast that easily compensated for these differences. But pale lagers are showcases for malt character, and small differences in the malt mean big differences in beer taste.

Brewers adapted and used what they had. They soon found that a small addition of corn or brewer's rice to the mash lightened the beer, smoothed out the husky astringency of the six-row malt, and gave the beer a crispness similar to that of the European pale lagers. Even though using these grains required the purchase, operation, and maintenance of additional equipment (cookers, storage silos, and conveyors), almost every American brewer did it. Some say they overdid it, as the percentages of adjuncts in the beer rose over the years. Is a beer that is 30 percent corn still a pilsner?

Microbrewers say adjunct grains are cheap substitutes for barley malt. In terms of yield, corn and brewer's rice are less expensive than two-row barley, but they are still high-quality grains. Similarly, six-row barley is not inherently inferior to two-row; it is just not as well suited to the brewing of some styles of beer. Mainstream brewers have adapted their brewing processes to six-row barley. The difference is in the beer those processes produce.

Another difference between microbrewers and mainstream brewers is the practice of high-gravity brewing. The alcohol content of a beer is mainly dependent on the ratio of fermentable sugars to water in the wort, which determines the specific gravity of the wort. A higher gravity means more alcohol.

Large commercial brewers, in their constant search for ways to peel pennies off the costs of brewing, discovered that they could save money by brewing beer at a higher alcohol content and carefully diluting it later. To do this, a brewer adds a calculated extra amount of malt, rice, corn—whatever "fuel" is used—to boost the beer to 6.5 percent alcohol by volume (ABV) or higher. When the fermented beer has been filtered, water is added to bring the ABV down to the target level of 4 to 5 percent.

How does this method save money? It saves energy and labor costs during the brewing process by effectively squeezing 1,300 barrels of beer into a 1,000-barrel brewkettle. Although 1,000 barrels are boiled, 1,300 barrels are eventually bottled. It also saves money by allowing more efficient use of fermentation tank space: 10,000-barrel fermenters produce 13,000 barrels of beer. It sounds great, so why not do that with every beer? Because the high-gravity process can produce some odd flavor and aroma notes during fermentation. That's what brewers aim for in big beers like doppelbocks and barley wines. But these characteristics are out of place in a pilsner. I also feel that beer brewed by this high-gravity method suffers from a dulling phenomenon similar to "clipping" in audio reproduction: The highs and lows are clipped off, leaving only the middle.

With a studied nonchalance, big brewers keep this part of their brewing process away from the public eye. To tell the truth, of all beer styles, American mainstream lager is probably the style least affected by this process. It is mostly a practice that just seems vaguely wrong, and you won't see any microbrewers doing it.

So now you know how beer is made, and a few of the differences in how the big boys and the little guys do it. It's probably time for you to do a little field research. Have fun!

The Capital Area

Route 15 runs north from the Mason-Dixon line, past Gettysburg, through farms and orchards, meets the Susquehanna across the river from Harrisburg, and then follows the river north. To the east lies Pennsylvania Dutch Country; to the west, the land is furrowed with seemingly endless green ridges and valleys. But Route 15 and the Susquehanna wend their way north, piercing the ridges, seeing farms, busy rail lines, and the increasingly heavy traffic of the state's capital.

This is the route Robert E. Lee planned to use in his campaign to take the Civil War to the North, to strike into the relatively undefended areas of Pennsylvania and force the North to sue for peace. Thanks to overwhelming Union forces (and a certain amount of battlefield luck) at Antietam the first time, and a bad decision at Gettysburg the second time, Lee's plan failed, and instead it was the Union's William Tecumseh Sherman who marched into the Confederacy's heartland and brought the war closer to an end.

Had Lee succeeded, Harrisburg was a sure target. Not just because it was a state capital, but also because of its position astride the Susquehanna River. Bridges still play a major role in Harrisburg's everyday life: Highways, railroads, and footbridges keep this city moving. When I'm in town, I usually cross the river at least twice in the course of the day; there's too much of interest on both sides not to.

The major industries here are government and tourism; agriculture plays a picturesque third place. Harrisburg celebrates the Susquehanna with Riverfront Park, 5 miles of gardens and memorials along the river. The seat of government offers tourists the architectural glories of the State Capitol and a look at the history of the state at the State Museum of Pennsylvania. Once a year, the state's farmers come to Harrisburg for the six-day Pennsylvania Farm Show, complete with animals, vegetables, crafts, and outstanding food. The headquarters of the Pennsylvania

185

Liquor Control Board (PLCB) are here, too, keeping an eagle eye on what our beloved brewers are doing.

The National Civil War Museum is also here, close to Gettysburg and in the heart of what Lee so urgently wanted. Gettysburg is the foremost historical attraction in the area, drawing thousands of visitors every day in the summer to relive the pivotal battle of the Civil War. You can walk or drive the battlefield and see what small accidents of geography made the battle: the high ground of the series of ridges that allowed the hard-pressed Union forces to fall back to successive positions of strength, the shattered rocks of Devil's Den that made such perfect protection for Confederate sharpshooters, and the cool flow of Spangler's Spring that legendarily brought temporary truce to the battle of brothers. The Appalachian brew-pub in town is right beside Lee's Gettysburg headquarters.

Carlisle is a beautiful, little town with a history of its own. It was the home of two signers of the Declaration of Independence and the location of the Carlisle Indian School, where Jim Thorpe got his education. At Carlisle Barracks, you can visit the Army's Military History Institute, a library with a huge collection of Civil War photographs.

This area is more often driven through than driven to. With the Pennsylvania Turnpike and Interstates 80, 81, and 83 passing through, the area is continually crisscrossed by travelers. But take an exit, take a drive, then stop for a beer. You may just find something you like.

Appalachian Brewing Company, Harrisburg

50 North Cameron Street, Harrisburg, PA 17101
717-221-1080
www.abcbrew.com

Old and worn but beautiful. That describes the Appalachian Mountains. These folded ridges, eroded remnants of sky-piercing peaks, thrust north into the state from Maryland and then make a bend to the northeast, curving around the state capital at Harrisburg. Compared with mountain chains in the West, and even New Hampshire's Presidential range, Pennsylvania's mountains stand head and shoulders *below* the rest in terms of sheer altitude. In my admittedly prejudiced view, they bow to no mountains when it comes to the beauty of their vistas and foliage.

Appalachian Brewing Company is less than fifteen years old, yet it is also old and worn . . . but beautiful. The building is a massively built print shop dating from 1918 that took two years to renovate. The brewhouse is recycled from Vancouver Island Brewery in British Columbia. Appalachian's bottler is a used German classic, a Holdefleiss long-tube filler.

Beers brewed: Year-round: Trail Blaze Organic Nut Brown, Purist Pale Ale, Water Gap Wheat, Jolly Scot Scottish Ale, Hoppy Trails IPA, Mountain Lager, Susquehanna Stout, Broad Street Barleywine. Seasonals: Zoigl Star, Abbey Roade, Celtic Knot Irish Red, Peregrine Pilsner, Anniversary Maibock, Kipona-fest, Dom Blonde Kölsch, Hinterland Hefe-Weizen, Rauchbock, Pennypacker Porter, Grinnin' Grizzly, Volks Weizenbock.

Like the Appalachians, this brewery is also eye-catching. The building was designed for function, to hold massive machinery, yet there is a beauty in its solid construction, huge timbers, glowing hardwood floors, and wide-swinging front doors. This is one of the biggest places you'll ever feel comfortable in. With its high ceiling, the great depth of its main room, and the massive tanks behind the glass wall to the right, one thing Appalachian has is plenty of room. But it's not impersonal because of the organic feel of the worn wood.

I used to say that brewmaster Artie Tafoya is also recycled, having built his reputation in the Colorado brewing scene . . . but these days, Artie's reputation is all about Appalachian. He's reinvented himself, and ABC has changed as well.

"A lot has changed," he emphasized as we sat in the quiet bar, drinking coffee before the doors opened on a cold winter morning. "We've got eight big new tanks [the old ones were starting to have maintenance problems], we upgraded the mash tun with powered rakes and a new grist arm. We've got certification as an organic brewery now; we put in a separate mill and grist case for the Trail Blaze. We've got new beers, we're doing new sodas."

The sodas I knew about; they've actually been showing up in my local supermarket in its "Pennsylvania Preferred" section of locally made items. I'd had the root beer, so Artie sampled me on the ginger beer (properly hot and spicy, a bit cloudy, and not overly sweet; I'd like to get this in bed with some rye whiskey) and the diet root beer. "We tried six different sweeteners," Artie said. "We chose stevia. It really makes a difference."

But you don't really want to know about sodas, right? So let's talk about those new beers. The one at the top of my list is the Zoigl Star, an unfiltered lager that's available at ABC from January through spring. It's rich in flavor, with a broad hops character, a deep maltiness, and a slight yeasty edge, a rustic quality. "It's a traditional style in Germany," Artie said. "We were there, drank it, and loved it. The *zoigl* is a six-pointed star (from alchemical tradition) that was hung on houses that had fresh beer for sale (learn more about this unique beer at www .zoigl.de, which also has pictures from Artie's trip).

The Pick: I just love the Zoigl Star. It's an excellent example of unfiltered lager, with all the hallmarks that make them so special: intense flavor, great body, and a liveliness you don't get in filtered beer. Hurry back, January! Water Gap Wheat is a wheat ale, generally one of the dullest, blandest styles of American craft brewing. But Water Gap surprises with a fresh graininess and subtle fruity notes. Try one.

Then Artie popped a two-year-old 12-ounce bottle of Broad Street Barleywine and proved just how nice a job ABC can do on the big beers. It was just a mellow as aged cheese: deep complex malt character, layers of ripe fruit that weren't bright and shouty, a wonderfully nuanced beer.

The new beer with the most potential, though, might be the Trail Blaze Organic Nut Brown. It's been successful, and the brewery's equipped to do more organic beers. "It's the only all-domestic malt beer we make," Artie said, "and it adds 20 percent to the costs by using organic ingredients. We might go with more organic beers; it would be nice to go organic on the Water Gap Wheat. But how do you change your best-seller?!" It's a tough call, but the kind of people who are buying the beer because of the affiliation with the Appalachian Trail might have strong opinions about it.

Some of the biggest business Appalachian is doing these days isn't even with their own beer. The Abbey Bar, on the second floor, features a selection of about fifty Belgian specialty beers in bottles, and it's become very popular. "The Abbey is a whole different place," Artie said, "and it's worked out a lot better than we'd hoped. It's become a destination on its own."

The brewpub is busy almost every day. The food's great and draws a good lunch crowd. The second-floor deck is a very popular spot in the summer evenings. The parking has expanded, with 140 spaces out back in the lot.

"We did a lot of great things in 2007 on cost cutting," said Artie, "and that's carried us forward. Things are great. We're looking at other locations, not too far away, brewing locations." I asked him about the long-talked-about Lancaster possibility, but all he would say is that it's not a dead issue.

"Nothing could surprise me anymore," said this experienced brewer-owner. After all his years in the business, that doesn't surprise me, either.

Opened: January 1997.

Owners: Shawn Gallagher, Jack Sproch, Artie Tafoya.

Brewers: Artie Tafoya, brewmaster; Jay Kendig, head brewer; Emily Block, Scott Koon, Tim Shaughnessy, brewers.

System: 36-barrel "highly modified" Alliance brewhouse, 10,000 barrels annual capacity.

2009 production: 3,800 barrels (and almost that much in soda).

Brewpub hours: Sunday through Thursday, 11 AM to 11 PM; Friday and Saturday, 11 AM to midnight.

Tours: Saturday at 1 PM, or by appointment.

Take-out beer: Growlers, six packs, cases, and kegs.

Food: A full menu of fresh and innovative pub food. For starters, try the Classic Poutine, a Montreal import of fries with cheese curds and gravy made with ABC's own stout, or the Brew Wings with locally made sauces (try the Root Beer BBQ—no kidding), and add some Appalachian classics like Brewer's Cheddar Ale Soup and Pennsylvania Dutch pretzel logs in the mix. Fresh salads and hearty sandwiches make up the lunch and light dinner options. The steak and portabella salad, Hog Wild (pulled pork sandwich), or ribeye sandwich will surely fill you up. Really hungry? Try the Drunken Shepherd's Pie, beer-battered fish and chips, or the more conventional steaks, crab cakes, or pizzas. The full menu is available all the time.

Extras: Full liquor license. The second-floor Abbey Bar (opens at 5 PM, seven days a week) is Harrisburg's premier Belgian beer bar, with around fifty Belgian specialty beers in bottles; the full ABC menu is available. Live music every week, featuring regional and national acts on weekends, plus open stage nights; check the Web site for schedules. Nine-foot billiard tables (pay by the hour; free on Sunday and Tuesday nights). Rooftop outdoor deck with a view of the Capitol Building. Banquet facilities for parties of 25 to 550 in the Gallery banquet room.

Special considerations: Kids welcome. Vegetarian meals available; try the walnut-stuffed eggplant entrée.

Parking: Off-street lot behind building and metered on-street parking.

Lodging in the area: Comfort Inn Riverfront, 525 S. Front St., 717-233-1611; Holiday Inn Express, 4021 Union Deposit Rd., 717-561-8100; Milestone Inn, 2701 N. Front St., 717-233-2775.

Area attractions: The *State Museum of Pennsylvania* (Third St. between North and Forster, north of the Capitol, 717-787-4978) has a wide range of exhibits on industry, art, science, archeology, and of course, Pennsylvania history. You might be surprised to find the *National Civil War Museum* (Reservoir Park, 717-260-1861) in

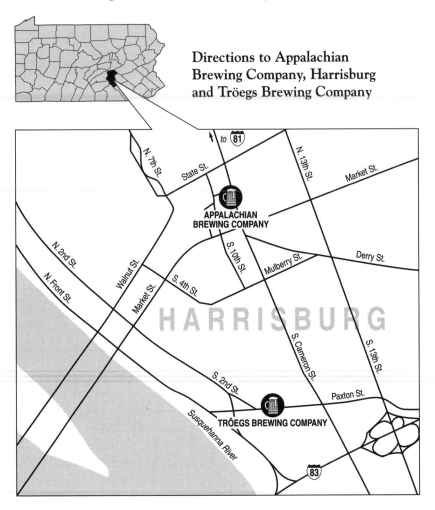

Directions to Appalachian Brewing Company, Harrisburg and Tröegs Brewing Company

Harrisburg, but it's been well received and noted as an unbiased look at this convulsive period of American history. The **State Capitol** offers free tours every day of the week to view the grand architectural features of this massive stone structure. **Riverfront Park** hosts a number of festivals; call the mayor's office (717-255-3040) for more information. There's lots going on over on **City Island**, in the middle of the river: trails, swimming, and Metro Bank Park, home of the Harrisburg Senators minor league baseball team (717-231-4444; www.senators baseball.com). You may want to time your visit for January to catch the **Pennsylvania Farm Show** (717-255-3040), a huge and friendly display of the state's agricultural bounty, from fancy chickens to butter sculptures to draft horse pulling competitions—and the food is fantastic! Fair warning, though—Pennsylvanians have a superstition about

"Farm Show Weather": Winter often seems to save its worst for that week. Nearby **Hersheypark** (800-437-7439) is a treat for roller coaster fans. **Hershey's Chocolate World** (800 Park Blvd., 717-534-4900) offers a tour ride that exhibits the chocolate manufacturing process in a nonfactory setting.

Other area beer sites: McGrath's Pub (202 Locust St., 717-232-9914) has great food, well-cared-for draft beer, and a good-looking bar. Don't be fooled by the Irish name or unassuming streetfront: **Shady McGrady's** (204 Vebeke St., 717-232-7050) might have the best beer selection in Harrisburg, and you can get it to go, too. Fair warning: Smoking is still allowed here. **Stocks on 2nd** (211 N. Second St., 717-233-6699) is more a restaurant, and a fine one, but good beer's always welcome with a fine meal. The **Pep Grill** (209 Walnut St., 717-236-6403) has carried ABC beer from day one: Get a gyro and relax in this friendly dive. **Cragin's Brickhaus** (229 N. Second St., 717-233-4287) is a bit rowdy but does have some good beers on. **T. Brendan O'Reilly's** (800 E. Park Dr., 717-564-2700) isn't just the Irish joint the name suggests; like Shady McGrady's, they've gone well beyond Guinness in their offerings. **Zembie's** (226 N. Second St., 717-232-5020) was one of my farthest-flung regular stops when I lived in Lancaster in my twenties. It's become more sports-oriented, but it's still a good old-school bar, with just enough beer to get you by.

Tröegs Brewing Company

800 Paxton Street, Harrisburg, PA 17104
717-232-1297
Late 2011: **200 E. Hershey Park Dr.**
Hershey, PA 17033
www.troegs.com

What's in a name? Tröegs is certainly an odd one. It's a loose combination of brewery partner Chris Trogner's adolescent nickname "Trogs" and a *kroeg*, a Belgian slang word for pub. Even in central Pennsylvania, where you run across names like Hocker, Ochtemaier, and Fishburn,

Tröegs sticks out. How do you pronounce it? You can pretty much say it any way you want as long as it gets you one of these beers!

Tröegs's logo proudly proclaims, "Hand Crafted by the Tröegs Brothers." Chris and John Trogner have carefully put together a technically proficient brewery in the middle of the state capital, Harrisburg. There's a well-thought-out brewhouse and fermentation hall, spotless in stainless steel and white plastic and epoxy.

At least, that's what I wrote when these guys were first starting out. It was even true five years ago. It's not true anymore. Oh, the brewhouse and fermentation hall are still spotless, and they're eminently well planned and technologically advanced.

Beers brewed: Year-round: Tröegs Pale Ale, Hopback Amber, Dreamweaver Wheat, Troegenator Doublebock. Seasonals: Sunshine Pils, Mad Elf, Dead Reckoning Porter, Flying Mouflan, JavaHead Stout, Nugget Nectar. The Scratch beer series was up to twenty-five beers when I wrote this and had spawned the Splinter series of sour, wild, wood-aged beers. These are rarely available anywhere but the brewery.

But the image I carry of Tröegs now is a grinning John Trogner in the door of their newly constructed hops refrigerator, standing in front of stacks and stacks of bales of Nugget hops.

"Nugget Nectar and Mad Elf are beasts," he admitted. "When we expand the brewery, those are the two that drive it." Those two seasonals, and the early summer bulge of Sunshine Pils, make things move at Tröegs, and the releases of Mad Elf and Nugget Nectar are major events in the beer geek firmament. Tröegs has a national reputation, and it's not for the carefully consistent middle-of-the-craft-road beers they brewed when they started.

The funny thing is, I remember John and Chris clearly under some strain five years ago, grimacing as they wondered how they would keep up with burgeoning demand. The brewery's grown at about 30 percent a year for quite a while, which means they always have to be planning three years in advance. They've expanded into almost the entire building at this point, when they used to rattle around in the front bay. They have a crushingly busy tasting room—no, a pub with no food (more on that shortly)—and take-out business; they have a busy schedule of appearances and events; they have two different series of specialty beers going, the Scratch experimental beers and the sour-funky Splinter series; and Nugget Nectar just keeps booming.

So why are John and Chris so cool these days? "What we thought was our perfect world has changed," John told me. "Instead of being about sales or size, it's about lifestyle: ours and everyone's here. We're bringing in people with personalities and letting them show through.

"We had no idea what we were doing when we started," he admitted. "We just tried to work harder to make it happen. We're working a lot smarter now. We're making more beer, a lot more, but it's not as much work. Emergencies aren't nightmares anymore, they're just things you deal with."

One of the things they're dealing with is some unexpected growth. "We saw the economy shrinking [in 2008] and hedged our bets by opening markets in new states," John said, "but they took off, and our home market is growing as fast as any other. Turns out it wasn't a 'mature market' after all!

"That's great news," he continued, explaining that it meant that craft beer had reached a critical takeoff point. "There are more craft-focused bars, but there are also more craft handles at neighborhood bars, at VFWs. That's what driving it: It's selling because it's *there*. Better beer, more brewers, and sufficient time brought us to this tipping point."

That wasn't all. John tips his hat to the Internet, to BeerAdvocate, ratebeer, beer bloggers, and Facebook. "When there wasn't that network, there was just us going out there and yelling," he said. "Now that's amplified a thousand times with social networking. It's good and bad. The criticism's tough, but we're harder on ourselves than anyone else."

If you've read the previous editions, you may remember John shouting that there would not be a pub. What he actually said was, "And we won't build a pub. No pub!" Call it a tasting room, but what they have is a pub with no food. Or inedible food.

As brewery manager Ed Yashinsky put it, state law said they had to have a meal available for each of the thirty seats required in the tasting room by the brewpub regulation. "And we do," he said. "We have thirty small microwave pizzas in a freezer." He paused. "For $10 each." He paused again. "We don't recommend them." People tend to bring their own food, which I'm sure makes John happy. The pub also does a brisk business in take-out beer (cases in the back, which is under the brewery license . . .) and Tröegs gear, which I'm sure makes both John and Chris (and probably Ed) very happy indeed.

The Tröegs experience will be getting bigger, better, and farther east in late 2011. The brewery will move to a new location in Hershey, with more capacity, an outdoor seating area, and a 5,000-square foot tasting room right in the middle of the brewhouse. No word on food at this point.

Tröegs has come a long way from their early days of fairly cautious (though always well-crafted) beers: a pale ale, an ESB, a nut brown. You can hear the difference when you walk in the door, you can see the difference when you take the tour, and you can smell and taste the difference when you pour a glass.

Opened: June 1997.

Owners: Chris Trogner, John Trogner.

Brewers: John Trogner, brewmaster; Andrew Dickson, head brewer; Andrew Tice, Tim Mayhew, Jeff Jerman, Jeff Musselman, Bruce Tanner, brewers.

System: 25-barrel five-vessel Braukon brewhouse, 30,000 barrels annual capacity.

2009 production: 23,050 barrels.

Tours: Full guided tours every Saturday at 1:30, 2, and 2:30 PM. Please call for reservation. The tasting room is open Monday through Friday, 10 AM to 5 PM; Saturday, noon to 4 PM.

Take-out beer: Growlers, single 22-ounce bottles, six-packs, cases, and kegs (call for keg availability).

Special considerations: Kids welcome.

Parking: Large off-street lot.

Lodging in the area, Area attractions, Other area beer sites: See Appalachian Brewing, Harrisburg, on pages 189–91.

Appalachian Brewing Company, Camp Hill

3721 Market Street, Camp Hill, PA 17011
717-920-2739
www.abcbrew.com

Appalachian always planned on opening branches—brewing branches, said Artie Tafoya—and this was their second after Gettysburg. There's a nice bar to your left, and a restaurant dining room to your right that's popular with local families. The small brewery is on the bar side; you can tell right away it's not capable of supporting this place by itself, and it doesn't.

The big brewery on Cameron Street supplies almost all the beer. Artie himself comes over and brews here. "It's nice," he said. "I get to keep my hand in on a small system, I brew more what I want to." I'd had the Zojac's bock when I was in; it was good, and I told him so. He informed me it was done with a local homebrewer.

That's the kind of thing you'll find at small places like this. Even when they're part of big places like Appalachian.

Opened: August 2006.
Owners: Shawn Gallagher, Jack Sproch, Artie Tafoya.
Brewer: Artie Tafoya.
System: 5-barrel Newlands system, 260 barrels annual capacity.
2009 production: 100 barrels.
Brewpub hours: Monday through Thursday, noon to 11 PM; Friday and Saturday, noon to midnight; Sunday, noon to 8 PM.
Tours: None available (the brewery's all plainly visible from the bar).
Take-out beer: Growlers.
Food: See the listing for Appalachian Brewing Company, Harrisburg, on page 189.
Special considerations: Kids welcome. Vegetarian meals available.
Parking: Off-street lot.
Lodging in the area, Area attractions: See Appalachian Brewing Company, Harrisburg, on pages 189–91.
Other area beer sites: *Grandpa's Growler* (398 N. York St., Mechanicsburg, 717-766-0720) has a couple good craft taps and solid bottles, along with good pub food and a congenial vibe. My editor for these books, Kyle Weaver, and I always go to the **Brewhouse Grille** (2050 State Rd., Camp Hill, 717-737-0030) when I drop off a manuscript; the pizza's inventive and delicious, and there are always some good craft drafts. **Al's of Hampden** (4520 Valley St., Enola, 717-728-3840) may look like just another pizza joint—okay, it is, mostly, but they're also rocking ten craft taps and a few hundred bottles (takeout, too). The amusingly busy front wall of **Coakley's** (305 Bridge Street, New Cumberland, 717-774-5556) ushers you into a classic long bar with two dining rooms. You'll enjoy the topnotch comfort food (get the shepherd's pie), snappy bartenders, and craft beers from local brewers; then walk off your meal on this neat little stretch of downtown New Cumberland.

Beers brewed: Limited numbers of seasonal beers; recent ones included Zojac's Traditional Bock and Framboise.

The Pick: I got to taste the Framboise, too, and it was very impressive: aged nine months in oak, tart not sour, good oak depth, but nothing sticking out too far. If this is the kind of thing Artie's doing over here, more power to him.

Market Cross Pub and Brewery

113 North Hanover Street, Carlisle, PA 17013
717-258-1234
www.marketcrosspub.com

This is the brewery that refused to die. Before Jeff Goss talked Kevin Spicer into brewing on it (and it didn't really take much talking to get the advanced homebrewer onto a real system), this was the brewhouse for Whitetail Brewing, a brewery that had at least two lives. Whitetail brewer Wade Keech told me that before that, the brewery had been the original brewhouse built by English microbrewing pioneer Peter Austin, back in the late 1970s, and used in his first microbrewery, The Long Barn.

That's some pedigree, but Market Cross is up to it. Jeff Goss was a food services major from Penn State who wound up working for a computer company. Then he got married and had a daughter (Ashleigh), and decided he wanted to settle down and watch her grow up. Market Cross was the result. He named the pub for the main square in the United Kingdom's Carlisle, also an old market town.

It was a conscious decision he made after having been there. "I wanted to re-create that community feel in the pubs in the UK," he told me, "and I like to think we succeeded. Our customers, our regulars, are lawyers, plumbers, colonels from the Barracks, truck drivers."

It's certainly a lot better now than it was when Goss bought the building. His wife, JoAnne, is from Carlisle and remembers what it was. "The Boiler Room," Jeff said, laughing. "They had Bud, Busch, and fights every week." There hasn't been a fight in here in years, but it's still all about beer: Market Cross has one of Pennsylvania's increasingly rare beer-only licenses, and Jeff proudly points out that it is malt beverage license E2, the second one issued by the state after Repeal.

So why the emphasis on beer variety that would finally lead to a brewery out back? "I thought, if we only have beer, let's do the best we can," Jeff said.

Beers brewed: Market Cross Red and Olde Yeller IPA are usually on, other beers rotate, usually two or three on at a time plus cask: Pub Porter, Bessie's Brown Ale, Lion-Heart Lager, Scarlet McSteamy, Naked Porter, Tell Me Rye, Midsummer Knights Wheat, Blue Mountain Maibock, Excaliber Imperial Stout.

They opened with a selection of 60 beers that has grown to more than 250, plus the house beers.

The house beers have been around longer than the brewery. "I hooked up with Wade when he was still brewing down in York," said Jeff. "Kevin came up with the recipes for the Red Ale and the Porter, and Wade brewed them for us." When Keech lost his lease in York, Goss offered the back building as a new home for Whitetail. And when Keech finally gave up after much heartache, Goss took over the brewery and let Spicer, a local high school geoenvironmental science teacher, take over the brewing.

The Pick: Tell Me Rye, indeed; tell me rye so many other beers like this at other brewpubs taste like tainted fizzy water, when this tastes like beer—distinctive beer, and pint-poundable. If you've never had a rye beer before, this is a good place to start.

"We go to the festivals," Goss said. "We're the little guy, not like the big craft brewers with the fancy logos and glassware. But we don't have to be financially cautious about our beer. It's just part of what we do, so Kevin can stretch a little."

That's where beers like Tell Me Rye come from, a hazy "American rye" beer that lets the flavor of the grain come through. Kevin's Olde Yeller IPA ("You'll cry when the beer's over" is the standard joke on that one) is a light yellow beer that shocks you senseless with 7-plus percent ABV and hops sticking out all over.

What's it like, brewing on Peter Austin's original system? "It really is home brewing. It's a *very* manual system," Kevin said. "I carbonate the beer by rocking the kegs; about 250 rocks does it."

But that's not Ringwood yeast in there anymore. "We get yeast from Appalachian Brewing," Kevin said. "Appalachian and Tröegs have been a big help. Artie Tafoya told me when I started, 'I *want* you to brew good beer, right out of the gate!' He knows that good beer at every brewpub, helps every brewpub." True, but the only place you're going to find this good beer—except for the occasional festival—is here at the pub. You won't even find it at the newer Market Cross location down in Shippensburg (105 W. King St.).

Things change. Little Ashleigh, who was the reason Jeff settled down, is all grown up now, part owner of Market Cross, and Kevin was planning a Matrimoniale for her wedding. The pub no longer makes the Raspberry Porter I loved; the extract is not available anymore, and they can't find one as good (that's why there's Naked Porter). Business has picked up, and they now have bands playing on the roof of the brewery some weekends (and do a keg drop off the roof at midnight on New Year's Eve).

But some things don't change. Market Cross is still beer crazy, and Kevin's creations are still pretty darned good for coming out of an

**Directions to
Market Cross Pub
and Brewery**

ancient brewing system in a garage out back. The Excaliber I had last time was a big mouthful of toffee and molasses, tempered by bitterness and alcohol: a big beer indeed.

When it's all about the beer, you know you're going to have a good time. Trust me—this place is all about the beer.

Opened: Pub opened April 1, 1994; brewery resumed operations as Market Cross in September 2002.

Owners: JoAnne and Ashleigh Goss.

Brewer: Kevin Spicer.

System: 10-barrel Peter Austin brewhouse, 1,000 barrels potential annual capacity.

2009 production: 150 barrels.

Brewpub hours: Sunday through Thursday, 11 AM to midnight; Friday and Saturday, 11 AM to 1 AM.

Tours: Monday and Thursday nights, 6 to 8 PM.

Take-out beer: Growlers; six-packs of nonhouse beers also available.

Food: Market Cross has the usual bar food, well executed and fresh, as well as a strong selection of the best of English pub food: fish and chips, cottage pie, shepherd's pie, bangers and mash, and beef and Guinness. Solid, belly-mortar food.

Extras: Real darts, big-screen TV, frequent live music (check the Web site for schedule), and "Singin' Wingin' Wednesdays." Really.

Special considerations: Kids welcome. Vegetarian meals available.

Parking: On- and off-street parking easy to find.

Lodging in the area: Carlisle House B&B, 148 S. Hanover St., 717-249-0350; Country Inn and Suites, 1529 Commerce Ave., 717-241-4900; Jacob's Resting Place B&B, 1007 Harrisburg Pike, 888-731-1790.

Area attractions: Carlisle is simply a nice town to stroll through, neatly kept with an attractive town square. It is also well known for an annual series of automobile flea markets run by **Carlisle Productions** (717-343-7855, www.carsatcarlisle.com), where car enthusiasts buy and swap car parts from vintage autos and hot rods. There is a different market each month from April to October. The **Trout Art Gallery** (on High Street on the Dickinson College campus, 717-245-1711, www.dickinson.edu/trout) has a variety of art including classical Greek, African, Oriental, and modern American. **Carlisle Barracks**, one of the oldest permanent army posts in the United States, is home to the Army War College, the Army's Military History Institute, and the Army Heritage Education Center (717-245-3641, www.usahec.org), which displays the assortment of military hardware you'll see along I-81. You can walk among those exhibits—which include reconstructions of outposts from America's wars, from the French and Indian War to Vietnam—or visit the Army Heritage Museum. The institute's collections are open to researchers and genealogists; extensive digital collections of photos and documents also are accessible via the Web site or the education center. The center and the institute are not on the barracks grounds, so no DOD sticker is required. The fly fishing on the Yellow Breeches Creek is world-class; you can contact the **Allenberry Resort Inn** (1559 Boiling Springs Rd., Boiling Springs, 717-258-3211) about their trout-fishing seminars and weekend packages—or their dinner theater specials at the Allenberry Playhouse. If you'd rather wade in on your own, get in touch with the folks at **Yellow Breeches Outfitters** (2 First St., 717-258-6752, www.yellowbreeches.com), on the lake in Boiling Springs; their Web site includes links to stream condition reports.

Other area beer sites: There are three places in Carlisle. **Alibi's Eatery and Spirits** (10 N. Pitt St., 717-243-4151) is all about the beer, but like Market Cross, they don't realize it—they think they're about martinis. Don't argue with them, just praise them for their laserlike focus on Pennsylvania beers—we like that! **Café Bruges** (16 N. Pitt St., 717-960-0223) is equally focused on *Belgian* beers. They have authentic Belgians on draft and in bottle, they know what they're doing with them, and the food's excellent. This is a place worth going out of your way for. Finally, the **North Hanover Grille** (37 N. Hanover St., 717-241-5517) is the relaxed choice: good beer, nice folks, maybe not as crazy about the beer, but sometimes I like that. Outside of Carlisle . . . Cathy and I discovered the **Boiling Springs Tavern** (First and Front Streets, Boiling Springs, across from Yellow Breeches Outfitters on the lake, 717-258-3614) recently and enjoyed the food, service, vibe, and beer immensely. Nice place, indeed, and well off the beaten track.

Appalachian Brewing Company, Gettysburg

401 Buford Avenue, Gettysburg, PA 17325
717-334-2200
www.abcbrew.com

General Robert E. Lee led his Army of Northern Virginia up the Appalachian front to Pennsylvania in 1863, his second attempt to bring the war to the North. It was a bold, swift stroke, the kind he was known for. But his genius failed him at Gettysburg, as the Union forces gathered swiftly to block his advance and tenaciously held the high ground against all assaults. The cream of Lee's army was broken in the battle, and he would never attempt to take the war north again.

Lee watched the battle unfold and fall apart from his headquarters, a stone house rented at the time by Mary "Widow" Thompson and her family, and ironically owned by the fiercely antislavery, anti-Confederacy politician Thaddeus Stevens. Whether

Beers brewed: Limited numbers of seasonal beers brewed here: Karma California Common, Tripelocity, Vanilla Porter, Obbie's Grand Cru, Shimmelfenig Smoked Ale, Imperial Stout. ABC's regular offerings are also pouring.

this occupation contributed to Stevens's radical plans for subjugation of the South after the war is a teasing question.

Artie Tafoya led Appalachian Brewing Company south down Route 15 almost exactly 140 years later in an attempt to bring ABC's style of brewpub to more communities. It was also a bold, swift stroke: The whole thing took place in a matter of weeks (though there were months of delay in beginning brewing operations as the PLCB slowly untangled the mess of regulations around the premises).

The Pick: The one beer I did get to taste that was brewed at Gettysburg was the Imperial Stout. It was smooth as glass and not huge, contrary to the current trends to make imperial stouts bigger, blacker, and boozier. All the components are here, and none of them goes over the top.

Artie's army has prevailed where Lee's did not, and symbolically, ABC's Gettysburg brewpub is only a few steps from the museum that Lee's headquarters and Stevens's house has become.

"We had always hoped to franchise the Appalachian brewpub idea," Artie explained. "But you can't really franchise until you've done it yourself; you have to be multiunit first. No one wants to be the beta site for your expansion plans. So we did that. This was an operating restaurant, and we came in and made it an ABC brewpub in a month.

"We're looking for more opportunities like this," he added. "We're looking at some right now. We intend to put a brewery in each one. We had a chance to pick up two small systems recently, and we've put them in storage till we need them." One of those is now at ABC's second expansion site in Camp Hill.

It's not a small system here: ABC Gettysburg got a 10-barrel Mueller brewhouse. "Mueller," Artie noted, "that's the good stuff." But it's still smaller than the big system up in Harrisburg, and that has advantages. "We'll still have the majority of the beers brewed in Harrisburg," Artie noted. "But here we'll be able to do smaller batches of big beers we couldn't really do at Harrisburg: doublebocks, imperial stouts, triples." Now that sounds interesting.

The origins of that Mueller brewhouse are interesting, too. Mueller is a company known for their work making tanks for the dairy farming industry; they are accomplished masters at stainless steel fabrication. There aren't many Mueller brewhouses out there, and this one has an interesting provenance. It was originally built for the Jack Daniel brewery. The Jack Daniel Company jumped into microbrewing back in the mid-1990s—when it seemed like everyone was jumping into it—and for three years produced some pretty darned good beers. Their Christmas beer was exceptional, a cherry-spiked malt mama that aged well: I had an excellent example that was five years old.

The brewhouse isn't the only thing that's smaller than in Harrisburg. This pub's much smaller, though there is a large banquet room downstairs. There's a game room, too, right beside the brewhouse. But you'll find the main bar and dining room upstairs, looking out across the battlefield.

Out across the battlefield . . . Artie, like Lee, sees the battle shaping and knows it's all on his shoulders. "I figure I can go do something else," he said, shrugging, "or I can take this as far as it can go. I've got great staff. We work hard at excellence. My partners are great; they trust my decisions and help out where they can. This brewpub, the planned brewpubs, open new ground for the bottle and kegged product; people see it, drink it, and then go buy it."

Artie Tafoya and ABC have taken the high ground in Gettysburg, and they're staying till the fight's won.

Opened: August 2003.
Owners: Shawn Gallagher, Jack Sproch, Artie Tafoya.
Brewer: Artie Tafoya.
System: 10-barrel Paul Mueller Company brewhouse, 1,200 barrels annual capacity.
2009 production: 100 barrels.
Brewpub hours: Sunday through Thursday, 11:30 AM to 10 PM; Friday and Saturday, 11:30 AM to 11 PM.
Tours: Every day at 5 PM, plus 1 PM on Saturdays.
Take-out beer: Growlers, six-packs, and twelve-packs.
Food: See the listing for Appalachian Brewing Company, Harrisburg, on page 189 for identical menu.
Extras: Full liquor license. Billiard room (pay by the hour for tables) with darts. ABC also offers banquet facilities for parties of 25 to 125 in the Gallery banquet room. Located just steps from General Lee's Headquarters and museum at the edge of the historic battlefields.
Special considerations: Kids welcome. Vegetarian meals available.
Parking: Lots beside the building and across the street.
Lodging in the area: A Quality Inn is right beside the brewpub, 401 Buford Avenue, 717-334-3141; Comfort Inn, 871 York Rd. (717-337-2400); Best Western Gettysburg Hotel, historic hotel on Lincoln Square, established 1797 (717-337-2000); The Inn at Herr Ridge, 900 Chambersburg Rd. (800-362-9849); Lightner Farmhouse, historic B&B, 2350 Baltimore Pike (717-337-9508).
Area attractions: The **Gettysburg National Military Park and Cemetery** (717-334-1124, www.nps.gov/gett) are naturally the main draws

in Gettysburg; the entrance to the park and the new museum and visitors center is at 1195 Baltimore Pike. Guided and self-guided walking and auto tours are available there, including private tours with licensed battlefield guides. The center also has a museum and the newly restored Cyclorama, a 365-foot painting of Pickett's Charge done in 1884 that surrounds the visitor in a circle. Another site of interest to military history buffs of a different era is Dwight D. Eisenhower's Gettysburg farm, preserved as the **Eisenhower National Historic Site** (717-338-9114, www.nps.gov/eise); the only access is by a shuttle bus to the site from the battlefield museum and visitors center. When you're tired of battles and history, there are other things to do. In nearby Hanover, **Utz Potato Chips** (900 High St., 800-367-7629, www.utzsnacks.com) offers free tours showing the production of their delicious chips. There's good antiquing in New Oxford (about 8 miles east on Route 30). **Ski Liberty** in Fairfield (southwest on Route 116, 717-642-8297) has a 606-foot vertical drop, snow-making, ski school, night skiing, restaurant and lounge, and day care. **Caledonia State Park** (west on Route 30, 717-352-2161) offers camping, fishing, swimming, hiking, golf, and 10 miles of cross-country skiing trails.

Other area beer sites: The **Blue Parrot Bistro** (35 Chambersburg St., 717-337-3739) is a relaxed oasis off the square, away from the hustling tourist trade. You'll find a couple local taps and some good whiskeys. I was quite taken by the **Springhouse Tavern at the Dobbin House** (89 Steinwehr Ave., 717-334-2100), built in 1776. The Springhouse Tavern is downstairs in a rough stone cellar, where the bar itself (complete with after-hours wooden "fences" to lock up the liquor) dates from "before 1818." It's all lit with low lights and lots of candles, and you can hear the actual spring trickling in the corner, and they usually have a Tröegs beer on tap. Artie also recommended **Mamma Ventura's Restaurant and Pizzeria** (13 Chambersburg St., 717-334-5548) as a friendly place for a quick bite and a beer; the bar's downstairs. Out of town, you'll find an outstanding selection of German and German-style beers at the **HofbrauHaus** in Abbottstown (just west of the town square on U.S. 30, on the north side, 717-259-9641). It's clean and neat, and the food is delicious. **KClinger's** (304 Poplar St., Hanover, 717-633-9197) is an excellent big city-level multitap beer bar with limited-release beers, vintage beers, and a whole boatload of attitude. It's a must-stop.

Roy-Pitz Brewing

140 North Third Street (in the back)
Chambersburg, PA 17201
717-496-8753
www.roypitz.com

Chambersburg had a craft brewery back in the early days of Pennsylvania craft brewing: Arrowhead Brewing, which was open from 1991 to 1997, too early for my first *Pennsylvania Breweries* (though they were in, kind of, as Rock Creek, a Virginia-based brewer that had bought the facility). I remember their beers fondly—Red Feather Ale, Arrowhead Brown, Coal Tar Stout—and the owner-brewer, Fran Mead, was widely considered to be one of the nicest guys in brewing. Part of Arrowhead's failure, though, was a complete lack of acceptance in their hometown. You had to travel about 30 miles to find an Arrowhead tap or bottle.

Fast-forward to today, and Chambersburg has a hometown brewery once more. It's pleasing to note that Roy-Pitz is getting more local love right out of the gate. "Norland Pub and the Orchards keep us on regularly," owner-brewer Jesse Rotz told me. "Dilly's and EJ's have us on most times. But anyone around here who's interested in craft beer comes out of the woodwork to find us. Growlers here at the brewery are 20 percent of our sales."

His partner, Ryan Richards, then admitted, "It's been tough around here; it's a Bud town," which is the same thing Fran Mead told me when I visited years ago. He probably knew it all too well; Arrowhead was just down the street from the local Bud wholesaler. "And there's nothing west of here till you get to Pittsburgh," Ryan added. (That's not quite fair to the excellent Jean Bonnet Tavern in Bedford, but otherwise it's pretty accurate: Leave Chambersburg to the west on Route 30 and it gets sparse abruptly, although the drive up over the mountains to Breezewood is exhilaratingly winding and beautiful.)

Beers brewed: Year-round: Old Jail Ale, Best Blonde Ale. Seasonals and specials: Lovitz Watermelon Lager, Lay Down Stay Down, Gobbler Lager, Ludwig's Revenge, Doc's Double Pale Ale, White Horse Hefeweizen, Ichabod Crane's Midnight Ride, Daddy Fat Sacks Imperial IPA, Truly Honest Ale, Chicken Leg Oatmeal Stout, Ice Fest Ale, McKulick Scottish Red Ale.

Jesse and Ryan know about that sparse gulf to the west, and about how the Conococheague Creek winds through town, and, well, all about Chambersburg—they grew up here. "We met in second grade," Jesse said. "At Corpus Christi School, just down the street," Ryan added, and they both laughed. "When we got to high school," Ryan said, "we used to joke about running away and starting a brewery."

The funny thing is, after a year in college, they came home and started talking about a serious look at the brewery idea. They both switched majors to business and "started to homebrew like mad," said Jesse. "We really threw ourselves into it. We learned a lot about conditioning and fermenting."

The Pick: Old Jail Ale memorializes the 1818 Old Jail, one of the few buildings to survive when the Confederate Army burned Chambersburg in 1864. It's the local favorite and the first recipe Jesse and Ryan put together: a nutty, slightly roasty brown ale, an honest, well-made beer with just enough flavor to crack a market that's new to craft beer, or to entice a craft beer veteran to have a few on a lazy afternoon.

After college, they briefly worked at Victory (in the kitchen), then got jobs at the Twin Lakes brewery, just over the border in Delaware, brewing with Mark Fesche. Fesche was an experienced brewer who told them that if they were serious, they should take the short brewing course at the Siebel Institute in Chicago. After taking the course, Ryan went on to further study at Doemens Academy in Gräfelfing, Germany, and Jesse hit the streets of Chambersburg looking for funding.

Jesse's work soon convinced them that their plans for a brewpub weren't realistic. "We'd been planning a brewpub since the second year of college," he said, "but it was just too much money. So I hit 'delete' on three years of planning work, and we got realistic."

"Realistic" meant hitting up family, friends, and anyone who had money for loans. "We got in just before the recession hit," Ryan told me. "We made it by the skin of our teeth. I just wish we would have asked for about four times as much!" They put aside visions of a beautiful brewhouse and moved into the basement of an old hosiery factory, built in 1906. It's a righteously solid building with huge old beams, though, and the basement stays cool all year.

Realistic also meant getting a used brewhouse cheaply . . . but it was in Anchorage, Alaska, and no one wanted to pay the freight to get it to Chambersburg. "We had a friend in the onion and fish business," said Jesse. (Did you know there was an onion and fish business?) "He took a truckload of onions up to Anchorage, got a load of fish, and we rigged the brewery onto the back of the truck." Opening a brewery, folks, you do what you have to do.

What they had to do, by this point, was sell some beer. "The first batch took twenty-four hours, getting acquainted with the new brewery and the changes we'd made to it," said Ryan. "We needed that first batch to work, because we had to sell it!"

As you know by now, everything worked out. Not only does Roy-Pitz have a toehold in Chambersburg, but they're also doing pretty well in the Philadelphia market, led by their seasonal Lovitz Lager, a watermelon-flavored brew that really caught on. Those growler sales are setting their base market well, and it's only a matter of time before the Chambersburg market expands for them.

If you're wondering about the name, Roy-Pitz, it's been the source of much conjecture. Jesse and Ryan originally had a story on their Web site about conjoined twins, thunderstorms, and mad brewing in the 1700s . . . but they told me that "Roy" and "Pitz" were their grade school nicknames. Then they laughed and said that every time someone asked the question, they gave a different answer. Shades of the Rolling Rock "33." It's about time Pennsylvania had another brewery conundrum!

Opened: May 2008.
Owners: Jesse A. Rotz, Ryan C. Richards.
Brewers: Jesse A. Rotz, Ryan C. Richards.
System: 10-barrel JV Northwest system, 1,080 barrels annual capacity.
2009 production: 500 barrels.
Tours: Taproom open for informal tours, sampling, and growler sales: Monday through Friday, 4 to 8 PM; Saturday 1 to 5 PM.
Take-out beer: Growlers and kegs (call for availability).
Parking: Large free lot behind the building.
Lodging in the area: Craig Victorian B&B, 756 Philadelphia Ave., 877-236-3399; Four Points by Sheraton, 1123 Lincoln Highway East, 717-263-9191; Quality Inn and Suites, 1095 Wayne Ave., 717-263-3400.
Area attractions: The **Old Jail** (175 E. King St., 717-264-1667), mentioned in The Pick, is probably Chambersburg's biggest historic attraction, home to the county historical society and a museum featuring a gun collection, pioneer kitchen, and genealogical library. The society also cares for the **John Brown House** (225 E. King St.), where the radical abolitionist met with Frederick Douglass and planned his Harpers Ferry raid in 1859; tours are available—call the society for schedules. Otherwise . . . walk the historic town center, ride or walk the downtown rail-trail (find details at www.TrailLink .com), and get out into the countryside. If you're a fly fisher, the

area's limestone spring creeks offer challenging trout fishing; check out guides at www.limestoner.com and www.fallingsprings.com. If you're looking for a split-bamboo rod, Wyatt Dietrich makes his **Dream Catcher rods** right in town (416 Cumberland Ave., 717-372-8252, www.bamboorods.net).

Other area beer sites: *EJ's Grill* (346 Lincoln Highway East, 717-263-1137) is probably your best bet for craft in Chambersburg and has a nice bistro atmosphere to boot. *Norland Pub* (454 Norland Ave., 717-264-9115) and *The Orchards* restaurant (1580 Orchard Dr., 717-264-4711) always have Roy-Pitz beers on; The Orchards offers upscale fine dining, and Norland is a comfortable bar with good pub grub. *Market Cross Pub* (105 W. King St., Shippensburg, 717-532-3967) is only 12 miles away and carries Market Cross drafts and the same good selection of bottled beers the Market Cross brewpub has.

A word about . . .

Beer Traveling

First things first: "Beer traveling" is not about driving drunk from brewpub to brewpub. Beer outings are similar to the wine trips celebrated in glossy travel and food magazines; they're pleasant combinations of carefree travel and the semimystical enjoyment of a potion in its birthplace. Traveling to Munich or London may be more romantic and exciting than traveling to—no offense, guys—Meadville or Chambersburg, but every place has its merits. For instance, you can hop in a car and be in Chambersburg drinking fresh Lovitz Lager five hours after rolling out of any driveway in the state, and all it will cost is about thirty bucks in gas and tolls. Life's a series of trade-offs.

Besides, beer traveling is sometimes the only way to taste limited-release brews or brewpub beers. You're about to read about one of those at Bullfrog Brewery: The beer sold out in twenty minutes, and it was gone. Tröegs regularly releases brewery-only beers. Beer is usually freshest at bars and distributors near the source. And the beer you'll get at the brewery itself is sublimely fresh, beer like you'll never have it anywhere else—the supreme quaff. You'll also get a chance to see the brewing operations and maybe talk to the brewer.

One of the things a beer enthusiast has to deal with less often these days is the perception that beer drinkers are second-class citizens compared with wine and single-malt scotch connoisseurs. Time was, the vacationer who was taking off for Napa or Islay would look down on the poor schlub who was going to Philly for brewery visits. Nowadays, events like Philly Beer Week draw tens of thousands of people, the mayor taps the opening keg, beer reigns in the finest restaurants in town . . . and your friends say, "You're going to Philly Beer Week? *Cool!*"

Still, beer does have a simpler cachet. Beer gear, the souvenirage of brewery affiliation and the attire that proudly proclaims where you've been, tends to be of the T-shirt and ball cap type. We like that. I have more brewery T-shirts than I could wear in half a year; the hall closet vomits caps when I open the door. We look casual. Well, what of it? Don't let it bother you, just relax and have another sampler of White Magick of the Sun; Justin's pouring it right off the zwickel.

When you're planning a beer outing, you need to think about your approach. If you want to visit just one brewery, or perhaps tour the

208

closely packed bars around Nodding Head in Center City Philadelphia, you can first settle in at a nearby hotel. Get your cab fare or your walking shoes ready, and you're set to work your way through the offerings. If you plan to visit several breweries in different towns, maybe making the run from Otto's to Berwick, it is essential that you travel with a nondrinking driver. And when you're looking for that brewery in a mess of industrial buildings, here's a tip for you: Look for the grain silo; it's a dead giveaway.

You should know that the beer at brewpubs and microbreweries is sometimes stronger than mainstream beer. Often brewers will tell you the alcohol content of their beers. Pay attention to it. Keep in mind that most mainstream beers are between 4.5 and 5 percent ABV, most craft beers start at 5.5 percent and head north from there, and judge your limits accordingly. Of course, you might want to do your figuring before you start sampling.

About that sampling: You'll want to stay as clear-headed as possible, both during the day, so you can enjoy the beer, and the morning after, so you can enjoy life. The best thing to do is drink water. Every pro I know swears by it. If you drink a pint of water for every two pints of beer you drink (one to one's even better), you'll enjoy the beer more during the day. Drinking that much water slows down your beer consumption, which is a good thing.

Drinking that much water also helps keep away the *katzenjammers*, as the Germans call the evil spirits that cause hangovers. Just remember that if you do, you'll probably also want to follow the sage advice apocryphally attributed to President Ulysses S. Grant: "Never pass up an opportunity to urinate." There is, however, no substitute for the simple strategy of drinking moderate amounts of beer in the first place.

Beer traveling is about enjoying beer and discovering the places where it is at its best. You could make a simple whirlwind tour of breweries, but I'd suggest you do other things, too. I've always enjoyed trips to breweries more when we mixed in other attractions. Beer is only part of life, after all; a great part, but generally the people enjoying it with you are even better.

The Appalachian Ridge

The Appalachian Mountains snake their way through Pennsylvania from southwest to northeast, sinuous curves of short but steep ridges that run for miles. They framed the early history of the state, keeping large settlements in the southeastern corner around Philadelphia. The front line of the mountains was such an obstacle that even on a map with no terrain, you can still make out the shapes of the ridges by how the state's highways follow the valleys; the state forest lands bend with the ridges, too. As anyone who travels from Harrisburg to Penn State can tell you, getting over the Appalachian ridges is still an obstacle.

Start at Altoona and drive north, up the new I-99, past State College, then follow I-80 all the way over to the Delaware River border with New Jersey. As you do, you'll follow the mountain ridgelines, and you'll also drive within 15 miles of fourteen different breweries. I'm always struck by the miles and miles of unbroken ridgeline as I make this drive. Make your way southwest of Selinsgrove to Lewisburg on Route 522 and you're flanked by ridges on your left and right—steep, forested walls, a channel without an exit.

Getting over those ridges can be a challenge—or a thrill. For those of you who, like me, find driving winding mountain roads a pleasure like few others, make one of my new favorite runs: Start with lunch at the Bullfrog (you can get a growler if you're the driver). Then run down along Route 220 past Lock Haven, get off on Route 64 to Clintondale, and go about 3 miles south to the turnoff for Pike Road, Route 445. You'll cruise along the rushing waters of Roaring Run, then make a steep climb (get the miles of view to your left as you do), go over the top and down two switchbacks into Madisonburg . . . but the fun's not over. Turn left and stay on Route 445, go about a mile and a half, and follow it again on a right turn. You're headed for the Millheim Narrows, with steep rock walls on either side; rushing right beside you is none other than Elk Creek, and that is where you wind up, coming right into Mill-heim beside Elk Creek Café and Aleworks. I'm not sure if I'm going for the beer or the drive anymore.

You can find natural beauty all along this stretch of mountains. There are scenic vistas, secluded glens and glades, the high lakes and birch woods of the Poconos, the deep ravines of the "Grand Canyon of Pennsylvania," the mountain bike trails and rafting rivers that have made Jim Thorpe an outdoor sports mecca.

Anglers and hunters will find the state a rich preserve of fish and game in a tranquil setting of pine, oak, and mountain laurel, the state flower. For information on seasons, licenses, state game lands, and stocked lakes, contact the Game Commission (717-787-4250, www.pgc.state.pa.us) or the Fish and Boat Commission (717-657-4518, www.fish.state.pa.us).

Hikers and campers enjoy Pennsylvania's extensive system of trails and state campgrounds. The Appalachian Trail runs west along the front ridge of the Appalachians, then heads south between Gettysburg and Harrisburg. There are short hikes to scenic sites at Dingmans Falls in the Delaware Water Gap National Recreation Area and at Hawk Mountain Sanctuary. In the skies over Hawk Mountain, autumn migration routes converge, making the sanctuary an ideal spot for observing migratory hawks, eagles, and other raptors.

Pennsylvania has an extensive state park system, largely thanks to Gifford Pinchot, a Reform governor who was a well-known conserva-tionist and one of the commonwealth's great politicians. (Pinchot was also an ardent prohibitionist who presided over the creation of the byzantine regulations of Pennsylvania's Liquor Code, but nobody's per-fect.) You can get information about Pennsylvania's state parks from the Bureau of State Parks (800-637-2757). Be forewarned that drinking is forbidden in state parks, and the rangers take it pretty seriously.

You can canoe on rivers like the Delaware, Lehigh, Juniata, and Susquehanna. For the more experienced whitewater aficionado, Pine Creek runs the Grand Canyon of Pennsylvania and is rated as a Class III trip. If you're traveling in winter, take your skis. Pennsylvania has more than thirty downhill ski areas, some with vertical drops of over 1,000 feet.

There is some concern about the preservation of this natural bounty. A new energy boom is taking place in Pennsylvania as the natural gas deposits of the Marcellus Shale layers are exploited, using a technique called hydrofracturing. Gas exploration is bringing millions of dollars to areas like Williamsport and Washington, but residents and environmentalists fear that the chemicals used in hydrofracturing will pollute Pennsylvania's groundwater.

I would urge anyone who would dismiss this too quickly to hop on your bike and ride the D&H Rail Trail from Herrick Center down to Carbondale. All along the trail are historical markers showing how acids and salts from coal mines abandoned more than a hundred years ago still leach into the streams, and heaps of wasterock form barren hills along the trail. Pennsylvania's last energy boom had effects that still are with us. Preservation of the beauty we have left is a goal worth thinking about.

Marzoni's Brick Oven and Brewery

165 Patchway Road, Duncansville, PA 16635
814-695-1300
www.marzonis.com

I don't like going to brewpubs until they've been open for at least three months. It gives them a chance to "shake down," learn the quirks of their brewing system, bring the whole service picture into focus, and firm up the menu. You often get a radically different impression on a second visit if you visit too early.

But when I had a chance to visit Marzoni's less than two weeks after they opened, I grabbed it. I'd heard about Marzoni's—that it was a new idea, a new *concept* from the Hoss's restaurant chain—and I was intrigued by the whole idea of a brewpub in Altoona (or really close to Altoona; Marzoni's is in Duncansville, just south of Altoona, where Hoss's headquarters are located). This would be the third time someone tried to open a brewpub in Altoona, and I wanted to see if these guys actually had opened their doors, unlike the other two.

Beers brewed: Year-round: Locke Mountain Light, Marzoni's Amber Lager, Highway 22 Wheat, Patchway Pale Ale, Avalanche IPA, Stone Mason Stout. Seasonals: Altbier, Scotch Ale, Dortmunder, Irish Red, Hoppy Saison, Lichtenhainer, Doppelbock, Mark's Mash-Hopped Pale Ale, Wheat Wine Kölsch, Octoberfest, Raspberry Wheat, Anniversary Ale, and a lot of others.

They were open, all right. They were so darned open that we wound up three rows back in the parking lot in the middle of a cold, windy day. Hey, good sign!

It was prophetic. Uncle Don and I walked past an antique delivery truck into a gleaming restaurant, past a hostess station perched under an immense suspended locomotive driving wheel, and through to the bar, a bar that shone with polished wood. Service was quick, friendly, and competent; we had two samplers and even a fairly decent presentation on the beers. That's amazing for just ten days open.

The Pick: If I had to pick a regular, I'd go with the Avalanche IPA. "I like hops," Bill said with a grin when I looked at him after my first sip, and he sure does. This a hoppy beer, with the gutsy body underneath to support it. Better hope it doesn't sweep you right off the mountain.

But I have to be honest: The beer, for ten days open by a brewer who was solo on his first commercial job, simply blew me away. Bill Kroft had managed to put together a full slate of beers that were at least competent, some of which were quite good, and only one clinker, an odd-tasting hefeweizen.

"I'm kind of stuck brewing that with a dried yeast," Bill explained to me six months later, when I told him about my disappointment with the hefeweizen. "The guy we got in to set up the system brewed a batch of hefe with that dry yeast, and people got used to it. I don't really like it, but people drink it, so like I said, I'm kind of stuck."

Bill, buddy, if that's the only problem you have, you're way ahead of the game! Bill gave me his story, and it's a classic. He was a Hoss's employee for years, worked his way up from dishwasher to general manager. But he'd also been homebrewing for eight years. "When this concept came up," he said, "I threw my hat in the ring. I couldn't believe it when they let me have the job. I still feel like a kid at play doing this, a homebrewer gone wild."

He's completely self-taught, too. "Oh, I talk to Charlie Schnable over at Otto's," Bill said, "I ask questions on the ProBrewer Internet forum, and I do a lot of reading." That's kind of like somebody driving a big rig cross-country after watching *Smokey and the Bandit* three times and hitching a ride home from college on a chicken truck. It only makes the quality of the beer more amazing.

The beer makes the restaurant even nicer, and that's a big job, too. With more than forty restaurants, the people at Hoss's know what they're doing, and while Marzoni's was a new concept and a new menu for them, the basics—solid service and good food value—stayed the same. The whole idea of Marzoni's is that the Campbell family figured they had put as many Hoss's as they could into a market that they could

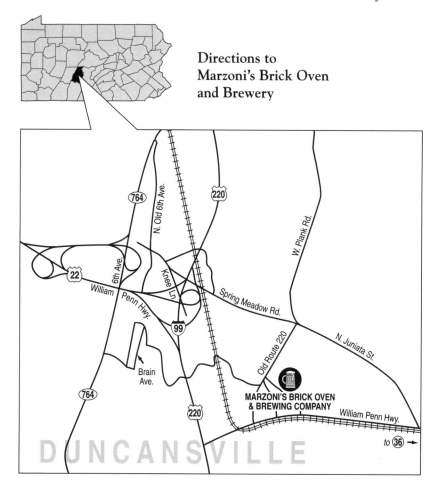

**Directions to
Marzoni's Brick Oven
and Brewery**

realistically control. They wanted to continue to expand, but they didn't want to go farther from Duncansville than they already had or "cannibalize" the territory of any existing restaurants. Marzoni's is the possible solution: a completely different menu and image, with a brewery and full bar (the Hoss's restaurants have no booze).

They tried a second Marzoni's, in the northern Pittsburgh suburbs, without brewing on-premises; the beer was trucked over from this one. It didn't work out, although it may not have been the best of locations. Bill said the feeling in the company was that "the concept's sound, but it's on hold right now with the economy situation."

Things looked much the same when I stopped in this time as they did that first time, six years earlier. There were a couple new beers, but the regulars were still selling well. Bill still makes some new stuff; he had a quite tasty Belgian IPA on. He also did two collaborative brews with

Scott Smith of East End—two rare German beer types, gose and lichten-hainer—which I managed to taste earlier at Bocktown Beer and Grill in Pittsburgh. They were eye-opening and every bit as extreme as you could ask.

Stop in for a beer and a sandwich if you're in town to see the Curve (railroad or baseball). It's a great place to rest a bit before heading back over the mountains.

Opened: November 2003.

Owners: Bill and Nancy Campbell.

Brewer: Bill Kroft.

System: 10-barrel Liquid Asset brewhouse, 1,200 barrels potential annual capacity.

2009 production: 600 barrels (est.).

Brewpub hours: Sunday through Wednesday, 11 AM to 10 PM; Thursday through Saturday, 11 AM to 11 PM.

Take-out beer: Half-gallon and gallon growlers; sixtels and half-barrel kegs.

Tours: On request, subject to brewer availability; will schedule for larger groups.

Food: Brick-oven pizza is the big draw, but the pasta and sandwiches are excellent as well. My daughter was overwhelmed by her meatball sandwich: "It's huge!" she admitted. The portabella parmesan panini is a delicious crusty mouthful of mushroom.

Extras: Seventeen TVs. Private banquet rooms available. Mug club.

Special considerations: Kids welcome. Vegetarian and gluten-free menu items.

Parking: Large free lot.

Lodging in the area: Comfort Inn, across the parking lot, 814-693-1800; Rolling Rock Motel, 2590 Old Route 22, 814-695-5661; Iron Corbel Inn B&B, 703 Allegheny St., Hollidaysburg, 814-696-0324. The Jean Bonnet Tavern (see below) also has rooms.

Area attractions: There are two very reasonable family-style amusement parks near Altoona. *Del Grosso's Park* (Exit 41 off I-99, Tipton, follow the signs, 814-684-3538, www.delgrossos.com) has the feel of an old-style "family" amusement park but is fun even for jaded teenagers, with miniature golf, go-karts, and mountains of what is possibly the best amusement park food in the country. (This is the same Del Grosso's as the delicious spaghetti sauce available in Pennsylvania grocery stores; try some—they're very good.) *Lakemont* (700 Park Ave., Altoona, 814-949-PARK, www.lakemontpark.com)

is like a really big county fair, with a lot of older, classic rides, including a large wooden coaster, a gas-powered antique auto ride (running at antique speeds, too), and a very special attraction: Leap the Dips, the world's oldest roller coaster and the last of a type of coaster known as a side-friction figure eight. No seat belts, no high speeds or huge drops, but my son and I found that the constant side-to-side banging and crashing and the short, abrupt dips and rises of the tracks had a quaint but real excitement all their own. Not to be missed and dirt cheap—five of us got in for under $30. The **Altoona Curve** AA baseball stadium (right next to Lakemont, 814-944-9800) is a beautiful little ballpark (with $4 beers!) with a great view of the roller coaster and the mountains. The baseball team is named for the famous **Horseshoe Curve National Historic Landmark** (6 miles west of Altoona on local roads, follow signs, visitors center telephone is 888-4-ALTOONA), the sharp horseshoe-shaped bend that allowed railroad travel over the steep ridges of central Pennsylvania. This engineering marvel and work of surveying genius was considered vital to the country's World War II war effort and was a prime target of the German saboteurs who came ashore on Long Island in 1942. There is a funicular up to the tracks, where more than fifty trains pass by each day, diesel-electric engines thundering. Just as vital to rail travel, and an even greater engineering feat, though nowhere near as well known as the curve, are the nearby **Gallitzin Tunnels** (411 Convent St., Gallitzin, 814-886-8871), dug through the rock of the mountains by immigrant laborers in the early 1850s. This is one of the best sites for train-watching in Pennsylvania, as trains rumble out of the twin-track tunnel into the rock cut. The nearby museum, with restored 1942 caboose, tells their story. *Raystown Lake* is the largest man-made lake completely in Pennsylvania (part of Pymatuning Lake is in Ohio), and it supports a wide range of water activities: fishing, boating, water-skiing, swimming. You can rent boats at the **Seven Points Marina** (near Hesston, 814-658-3074, www.7points marina.com). After you're done jaunting about, come back to Altoona for a snack: tour the **Benzel's Pretzel Bakery** (5200 Sixth Ave., 814-942-5062) and watch as 5 *million* pretzels are made every day. Takes a lot of beer to eat those pretzels . . .

Other area beer sites: You've probably picked up by now that I love old, authentic bars, and the **U.S. Hotel** (401 S. Juniata St., Hollidaysburg, 814-695-9924) is a gem: a real old Pennsylvania hotel bar, complete with massive wood backbar, mosaic and tile floor and walls, some beautiful "bunch o' grapes" lamps over the bar, and an authentic "gentleman's trough" at the base of the bar—a tile trough with running water to take the place of unsightly (and hard-to-hit) spitoons! The beer's not amazing, but the place is great. The **Altoona Hotel** (3830 Fifth Ave., Altoona, 814-944-5521) delivers a great selection of whiskeys and gins, and an adventurous selection of beers, in a bistro atmosphere with an ambitious menu. The **Knicker-bocker Tavern** (3957 Sixth Ave., Altoona, 814-942-0770) is a fun place to eat, drink, and relax. They have great bar food, a beautiful courtyard dining area, a neat little old-style bar, and probably the best selection of beer within 30 miles. But 34 miles away is the **Jean Bonnet Tavern** (6048 Lincoln Highway, Bedford, 814-623-2264), a colonial-era stone-built tavern that focuses on Pennsylvania drafts, and they have a fantastic selection as well. Protestors of the Whiskey Rebellion raised a liberty pole here in 1794; General/President Washington's punitive expedition to put down the rebellion, the "Watermelon Army," camped here later that year on its way to Pittsburgh. If you're traveling off the interstates and find yourself rolling across the state on Route 22 (I recommend it: some gorgeous vistas), stop at **Boxer's Café** (410 Penn St., Huntingdon, 814-643-5013) in Huntingdon. The beer picks are small but well made, the food's quirky and tasty, and the unique stone backbar is astonishing. One other place: I keep hearing good things about the **Windber Hotel** (502 15th St., Windber, 814-467-6999), although I couldn't squeeze it in this time. Sounds like it would be worth your while.

Otto's Pub and Brewery

2235 North Atherton Street
State College, PA 16801
814-867-6886
www.ottospubandbrewery.com

State College was the site of one of the state's first brewpubs, Happy Valley, way back in the late 1980s. With one of the largest college campuses (and faculties) in the country nearby, Happy Valley should have been a natural, but it failed fairly soon. As is often the case, that failure put a bad light on the idea of another brewpub in the area. The ongoing farce of the "planned" Red Bell brewpub in the town didn't help people take brewpubs seriously.

So I was kind of surprised to hear that Bullfrog brewer Charlie Schnable had left Williamsport to open a brewpub called Otto's (named for Charlie's cat) in State College. Hope it works for him, I thought, torn between the pessimism engendered by the bad mojo surrounding brewpubs there and the natural optimism that, darn it, State College was a *perfect* town for a brewpub, hoodoo or not.

Charlie and Otto's broke the hoodoo wide open with a success that just couldn't be stopped. Eventually, the biggest problem for Otto's would be the limited parking in the tightly bound property, especially after adding a small outdoor beer garden and an external beer cooler.

I toured the brewery with Charlie on a recent visit. He's working on one of the last of the Bohemian Monobloc systems, with the company's signature gleaming copper cladding, a previously unused model that was displayed at trade shows. The Monobloc was Bohemian's finest system, when the company finally got it right, just before folding. Charlie had brewed on a Bohemian system at Bullfrog and was obviously pleased to have one again.

Tour over, we sat down and ran the taps. What I tasted was twelve great beers, and one of them, the Flanders Red, was phenomenal. What made it all the more impressive was that the Flanders Red was Charlie's first try at a "bug beer," a beer intentionally inoculated with bacteria to produce effects similar to those in the sour beers of Belgium . . . and he'd nailed it. I'm afraid I might have lost my professional composure and whistled and stamped the floor.

Another time, I stopped in for lunch with a local friend, Sam Komlenic. Sam got the pilsner, which he'd been drinking for the past week; I got a cask-conditioned Arthur's IPA (named for Charlie's other cat). Both were so good we kept passing them back and forth. (Charlie has cask ales down by this point, with two beer engines going most times.)

Then Charlie saw us and brought us samples of his new Tripel D: a beefed-up version of his explosively hoppy Double D IPA, fermented with a Belgian yeast. We forgot the other beers and dove headfirst into

Beers brewed: Year-round: Helles Lager, Apricot Wheat, Mt. Nittany Pale Ale, Red Mo Ale, Double D IPA, Arthur's Nut Brown Ale, Black Mo Stout. Seasonals: Black Raspberry Wheat, Imperial Stout, ESB, Barley Wine, Oktoberfest, Abbey Dubbel, Apple Barrel Brew, Arthur's Rye Ale, Arthur's Best Bitter, Arthur's Robust Porter, Duffinator Double Bock, Hefeweizen, HellKat, Honey Weiss Triple, Maibock, Mom's Elderberry Stout, Roggen Bier, Spring Creek Lager, Schwarzbier, Sumatra Stout, Winter Warmer, Belgian-Style Wit, Pilsener Lager, Flanders Style Red Ale . . . plus more to come.

this roller coaster–fun ride of a beer: spicy, sweet, and blessed with a beautifully appropriate hop aroma. Genius.

Lunch was pretty good, too, as it always is. They try to be as local as possible at Otto's and run a great series of local food alerts on their e-mail list. Grass-fed beef cheesesteaks, local pork from Hogs Galore in Phillipsburg, local produce in season— and it's not just the food. Mom's Elderberry Stout is really made with elderberries that Charlie's mom grows and cuts, a delicious stout with just a hint of the medicinal, blackberry notes of the fruit. The Keewaydin Cider you see offered at the brewpub is another one of Charlie's projects, pressed from apples in Frenchville, and it may get quite a bit bigger in the next couple years (you have to drink it on-premises because of an odd wrinkle in the state liquor laws, but you can buy it at Wegmans and in cases at Pletcher's in State College).

The Pick: Man, that's tough. Oh, why not: Double D IPA. Just because I think there are too many beers like this around doesn't mean I can't like a good one, and this is. There's a ton of big, fat hop flavor in here, honeyed with malt-a-plenty; it's maltilicious with plenty of hop dressing; it's bulging with hops, psycho-hops, and maniacal malt . . . and I'm rolling in it like it's catnip. I can't stop! (It's fun when Charlie slips the Belgian to it and makes Tripel D, too.)

All this good stuff, along with a ton of fun, great service, and a more mature atmosphere than at most of the bars in this very-much-college town, left Charlie and his partner—father-in-law Roger Garthwaite— running hard just to keep up with record sales. They decided to look for larger accommodations, as much for the brewery as the restaurant.

They found them just a bit down the hill at a defunct Quaker Steak and Lube restaurant that they were able to pick up at a rock-bottom price. "We had to do it," Charlie said, "or someone else would have." They signed the papers in early 2010 and should be moved in by the time this edition sees print. The new place is much bigger and has a lot more parking. It also has room for an expanded brewery, and the 12-ounce bottles of Otto's beer may see a wider market.

Next time you get up to State College—to go back to school, take your kid back to school, or go to a Nittany Lions game—stop in at Otto's and have some of this great beer and great food. Try a Black Mo Stout, named for the local Black Moshannon Creek. Get one of those grass-fed cheesesteaks and try a bottle of Keewaydin. There's a little something for everyone at Otto's.

Opened: September 2002.
Owners: Charles Schnable, Roger Garthwaite.
Brewers: Charles Schnable, Chris Brugger.

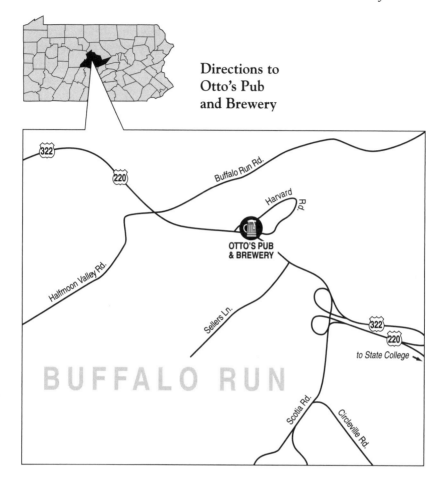

Directions to
Otto's Pub
and Brewery

System: 10-barrel Bohemian/Specific Mechanical brewhouse, 5,000 barrels potential annual capacity.

2009 production: 1,800 barrels.

Brewpub hours: Sunday through Wednesday, 11 AM to midnight; Thursday through Saturday, 11 AM to 2 AM.

Tours: On request, subject to brewer availability

Take-out beer: Growlers, 12- and 22-ounce bottles; sixtels, half kegs; call ahead for keg availability.

Food: Hey, it's a college town; things are a little different. For one, there are some serious vegetarian meals here, not just tossed salad and cheese pizza. The walnut barley burger, risotto balls, and butternut squash ravioli make for real choices. There's still stuff for Mom and Dad, like the grilled salmon with lemon-hops butter, grilled ribeye, and those pasture-raised burgers.

Extras: Live music several times a week; call for schedule. E-mail newsletter, with the latest local food options. Outdoor patio, weather permitting. Penn State football games (and other events, if necessary) on six TVs. Otto's has an interesting twist on the mug club idea: the Pub Club, with a lifetime membership for $150. Beers and growler refills are discounted, food and merchandise too, and there are special Pub Club beer dinners.

Special considerations: Kids welcome. Serious vegetarian meals available.

Parking: Large on-site lot.

Lodging in the area: Carnegie House, 100 Cricklewood Dr., 814-234-2424; The Penn Stater, 215 Innovation Blvd., 814-863-5000; Quality Inn, 1274 N. Atherton St., 814-234-1600.

Area attractions: The biggest attractions in State College are connected to Penn State, and there are a lot, ranging from museums of football, entomology, and minerals and gemstones to the sports events at the college (and when there's a football game in Happy Valley, you'd better have a ticket and motel reservation lined up well in advance!) to the two college golf courses open to the public (814-865-GOLF for fees and tee times). Get the inside information from the **Centre County Convention and Visitors Bureau** (800-358-5466, www.visit pennstate.org). **Tussey Mountain Ski Area** (in Boalsburg, 814-466-6810, www.tusseymountain.com) has a vertical drop of 550 feet, snowmaking, night skiing, ski school, restaurant and lounge, and day care. Also in Boalsburg is the **Pennsylvania Military Museum** (814-466-6263, www.pamilmuseum.org), a thoughtful and well-done museum honoring the state's soldiers from pre-Revolutionary times to the Persian Gulf War, with a focus on the Pennsylvania 28th Division's history in the two world wars. There's an oddly old piece of history on the other side of Route 322 from the Military Museum: the **Boal Mansion** (814-466-6210), home to nine generations of the Boal family. The altar, religious relics, and explorer's cross from the Columbus family chapel in Spain are in the mansion, as is Columbus's desk. Follow Route 22 southwest from Lewistown to **Raystown Lake** (888-RAYSTOWN, www.raystown.org), the largest man-made lake inside Pennsylvania and a great hunting, boating, swimming, and fishing area. **Lincoln Caverns** (814-643-0268) are in nearby Huntingdon, with tours through the two caves, gem panning, and picnic areas. **Penn's Cave** (5 miles east of Centre Hall on Route 192, 814-364-1664, www.pennscave.com) is a rare water-filled cave, toured by boat. There is also a wildlife sanctuary with bears, mountain lions, elk, and wolves. Penn's Cave is a little like South of the Border in that the signs are hard to miss once you get northwest of Harrisburg. **Grice Clearfield Community Museum** (119 N. Fourth Street, Clearfield, 814-768-7332), open Memorial Day weekend through the end of September, has a neat collection of classic cars. Otto's Black Mo Stout is named for Black Moshannon Creek, which runs into the lake at **Black Moshannon State Park** (4216 Beaver Rd., Philipsburg, 814-342-5960). The streams that feed the lake drain through the sphagnum moss of Black Moshannon Bog, picking up so much tannin that the water of the lake is perfectly clear, yet as brown as strong tea, endlessly entertaining to me as a child when I swam here (and still pretty funny the last time I did it). The park offers a range of recreation: swimming, camping (rustic and modern cabins, too), fishing, hunting, snowmobiling, hiking, ice skating, and cross-country skiing.

Other area beer sites: Zeno's (100 W. College Ave., 814-237-2857) is the original State College beer bar, with a great selection of draft beer, "located directly above the center of the earth." The other spot for beer in State College is **The Deli** (113 Heister St., 814-237-5710), a favorite of Charlie's and just about everyone else with a beer lust. There's a branch of the **Mad Mex** beer-o-philic restaurants in the Days Inn Hotel (240 S. Pugh St., 814-272-5656). Just outside of town is **Olde New York** (2298 E. College Ave., 814-237-1582), owned by the folks who used have the beloved Schnitzel's Tavern in Bellefonte. It's no Schnitzel's, but the beer's very good, and there's an extensive bottle shop for take-out. **Denny's Beer Barrel Pub** (1423 Dorey St., Clearfield, 814-765-7190) has improved their beer selection, but that's still not why you're going there. It's for the immense "challenge" burgers they serve, in 2-, 3-, 6-, and 15-pound sizes. No kidding, the big one's over half the size of a case of beer. They will make a 100-pounder for charity events. Wow!

Gamble Mill Restaurant and Microbrewery

160 Dunlap Street, Bellefonte, PA 16823
814-355-7764
www.gamblemill.com

I was at the State College Microbrewery Exposition one year, a great beer fest that's sadly no longer around, and ran into someone I knew from the area just as the first session was ending. "Help me out," I asked him. "I want someplace I can get a good dinner with a good beer that isn't going to be crazy tonight." He sized me up, rubbed his chin, and said, "For you? Schnitzel's, in Bellefonte."

Schnitzel's was a great little German restaurant in a historic old hotel, right by Spring Creek. I had a significant beer experience that night that I wrote about in *All About Beer* magazine. I loved the place, loved the town, took friends there year after year, and kept returning. I would drive 30 miles out of my way to stop in for a beer, just to soak up the atmosphere and walk the streets of this classic central Pennsylvania small town.

But in 2006, the historic old hotel burned to the ground. The town was still there, but for me, it had lost its heart. I followed the news, and people talked about replacing Schnitzel's with an Applebee's. As if!

Then, early in 2010, I got an e-mail from my buddy Sam Komlenic (who had called me with the news the morning Schnitzel's burned). The Gamble Mill Restaurant, in Bellefonte, was adding a brewery. They had the brewhouse already in-house, they had a brewer lined up, and the restaurant was a long-established concern. So I'm breaking my own rule (again) by putting a brewery that had not yet opened in this edition. Consider it my tribute to Schnitzel's.

Dave Fonash owns Gamble Mill with business partner Paul Kendeffy as the Fonash.Kendeffy Restaurant Group; the group also runs Zola New World Bistro in State College and Alto in Lemont. Kendeffy is the chef, Fonash is the sommelier (and a State College native and PSU graduate), and the restaurants have met with acclaim in central Pennsylvania.

Why mess with success by experimenting with a brewery? "We wanted to add a brewpub because it's a great fit for a building," Fonash told me. "It's an old gristmill and built very solidly. It's early Americana, a late-eighteenth-century building rebuilt in 1802." The building is solid and striking after years of restoration in the 1970s and 1980s, and I've seen brewpubs in similar buildings that seemed absolutely organic.

His other reason touched me. "We think it's going to benefit the community," he said, and made clear that he meant that benefit in terms of access to fresh-brewed beer, adding, "People can get to Elk Creek or down to State College, but there's a gap in between." That's an example of the place Gamble Mill has in the area; Elk Creek owner Tim Bowser once worked at the restaurant.

Gamble Mill had a devoted clientele, and Fonash and Kendeffy don't want to change it too much. "We have changed the menu to a more American theme," he said. "We kind of 'casualed it down.' But we haven't changed the interior at all. We are going to stick to the wine program as it is. We want killer wine *and* great craft beer."

What great craft beers will be brewed is still up to brewer Mike Smith, a Centre County native and Penn State graduate who's returning to the area after brewing at Dogfish Head and Ithaca Brewing. Fonash's own tastes are pretty broad. "I like Belgian styles, I like Cascade-hopped IPAs, I'm really pretty open," he said. "I like beers across the board."

Looks like I'll be going out of my way to get to Bellefonte once again. Maybe I'll see you there.

Opened: Restaurant opened 1986, changed owners 2008; planned opening of brewery by late 2010 (call ahead).

Owners: Fonash.Kendeffy Restaurant Group.

Brewer: Mike Smith.

System: 7-barrel JV Northwest system, 750 barrels annual capacity.

2009 production: None.

Brewpub hours: Closed Sunday. Restaurant is open Monday through Saturday, 11:30 AM to 2 PM, and 5 PM to close. Hours will probably expand with brewery operations; best to call ahead.

Tours: On request, depending on brewer's availability.

Take-out beer: Growlers

Food: A full range, from pubby appetizers to dishes like the restaurant's signature seafood strudel, butternut ravioli, and wild-caught salmon, with a nice selection of flatbreads and juicy burgers. The restaurant's carefully chosen wine selection has won awards from *Wine Spectator* and *Wine Enthusiast.*

Special considerations: Gamble Mill is more of an adult venue. Vegetarians will find a range of dishes beyond the usual salad and pizza.

Extras: Monthly wine dinners; will be adding beer events. Monthly live
music program; call for schedule.

Parking: Large off-street lot across the street.

Lodging in the area: Reynolds Mansion B&B, 101 W. Linn St., Bellefonte, 814-353-8407; Riffles and Runs B&B and Outfitters (a special place for anglers), 217 N. Spring St., Bellefonte, 814-353-8109.
See the listing for Otto's on page 222 for more suggestions.

Area attractions: The gushing spring that gave Bellefonte its name
(supposedly suggested by the French statesman Talleyrand while he
was in exile in America and doing a bit of land speculation in Pennsylvania) is the centerpiece of *Talleyrand Park*, which also is home
to the *George Grey Barnard Sculpture Garden*. Barnard was born
in Bellefonte in 1863, and there is a casting of the head of Lincoln
he sculpted in the garden. Spring Creek is just one of the great fly-
fishing streams (the others are Penns Creek, Little Fishing Creek,
and the Little Juniata River) around Bellefonte. *Riffle and Runs
B&B and Outfitters* (see above) caters to anglers, and there are two
fly-fishing shops in State College: *Flyfisher's Paradise* (2603 E.
College Ave.) and *TCO Fly Shop* (2030 E. College Ave.).

Other area beer sites: See the listing for Otto's on page 223.

Elk Creek Café
and Aleworks

100 West Main Street, Millheim, PA 16854
814-349-8850
www.elkcreekcafe.net

I thought I had heard from Tim Bowser pretty early on about this project.
Tim contacted me in the late fall of 2005 with a bunch of questions, and
we met one night at Selin's Grove Brewing Company (twist my arm,
Tim) and talked at the bar for a while about his idea. He was all about
local, sustainable food, about fitting a brewpub into a community—"one
farther out than this one," I remember him saying. At that time, he was
running the building in Millheim as Equinox, a coffeehouse with live

music, and once I found out where Millheim was, I was pretty impressed that he'd stayed open. Millheim may not be in the middle of nowhere, but on a clear day you can glimpse it from there.

When I sat down with him and brewer Tim Yarrington and got the whole story, it turns out he'd been working on this project for almost twenty years. It started back when he'd gone to agricultural college after growing up on a farm. "I didn't care for the reigning paradigm," he said; really, he did, he's a thoughtful kind of guy.

Beers brewed: Year-round: Winkleblink Ale, Great Blue Heron Pale Ale, Elk Creek Copper Ale, Brookie Brown Ale, Poe Paddy Porter, Double Rainbow IPA. Seasonals: Penn's Valley Pilsner, Crickfest Bier, Duckwalk Dunkelbock, Homegrown IPA, Re-Session Ale, Big Trout Oat Stout, Olde Millheim Strong Ale, Gambol + Gyre Golden Ale, Wee Heavy, Mid-State Trail Ale, Anniversary Ale, Colyer Kölsch.

So he founded the Pennsylvania Association for Sustainable Agriculture in 1992. "It started as a resource for farmers," he said, "finding and creating local markets for grass-fed beef and dairy and organic produce. Sustainable agriculture is community-based, local. Shipping organic food thousands of miles isn't sustainable."

The second stage is the pull in the other direction. "When people get to know the local farmers, meet them," he said, "they'll support them, and they'll pay a little more for the food. That doesn't just work for a farm; it works for a brewpub, too."

Bowser bought the building in 1999. "The brewpub was the ultimate goal, even then," he said, "but the area wasn't ready for it. We went with a food-based business, the coffeeshop." Music was an important part of Equinox, and it would become a key part of Elk Creek—the "fourth leg" in Bowser's plan, along with local food, house-made beer, and a comfortable gathering place. That would be Elk Creek.

But he needed a brewer. "I wrote a nontypical want ad, focusing on what we were trying to do more than technical requirements," he said. "I figured we'd get a young guy with lots of heart and no experience. I got résumés from four brewers with GABF gold medals." There was a new feel in brewing, he thinks, more about quality and less about commercialism.

"Beer is becoming part of the cultural vernacular," Yarrington chimed in; he's pretty thoughtful, too, and definitely experienced. "I thought it had happened, but when I got here, I saw how deep it was. People are proud of it, they want to have a favorite, they want to have an opinion."

When he got here, Yarrington had his eyes opened. "I came down through the Narrows and saw the town, and I thought, no way," he said. "This is the most daring thing I ever saw someone try to pull off. I wanted this to work, because I think this is what our business should be:

small breweries in locales, being individual, being unique, fresh beer in every burg."

He tried to talk Bowser out of hiring him full-time, but he got sucked in, fell so hard for Penns Valley that he moved here. They worked out that Yarrington would brew part-time and continue to consult, and it's worked. "It's exciting," he said. "It's been really good."

It took him a while to get the brewing system and the water dialed right in, but the last time I was there, the beers were outstanding. Tim doesn't do big beers very often; he does 3.5 to 6 percent beers, and he's all about balance. "What's the point, if we all do big beers, if we all do sour beers?" he asked. "We all do what we do. I don't want to be all things."

The four legs are strong. The food is local and sustainable as much as possible, and that counts for what comes out as well as in: fryer oil goes biodiesel, kitchen waste feeds chickens, and almost everything else goes into recycling bins. Elk Creek is a zero-waste operation. Draft beer in reusable growlers and kegs helps, of course.

The gathering-place aspect is strong. People come here and talk while they drink; I've seen it every time I've been in. The live music is working very well. "The majority are local acts," Bowser said, "but it's evolving. I try to keep it authentic roots music, blues and jazz. We've had acts we had no business getting, but they play here, and then they want to come back."

I know the feeling exactly. Elk Creek is near the top of a private list I keep: places I wish were where I live. We all need a gathering place, with sustainable food and good live music. And of course, fresh beer in every burg. Every burg should be as lucky as Millheim.

The Pick: I do like the Porter, and the Pilsner's great, but the Great Blue Heron has a smart shot of hop aroma, light-medium body, and a solid bitterness that make it a real drinker. Try it next time, and don't overlook the Elk Creek Copper, either.

Opened: December 2007.
Owners: Elk Creek Café + Aleworks LP, Tim Bowser general partner.
Brewer: Tim Yarrington.
System: 8.5-barrel Cask Brewing system, 400 barrels annual capacity.
2009 production: 350 barrels.
Brewpub hours: Wednesday and Thursday, 4 to 10 PM; Friday and Saturday, noon to 11 PM; Sunday 11 AM to 2 PM. Special events may change the schedule on Sunday; check the Web site.
Tours: On request.
Take-out beer: Growlers, sixtels.
Food: "Nouveau Dutchie" cuisine. As locally sourced and from scratch

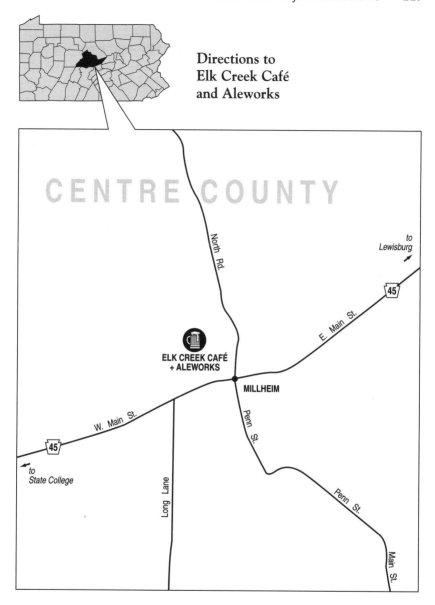

Directions to Elk Creek Café and Aleworks

as possible; pork and trout come from local sustainable farms, and even the Alaskan salmon is wild-caught by a local fisherman. Chef Mark Johnson takes all this great stuff and creates new dishes all the time. Fresh, grass-fed beef and pork make an amazing difference. Try the shrubs: flavored sweet vinegars mixed with ice and seltzer—wickedly refreshing.

Extras: Lots and lots of original, live music. No televisions.

Special considerations: Kids welcome, but there's no separate children's menu. Vegetarian and vegan dishes are always on the menu.

Parking: On-street parking and municipal lot (follow signs).

Lodging in the area: The Three Porches B&B, 161 E. Main St., 814-349-7275; Inn on the Sky, 538 Brush Mountain Rd., Spring Mills, 814-422-0386; Aaronsburg Inn, 100 E. Aaron Square, Aaronsburg, 814-349-8626; Woodward Crossings, 178 Jackson Hill Rd., Aaronsburg, 814-349-4484.

Area attractions: When I'm in Penns Valley, I get a ton of satisfaction from just looking at the scenery. At **Bald Eagle State Park** (along Route 150 near Howard), you'll find hiking trails, swimming, fishing, boating, hunting, a full range of winter activities, camping, a rustic inn, and hey, where else can you stay in a yurt? The drive down to Millheim on Route 445 from the park isn't just scenic; with the switchbacks north of Madisonburg and the run through the Millheim Narrows, it's downright thrilling. **Penn's Cave** is here, the only water cave in the country; you tour it by boat (222 Penns Cave Rd., Centre Hall, 814-364-1664, www.pennscave.com), and if you miss the multitude of signs along the road, you must be asleep. If you like your porter, head out to its namesake: **Poe Paddy State Park**, which lies between Poe Mountain and Paddy Mountain, if you were curious about the name. The park, created by the CCC in the 1930s, offers hiking (part of the Mid-State Trail) and a bike rail-trail, picnicking, and snowmobiling, and the fly fishing on Penns Creek is nationally renowned. Maybe it's just me, but I really like the little **Penns Valley Meat Market** just up the street; not much to look at, but they smoke their own meats, make their own jerky and sausage, and roast their own peanuts. It's great stuff, and I never leave Millheim without some.

Other area beer sites: Better head down to State College; see the listing for Otto's on page 223.

Copper Kettle Brewing

339 Fairground Road, Millmont, PA 17845
270-342-1638
www.ckbrewery.com

When does homebrewing cease to become a hobby? At what point have you become a *brewer*? When does what you do for fun become a job?

For the PLCB, it's a clear line: It's when you sell your beer, at which point you'd better have a license and be a brewer. For Harold Kerlin and Russ Eisenhuth, the answers are fuzzier, and you get the feeling that fuzzy is just fine with them. These two are Copper Kettle Brewing, which is a 1-barrel brewkettle in Russ's basement, with four 1-barrel tanks. "We'll do 40 barrels of beer in 2009," Harold told me. Even though they are licensed and selling beer—in that order!—it sounds like they're still having a lot of fun.

I was talking to Harold where he works during the day, Bucknell University, in the engineering lounge (I was there so my son could tour the campus). He and Russ both work for the university: Harold maintains the telecommunications system, Russ repairs computers. They're both electricians and have worked together for years.

They also homebrewed together. "We were making beer," Harold said, "and people wanted to buy it. We knew that wasn't legal. But then we won the northeast regional of the 2006 Samuel Adams Longshot competition with the porter, and we started thinking about going into business." The beer he calls "the porter" is the Potbelly Porter they make, and it's quite a good beer.

They were making more and more homebrew and giving it to friends to try. One of them was Mike Purseil, who owns the Bull Run Inn in Lewisburg, and he wanted to sell it. Hey, we've got an outlet, Russ and Harold thought, and that's what pushed them over the top. They filed in 2007, put together the brewhouse (the vessels were scrap stainless steel from a Chef Boyardee plant), and got their brewing license in May 2008.

Officially, they were brewers, in an unofficial, size-based category known as "nanobreweries." Loosely

Beers brewed: Year-round: Potbelly Porter, Lucky 393 Grand Cru. Seasonals: Celebration Wheat, Eislin Double.

The Pick: The first Copper Kettle beer I had was the Potbelly Porter, and it's my favorite. Solid malt but not thick, a little chocolaty, and leads you to have another— that's practically my definition of "porter."

defined, a nanobrewery is one that brews in batches of less than 3 barrels and sells beer off-premises. Copper Kettle is one of three nanobreweries in Pennsylvania—along with Breaker Brewing and Berwick Brewing—that are within 75 miles of each other.

But it still sounds a lot like homebrewing! "We both work full-time, and I have a four-year-old son," Harold said, "so finding time to brew is always an issue. We need an hour to mash, an hour to sparge, an hour to boil, an hour to bottle, and two hours to clean. We're hand-bottling, and of course, we have to sample every batch. That's the fun part!"

They decided they were going to bottle rather than keg because both of them liked bottle-conditioned beers. "You can't do that in a keg," Harold said. It's all hand-bottling, and the labels were designed by Russ's wife.

"It's still fun," Harold told me, and the distinct twinkle in his eye showed me it was true.

What about the future? "We can eventually expand," he said. "It's not a lot of money, and we can piece together a 3-barrel system and a small bottling line. Draft would be good, but there's just not enough beer to keg. As long as people keep buying it, we'll keep making it."

That's how they got into this in the first place: making beer people wanted to buy. If enough people want to buy it, they'll have to make another step. For now, though, Harold and Russ are still a little fuzzy about that line between homebrewer, hobby, job, and business . . . and it doesn't seem to bother them at all.

Established: May 2008.
Owners: Harold Kerlin, Russ Eisenhuth.
Brewers: Harold Kerlin, Russ Eisenhuth.
System: 1-barrel custom-built brewkettle, 50 barrels annual capacity.
2009 production: 40 barrels.
Tours: By appointment only.
Take-out beer: Cases of 12-ounce bottles.
Parking: Limited off-street parking.
Lodging in the area: Maison Boisee, 389 Paddy Mountain Rd., Millmont, 570-922-4164; Lewisburg Hotel, 136 Market St., 570-523-7800; Mifflinburg Hotel, 264 Chestnut St., 570-966-5400.
Area attractions: Check out the **Campus Theatre** in Lewisburg (413 Market St., 570-524-9628, www.campustheatre.org), a real old-time movie palace that will make you understand why movies were magic back in the 1940s, showing first-run films, foreign films, and other

events. See the listings for Elk Creek (page 230), Selin's Grove (pages 247–48), and Bullfrog (page 237) for more suggestions.

Other area beer sites: The *Bull Run Inn* (605 Market St., Lewisburg, 570-524-2572) has a decent bottle selection (including Copper Kettle) and good food. *Vic's Pub* at the Victoria House restaurant (2167 Old Turnpike Rd. Lewisburg, 570-523-8090) has a good selection of taps, a comfy pub feel (and pub menu), and serious Quizzo on Thursday nights. The *Scarlet D Tavern* at the Mifflinburg Hotel (see above) also carries Copper Kettle and eleven drafts. Otherwise, Elk Creek, Old Forge, and Selin's Grove aren't too far away.

Bullfrog Brewery

229 West Fourth Street
Williamsport, PA 17701
570-326-4700
www.bullfrogbrewery.com

I knew the American brewing revolution was finally in full swing in Pennsylvania when I found out that a brewpub was opening in Williamsport. From Scranton to Erie to Rochester, New York, stretched a great Bermuda Triangle of malt, where interesting beer did not, seemingly could not, exist. Some places offered Genesee Cream Ale as if it were the answer to prayer. It's gotten much better these days, but at the time I found it hard to believe that someone had taken the chance of planting a brewpub on such barren ground.

But the rumors were true: Billtown had a brewpub. One man's barren ground is evidently another man's open market. I stopped in for the first time shortly before Bullfrog opened, when the gleaming Bohemian brewhouse had been installed in the front windows. I took a look around as brewmaster-to-be Charlie Schnable (now brewer-owner at Otto's in State College) sanded the hardwood floors. The old building was well constructed, with glass all around the dining area and solid beams down below. The sunlight through the glass made the place cheery, even though it had no furniture or lights and the walls were unpainted.

Now that the Bullfrog has been up and running for almost fifteen years, it's an even happier place. It's become a big part of Williamsport's cultural scene, and business is good. I was in not long ago, running samples with brewer Terry Hawbaker, when a woman at one of the "high-hat" tables nearby saw the multitude of little beers on our table. "What's that?" I heard her say. "I want some of those little beers!" Not only did she get a sampler, but she passed it around to her tablemates as the waitress, busy though it was, cheerfully stood by and explained every beer to them. Nice work by the waitress—that's how you get people going on craft beer.

Beers brewed: Year-round: Billtown Blonde, Apricot Wheat, Double Coffee Stout, Edgar IPA. Seasonals: Friar Frog Dubbel, Smoked Porter, Wolfsblood Scotch Ale, Busted Lawn Mower Saison, Old Toad Barleywine, DREAD double red, Deuane Nitro DIPA, Nut Brown Ale, Fast Eddie's Pale Ale, Beekeeper, and way too many others to list. Kegs Gone Wild series taps a new wild-aged beer every Friday. Terry is constantly experimenting with new barrel-aged sour beers.

After Charlie moved on, Bullfrog had some retention problems with brewers, including one who stayed less than a week. Then Terry came in from Black Rock, a failed brewpub in Wilkes-Barre, where he had been brewing anything that took his fancy and brewing it well. Terry told me he liked Williamsport, liked the Bullfrog, and plans to stay. They're lucky: He's one of the better brewers in Pennsylvania, and with the competition, that's saying something.

Still, Terry's . . . not unique, maybe, but exceptional. He's wringing beers out of this brewery system that are bringing people from hundreds of miles away, just for those beers. When he did his first release of bottles on his sour raspberry beer—an exquisite beer, for sure—he figured on starting to sell at 11 AM, when the brewpub opened. He and assistant Nate Saar happened to look out the window at 7 that morning, and there were people standing at the door.

Terry went to the door and asked them, "What's up? Can I help you?" Turns out they were already in line, waiting for the beer. "I was . . . " he began, then grinned and shook his head. "I mean, what were they doing? I offered them a cup of coffee and kept brewing." At 11, the doors opened and it was madness. Three hundred 750-milliliter bottles sold out in twenty minutes, at $20 each. The GABF gold medal Terry won for his Beekeeper barrel-aged sour in late 2008 really lit the beer geek beacon at the Bullfrog.

He's stoking the flames with a barrel-aging program that takes advantage of the leftover flavors in bourbon and wine barrels, the wood flavors in new French oak barrels, and the microflora in used barrels, the stuff that makes sour or brett beers with the complex flavors the *über*-geekerie love. Okay, I like them, too: Terry sampled me on his Magic Beans, a sour chocolate beer, which sounds horrible but tasted like a revelation, an amazing blend of flavors and sensations.

He also runs the absolutely insane Kegs Gone Wild program at the brewery. He takes the kegs that have held the sour or brett beers from the barrel program and, without cleaning them, puts other beers in the kegs: the Billtown Blonde, the Smoked Porter, even the Edgar IPA. "I was nervous about using the kegs after having the wild beers in them," Terry said, "so I just went ahead and tried the wild thing, and it's turned into a beast. It's an insane risk, and it still is; the beers are in there for a year. But the owners don't even blink anymore."

The Pick: Old Toad Barleywine isn't on that often, but when it is, it's a big malty fist inside a smooth-as-silk glove, like sweet oil on the tongue. Every day? Tough call, but I'll go with Edgar. Even I like a good hoppy IPA sometimes, and this is a good . . . hoppy IPA.

The stuff's brilliant—if you like that kind of thing—and people come to Williamsport just to drink it. But the other beers are great as well. The Smoked Porter is smoked just so, tasty but not overpowering. Edgar IPA is in the bright, hops-crisp Pacific Northwest style, very popular and easy to love. The Double Coffee Stout—my nightcap after a long day of beer travel—was as intense as any coffee beer I've ever had.

It's not just the beer, though. The Bullfrog has the touches, the menu, the attitude that makes it one of my favorites. The doubled beer boards are still there: Blackboards hang from the ceiling with the current house beers and upcoming events written on them, and someone cleverly writes backward on the backside of the slates so that they are legible in the large back mirror! The tap handles are hand-carved by a local woodworker. My favorite is the one for the root beer—simply a spreading root, sanded and polished.

From the gleaming brewkettle to the hand-carved taps, Bullfrog is a brewpub that would look good anywhere. With other breweries popping up in the old "Beermuda Triangle" (two in town, and more down the river and over the line in New York), this has become one of the hottest beer spots in the Keystone State.

Opened: August 1996.
Owners: Bob, Harriet, and Steven Koch.
Brewers: Terry Hawbaker, head brewer; Nate Saar.
System: 10-barrel Bohemian brewhouse, 1,000 barrels potential annual capacity.

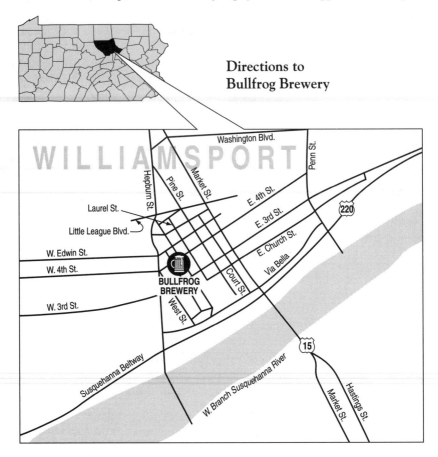

Directions to Bullfrog Brewery

2009 production: 700 barrels (est.).

Brewpub hours: Monday through Thursday, 11 AM to midnight; Friday and Saturday, 11 AM to 2 AM; Sunday, 9 AM (for brunch) to midnight.

Tours: The brewhouse is right there in the restaurant; step up and have a look.

Take-out beer: Growlers, sixtels (call ahead for availability), and limited-release 750-milliliter bottles.

Food: You'll find hand-cut steaks, innovative sandwiches, a range of salads, and fresh seafood. When possible, local providers are used for supplies. Bullfrog also serves some very healthy items, including a variety of vegetarian dishes.

Extras: Full liquor license, including a fine selection of wines and the area's most extensive selection of scotch, tequila, and bourbon. Private rooms available for parties and banquets. Lots of live music, several times a week (call or check Web site for schedule).

Special considerations: Kids welcome. Vegetarian meals served.

Parking: Limited on-street parking. Municipal parking lot one block south.

Lodging in the area: Genetti Hotel and Suites, 200 W. Fourth St., 570-326-6600; Holiday Inn, 100 Pine St., 570-327-8500; Peter Herdic Inn, 411 W. Fourth St., 570-326-0411.

Area attractions: The brewpub is right across the street from the **Community Arts Center** (220 W. Fourth St., 570-326-2424, www.caclive.com), featuring live music, movies, live theater, and cultural shows. Williamsport is the birthplace of Little League baseball and home of the annual Little League World Series in August. The **Peter J. McGovern Little League Museum** (next to the World Series field on Route 15, 570-326-3607, www.littleleague.org) has batting cages, Little League history, and major leaguers' Little League uniforms and equipment. Take a Susquehanna River ride on the **Hiawatha** (800-248-9287, www.ridehiawatha.com), a paddle-wheel riverboat. The **Taber Museum** (858 W. Fourth St., 570-326-3326, www.taber-museum.org) tells the story of Williamsport's heyday as a lumber boomtown and also has an art gallery and an outstanding exhibit of toy trains. As a former librarian, I have to tell you about the **Brodart Book Outlet** (500 Arch St., 570-326-6480), a supplier of leased library books that sells the returned titles for insanely low prices. In nearby Woolrich, you'll find the **Woolrich Mills** factory outlet (570-769-7401) and some outstanding bargains. If you go south from Williamsport on Route 15, stop at the scenic overlook, where you can see the whole valley stretching out for miles. Farther down the road near Allenwood is **Clyde Peeling's Reptiland** (800-REPTI-LAND, www.reptiland.com), a reptile zoo with snakes, lizards, tortoises, frogs, and alligators. It's a Pennsylvania classic. For more ideas, call the **Lycoming County Visitor Information Center** (800-358-9900).

Other area beer sites: As with other brewpub towns in this edition, Williamsport's bar scene has really come up a notch. **Kimball's Pub** (972 Second St., 570-322-1115) is a bit basic in décor, but the folks there are really friendly, the drafts are good, and the bottle selection will probably surprise you. The **Wegmans** in town (201 William St.) is one that has successfully navigated the PLCB's regulations to be able to sell beer. The **J Bar** at the Holiday Inn (see above) has upgraded their selection of draft beers. **Franco's Lounge** (12 W. Fourth St., 570-327-1840) has excellent fresh-made food, smart service, and a selection of wines and beers that draws me in every time. **Rumrunner's** (341 Market St., 570-322-0303) has live music, solid Italian food and seafood . . . and about 105 different rums, some of them pretty awesome. They've got the fruity, spicy stuff you see everywhere; try some of the excellent aged rums. The bar at the **Genetti Hotel** (see above) is a bit plush, but the taps are sound . . . and with the Bullfrog a block away in one direction and Franco's two blocks the other way, you've got yourself a pubcrawl going.

Bavarian Barbarian Brewing Company

429 West Third Street, Williamsport, PA 17701
570-322-5050
www.bavarianbarbarian.com

Brewing kept knocking on Mike Hiller's door, but when he answered, it was only to let brewing in for a visit. He had other plans.

"I worked at Legend Brewing in Richmond from 1997 to 2001," he told me. "I hadn't really been big into beer. I just took the job to support an acting career." He sold beer for a year with Legend's distribution company, then took a job in the brewery.

He liked it. "There was a great crew of brewers there," he said, "and I'm a creative person. I like making something with my hands and then watching people enjoy it. I liked going up into the taproom and seeing people drink the beer I'd been making."

Mike's wife, Kira, got accepted at Harvard for a graduate program, and they decided that was too good to pass up. They moved to Boston, where brewing knocked again. Mike picked up a job working part-time at Cambridge Brewing with Will Meyers, yet another opportunity many wannabe brewers would sell an organ to get.

But not Mike: He took work as a welder and carpenter for a scenery company. "I welded the cockpit of the *Millennium Falcon* for a Star Wars exhibit that's still out there," he said. He still missed brewing

Beers brewed: Year-round: Hammerin' Ale, Headbangerz Brown Ale, 2X4 IPA, Steel Drivin' Stout. Seasonals: Square Feet Wheat, Hard Times Belgian Farmhouse Ale, Weldspatter IPA, First Snow Ale.

a bit, so he cobbled together a homebrewing setup from two turkey deep fryers. That satisfied him.

Then brewing broke down the door and stormed into Mike's life in the form of *Brewing Up a Business*, Sam Calagione's book about starting Dogfish Head Brewing. "I read that book in two days," Mike said, "and then I met Sam at an event in Boston. I talked to him as much as I could, and he gave me his card and said, 'Call me with questions.' It inspired me."

Mike worked on a business plan for nine months, then shopped it around here in his hometown. He found investors, got the building and the equipment together, and started making beer under the Bavarian Barbarian name.

About that name . . . "I found out that Hiller was a Bavarian name," Mike said, "and I had long hair and a beard at the time; I looked like a barbarian. Besides, Bavarian Barbarian—it's got alliteration *and* it rhymes!" Maybe, but it's not that easy to say after you've had a few.

He's got very definite ideas about why he's not running a brewpub. "I can take criticism on the beer, I love it," he said. "But food, I don't care about that, so I couldn't take criticism on it well. We're brewing for the people here, and we take the beer to where they are, rather than them coming to me.

"That's why we make the beers we make," he continued. "Brown ale, wheat, Hammerin' Ale . . . again, it's the people's beer, more accessible to people who aren't beer geeks. People want a West Coast–style IPA, so we're working on that [the 2X4 IPA is the result]. It's a broader market. I want to do beers no one else does, without being extreme about it. It's working okay here; it's time to push out."

All that said, he does have the brewery open so the people can come to him. There's a tasting room, the Horde Room, a little oasis of comfort off to one side of the huge open space that's the brewery, with a bar, couches, carpet, music. When you look at it, there's a strong resemblance to the theater set of a one-man show, a room with an open side. Maybe it's Mike's acting career, knocking at the brewery door.

More likely, it's just a reflection of that big, open space. Brewing's moved in, and Mike Hiller hasn't been the same since. Sample his obsession.

Opened: July 1, 2007.
Owners: Kira Gay and Mike Hiller.

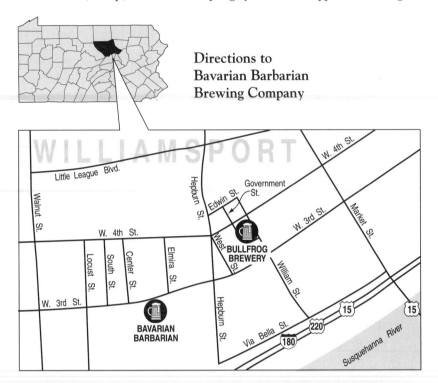

Directions to Bavarian Barbarian Brewing Company

Brewer: Mike Hiller.

System: 10-barrel Stromberg Systems brewhouse, 1,000 barrels annual capacity.

2009 production: 300 barrels.

Brewpub hours: The Horde Room is open Tuesday through Thursday 2 to 6 PM; Friday 2 to 8 PM; and Saturday 9 AM to 8 PM, with free samples.

Tours: Mike has suspended tours for the time being; check the Web site for updates. The brewery can be observed from the Horde Room.

Take-out beer: Growlers and cases of 22-ounce bottles available for take-out in the tasting room.

Special considerations: The brewery has no A/C in the summer and limited heat in the winter, so dress appropriately. Kids are welcome, accompanied by an adult.

Parking: On-street parking.

Lodging in the area, Area attractions, Other area beer sites: See Bullfrog on pages 237–38.

Abbey Wright Brewing at the Valley Inn

204 Valley Street, Williamsport, PA 17702
570-326-3383
www.thevalley-inn.com

You have to make some decisions when you get here. First, are you in Williamsport, South Williamsport, or Duboistown? I've seen all three towns associated with this place, and the post office makes no distinction in the zip code. The locals call it Mosquito Valley, just to add to the confusion.

Next, you have to decide if you're looking for the Valley Inn or Abbey Wright Brewing. Because if you're looking for Abbey Wright, you won't see any evidence of it on the outside. This place has been the Valley Inn for quite a bit longer, about twenty years, and that's what everyone knows.

Then once you get inside, it's more decisions. Do you want house beer or one of the twenty-two taps of guest beers (mostly mainstream, but craft, too), are you going to sit at the bar or a table, shoot pool or not . . . the usual bar decisions.

And then there's the really important decision: How do you want your wings? There's Mild, Hot, Extra Hot, Suicide, Cajun, Teriyaki, Italian, BBQ, BBQ Hot, Garlic, Gold & Tangy, and Gold & Tangy Hot, so you've got some thinking to do before you order. I dove into the BBQ Hot, and they were some of the best wings I'd had in a long time. The Valley Inn gets them fresh, never frozen, and they were juicy.

"We'll sell a lot of wings tonight," Jim Wright told me as we stood in the brewery, where he was fiddling with a pump. "Hundreds of pounds. People like Wing Night." Tuesday and Thursday are Wing Nights, when wings are on sale for 15 cents each. (Take my advice—pay extra for the big wings. Lots of meat on those bad boys!)

That's the story here at the Valley Inn. This is a bar, first and foremost, with a good pubby menu (it's

Beers brewed: Alpha Deuce IPA, Irish Red, Cold Hop Pale Ale, Saison, Nut Brown Ale, Porter, Kosmic Kölsch. Seasonal: Vanilla Latte Stout, Raz-Berry Wheat.

The Pick: The Nut Brown Ale was the beer I liked when I first visited, and Jim's was good, too: smooth, not overly sweet, pint-drinkable, just the way you want it to be.

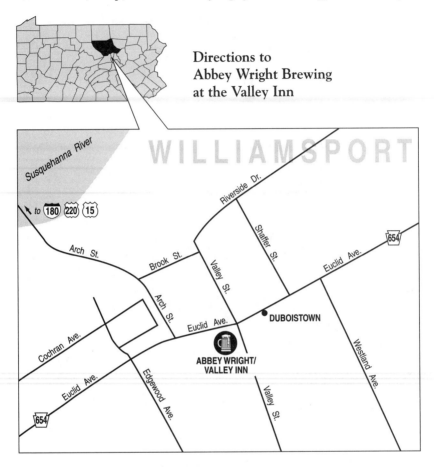

Directions to
Abbey Wright Brewing
at the Valley Inn

never going to get a medal from the American Heart Association, but if you're at Wing Night, you have to have known that going in). Jim and Ellen Wright ("Abbey Wright" is from Ellen's maiden name and Jim's name) told me about how they've tried to make it a place where people feel welcome and make the banquet hall a special place for celebrations, from weddings to funerals and all the happy times in between. The banquet hall was really nice; they took me in during a wedding, and I almost got swept up in the celebration by a couple of high-spirited bridesmaids.

The house-brewed beer is a sideline. Most of the regulars don't drink it or know much about it. That's fine with Jim. "It's a hobby," he said. "It's maybe 1 or 2 percent of my beer sales. I had hired a brewer at first, but that just didn't work out. It didn't make sense to have someone doing it when we weren't selling that much."

I kind of admire Jim for not abandoning the brewery or selling it; he could probably get a good price right now in this tight market for used brewery equipment. Other places have. But Jim's doing something he likes doing. "It's fun and I'm getting better at it. I dumped two of my first six batches," he admitted. "I can afford to do that, but I couldn't afford to sell those two!"

Sitting at the bar, eating those big, old wings and sipping a pint of porter, I'm thinking that being a bar first and a brewery second . . . isn't so bad once in a while. There's lots of ways to skin the craft-brewing cat, and this is just another.

Opened: May 2006.

Owners: Jim and Ellen Wright.

Brewer: Jim Wright.

System: 7-barrel Newlands brewhouse, 1,000 barrels annual capacity.

2009 production: 120 barrels (est.).

Brewpub hours: Seven days a week, 11:30 AM to 2 AM. Call about major holidays.

Tours: If you see Jim, ask. Don't do what I did and just walk into the brewery!

Take-out beer: Growlers ($2 off on Fridays).

Food: Well-done bar food. In addition to the excellent wings, they have fresh-cut fries that are so good you should skip the ketchup, plus the Williamsport sandwich, called the Cosmo, a toasted cheese sandwich with lettuce and tomato. This simple description doesn't do it justice; get one and find out what it's about.

Extras: Wing Night on Tuesdays and Thursdays; $1.99 burgers and fries on Wednesdays; live music on Fridays. Large banquet room. The kitchen is very flexible about working with your recipes.

Special considerations: Kids welcome during regular dining hours. Even a bar-food menu can have vegetarian meals; you'll find salads, pizzas, veggie burgers, and the Cheese Cosmo.

Parking: Large off-street lot.

Lodging in the area, Area attractions, Other area beer sites: See Bullfrog on pages 237–38.

Selin's Grove Brewing Company

121 North Market Street, Selinsgrove, PA 17870
570-374-7308
www.selinsgrovebrewing.com

What was once a novelty in this small Susquehanna town—a bar where they make their own beer and don't let you smoke—has become normal. "People know where we are," co-owner/cobrewer Heather McNabb said. "We're part of people's lives, well knitted into the community."

It's no surprise. Selin's Grove was about knitting people together from the beginning. Right away, I liked the low-volume background music and lack of television. Heather and Steve Leason said they wanted people to "practice the art of communication," something that all too many pubs make impossible. It's worked really well.

The couple started out homebrewing in Maine, then moved to Colorado, where they worked for the burgeoning New Belgium brewery for two years. With that experience, they came to the Susquehanna Valley to make their dream of a small brewpub happen. The brewpub occupies the basement of the Snyder mansion, which until recently was run as a museum attraction by Heather's parents. "We're here because we could afford it," Heather cheerfully admitted.

Steve and Heather are like that. They work with what they have to get the results they want. They don't—*can't*—throw money at every problem, so a lot of thought goes into everything. They started brewing on a Frankenstein-like 3-barrel brewhouse, cobbled together from various reused stainless tanks and vessels, because that's what they had. With that much brewing experience between them, though, the size of the system didn't matter.

They did eventually move brewing out of the house (they had to; the steam and heat weren't good for the old building) into an eighty-year-old garage

Beers brewed: Year-round: Captain Selin's Cream Ale, Scottish Ale, I.P.A., Stealth Triple, White Horse Porter, Organic Baltic Porter, Organic Shade Mountain Oatmeal Stout, and one of three fruit beers: Kriek, Saison de Peach, or Framboise. Seasonals: Wit, Market Street Fest Lager, Wilder's Hefe Weizen, S.N.A.F.U. I.P.A., Olde Frosty IPA, Snake Drive Stout, Razzmerry, Pilsner, Mai-Bock, St. Fillian's Barleywine, Solstice Dubbel, Hoppy Monk, Hop Nouveau, and the list is still growing; call for current taps. Selin's Grove has two beer engines and cask-conditions some of its beers for hand dispense.

in the back, on a used 7-barrel system. On New Year's Day 2009, the kettle cracked. "It was a great start to our thirteenth year!" Heather said. "We got a guy in to weld it, and the cracks just spiderwebbed out. Panic! We got another welder, who laid big patches on it, and that held till we got the new one. My advice to a starting brewer: Get used tanks, you can get a used mash tun and pumps, but get a new kettle—it's the heart of the brewery." Their new direct-fire kettle was made to their design by Sharpsville Container in western Pennsylvania.

The Pick: The Shade Mountain Oatmeal Stout is a lighter-bodied yet intensely flavored stout, possessed of smooth body with a real roasted barley bite—a great all-around stout. The St. Fillian's is very broad and full of malt, with a pleasing touch of butterscotch, fruitiness, and alcohol heat, and it only gets better as it ages. The Kriek is just phenomenal, like eating a sour cherry pie. Once I tasted it, I knew I was leaving the pub with a growler of that beer, one way or another.

It was all worth it, because the beer is knock-your-socks-off stuff. Heather and Steve both brew, and it's impossible to tell who brews which beer. ("Steve's a more meticulous brewer," Heather said. "I'm very relaxed.") I tried nine beers the first time I visited Selin's Grove (the plain black taps are marked with masking tape and marker), and seven of them were exceptional. My notes have phrases like "reaches out and grabs you" (Old Trail ESB), "real beer" (Cream Ale), and "Wattabeer! Smooth and silky, yet fathoms deep" (Shade Mountain Oatmeal Stout).

It hasn't changed in thirteen years. I had a glass of the Framboise this time, and it was rich, fruity, and a bit nutty. "Don't try this unless you want to be assaulted by fruit," I wrote. I once took a growler of Selin's Grove Kriek to a beer event at the Grey Lodge Pub in Philly, and people got on their knees and bowed down to the beer.

I asked Heather how they got all that fruit flavor into the beers. "It's proprietary," she said and frowned, and I thought it was because she hated how corporate that sounded. Then she sighed, and added, "There's puree and whole fruit, that's part of the equation. But there's so much waste. Costs aren't as important at this scale; we just look the other way and do what we want, and it works out. You do it to make good beer, and if it brings people in, that's great; we don't spend the money on advertising."

The food's pretty great here, too. Sara Maul ("The keystone," Heather called her. "She's been here since the first year.") and Scott Bordner are passionate about food and fit well in the brewpub's vibe. The kitchen is tiny but as tightly organized as a ship's galley, and only the necessary appliances fit in. "Just because it's a micro*brewery* doesn't mean you have to have a micro*wave*," Steve noted acerbically, and I applaud the sentiment.

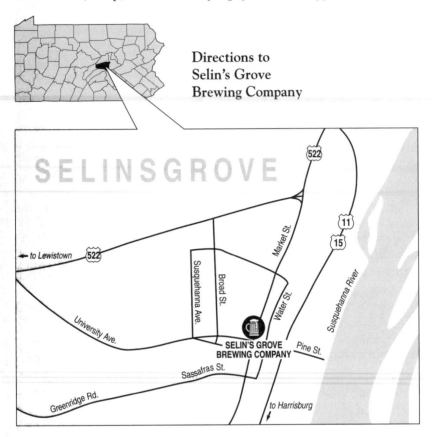

Directions to
Selin's Grove
Brewing Company

I also applaud how they have tried to use local foods wherever possible, something that naturally fits into the whole idea of a brewpub. Bread is from a local bakery, there's a plate of local cheeses, and a lot of local produce is used in the summer. "People want to have a connection with who's making the stuff they put in their mouths," Heather said.

If you wondered about the dog and treadmill symbol for the brewpub, it's all about Selinsgrove. When Steve and Heather decided to open here, they delved into Selinsgrove history, looking for evidence of a brewing heritage. They came across a few mentions but were more interested in something else they found. A man named Mathias App had a distillery in Selinsgrove in the early 1800s. He had a water pump at the distillery that was powered by stray dogs in a wheel, and he paid small boys to catch dogs for him. Heather and Steve liked this image of a dog-powered distillery so much that they made it the symbol of the brewery.

A quirky symbol, beers where they don't count the cost, a kitchen the size of a walk-in closet that produces fresh delicious food from local ingredients, twelve great beers, a pub "too small to have darts"—and all of it tucked into the cellar of a historic mansion in a small town by a river. Is it any wonder it's knitted into people's lives?

Opened: December 21, 1996.

Owners: Steven Leason, Heather McNabb.

Brewers: Steven Leason, Heather McNabb ("Mostly as helper now," she said).

System: 8.5-barrel custom-fabricated (in Pennsylvania) brewhouse, 380 barrels potential annual capacity.

2009 production: 300 barrels.

Brewpub hours: Wednesday and Thursday, 11:30 AM to 11 PM; Friday and Saturday, 11:30 AM to midnight; Sunday, 11:30 AM to 8 PM. Closed Monday and Tuesday.

Tours: By appointment; please e-mail through the Web site.

Take-out beer: Growlers.

Food: Sandwiches, from-scratch soups, and salads make up the bulk of the menu, along with one weekly hot entrée special. The emphasis is on healthy, great-tasting food, sourced locally when possible, and with vegetarian options. Desserts are from Emma's, down the street, run by former Selin's Grove cook Emma Renninger. A very good house-made root beer, organic coffees, and teas round out the menu for kids and nondrinkers.

Extras: Selection of Pennsylvania wines (Mt. Nittany, Brookmere, Shade Mountain) available, plus Keewaydin Cider from Otto's owner, Charlie Schnable. Live music every other week: bluegrass, swing, folk, blues, and much more; call for schedule. Assorted books, magazines, tavern puzzles, backgammon, and chess. Anniversary party on the winter solstice is a special night.

Special considerations: Kids welcome. Many vegetarian meals available, including selections to suit full vegans.

Parking: The entrance to the brewpub is actually in the rear, not on Market Street. Parking is available on Market, then you simply walk through the side garden to the rear entrance. There is also a parking lot off Strawberry Alley.

Lodging in the area: Selinsgrove Inn, 214 N. Market St., an easy walk to the brewpub, 866-375-1700; Potteiger House B&B, 8 W. Chestnut St., half a block from brewpub, 570-374-0415; Country Hearth, 710 S. Route 11/15, 570-374-8880.

Area attractions: Small museums and restored homes abound in the central Susquehanna Valley. The ***Mifflinburg Buggy Museum*** (523

Green St., Mifflinburg, 570-966-1355; www.buggymuseum.org) displays carriage-making techniques; open Thursday through Sunday from April through October. The **Joseph Priestley House** (472 Priestley Avenue, Northumberland, 570-473-9474, www.joseph priestleyhouse.org), the home of a wide-ranging thinker who discovered oxygen, founded the Unitarian Church in America, and influenced the writing of the Constitution, has been restored for visits. For more outdoorsy fun, the Susquehanna has plenty of boat ramps; **Middle Creek Lake**, south of Selinsgrove, is a stocked fishing lake, and state game lands are scattered along the river. **Creekside Ventures** (617 S. Market St., Selinsgrove, 570-374-4653, www.creek sideventuresllc.com) offers canoe and kayak rentals, with pickup service and lodging.

Other area beer sites: BJ's, just one block from the brewpub (17 N. Market), is a steak and rib restaurant with several micros on tap. **McGuigan's Public House** (266 Market St., Sunbury, 570-286-5002) is a lovingly restored corner bar with a very good selection of bottles, small but interesting tap offerings, and a shockingly good whiskey selection. **Brasserie Louis**, up the river in Lewisburg (101 Market St., 570-524-5559), is high-end dining, but the bar has a surprising selection of about a dozen Pennsylvania craft beers. **Old Forge Brewing** in Danville (see next listing) is quite close as well.

Old Forge Brewing Company

282 Mill Street, Danville, PA 17821
570-275-8151
www.oldforgebrewingcompany.com

OLD FORGE
BREWiNG COMPANY

The first time I visited Old Forge was only three months after they opened, at the end of a long day of brewery visits with Mike "Scoats" Scotese, the owner of the Grey Lodge Pub in Northeast Philadelphia. We were lining up beers for an Upstate Beer Dinner we were doing at the Lodge as part of Philly Beer Week, and we'd sampled beers at One

Guy (as Berwick Brewing was then known), Bull-frog, Bavarian, and Elk Creek. I knew that Damien Malfara was a new brewer, in a new location, and I guess we had low expectations.

It's not an overstatement to say that we were blown away, by both the beer and the food. Damien's alt was spot-on; he asked for comments, and I think the only thing I said was "Make more." It was one of the best sets of sample beers from a new brewpub I can remember. We split a chicken quesadilla that was wonderful: tasty, juicy beer-marinated chicken, gooey melted locally made cheese, bits of meaty bacon, and a surprising mix of sautéed apples and leeks. It was not just well executed, it was imaginative.

I've been back, and I believe that combination might be Old Forge's signature, along with a real integration with a community of surprising talents. You'll notice one example as soon as you walk in the door: the big umbrella-like mug rack for the overflow of the brewpub's mug club. It's not just keeping the mugs hung up out of the way, it's intriguingly decorated, it spins (slowly!), and it's a conversation piece. That's the work of Keith Kocher, of Lightstreet Custom Woodworking, who also did the mug rack behind the bar, the bar itself, the booths, the tables, and the slick shelves upstairs. The mugs on the racks, as well as the plates and bowls, were made at M. Hart Pottery by Mike Hart. J. Mark Irwin, local sculptor at the Irwin Sculpture Studio, did the tap handles. All imaginative and well executed.

Damien is a big supporter of personal craftsmanship and of not set-tling for the easy, generic choices. "It's about working with your hands, the combination of art and science," he said, which is where the Old Forge name came from. "I don't go to chain restaurants. I'll take a risk, maybe get a bad meal sometimes, to take a chance on something amazing."

He seems like a natural for a brewpub, doesn't he? But it found him, not the other way around. Damien was selling scientific instruments in 2005, based in Philadelphia, where he grew up. He was married to Maria. He liked good beer, and there was plenty in Philly. Things were good. Then Maria got accepted at Bloomsburg University for graduate work in education for the deaf, so they moved.

"It was great, she could walk to school," Damien said, and he could still travel for his job. "But driving to Selin's Grove and the Bullfrog for a beer was tough! Then I started thinking that with the university, and Geisinger [Health System in Danville], that might be a good opportunity. I started looking for properties and upped my homebrewing game. I put a deadline on it: We had to be open by the end of 2008."

He made the deadline by twenty-six days, largely because the guy who took their wedding pictures, Gordon Wenzel, owned the building they're in now. They'd met, Damien had looked at some spots but nothing worked. Then Gordon called: This property, which was a Mexican restaurant, was available.

"We took it and kept the kitchen," said Damien. "It sped up the process a lot and saved us a ton of money, which let me buy new brewing equipment. Only I got three fermenters when I wanted four; I thought I needed four. Turns out I was right, but what I really need is space. We're looking at some options for that." He's since secured some more space from Gordon; enough to add that fourth fermenter (and 30 more seats, bringing the total to about 100).

Thing is, what Damien had been planning was a production brewery. "I had no restaurant experience," he said. "But when the opportunity came up, it was too good to miss, and this is a great way to test recipes. You can actually talk to people about the beers while they're drinking them. We can make it on something this size, and we're saving. We might open a production brewery down the road a while, probably in Danville. But not here and not now."

That's okay, because here and now's pretty good for local folks and beer travelers (it's not far off I-80 at all). Old Forge isn't big but it has gotten uniformly good reviews from beer enthusiasts who've stopped in. The opportunities for fresh beer continue to grow along the Appalachian ridge, in imaginative and well-executed ways.

The Pick: The first time I visited, Damien caught me not long after I'd been in Düsseldorf drinking *altbier*, and his Old Forge Alt was closer than many other American alts I've had—a lot closer. Malty-dry, fairly big but drinkable, and a clinching bitterness in the finish. Very nicely done, indeed.

Opened: December 2008.
Owners: Damien and Maria Malfara.
Brewer: Damien Malfara.
System: 5-barrel Premier Stainless, 750 barrels annual capacity.
2009 production: 300 barrels.
Brewpub hours: Tuesday through Thursday, 11 AM to 10 PM; Friday and Saturday, 11 AM to midnight. Closed Sunday and Monday.
Tours: The brewhouse is right there in the front window; have a look!
Take-out beer: Growlers.
Food: The emphasis is on fresh and local, like the selection of grilled cheese sandwiches made with local cheese on bread from the City Girl Bakery just up the street (a great coffeeshop for breakfast, by the

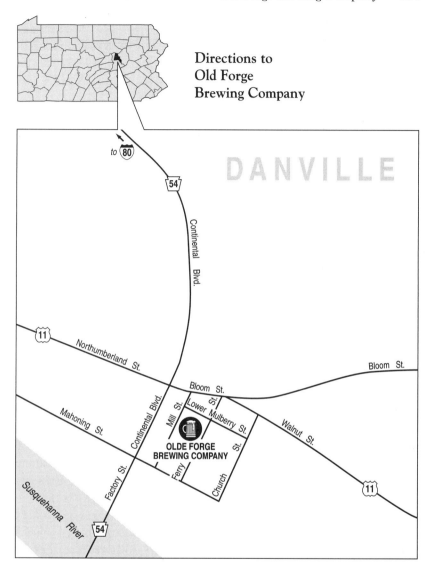

Directions to Old Forge Brewing Company

way), fresh produce in season from Mad Dog Farms in Bloomsburg, and the delicious soft pretzels from D&L Bakery in Mifflinburg. "We have a small freezer," said Damien. "Our cooks can't cheat!"

Extras: Live music every Thursday night, occasionally on other nights; check Web site for schedule. Free Wi-Fi provided. No TVs anywhere.

Special considerations: Kids welcome; a children's menu is offered. Vegetarian meals available.

Parking: On-street and nearby municipal lot.

Lodging in the area: Pine Barn Inn, 1 Pine Barn Place (walking distance), 570-275-2071; The Doctor's Inn, 101 W. Market St., 570-275-1821; Days Inn, 50 Sheraton Rd., Danville, 570-275-5510; Knoebels Grove Campground at Knoebels Amusement Resort, 391 Knoebels Blvd., Elysburg, 570-672-9555.

Area attractions: Danville has a nicely recovering downtown; I like just walking along Mill Street. As mentioned above, the **City Girl Bakery** is just up on the corner (252 Mill St.) and is open at 8:30 with exceptional coffee and fresh bread and pastries. **T and J Train Junction** is just two doors down (290 Mill St., 570-850-1284) and has a great selection of model railroad equipment, including a small operating layout; it's a fun place to browse with your kids. If you really want to be a hero to the kids, take them to **Knoebel's Amusement Resort** (391 Knoebels Blvd., Elysburg, 800-487-4386; www .knoebels.com), only fifteen minutes away. It's not expensive (free admission, you pay by the ride), you can bring food in (or buy theirs, which is delicious) and picnic, you can swim, you can even camp there. My kids love it and so do a lot of others; it was recently rated the fourth-best amusement park in the world, and its Phoenix coaster was rated fourth-best wooden coaster. Ever seen one of those German Army motorcycle half-tracks from World War II and assumed they were a joke? They're not, and you can see one at **Bill's Old Bike Barn** (7145 Columbia Blvd., Bloomsburg, 570-759-7030, www.billsbikebarn.com), along with more than a hundred other restored motorcycles and memorabilia from the 1939 New York World's Fair. The power company PPL Corporation has parks on company land across eastern Pennsylvania; one, **Montour Preserve** (570-437-3131, www.pplweb.com/montour+preserve), is not far from Danville and offers hiking, an actively supported geocaching program, fishing, and boating (electric motors only). Other beautiful parks are **Ricketts Glen State Park** and the **Weiser State Forest**. See the listings for Copper Kettle on pages 232–33 and Bullfrog on pages 237–38 for more suggestions.

Other area beer sites: See Copper Kettle and Bullfrog. As Damien said, "We need more!"

Berwick Brewing Company

**328 West Front Street
Berwick, PA 18603
570-752-4313
www.berwickbrewing.com**

Berwick Brewing goes back to the fall of 2009, when One Guy Brewing became Berwick Brewing after Tom Clark formally joined Guy Hagner as a partner. Actually, it goes back to early 2008, when Guy opened the doors of One Guy. (I was involved—a little—even earlier than that; my kids and I put in two days of work to help Guy get the brewery going. Full disclosure: we were paid in pizza.) Before *that*, Guy was the brewer-manager at Franconia Brewing in Mountain Top, which closed after less than a year. Tom, meanwhile, had opened Red Bank Brewing in New Jersey about the same time, which also closed . . . about the same time.

But Tom and Guy go back much, much further than that. Tom Clark has been involved with some of the earliest names in eastern craft brewing. After a college semester in the UK that made him "a confirmed ale drinker," he fell into brewing. He got a job at the Manhattan Brewery, met Jay Misson at the Vernon Valley brewpub, and eventually opened a homebrew shop in Red Bank, selling malt to Dave Hoffman, who would open Climax Brewing in New Jersey, and Tom Baker (see the entry for Earth Bread + Brewery).

That's about the time he met Guy Hagner. Guy had been at Pabst's New Jersey brewery just before it closed. He parlayed that into a job at Dixie Brewing in New Orleans. He worked at The Lion after that, and then got the idea for Franconia Brewing. It maybe wasn't the best idea; the collapse of Franconia left Guy and his family deep in personal debt. He scraped by for the next few years on part-time brewing jobs, selling CDs on eBay, and working for Tom, taking apart closed breweries in the United States and Germany.

Tom had continued to brew, and then his sideline of finding and reselling used brewing equipment

Beers brewed: Regulars: Berwick Lager, Front Street Wheat, Bill's Porter, Hondo Keller Bier, Atomic Punk IPA. Seasonals: Peach Wheat, Oktoberfest, Barley Town Stout (nitro). Rotating specials: Raspberry Imperial Porter, Bourbon-Barrel Imperial Stout, Molly's Best Brown Ale, Dunkelweizen, Pils, Cinnamon Boldy . . . and more coming.

turned into a full-time business. He and Guy accumulated spare bits of equipment that might be useful down the road: tanks, pumps, and the like. The new brewhouse at Berwick mostly came out of that Pabst brewery where Guy had worked. (Tom worked there as a security guard once it closed, taking most of his pay in parts.)

The Pick: Hondo kicks butt. Keller Bier literally means "cellar beer," but what it really means is unfiltered beer, and unfiltered beer means more flavor, fuller body . . . *better* beer! Hondo is all that, and well made to boot. It's always my second beer, after whatever's new.

"Then Guy started talking about this project," Tom said, "and we looked at some buildings." "This project" was One Guy Brewing, a very small-scale brewery that Guy said he managed to put together for under $100,000. After Franconia, Guy had an understandable dread of debt and was determined to open with as little owed as possible.

But open he did, running solo (hence the One Guy Brewing name) with an odd business model that was neither brewpub nor production brewery. Guy figured to do mostly packaging—small kegs, growlers, and a small number of returnable bottles for local customers—with a rough taproom, serving beer by the glass, along with pretzels and hot dogs.

Berwick had other ideas. The taproom became a popular spot, even with limited hours, and most of the beer sold there. "This is bringing people back to Berwick," Guy said, "and Berwick sees it." There are good jobs in Berwick—the nuclear power plant upriver, Berwick Offray (the world's largest manufacturers of ribbons and the largest employer in Columbia County), and Wise snacks (where they make Cheez Doodles)—and people are happy to have a nearby place to go for craft beer.

Tom had loaned Guy some money close to the opening and helped him with the project. After the success of the opening, the landlord of the building asked Guy if he'd like to buy it. That's when Tom became Guy's partner. "Guy asked me in," Tom said, "and we bought the building. We had to; we needed to grow, and not just to 'the next level.' We needed to be able to pay ourselves."

Things moved into high gear, and One Guy became Berwick; there was more than one guy now! The rough taproom became a nicer place, partly as a result of the efforts of Tom's dad, Bill, who painted the German countryside murals you see there. (He also kept painting "BREW DARK BEER!" on the walls as he worked, and that's why there's a regular tap of Bill's Porter.) Then they added an outdoor beer garden with a great view of the Susquehanna River, expanded the taproom, put in a pizza oven, and opened a "music annex."

This is a big building, an old commercial bar, and one thing they have plenty of is room for expansion. By the time you read this, they will be running the new 7-barrel brewhouse, replacing the labor-intensive

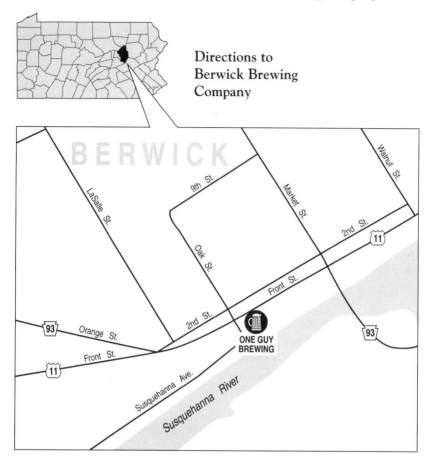

Directions to Berwick Brewing Company

1.5-barrel system Guy had cobbled together. The heat and steam are all generated by clean-burning Pennsylvania anthracite coal.

"The town has welcomed this," said Tom. "We took a building that would have been condemned and turned it into an attraction, a growing business. I think we'll outgrow the new brewery in a year. I'd love to be at 5,000 barrels in three years." The returnable bottles are back on the agenda, and Tom wants to bring in the half-liter/twenty-bottle crate that's standard for beer in Germany.

Berwick's not easy to get to. Once you get off I-80, you have to make a long climb over the mountain, drive through the town of Nescopeck, cross the river, and then find the brewery. Once you get there, though . . . you'll find it was worth the trip. Don't just make it once; there's new stuff happening all the time.

Opened: January 2008.
Owners: Tom Clark, Guy Hagner.

Brewers: Tom Clark, Guy Hagner, Steve Zourides, Tom Feeley, Kyle Kalanick.

System: 7-barrel custom-fabricated brewhouse, 1,000+ barrels annual capacity (est.).

2009 production: 250 barrels.

Brewpub hours: Tuesday through Friday, 3 to 11 PM; Saturday, 1 to 11 PM; Sunday, 1 to 7 PM. Closed Monday.

Tours: By appointment.

Take-out beer: Growlers.

Food: Berwick Brewing is currently cash-only; plan accordingly. The menu, with exceptions on special fest days—brats for Oktoberfest, corned beef and cabbage on St. Patrick's—is pizza, really excellent pizza. Try the Steve-o's Inferno, if you think you're man enough. I managed one slice before my tongue melted. If you see a sign saying "soupies" are available, get that pizza; they're made with a unique oil-cured, flat sausage from the Sunbury area.

Extras: Live music most weekends. The beer garden has a great view of the Susquehanna River and really captures a true German feel.

Special considerations: Kids welcome; let them try the Big Ben's blue birch beer from local Catawissa Bottling. Vegetarian pizzas available (the Margherita is great in the summer, with fresh basil grown in the beer garden).

Parking: On-street and off-street lot.

Lodging in the area: The White Birch Inn B&B, 1303 Market St., Berwick, 570-759-8251; The Inn at Turkey Hill, 991 Central Rd., Bloomsburg, 570-387-1500.

Area attractions: *Berwick Offray* has a ribbon outlet (2017 W. Front St., 570-784-1985) with a huge assortment; best to call ahead for open hours. The power company PPL Corporation runs the *Susquehanna Energy Information Center* (634 Salem Blvd., Berwick, 866-832-3312, www.pplweb.com: search on SEIC), down the hill from the nuclear power plant, to "take the mystery out of nuclear power." As nuke plants enjoy a muted renaissance in these green times, it's a good time to learn about them. PPL also maintains a number of environmental refuges near their plants; the *Susquehanna Riverlands* (same contact information) offers hiking, picnicking, and fishing. See the listing for Old Forge on page 252 for more suggestions.

Other area beer sites: The *Inn at Turkey Hill* (991 Central Rd., Bloomsburg, 570-387-1500) may be adding a brewery, and even if they don't, it's a good stop. Nothing else notable within half an hour, other than Old Forge in Danville.

Breaker Brewing Company

50 Powell Street, Plains, PA 18705
570-392-9078
www.breakerbrewingcompany.com

Mark Lehman and Chris Miller have found fame—of a sort—in being small. The two men and the brewery they built in Chris's garage were featured in an *All About Beer* magazine story on nanobreweries, and the phone has been ringing off the hook ever since.

Not really. "We're getting one or two e-mails every week from guys who are interested in starting a nanobrewery," said Chris. "After the article came out, they started calling, too. Hey, guys, one thing you have to know about a nanobrewery is that you don't have a lot of time! Specific questions are okay, we want to help, but don't ask us for our whole plan. We don't really want to give it all away, and our plan probably wouldn't work for you anyway."

That's for sure. Chris and Mark aren't just any pair of homebrewers; they are do-it-yourself engineers without fear. The engineer part is what they still do now as day jobs—they're both engineers for Frontier Communications, the national telecommunications company—but the "without fear" part comes from when they both worked at a Volkswagen repair shop outside Hazleton.

"We both liked Volkswagens," Mark said. "This guy gave us jobs, and we worked on them all day. He made things work. He would do things like chain a car to a tree and drive it away to straighten the frame. That's where we learned "no fear." You need something done? Just do it. You can't do it? *Just do it.* No fear."

Look around the brewery in Chris's garage, and you can see it was a lesson they learned well. Their brewery is built around some 55-gallon stainless steel drums they bought at a scrap yard. (They have since upgraded to 100-gallon tanks; the originals went to another nanobrewery.) "We bought the parts and we put it together . . . slowly," said Chris. "It's our design, built right here. No kit, no plans,

Beers brewed: Year-round: Anthracite Ale, Goldies Blonde Ale, Olde King Coal Stout, Malty Maguire, I(heart)PA (IPA), Lunch Pail Ale. Seasonal: 16 Ton Imperial IPA, Goldies Strawberry Blond Ale, Pot Belly Pumpkin Ale, Belsnickler Ale, Quiet Canary Saison, Black Mariah.

and no loans." Their keg washer was built the same way, and when they decided to automate it, they used what they had: a cheap temperature probe from a supply catalog and the control panels off two old microwave ovens (with the door handles still on them).

They hand-bottle their seasonals in 22-ounce bottles, using homebrewing equipment, something Berkshire Brewing in Massachusetts did successfully for years on a much bigger scale. "We make all our labels on my home computer printer," Chris said with a grin. "There are ways to do this cheaply. You don't have to buy labels from printshops."

They're also smart enough to charge enough for their beer. At their size, the temptation is to sell cheaper because your labor costs aren't coming out of your pocket, just your free time. But their per-bottle costs are higher, and their beer is rarer—there just isn't that much of it to go around. They need to charge more, and they do. "No one's batting an eye," Mark said.

That's part of the opportunity Mark and Chris saw. "The craft beer market is exploding around here," Chris said. "Bars are putting more taps in, and they want more local beer. That's working in our favor, but we don't want to go too highbrow on them. We're telling them, 'Look, this is your beer—it's made right here in the Valley.' Plains Township is all for it; they want us to do well, they want us to expand and stay here when we do. There's a guy down at the offices who sends us commercial real estate listings he sees that might be good."

They're working on keeping those local links strong. The name Breaker is for coal breaker, the towering machines that broke up coal from local mines into chunks sized for homes and factories. "You couldn't go 5 miles around here without seeing one," Mark said. "Everyone worked in the mines. We've got our beer names linked to coal—Anthracite Ale, Olde King Coal, Malty Maguire, Lunch Pail Ale—and people love it."

The beer isn't just paint-by-numbers stuff getting by on local good-will for the cute, plucky brewery, either. They don't fit neatly into stylistic pigeonholes. The stout is brown, not black, and has a roasted bitterness tempered by a dry graham cracker note. Anthracite Ale is an ale but reminds you of a bock, yet it's got a hoppy edge. The only one that's kind of close is the I(heart)PA, and even it's not cautious.

"We're not trying to make what's already being made," Chris said. "Making the same thing, that's no fun. As long as we're brewing and

The Pick: I don't like picking seasonals, but Belsnickler— named for the Pennsylvania Dutch and Appalachian Christmas figure perhaps best described as "Santa Claus's evil twin"—is just too good to ignore. This handful of malts, yeasts, and Belgian sugars turned out as good as many Belgian ales I've had: spicy, sweet but dry on the end, with a hint of anise. Very impressive for a small, young brewery.

people like it, and we don't have to answer to anyone, no boss . . . that's great."

They've built a new, larger brewing system, with larger fermenters, and they're looking for a building or land so they can get out of the garage. "We're thinking about a pub," Chris allowed. "The margins are better. But we don't want to have to get that big loan. We still want to go slowly."

The Valley may not want to let them. Breaker may be another nanobrewery that won't get to stay nano much longer.

Opened: April 2009.
Owners: Chris Miller, Mark Lehman.
Brewers: Chris Miller, Mark Lehman.
System: 3-barrel custom-built brewhouse, built by Chris and Mark. "We could do about 300 barrels a year . . . downhill . . . in a hurricane."
2009 production: 60 barrels (est.).
Tours: Not allowed by zoning.
Take-out beer: Sixtels only; call for availability.
Parking: None; zoning again.
Lodging in the area, Area attractions, Other area beer sites: See The Lion on pages 16–18.

Barley Creek Brewing Company

Sullivan Trail and Camelback Road
Tannersville, PA 18372
570-629-9399
www.barleycreek.com

The Poconos may not have the biggest vertical drops or the deepest powder (or any powder), but they are the heart of a gorgeous region located close enough to several major urban areas to be an easy weekend trip for many people. You can ski in the Poconos without fighting your way through an airport with your skis or white-knuckling it up the interstate to New England with one ear cocked for the radar detector's whine. You can relax, get in your skiing, and still have time for a trip to Barley Creek.

Barley Creek has never stood still. You'd think they'd have it made, perched halfway up the side of Camelback Mountain, downhill from a big ski resort, uphill from The Crossings outlets. Why change something that's likely perfect? But after fifteen years, Trip Ruvane is still tinkering, still working on making Barley Creek bigger and better.

"I stay in it because I haven't got it right yet," he told me recently. "Almost! But not right. Look, our location on that road? It's great. But our location as an area? Real seasonal. Winter is a gold mine up here, we're packing them in. Summer is a silver mine, almost as good. The rest of the year, I try to figure out how to keep everyone employed."

Beers brewed: Year-round: Navigator Golden Ale, Angler Black Lager, Antler Brown Ale, Cliffhanger Light Ale, Rescue IPA. Seasonals: Iron Arm Belgian-style Witbier, Traveler Foreign Stout, Wanderlust Chocolate Porter, Intrepid Irish Red, Expedition Strong Ale, Mountaineer Mai Bock, Summerfest Lager, Discovery Amber Lager, Harvest Moon Oktoberfest, Old 99, Sullivan Trail Oatmeal Stout, Winterfest Lager.

Barley Creek is designed like a tall-peaked wooden ski chalet, airy and open with miles of overhead space. The stone foundation and cellar remain from the old farmhouse that was there. Upstairs, much of the exposed wood—solidly thick beams and paneling—was salvaged from old buildings, and a glass wall gives passing motorists a striking view of the brewery's tanks.

It's been changing since year one. The layout was changed first: The main bar was pushed out into the room and became an island. Then Trip began pushing at the edges. The building expanded into the parking lot (and why not, the lot was huge), then a deck was added. Then came the whiffleball stadium—really, a whiffleball stadium.

"I struck out Chase Utley there," Trip said with a grin that just dared you to tell him he was lying about striking out the Phillies' star second baseman. Utley was in, sure enough, and Trip talked him into a few at-bats. "I fanned him!"

This past year, they enclosed the deck to create the Onyx Bar. It's a lot more room, and the exterior walls are like big garage doors with glass panels (there's a story on how they got there, too, involving Trip, a truck, and a blinding snowstorm; buy him a beer sometime and ask him about it). You can see out in winter, and in summer they are rolled up to reclaim the deck atmosphere. The bar itself lights up with a soft glow.

But it's not just the building: The beer's changed, even the philosophy. "We've pulled back from trying to sell beer farther out," Trip said. "We sell 90 percent of our beer in-house now. We're on tap in about seven accounts, and it's at the point where they have to come pick it up if they want it."

It's still a Peter Austin system, but they dropped the Ringwood yeast after the first year. There's a new lagering tank, a new glycol chiller, and a new set of beers coming out of the brewery. The only name I recognized was the Antler Brown Ale. The Rescue IPA was the hoppiest beer I'd ever tasted at Barley Creek, and Trip laughed at the look on my face.

The Pick: The Rescue IPA is just barely hanging onto balance, stuffed full of citrus-smacked bitterness. It's thrilling. But I also like the smooth drinking action of the Angler Black Lager—a good, roasty body with just a touch of sweet on the end. It's relaxing.

Chef Jacobo Hernandez has built a great new menu that should satisfy appetites from kids to sophisticates. We sampled some food, and the freshness of the flavors was striking—nothing dull or muted; it snapped in the mouth. Trip brought out a hot dish of the Wicked Chip Dip, a hot, gooey, cheesy appetizer of chili over cream cheese that has always been a favorite of mine. The chef had tuned it by adding a topping of fresh tomatoes; wicked good.

"We want to win some more food awards," Trip said, and I know he's always seen the menu as a solid key to success. "They get our name out there. When everyone in Monroe County can give tourists directions to the place, then we've done our job."

He hasn't gotten there quite yet. Not everyone knows where Barley Creek is—not yet—and spring and fall are still a bit thin; copper mines, maybe. But he's almost there. As long as Trip's still chasing success, Barley Creek will just keep getting better and better, halfway up the mountain.

Opened: December 1995.
Owners: Trip and Eileen Ruvane.
Brewer: Tim Phillips.
System: 10-barrel Peter Austin brewhouse, 2,500 barrels potential annual capacity.
2009 production: 999 barrels.
Brewpub hours: Seven days a week, 11:01 AM to "late night, even later in ski and waterpark season."
Tours: Seven days a week at 12:30 PM and by appointment.
Take-out beer: Six-packs and cases of 12-ounce bottles, 22-ounce seasonal specialty bottles, growlers, and kegs (call ahead for availability).
Food: Barley Creek offers a wide menu: homemade soups, imaginative appetizers, hearty sandwiches, pub fare, fresh desserts, seafood, pasta, big steaks, daily specials, and a kids' menu. They've really homed in on food quality, and the samples I had were top-notch.

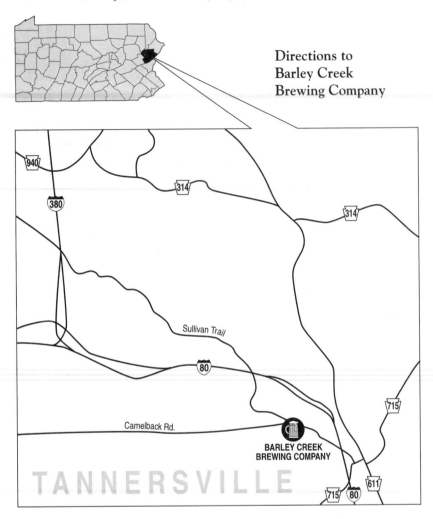

Directions to Barley Creek Brewing Company

Extras: Gift shop. Occasional live music (check Web site). Indoor-out-door deck. Two full bars. Mug club. Foosball, high-tech video arcade, great TVs for watching sports (and playing Wii), bar games, and metal ring puzzles. World's first whiffleball stadium ("We'll be ready when they start ESPN 5," Trip said). Great Pocono Wing-Off (third Sunday in August), baseball bus trips, concerts, a golf tourna-ment . . . Check the Web site, because there's always something going on.

Special considerations: Kids welcome. Vegetarian meals available.

Parking: Plentiful on-site parking.

Lodging in the area: The Chateau Resort, 300 Camelback Rd., Tannersville, 570-629-5900; Cranberry Manor B&B, 114 Cherry Lane Rd., East Stroudsburg, 570-620-2246; Countryside Cottages, Bartonsville Ave., Stroudsburg, 570-629-2131.

Area attractions: The major ski areas—*Camelback*, *Jack Frost*, *Split Rock*, *Shawnee*, and *Big Boulder*—are all within a thirty-minute drive. Camelback also has a warm-weather water park, *Camel Beach*, which adds a few thrills every year. Golf courses dot the area. *Pocono Raceway*, home to a number of NASCAR and motorcycle races, is about twenty minutes away. There are state campgrounds and game lands all around, well-stocked lakes and streams, hiking and biking trails, swimming, golfing, canoeing and rafting expeditions. Explore the scenery of the *Delaware Water Gap* and the mountains, the rushing beauty of Bushkill and Dingmans falls, and the Appalachian Trail. If it rains, *Summit Lanes* (Route 940 west of Mount Pocono, 570-839-9635) has thirty-six lanes of great bowling. *The Crossings* (570-629-4650, www.premiumoutlets.com) is a major shopping mall with more than a hundred brand-name outlet stores, and it's right at the bottom of the hill. There are also a yearly jazz festival and blues festival. Call the *Pocono Mountains Vacation Bureau* for more information (800-POCONOS, www.800poconos .com).

Other area beer sites: *Pub in the Pines* (on Route 940 in Pocono Pines, 570-646-2377, with the great Web site URL www.breakfastking .com) has fifteen taps and also serves a good breakfast for any early risers. If you want to go to town, in Stroudsburg you'll find the *Sarah Street Grill* (Fifth and Sarah Sts., 570-424-9120), a nice place for dinner and a beer, and *Flood's* (732 Main St., 570-424-5743), an Irish place, if that's more to your liking.

ShawneeCraft Brewery

Shawnee Inn, River Road
Shawnee-on-Delaware, PA 18356
570-424-4000, ext. 1295
www.gemandkeystone.com

Fidelis in Naturam, in Artem Fidelis (True to Nature, True to the Craft). That's the motto of ShawneeCraft. I'll tell you, there aren't many little craft breweries running around with a Latin motto. But just look at this place. You've got an old-school Pocono resort backing it up. The address doesn't even have a street number, because everyone in the area knows where the Shawnee is. The brewery's logo is a combination of Asian symbols for wood and water. The doors to the brewery are oversize, heavy wood, braced with black hand-hammered iron, and centered with that mystical logo, looking like something out of *Lord of the Rings*. If ever a small brewery deserved a Latin motto, this is it.

Brewer Leo Bongiorno came here seeking sanctuary. He'd been kicking around, brewing in the New York City area, but on September 12, 2001, he started making plans to get his family out of there. He'd started a company with his buddy Chuck Williamson to plan a brewery, and this was the time. They opened Butternuts Beer and Ale in Garrattsville, New York, out in the woods southwest of Cooperstown.

"We were incorporated for ten years," Leo said, "and we were still friends. I said to him, 'Let's divide and conquer.' I took a buyout, and it was all amiable." Leo started looking for his future, and saw a notice on the Probrewer forum from Pete Kirkwood at the Shawnee Inn. They met, they liked each other, and Leo decided to stay in the Northeast. That was in September 2007.

Pete's idea to put a brewery in the resort's flood-damaged hockey rink grew out of his family's desire to create something different at Shawnee. What emerged was a desire for handmade authenticity, a Pocono Gothic Revival. "I felt people were craving something real," he said. "People come here because it feels real. McDonald's are all the same; enough of

Beers brewed: Regulars (for now): Gold Lager, Session Porter, India Pale Ale, Biere Blanche, V.S.O.P. Seasonals and specials: Entire Porter, Pumpkin Saison, Bohemian Pilsner, E.S.B., Honey Triple, Bourbon Porter, Vienna Lager . . . and that's just the start.

that, we want something with a sense of place. The best things are made by hand. Out with the old, in with the older!"

ShawneeCraft is the core concept for a line of products. "We have an Amish furniture maker in Ohio who's making a ShawneeCraft line," Pete said. "We're growing herbs organically and sustain-

ably, we're going to start honey production, we're involved in local food co-ops. The brewery doors were made locally. We want to spread the wealth locally."

The brewery and the beers are the flagship of the ShawneeCraft idea. "The brewery is visible, it's exciting," Pete said. "I don't want this to be just a golf course brewery, but I don't want to make anything extreme, either. We're looking for elegance."

The brewery represents an absolute obsession with recycling and reuse. The brewhouse is used (as many are), and there are four heat exchangers (some parts reclaimed from the hockey rink) to wring every last bit of reclaimable energy out of the system. The spent grain is com-posted in the gardens, and all the barrels for aging beer are reused.

The resort even recycled their tavern, a franchise of the Sam Snead's Tavern chain. They bought that back and reopened as The Gem and Keystone, a showplace for the beers, including racking space for the extensive barrel-aging program Leo has planned.

"Extensive" is an understatement. The first rumor of Shawnee I heard was about "some guy opening a brewery at a ski resort in the Poconos that's going to be all barrel-aged beers," and it's not that far off. Leo had 28 barrels when I visited and planned to have 100 "working" barrels by the end of 2010. That's ambitious, especially when you hear Leo describe the area as "the Miller Lite Parkway."

He chuckled. "We got a lot of converts," he said, "and we're very close to New York and Philadelphia. Right now we're making session beers for the tavern, but long-term, it's about making beers like the small brewers of Flanders." The beers you'll read about here are really pulling duty as barrel conditioners, preparing the wood for the beers Leo and Pete are really planning.

"Our first real flagships will be out in [late 2012]," Leo said. "We're culturing up wild yeasts from other beers and White Labs." That doesn't mean the beers that are out now aren't good; the ones I had ranged from good to exceptional. The Pumpkin Saison that was on when I visited, made with Shawnee-grown pumpkins, was arresting in its blend of pumpkin spices and saison yeast effects, with a high-in-the-mouth glow of light pine–ginger–spice mélange. Leo told me that glow came from fresh mace grated off organic nutmegs. It was unique and wonderful. New flagships or not, I hope that Pumpkin Saison comes back. I know I'll be back before late 2012.

Opened: September 2009.

Owners: The Kirkwood family.

Brewers: Leo Bongiorno.

System: 8.5-barrel DME brewhouse, 1,000 barrels annual capacity.

2009 production: Not available.

Brewpub hours: Sunday through Thursday, 11:30 AM to 10 PM; Friday and Saturday, 11:30 AM to midnight.

Tours: Call for an appointment.

Take-out beer: Growlers.

Food: You'll find a wide selection of locally raised meats and vegetables, sustainable seafood, and artisanal cheeses on the menu; these guys walk the walk. There is both a pub menu—sandwiches, nachos, and the like—and a dinner menu, featuring hearty dishes like lamb shanks over crispy gnocchi and root vegetable ragout, grass-fed beef and buffalo steaks, and nods to Pennsylvania favorites like trout and mushrooms. You'll also find exceptional vegetarian offerings from appetizers to entrées; try the vegetarian pot pie.

Extras: Live entertainment every weekend, live jazz jam every other Thursday; see Web site for schedule.

Special considerations: Kids welcome. Vegetarian meals available.

Parking: Plentiful off-street free parking.

Lodging in the area: You can stay right at the Shawnee Inn in high class: 800-SHAWNEE; The Deer Head Inn B&D (bed and diner) has jazz and drinks, too (see below), 5 Main St., Delaware Water Gap, 570-424-2000; Stonybrook Inn B&B, River Rd. and Worthington St., Shawnee on Delaware, 888-444-5240.

Area attractions: Shawnee Inn has a well-regarded golf course, the first designed by the legendary A. W. Tillenghast, and largely situated on Shawnee Island in the Delaware River. Tee times can be reserved online (www.shawneeinn.com/pa-golf-courses). Shawnee also sits at the southern end of the **Delaware Water Gap National Recreation Area** (www.nps.gov/dewa), 40 miles of land along the river that forms the border between Pennsylvania and New Jersey, right where it flows through the Appalachians. You'll find trails all through the area, including 27 miles of the **Appalachian Trail**. There are boat ramps, swimming areas, camping, and simply scenic driving. The

Pennsylvania side has a no alcohol policy; the New Jersey side is a bit more civilized, but it should be noted that water sports and drinking, in particular, don't mix. Wait till you're off the water to enjoy a cold beer. ***Chamberlain Canoes*** (in Shawnee on Delaware, 800-422-6631, www.chamberlaincanoes.com) rents and guides canoe, kayak, raft, and tube trips through the gap, from a fun afternoon float to three-day wilderness canoe camping. See the listing for Barley Creek on page 263 for more suggestions.

Other area beer sites: The ***Deer Head Inn*** in Delaware Water Gap (5 Main St., 570-424-2000) is actually noted in tourist guides for its classically huge marble urinal, thought to be one of the largest in the country. You gotta see it! Okay, okay, they have great jazz acts, too. See the listing for Barley Creek for more suggestions.

A word about . . .

Pennsylvania's Regional Foods

Pennsylvania is a patchwork quilt, an assortment of cultures and eth-nicities that remain strong and clear even in these modern, mobile times. It probably has something to do with the tendency of Pennsylvanians to *stay*. We have more retirees than any state other than Florida, and more people living in the same houses in which they were born than any other state, so there's not a lot of blending going on.

Various snide explanations exist for this phenomenon—too poor or too stupid to leave being among them—but I think it's because we know we can't get the right food anywhere else. Pennsylvania has a plethora of regional foods. Just my home territory, the Dutch Country, has more well-known and widespread regional dishes than some states. Let's take a look at each area.

Philadelphia loves soft pretzels, hoagies, scrapple, Tastykakes, and the tasty but odd combination of fried oysters and chicken salad, but the food that defines the city is the cheesesteak, invented at Pat's King of Steaks at Ninth and Passayunk.

You can't get a good cheesesteak if you're more than 60 miles from here. I know because I've tried, and it's been nothing but a futilely humorous proposition: The rolls are all wrong, the meat's either too chunky or ground up, and the stuff they put in them—green peppers, lettuce, *mint*? I'm sure H. L. Mencken would agree that a man who would put mint in a cheesesteak would put serpents in a baby's cradle.

A cheesesteak is nature's perfect food. A counterman explained it to my sister years ago, and she passed it along. "Well, hon," he said around his cigar, "ya see, your cheesesteak has got your four food groups. Ya got your bread, ya got your meat, ya got your cheese, ya got your onions, which is a vegetable." He paused at this point and grinned. "And ya got your grease, hon, which is *very* important."

I watched my latest one get grilled down at Frusco's in Northeast Philly (7220 Frankford Ave., not far from the Six-Pack Store, which offers the opportunity for matching your steak with a great beer). Order up: "Yeah, a cheesesteak wit', sauce." That's a cheesesteak with onions and sauce. Shaved, pressed steak goes on the grill, sizzling and popping, to be turned and lightly chopped with the spatula. A constant pile of onions is kept slowly cooking to one side, glistening and translucent.

When the steak's done, they take the roll, which some people believe is the key ingredient—they're wrong, but their hearts are in the right place—a roll that's soft but chewy inside, crusty and tough enough to hold the juices on the outside, and lay it over the steak. (Frusco's gives you the option to pay a buck extra for a roll from the local Sarcone's bakery; definitely take it for their excellent hoagies, but not the steak—too crusty.) Then watch the cook slip the big spatula under the steak, flip it over into his hand, slide a spatula of fried onions on it, and ladle in some hot pizza sauce if you want it. Then spoon a fat stripe of hot Whiz right down the middle.

Because that's what you have here, folks—the classic Philly cheesesteak is made with Cheese Whiz, liquid Velveeta. Oh, you can order it with different cheese if you think Whiz is beneath you; you can even be like John Kerry and order it with Swiss (major faux pas for the then presidential candidate and his handlers, and talked about for days in the Philly press). But Whiz it is, because it's premelted, it blends well with the sauce, and that bright orange just looks good on there.

Where's the best? Good way to start an argument. Eat your way to an answer! Pat's is the classic place to start, then on to Geno's, right across the intersection. Tony Luke's is a perennial favorite (you can also try Philly's secret sandwich there, the roast pork Italian; 39 Oregon Ave.), as is Jim's Steaks (South and Fourth streets).

You'll notice there are no phone numbers. Don't call; these folks are too busy to answer the phone. Go get your steak and eat it Philly style: on the sidewalk, bent at the waist, the steak angled down and away, so you don't get that very important grease on your clothes. Get a beer to pound with it. What could be better than Philadelphia Brewing's Kenzinger?

The Philly Suburbs are not as culinarily well defined, and no surprise there; we mostly came either from somewhere else or from the city, so you'll find plenty of good cheesesteak and hoagie joints out here. One thing we do have is a strong tradition of local meat packers in Montgomery County: Hatfield, Leidy's, Alderfer's. There's also an excellent independent German butcher out near Chalfont, Ernst Illg (365 Folly Rd., 215-343-0670). They all do meats, but the thing we love out here is *landjaegers*.

The landjaeger is a smoked sausage, with flattened links about 7 inches long and maybe an inch across at their widest. They come in pairs, connected by a twist of . . . well, we don't really want to know what that is, do we? Let's just say "casing" and keep our appetite for them. The sausage comes out of the process a dark brownish purple, flecked with white. The ones Ernst makes will keep for a week or so unrefrigerated; the ones from the big packers are more thoroughly smoked and will keep for at least two weeks.

They make an audible *snap* when you bite into them. Each mouthful is pungently smoky; landjaegers will smoke up a car in no time flat. They're chewy, just a little bit greasy, and wonderfully satisfying. There's not much to be said for them as an ingredient; they're just a snack, but most bars and convenience stores have a jar of them handy. You'll need something classically German with these meat sticks—try a Stoudt's Pilsner.

I've recently learned about another sausage specialty, thanks to Tom Clark at Berwick Brewing: "soupies." They're not from Philly, they're from Sunbury, but it makes more sense to put the two sausages together. Soupies are made with pork and spices, stuffed tightly into cow intestines, and salt cured. There are two odd things about soupies, to my way of thinking, anyway. First, they're slowly pressed flat and then aged under oil (not sure why on the flattening, but I guess the oil is to keep air away from them). The other odd thing is that apparently the only other place they're made is in Rhode Island. I'd love to know how this sausage, clearly a derivation of the Italian sopressata (also cured in oil), got from one of these places to the other. All you really have to worry about is how often they make it to Berwick Brewing, where they get sliced onto the pizzas and you wash them down with a cold glass of Hondo.

Pennsylvania Dutch Country is where I grew up, in Paradise, and we've got more regional foods than you can shake an Amishman at. Shoofly pie (wet and dry bottom), chicken pot pie, *schnitz* (soft, leathery, dried apple slices), the area's distinctive and individual pretzels and potato chips (see Stackpole Books' *Pennsylvania Snacks* for that whole bounty), red beet eggs (hard-boiled eggs pickled in vinegar and beet juice; they come out purple), and cup cheese.

Cup cheese? Never heard of that one? It's not very common anymore, but once you've developed a taste for it, there's just nothing like it. It's a cheese made by cooking the curds from soured skim milk. In fact, it dates back to German *koch' käse*, which means, simply, "cooked cheese." One Pennsylvania cheesemaker still makes it, Shenk's Foods (New Danville Pike, Lancaster, www.shenks.com), and they believe it came from Germany with the Mennonites and Amish in the 1600s. Shenk's has been making it since 1929. Oddly, the only other place I could find in the United States that makes anything like it is in Texas.

Shenk's makes it in three levels of sharpness—mild, medium, and sharp—and the sharp is funky enough to stand up to the fine pseudolambics out of the Bethlehem Brew Works. The cheese is quite runny, stickier than honey, and a light greenish yellow in color. The sharp is flagrantly fragrant, in the limburger range; the medium is quite firm; and the mild is a nose-teasing echo of the sharp. Cup cheese is very low-fat, yet still immensely flavorful. It spreads easily—until you try to get it off your knife, that is—and is delicious even on something as plain as a saltine cracker.

I don't know of any gourmet recipes that use cup cheese, and I don't know of any cookbook authors or "foodies" who rave about it. But every now and then I sit down with a good book, a sleeve of saltines, a glass of something serious enough to defend itself, like a Weyerbacher Blithering Idiot, and eat my way through a little tub of Shenk's sharp. Alone. Just me and the stink.

Northeast Pennsylvania has some Polish and Ukrainian specialties that people grew up with—*bigos* and *crusciki*—and there are the drool-inducing hot dog shops with their individual "Greek sauces" and mustards. But there are two traditions up here I'd like to take a quick look at: Old Forge pizza and Boilo.

Old Forge is a town just outside of Scranton; there's an exit off the far end of the northeast extension of the Pennsylvania Turnpike for it. The first time I came up here was with some friends, one of whom was bent on finding a bar he'd been to, Maxie's. When we finally parked, my pal Rich Pawlak vaulted out of the car and hailed a guy walking toward us with two flat boxes: "Old Forge pizza!" To which the guy replied with a grin, "It's da best!" Huh?

We went into Maxie's (a great little bar, by the way, at 520 S. Main St., 570-562-9948), and Rich revealed all. Old Forge is a little town that has an overabundance of pizza shops, all of which make a unique style of pizza—rectangular, but not the "Sicilian" you find elsewhere. He ordered us some "cuts" (not slices, cuts) and we sampled. You've got a medium-thick crust, but with a crunchy layer on the bottom, about a quarter inch thick; not crispy, but crunchy, almost like zwieback. Then there's a nice, soft doughy layer on top of that, covered with a fairly peppery, onion-studded tomato sauce with lots of mozzarella and American cheese melted right into it all.

Old Forge styles itself the pizza capital of the United States and doesn't really care that hardly anyone outside Scranton has ever heard of the place. After all, they've got that great pizza and we don't. You can find some of the best at Maxie's, Arcaro and Gennell's (443 S. Main St., 570-457-4262), Brutico's (432 S. Main St., 570-457-4166), Revello's (502 S. Main St., 570-457-9843), and Salerno's (139 Moosic Rd., 570-457-9920), and they go great with a cold, fizzy glass of Stegmaier.

Now, Boilo, on the other hand, is not something you're going to find in a pizza shop or even in a store. Boilo (sometimes spelled Boillo) is something you see in Northeast Pennsylvania, and even down into the Lehigh Valley, around Christmastime (or just cold weather). You'll see people at work passing around Ball jars that look like they're full of cider. It isn't quite moonshine, but it's still faintly illegal, though only if you buy it from someone else.

Boilo is a kind of mulled cider, but heavy on the mull. Actually, it's more like spiced whiskey with some juice tossed in. Traditionally, Boilo is made from dirt-cheap blended whiskey (something like Kessler's or one of the bulk-brand Canadians), spiced up with cloves and a cinnamon stick, and diluted with just enough water and orange juice to make it gulpable. We got ours last year in a Ball jar with a rusty lid: classic Boilo. You heat it up to drink it, and it sure does go down easily. Good Boilo's actually pretty decent punch.

I teased you all with a secret Greek sauce recipe in *New York Breweries*, but I'll let you have this Boilo recipe, passed along to me several years ago. "From Saint Clair, PA, the heart of the Coal Region, comes a 'Warming Holiday Beverage.' The tradition is to welcome guests with a warm glass of Boilo to warm them up from the cold outside."

Put the following in a pot: 3 cups water, 1 cup sugar, 1/2 cup honey, 1 tablespoon caraway seeds, 4 cloves, 5 cinnamon sticks, and 3 oranges, cut in quarters (squeeze the oranges over the pot, then put in the pot). Bring it all to a boil, hold at a boil for five minutes, then remove from heat. Add a 1.75-liter bottle of cheap whiskey, "the cheaper the better." Stir well and return to heat. As soon as it comes to a boil, remove from the heat. Cool overnight, then strain into jars. Add used cinnamon sticks to jars and seal. Serve warm, and it will make you warm, but "watch out, it can get you."

The Northwest Corner may have plenty of regional specialties, but the only one I found was bumbleberry pie, a pie we saw at any number of dinors—that's not a typo, that's how "diner" is spelled in the Erie corner.

I saw bumbleberry pie as far south as Ridgway, but the best piece I had was at a place in Erie.

Bumbleberry pie sounds like a mistake, and it may have been at one time, but it has become a regional favorite. It is simply a mixed-fruit pie, based on blueberries, but with other fruits mixed in: raspberries, blackberries, pears, apples, whatever the cook has in the pantry and has the courage to add. It's always a little different, but I've never had a bad piece. It also tends to be a fresh fruit pie, because to the best of my knowledge, no one has a commercial prepacked "bumbleberry" can out there!

Pittsburgh has the famous chipped ham that was invented at Isaly's, the hulking huge fried fish sandwiches that are still a Friday staple in Da Burgh, and the Primanti Brothers' "almost famous" sandwiches—sandwiches that got gubernatorial candidate Mike Fisher in trouble in the Philadelphia press during the 2002 campaign. "What's your favorite sandwich?" the press asked both Fisher and Philly homeboy Ed Rendell. Rendell knew the answer to that one straight from his gut: the cheesesteak! But I give credit to Mike Fisher for staying loyal to his Allegheny County roots and telling a dumbfounded Philadelphia press corps that his favorite sandwich was one from Primanti Brothers.

What is the Primanti Brothers sandwich? There are actually quite a few of them: egg and cheese, kolbassi and cheese, steak and cheese, fried bologna and cheese, ham and cheese (and there's a note at the bottom of the menu that extra cheese is available!), and so on. But it's not the cheese that makes it a Primanti Brothers sandwich, or the thick slices of Italian bread, or the paper wrap that is cut with the sandwich. It's the coleslaw and french fries that go *right in the sandwich* that make it a Primanti Brothers special.

They're in there to save time. The original Primanti Brothers shop was right down in the Strip District, Pittsburgh's food and produce terminal district. Truck drivers back in the 1930s would come rolling in, unload their trucks, and need a sandwich they could eat one-handed as they drove out for their next load. The story is that one driver, who was tired of getting the fries and coleslaw sides and not being able to eat them as they slid around the cab of his truck, asked the counterman to put them right in the sandwich. Genius.

Okay, maybe it's not genius. The sandwiches are huge, and you really have to muckle on to them to get them in your mouth. The coleslaw drips. But they sure are good, and at 2 AM, when you've been up at the

Church or Gooski's all night, there's not much that can beat them. You want a beer suggestion to go with that? Pal, if you're at Primanti's at 2 AM, I *suggest* that you call it a night! (If it's not quite that late . . . Primanti's has discovered craft beer. Check the taps and dive in.) Addresses for the Primanti Brothers shops are in the Pittsburgh bar suggestions.

Hey, there's a whole other *book* I could write, *full* of food from this state! I've barely scratched the surface. Now get out there and have something good—and local!—to eat with all this good local beer!

Northwest Corner

Y ou'll hear people tell you that Pittsburgh is really more like the Midwest than it is like Pennsylvania, with a more inland perspective, where the architecture, accents, and ethnic makeup are all more midwestern than they are East Coast. Maybe . . . but I sure don't remember seeing gorges and hills like that in most midwestern cities.

If I can get in ahead of the urban ethnologists, I'd like to propose that the Northwest Corner of Pennsylvania is more like New York. Upstate New York is washed by the Great Lakes; so it is with Erie. Western New York is rooted in trade and heavy manufacturing; Erie is a major crossroads for highways and builds locomotives. Upstate New York is big on boating, fishing, and hunting; we've got that here, too. And New York has more than a few vineyards; Erie is the Wine Coast of Pennsylvania. The Pennsylvania Wine Association places eight wineries in the Northwest Corner, some along Lake Erie, some inland. They are easy to find and visit (www.pennsylvaniawine.com). Some are more focused on competition, others on making lighter-hearted fruit wines. All of them make wines that Pennsylvanians can be proud of.

Lake Erie offers fishing for walleye, perch, smallmouth bass, salmon, and trout, and you can fish for the table or the sport. If you want to go out on the lake, you'll find licensed charter captains listed on the Pennsylvania Lake Erie Charter Captain Association Web site (www.plecca .com). If you want to fish the inland lakes and streams, contact the Fish and Boat Commission (717-657-4518, www.fish.state.pa.us) about licensing, stocking, and where you can fish on state lands.

If you're the more sedentary type, the region offers many miles of scenic driving. Take Route 5 along the lakeshore and the wineries; it's beautiful in ice or the full green of summer. Route 6 runs down into the Allegheny Forest, meandering through valleys and up hills. The fiery fall foliage of the northern tier rivals that of New England but draws far fewer people, leaving roads clear of leaf peepers; it's been a favorite of my parents for years. Along the way, well-kept small towns like Bradford, Warren, and St. Marys, the home of Straub Brewery, shine with quiet beauty.

Don't overlook the city of Erie itself. Even though it's not a rural paradise, Erie's lakefront site and Presque Isle State Park offer a natural beauty unique in the state. And though it's far from the urban bustle of Philadelphia and Pittsburgh, you'll find respectable shopping and nightlife.

I was really just kidding about folks up here being more like New Yorkers. They're Pennsylvanians, through and through. Just look at how they support their local breweries. Cheers!

Erie Brewing Company

1213 Veshecco Drive, Erie, PA 16501
814-459-7741
www.eriebrewingco.com

It's lonely up in the northwest corner by Lake Erie, where Erie is somewhat isolated by the lake and large swaths of thinly populated territory. It was especially lonely for Erie Brewing Company (EBC) when it was the only brewery around. EBC had its work cut out for it, bringing the gospel of good beer to a dry land. Things are better, now that the Brewerie brewpub is just down the street and Voodoo and Sprague have joined the scene, but it was a long, hard slog at first, and it's not surprising that EBC has gone through a lot of changes: beers, markets, packaging, direction, ownership.

One thing hasn't changed, though: From EBC's brewpub birth as Hoppers, back in January 1994 in the same train station where Brewerie is now, through to its incarnation as a packaging microbrewery, this town has loved Railbender Ale. Falling somewhere between an English old ale and a wee heavy, this big, malty beer has more than a touch

Beers brewed: Year-round: Railbender Ale, Mad Anthony's American Pale Ale, Presque Isle Pilsner, Misery Bay IPA. Seasonals: Ol' Red Cease & Desist Scotch Ale, Fallenbock, Heritage Alt, Erie Crude Oatmeal Stout, Maibock, DeRailed Black Cherry Ale. There have been a number of one-off versions of Railbender, and experimental beers are on their way.

more alcohol than regular beers. At 6.8 percent ABV, it is not your everyday sipping beer, but it is by far the brewery's best seller. They're a different breed up in Erie, and my hat's off to them.

The Pick: I loved the Smoke-bender, a nice tang to this full, smooth beer. But stick to the regular Railbender for an easy ride on solid malt rails.

EBC broke out of Hoppers early in 1999 after five years in that location, moving down to their 12th Street brewery: big and high-ceilinged, with plenty of glass, originally built to be an automotive emissions-testing facility before Pennsylvania canned that program. It worked out well for EBC when they got the place for a discount price, and local bars were happy to no longer have EBC selling their beer in competition.

Erie got off to a good start, selling beer locally and down in Pittsburgh. But things faltered a bit, and I noticed it was harder and harder to get through to people at the brewery. I wondered what was going on, particularly when they started going through brewers at a fairly quick pace.

There were business problems, mostly centered around a lack of capital. After some changes in ownership, Don Chadwick arrived on the scene from northern New Jersey. "Don was an accountant at big firms for about thirty years," general manager Jim Hicks told me. "At five o'clock, you quit work and went for a beer. He liked beer and knew someone in Erie who told him that the brewery needed capital."

The combination worked for Don and his Cardinal Equity Group, which explains why I found Railbender on tap at the Railroad Café in East Rutherford, New Jersey, and Don Chadwick drinking it. That's his local bar, and he wanted his beer available!

Don's been a steadying influence on the brewery, and Jim has supplied the energy, pushing a pilot brew series of experimental beers. "We wanted to do a draft-only series," he said, "but we realized that 22-ounce bottles were a better image for the *über*-geeks we were aiming at. They're also great for delis that want to do better beer; they take up less space in a facing than a six-pack."

Jim clearly wants to get the attention of beer enthusiasts, but it's frustrating. "Our biggest critics are the beer geeks," he admitted. "They don't like the sessionable, balanced beers. We still sell more of those."

Railbender may not be "sessionable" at 6.8 percent, but it is balanced and accounts for over 50 percent of sales. It's the brand people think of with Erie Brewing. So some of the first experimental beers were a series of "Bender" beers: Ryebender, Smokebender, and Oakbender. I got some of the Smokebender at a festival and thought the smoked malt tasted great in that big, malty body. Jim's thinking about an all-Railbender variety case, an idea I thought was simultaneously brilliant and amusing.

EBC is in thirteen states, though they sell 60 percent of their beer in the stretch of Pennsylvania between State College and the Ohio border. "We're in Oregon," said Hicks. "It's a tough craft beer market, but Railbender and Ol' Red do okay. We got a nice letter from the Rogue Ale House in Portland about Ol' Red."

Jim wants to see sales stay solid in the home market, and it's getting easier. "Craft beer acceptance is definitely on the rise," he said. "People here used to think that because the national chains and brands were so big, they must be good and anything local is crap. They're realizing that's not so now. Putting local beers on offer brings people in."

After sixteen years, Erie's caught up with its local brewery. It's not so lonely up here after all.

Opened: January 1994; production brewery opened February 1999.
Owners: Cardinal Equity Group; Don Chadwick, CEO.
Brewer: Shawn Strickland, brewmaster; Tim Schnars II, assistant brewer.
System: 20-barrel PSI Engineering brewhouse, 10,000 barrels potential annual capacity.
2009 production: 4,300 barrels.
Tours: Tour times change with season; check Web site. Tasting room and gift shop are open Monday through Friday, 10 AM to 5 PM.
Take-out beer: Growlers and cases.
Special considerations: Kids welcome with parents. Handicapped-accessible.
Parking: Plenty of on-site parking.
Lodging in the area: Spencer House B&B, 519 W. Sixth St., 814-454-5984; Glass House Inn, 3202 W. Sixth St., 800-956-7222; Boothby Inn, 311 W. Sixth St, 866-BOOTHBY.
Area attractions: *Presque Isle State Park* (814-833-7424) on Lake Erie is the closest thing Pennsylvania has to a seashore. This sand spit has some beautiful beaches undisturbed by boardwalks or hotels. It is a wildlife conservation area with trails, swimming, boating, fishing, and picnicking areas. New to the park is the *Tom Ridge Environmental Center* (same number, www.dcnr.state.pa.us/trecpi), an education center with interactive exhibits and the Big Green Screen, a four-story high screen that shows movies of the natural world. Right at the entrance to the park is *Waldameer Amusement Park and Water World* (877-817-1009, www.waldameer.com), an impressive array of traditional amusement park rides and tons of water fun. Visit the *Erie Maritime Museum* (164 E. Front St., 814-871-4596, www.flagshipniagara.org) and you might be able to see the reconstructed

Niagara, flagship of Oliver Hazard Perry's lake fleet in the War of 1812. The sailing brig has been designated as Pennsylvania's flagship and is sometimes away representing the state; call ahead to see if it is at its dock. The museum also has exhibits about lake sailing and the 1812 lake battle, including a reconstruction of part of the *Lawrence* that has been pounded by the guns of the current *Niagara* to demonstrate the effects of cannon fire on wooden ships. The **Erie Sea Wolves** (814-456-1300, www.seawolves.com) play baseball in the Class AA Eastern League; the **Erie Otters** (www.ottershockey.com) play hockey at the Erie Civic Center (809 French Street, 814-452-4857). You can also contact the **Erie Area Convention and Visitors Bureau** (814-454-7191, www.visiteriepa.com) for more information on local activities.

Other area beer sites: *Oscar's* (12th and Pittsburgh Sts. in the plaza, 814-454-4325) has been Erie's relaxed and comfortable multitap bar for years; the food's pretty good, and the beer just keeps getting better. *The Docksider* (1015 State St., 814-454-9700) has upped their beer game and still delivers an excellent series of live blues and folk acts; call for music schedule. *U Pick 6* (7520 Peach St., 814-866-2337) is both a bar and bottle shop (technically, all bottle shops in Pennsylvania are both), with a real sharp selection of craft and import beers. *Beer and Pop Discount Warehouse* (901 Peninsula Dr., 814-454-2337) is a distributor with a good selection of Pennsylvania craft beers, and it's Brewerie owner Chris Sirianni's family business.

The Brewerie at Union Station

123 West 14th Street, Erie, PA 16505
814-454-2200
www.brewerie.com

There was a note in the third edition about a place called Turnpike Brewing coming soon to Erie, a brewpub to be manned by Gary Burleigh, who'd previously brewed at Erie Brewing. It never worked out, but happily, Gary did find a brewpub job at the Erie train station when local beer scion Chris Sirianni opened up the Brewerie there. It's not all that surprising; Union Station has been an incubator of Erie's modern brewing, and the 1920s public architecture makes a grand façade for a brewpub.

Chris and Gary met in 2000 at Erie Brewing. Chris, whose family sells beer in town, was interning there and learning about sales. They got along, and in 2002 they started talking about maybe opening a brew-on-premises operation, a small brewery-for-hire where people could make homebrew-size batches of beer with top-notch equipment. Then Gary lost his job at Erie, and the talk got more serious. Why not a full brewpub? asked Chris, and they started looking for a place.

They found a quirky, triangular building on the shortest street in Erie, and the concept of Turnpike Brewing was born. But a mounting series of problems with that property, culminating in the building being rammed by an out-of-control car, led them to give up. "It just got complicated," said Chris. "And someone told me, get a place you can grow into. There was nowhere to grow there."

Beers brewed: Year-round: Uncle Jackson's Blonde, Major McNair's Nut Brown, Apparition Amber, Hopness Monster IPA, Railway Hefe Weizen. Seasonals: Winter White Blueberry White Ale, Gino's 3 Berry Wheat, Raspberry Pale, Apple Pie, Jacob's Head Porter, Heart On Chocolate Cherry Stout, Rye P.A., Mojo's Rocket Red, Mai Honey Bock, Big Climax Munich Lager, Oktoberfest, Shitzengiggle Kolsch, Dunkel Weizen, The Christmas Ale, Girl Stout Cookie, Big Trouble Dubbel, Grand Cru, Abbeycadabara, #3 Tripel.

As luck would have it, just as they gave up on that idea in the spring of 2006, Porters—the fine-dining beer bar that had gone into Union Station after Hoppers brewpub morphed into Erie Brewing—closed their doors. "It was perfect," Chris said. "The building didn't need structural work; the drains were already in. Hoppers had done well here. It just wasn't a fine-dining spot"—he gestured to the high, echoing ceiling—"and this isn't a fine-dining town. We planned a friendly place with good beer and good bar food."

Lucky for them, the Erie Redevelopment Authority was rededicating the area as a cultural and entertainment district at about the same time. The park in front of the station, flanked by the main post office, was expanded; buildings were renovated; and the city has been encouraging conversion of buildings to condominiums. Chris is excited about the possibilities. "The lake and the [Presque Isle] peninsula represent a huge potential attraction," he said, "and it hasn't even been tapped."

He and Gary formed their business, moved their little 3.5-barrel brewhouse into the same area where Hoppers had theirs, hired staff, cleaned and changed some cosmetic details, and started brewing. They opened in October 2006, and by April 2007, they had hosted a major beer festival, Erie's first in years. I drove out for it and had a great time.

I enjoyed Gary's beers, too, after the fest closed down and a bunch of us continued to hang out in the rotunda. I drank a few porters and looked around the room. A wide variety of folks were drinking, talking, having a good time: different ages, genders, races and ethnicities, sexual orientations. I felt good about beer and about the Brewerie. "It's totally non-discriminatory," Chris said, with clear pride. "Everyone sitting side by side, drinking beer."

Something else that Chris is proud of is the large selection of Pennsylvania guest beers and wines they carry. "We have no BMC [Bud, Miller, Coors] beers here and up to forty different Pennsylvania craft beers in bottles and cans," he said. "We do it to pay homage to Pennsylvania brewers and to do something no one else in Erie is doing.

"We only serve Pennsylvania wines, too," he added. "This is Pennsylvania's wine country, but when you go out, you don't see Pennsylvania wine! We may have lost some business because we don't have Yellow Tail, but we gained more overall because we have the local wines."

It's all part of that huge untapped potential. I've been going to Erie for beer visits for fourteen years now, and the town is more beer aware than it's ever been. That potential is about to be tapped, and Chris and Gary are handing them the glass.

The Pick: Hopness Monster has a great hop flavor without being overly bitter . . . until the end, when there's a twist of bitterness that lasts through the next swallow. The Girl Stout Cookie, a chocolate mint stout, was drinkable, not overly rich—more like a Thin Mint cookie, not a glass of hot chocolate with a candy cane, and it's a great name!

Opened: October 2006.

Owners: Chris Sirianni, president; Gary Burleigh, vice-president.

Brewer: Gary Burleigh.

System: 3.5-barrel Price-Schonstrom system, 600 barrels annual capacity.

2009 production: 400 barrels.

Brewpub hours: Monday through Thursday, 11 AM to 10 PM; Friday, 11 AM to 1 AM; Saturday, noon to 1 AM. Closed Sunday.

Tours: By appointment.

Take-out beer: Growlers, plus more than thirty bottled Pennsylvania craft beers for takeout in singles, six-packs, and twelve-packs.

Food: Chris was sure fine dining was a bad idea in this space, so this is a casual menu: pulled pork nachos, "red hot" fries (with blue cheese and hot sauce), burger and fries salad, ten kinds of burgers, the Mother Clucker loaded chicken sandwich, steaks, and seafood. There are real vegetarian options, too: stir fries, pasta primavera, three-pepper wrap, and hearty salads.

Extras: Dartboard, pool tables. Open-mike night Thursday, live music/ entertainment Friday and Saturday, 9 PM to midnight. Trackside beer garden on the upper level, with a full bar and live music in warm weather. "It's pretty cool when a train goes by," Chris said. "Everyone yells during the noise."

Special considerations: Kids welcome. Vegetarian meals available.

Parking: Ample parking around the park; free on weekends and after 6 PM on weekdays.

Lodging in the area, Area attractions, Other area beer sites: See Erie Brewing on pages 278–79.

Sprague Farm and Brew Works

22019 U.S. Route 6
Venango, PA 16440
814-398-2885
www.sleepingchainsaw.com

The first news about this brewery trickled out in early 2005: Brian Sprague had bought the old Weyerbacher system, and word was that he was going to open a "farmhouse brewery" outside Venango, along French Creek. Two things went pounding through the beer geek telegraph: a *farmhouse brewery*, wow, all saisons and bier de gardes and lambic and neat Belgian-French stuff with all that funkiness! And then . . . Brian who?

It's safe to say that the reality was not what any of us had imagined.

Brian Sprague was not a brewer. He was (and is) a petroleum geologist, who did chainsaw carving on the side, the stuff with full-size tree trunks. He was certainly not any kind of Belgian beer maker, and his farmhouse brewery was just that: a brewery in a farmhouse. Actually, it was in a barn.

But would we see farmhouse ales? "We plan to ease into the farmhouse ale idea," Brian told me

Beers brewed: Year-round: Rust Belt Amber, Hellbender Robust Porter, Ale Mary Wit, Fighting Scotchtoberfest, I.B.U.D. 59, Effin' Dunkelweizen. Seasonals: Blissberry, Kick Bock, Downtown Kenny Brown, Lightning Rod Farmhouse Ale, Gemaschlichkeit Wheat, French & Indian Corn Ale. All draft.

then, "as we must create a beer that will be accepted in the immediate area. Believe me, it will have flavor and character."

Finding all this out left me with a crooked smile on my face. This guy was definitely not like anyone else in brewing, and it was likely that what he did was going to be fun and interesting. He got some help at the start-up from Matt Allyn, as have other people in the area. ("The man's a brewing MacGyver," said Chris Sirianni at Brewerie. "He came in here and built us a kegwasher out of some pipes in about three hours.")

The Pick: I've liked Ale Mary from the first day I tasted it. The peppery tang—from peppercorns—is unlike any other witbier, and it gives Ale Mary a refreshing and arresting kick. Different, like almost everything else at Sprague.

Things came together right on schedule—unheard of!—and on July 14, 2006, Brian's birthday, Sprague Farm and Brew Works had their grand opening. It was an astonishing day. The property is beautiful, sitting on a bend of U.S. Route 6 overlooking French Creek. Trees line the driveway back past the house, then you come out and the barn brewery is right in front of you, and the blue sky goes on forever. You'll know you've got the right place when you see the oversize handle on the side of the silo that turns it, visually, into a giant beer mug.

Folks had flocked to this opening—a few beer enthusiasts, but mostly local folks and friends of Brian who had helped him build this place. I finally met the man, and it was a moment. When you meet Brian Sprague, you'll see he's not just a brewer and chainsaw carver. He's also ruggedly handsome, possessed of a good-natured sense of fun that's as broad as a barn, and he's in superb physical condition; I was shocked to learn he was only a year younger than I am. Brian and his wife, Minnie, are great testimonials to the active life.

We drank beers. The Ale Mary was a wit brewed with coriander, orange peel, juniper berries, and peppercorns; a wake-up wit. Hellbender Porter (named for the huge salamanders that live in French Creek) was big but friendly, bitter but not astringent, showing real signs of promise. I left with a great feeling about this place.

What Brian and Minnie have done since then is even better. They took the far end of the barn, an open space that had been cluttered with brewery stuff and odds and ends, threw a big blue tarp over the roof and foamed it for insulation and waterproofing, and went to work inside. They created a space they call Bierhalla, a beerhall in Crawford County style, with plenty of local breweriana and Brian's wood carvings. The stage is at one end, the bar at the other, and the high roof arcs overhead, framing a stained-glass angel with the legend "VENANGO." There's a small food service area, and they have Pennsylvania wines. The glasses

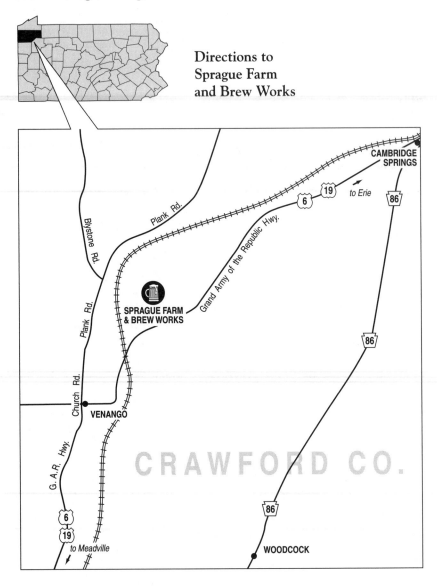

**Directions to
Sprague Farm
and Brew Works**

are half-pint (for the wine) and pint returnable cream bottles that Brian had to get from Canada, the only place still making them.

"You asked me two years ago what was next," Brian said, and laughed. "This! This is next! I saw the barn back in 1997, and I've been thinking about this ever since. The acoustics are great, too. This is where all the cool kids go! Well, it's pretty much the only place there is out here.

"We did this out in the middle of nowhere because we liked it here," he said. "I figured other people would like it, too. They have pride in the local beer, the local place. They come here a lot. It works out well for us; it's much better selling the beer by the glass!"

Minnie's doing most of the brewing, and she's getting good at it. Brian's still doing geology work—the money's hard to give up—and working on projects like the old milk truck he's using as a mobile draft dispensing unit for outdoor events (he's got a fire engine, too). They did have a draft tower built into an upright piano, which I loved, but that's been retired till Brian can get the insulation right; the beer kept warming up and getting foamy.

Brian and Minnie continue to do things their way. Other brewers take up causes, help local charities, encourage community involvement, do neighborhood cleanups—all good things. The Spragues want to clean up French Creek to protect the environment for the hellbenders, and part of that involves education sessions with Brian up to his waist in the creek, catching hellbenders and letting people see and hold them.

I'd love to know what's next.

Opened: April 2006.

Owners: Brian and Mary "Minnie" Sprague.

Brewers: Minnie and Brian Sprague.

System: 12-barrel VAFAC system, 400 barrels annual capacity.

2009 production: 325 barrels.

Brewpub hours: Thursday, 2 to 8 PM; Friday and Saturday, noon to 9 PM.

Tours: On request, subject to availability. Casual and kid-friendly.

Take-out beer: Growlers.

Food: Limited. For now, the Bierhalla offers a meat and cheese plate, Smith's hot dogs, chips and pretzels, and house-made beef brisket.

Extras: Live music every week; check the calendar on the Web site.

Special considerations: Kids welcome.

Parking: Slots at barn entrance reserved for handicapped parking; otherwise, park somewhere in one of their fields. Please don't park on the road; it's a narrow shoulder.

Lodging in the area: The farmhouse on the premises is for rent, but only as the whole thing, with kitchen and linens provided. "It sleeps eight, or more if you're friendly," Minnie said. Call the brewery for reservations. There's also Riverside Inn, 1 Fountain St., Cambridge Springs, 814-398-4645.

Area attractions: Sprague sits right on *U.S. Route 6*, one of the most scenic roads in the state (check out the PA Route 6 Tourist Association Web site at www.paroute6.com). It's a great drive that passes through or near some of the best attractions in the northern tier, all the way to the Delaware River. If you're in this area, either you're here for the three breweries or you're here for the scenery; enjoy. If you want something else, check the Blue Canoe listing on page 293 for the Oil Creek historical sites.

Other area beer sites: Not much. Like Brian said, this is where the cool kids go, because there's not much else.

Voodoo Brewing Company

215¹/₅ Arch Street, Meadville, PA 16335
412-468-0295
www.voodoobrewery.com

Is it Voodoo Brewery or Voodoo Brewing Company? According to Matt Allyn, some of the confusion is my fault. "When I started saying stuff to people about opening," he said, "I debated: 'Brewery or Brewing Company?' I thought Brewing Company was kind of boring. What did people say the most? Then when you wrote about it on your blog, you said, 'Voodoo Brewery opening soon,' and more and more people said that. So we did Voodoo Brewing Company, doing business as Voodoo Brewery. If you can't remember a name, and people call it something else, you need to go with that."

If you're going to be around Matt Allyn, you'll have to get used to that kind of constant analysis. His mind is in overdrive all the time; I've rarely seen the guy at rest. He's just thinking all the time—about beer, naturally, but he's also thinking about his businesses, about menus, about how to market beer in general and his beer in particular, about other people's restaurants, too: the hows, the whys, the "what's next."

Voodoo is a natural outgrowth of that fertile mind. "Why Voodoo?" Matt responded when I asked him where the name came from. "Voodoo is a name that rings a tone. Sometimes it spooks people, sometimes they like it. They'll say it two or three times and think about it. The White/Black Magick idea—it could have a good side and a bad side. I

Beers brewed: Regulars: Gran Met, Voodoo Love Child, Pilzilla, White Magick, Four Seasons IPA, Wynona's Big Brown Ale. Seasonals: Big Black Voodoo Daddy, Black Magick, Cowbell (an imperial chocolate oatmeal milk stout, "All the stouts in one glass!": nitro draft only).

don't want to be known as a Haitian brewery, but it needs to be good and hip and all that. It's been able to inspire people, it's fun, and people remember it."

Matt may seem to be shooting from the hip all the time, but like it says on the Voodoo Web site: "I brew beer not Web sites, nor can I spell or type, so be critical of the beer not the Web site." He thinks about marketing, he thinks about things to do with the big empty space in front of the brewhouse, but mostly he's thinking about the beer.

Take a look at those beers. You'll have to, because the brewery isn't much to look at—a small space in the back of an old furniture store, very bare-bones, although Matt and his fellow brewer Justin Dudek are always ready to tap a sample off

The Pick: Gran Met is excellent; Matt calls it a big biere de garde, I think it's closer to a triple, but it's overwhelmingly tasty. Voodoo Love Child, though . . . is Gran Met aged on Michigan cherries, passion fruit, and raspberries. That might sound like a mess, but it's magic, and wonderfully light to drink for a 10 percent beer. As my wife said, this would be great on a summer night as the fireflies come out.

the tanks. Those tanks (and barrels) are full of beers like Pilzilla, an oversize, unfiltered pilsner. "Pilsner" usually means something around 4.5 to 5 percent ABV, lighter-bodied, bitter but not overwhelming, and sublimely drinkable. Pilzilla is described as "nicely hopped at this point with 9 different kinds of hops at 10 additions and about 6.75%."

But talk to Matt, and he'll tell you it's not really that big a deal. "I didn't want to break the boundaries, like Sam Adams Imperial Pilsner," he said, referring to Jim Koch's big, sticky, 8 percent hopbeast lager. "I just wanted a bigger pilsner, unfiltered, flavorful, but drinkable. We're not trying to reinvent anything, we're not trying to clone anything, just trying to make beers that are slightly different from their interpretations. We make what we want, when we have the inspiration.

"The White Magick wasn't supposed to be a white beer," he continued. "It's of the original parameters of a witbier, but with a bunch of other stuff in it. Why does wit have to be just coriander and orange peel? It's a beer of spice. Pierre Celis says, 'Do whatever you want!' and he's the expert on it. We started with a platform and went from there."

Even on less exotic styles, Matt goes his own way, or goes on the ways of the past that others might have forgotten. Take Wynona's Big Brown Ale. "Most brewers make brown ale with things other than the malt called 'brown,'" Allyn said. "An English maltster told me that he didn't sell any brown malt to the U.S. market except for stouts, and he didn't understand it: 'We make brown malt for brown ale.' There's 100 pounds of brown malt in Wynona's. People taste it and say, 'This doesn't taste like most of the brown ales I drink.' That was the intention! I put the 'big' in there as a disclaimer."

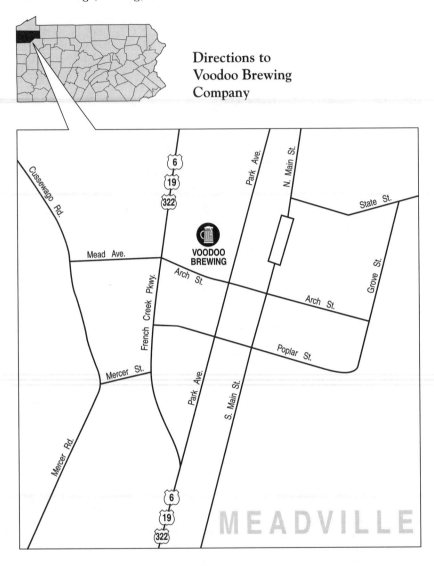

**Directions to
Voodoo Brewing
Company**

So that's what Matt wants to do. It remains to be seen whether he'll be able to. Every time he ships beer to Philadelphia or Pittsburgh, it's snapped up and drained in a matter of days. It goes quickly at home, too. "My next door neighbor at Voodoo, an orthodontist and his crew, love the beer," Matt said. "They're in there every weekend getting growlers!"

The problem is capital. "We're trying to put a pub in at Voodoo," Matt told me. "That would be a saving grace. But money got a lot tighter when the stock market crashed. We expected things to roll a little faster. Once the banks start letting people borrow and build, we'll do something."

Right now, he's able to do some things at Straub (where they have an in-house sign shop and a lab), thanks to his working there as brewmaster, and there's the possibility of a joint venture. That would be great for Voodoo, but Matt said the friendship with the Straubs is more important; if the joint venture is a dealbreaker, it's off the table.

"Voodoo is not going to go anywhere unless it's financially viable," he admitted. "We were treading water for a while, but it looks like we'll be able to do some swimming. We'll make the next step with either some Straub money or private investors."

Will Voodoo be able to work a little magic and hang on till the economy rolls around again? Given how good the beer is, I hope the spirits are favorable to the idea.

Opened: September 21, 2007.
Owner: Matt Allyn.
Brewers: Matt Allyn, Justin Dudek.
System: 10-barrel Pub Brewing system, 1,500 barrels annual capacity.
2009 production: 400 barrels.
Tours: By appointment only.
Take-out beer: Growlers.
Parking: Large garage out back.
Lodging in the area: America's Best Value Inn will do you right if you just want a clean place to sleep: 11237 Shaw Avenue, Meadville, 814-724-6366; Holiday Inn Express, 18240 Conneaut Lake Rd., Meadville, 814-724-6012; Wynken Blynken and Nod B&B, 468 Chestnut St., Meadville, 814-337-2018.
Area attractions: Meadville residents will proudly tell you that the zipper was invented here. Well, kind of—it was invented in Akron and perfected in Meadville by Gideon Sundbäck, a Swedish-born engineer who later formed his own Canadian zipper company . . . but he developed the zipper, lived, and is buried in Meadville. There is no zipper museum, though; sorry. Boating and fishing are big draws at **Conneaut Lake** (www.conneautlake.com), Pennsylvania's largest natural lake, and the **Pymatuning Reservoir in Pymatuning State Park** (724-932-3141, www.dcnr.state.pa.us), the state's largest manmade lake (Raystown Lake is the largest wholly inside the state; a part of Pymatuning Lake is in Ohio) and the state's largest park. The park has boating (rentals are available), fishing, swimming, camping and cabins, hunting, winter sports (including iceboating), picnicking, and a fish hatchery. The fish hatchery is a huge draw in the spring and summer, when thousands of people come to feed the fish

(feed is available), which swarm so thickly that ducks walk across their backs to compete for the food. It's something to see!

Other area beer sites: Matt's been teaching a beer school at the **Roff School Tavern** (13388 Leslie Rd., Meadville, 814-333-8641), and it's got the taps for the curriculum; get an education. **Chippers Pub** (253 Chestnut St., Meadville, 814-333-2122) has a broad selection of bottles and draft and a friendly atmosphere. Oddly enough, **Chovy's Italian Casual** restaurant (18228 Conneaut Lake Rd., Meadville, 814-724-1286) is a good place to drink beer in Meadville. There's also an exceptional selection of wines; that's actually what I wound up drinking when I visited.

Blue Canoe Brewery

113 South Franklin Street, Titusville, PA 16354
814-827-7181
www.thebluecanoebrewery.com

To get to Titusville, you have to take two-lane roads, no way around it. There are ridges to climb and rivers to cross and woods to pierce, kind of like the musical road to grandmother's house. When the nearest towns are Tionesta and Oil City, you know you're getting out there in Pennsylvania.

So when Thom Sauber opened Four Sons, a state-of-the-art brewpub, sporting schwarzbier, tripel, oatmeal stout, and witbier brewed by ace brewer Matt Allyn (an experienced brewer lured in from Erie Brewing), and a menu that's quite a bit beyond the common fare of Titusville bars, it was a bit of a shock. How would it work out?

For a while, it did, but then things kind of lost focus, Allyn left to open Voodoo Brewery in nearby Meadville, and business dropped off. On New Year's Day 2007, Four Sons closed, $400,000 in debt. Not good news for local craft beer drinkers, and not good news for local brewers, either; it almost always hurts everyone when places close, because it gives fuel to the "fancy-shmancy yuppie beer doesn't sell"

Beers brewed: Year-round: Flashlite Lager, Titusville Gold Lager, Classic 5 A.P.A., Heavy Kevy, Distorter Porter. Seasonals: Wits End Wit, Joe's Electric Bill Amber, Dubbel Trouble, Polish Thunder Oatmeal Porter, Spinal Tap (a double IPA, but don't call it that), Crazy Rye, Big Skye Special, and yes, Dead Tony's Trippel . . . with many more to come.

crowd. (Really, I still hear people say that. "Yuppie beer." In 2010. Amazing.)

But the building was still sitting there on a busy corner (location, location, location), the brewhouse sitting behind the glass, a brewpub just waiting to open again in this 1840s-era building (thought to have been a bank at one time, where John Rockefeller had an office on the second floor). It was just too tempting for Matt Allyn. He grew up in nearby Corry (where he went to high school with North Country brewer Sean McIntyre), and he wanted this to succeed.

The Pick: I'm going to go with Heavy Kevy. This was good the first time around, and it's still good, stupid good, no-brainer good, easy-to-drink good. It's sweet but not gaggy, it's smooth but flavorsome. Embrace it, but keep that 6.8 percent in mind.

"Jeremy Potocki and I designed the place," Matt said, "and we felt it was as much ours as it was Thom's." He and Jeremy (the once and current chef at the brewpub) got together with Bill Zimmer, a friend who'd been working at Big Sky Resort in Montana (Bill also went to school with Matt and Sean; who knew they had such a hospitality program at Corry Area High?), put together a plan and financing, and bought the place in April 2008. Matt's dad's presence on the Titusville Redevelopment Authority board had to have helped, but it really was a win-win for the town.

"It's a great little brewery, and I wanted to do business with my friends," Matt said. "To be able to get it back up and running has really bolstered the community. Stores that closed when Four Sons closed have reopened. If you care, and play it smart, and the customers know you care, you can do it. You can put a brewpub in any size town like that. We got it for a discount price, and we're paying all our bills.

"I think every small town can do this," he added. "There's money in these towns, but people have to go outside to do something nice. Now they can hang out here and feel like they're in a small pub downtown in some city. They like that."

The Blue Canoe name has spread all over the brewpub. There's a colorful mural across the front of the building with the whole outdoors theme. The concrete bar inside has been painted with a meandering river down along the ice rail.

Where did the name come from? "We were trying to come up with something that said 'outdoors,' that flowed well," Matt said. "A lot of the folks in our area are canoers. We're outdoors people; Jeremy and I do a lot of camping and canoeing. Blue Canoe flowed, the artwork was easy, and blue is a good, calming word. You want families to feel good about the name."

Justin Dudek's doing most of the brewing, over in the glass-enclosed brewhouse ("It's humid in the winter and really hot in the summer," he said), turning out beers tuned to the high and low expectations of a varied clientele. "We do the solid interpretations of well-known styles," said Matt. "At a brewpub, I don't want to make beers we have to explain to everyone. It's a lot more work."

The Flashlite Lager, for instance, is a credible light lager, but the Titusville Lager is noticeably bigger and more bitter. The Distorter Porter is solid, bitter, and has a bit of burnt malt bite to it. And if you remember Four Sons, you'll be glad to see Heavy Kevy, the renamed Heavy K, a happy Scotch ale that's full of malty goodness. There was even a batch of Dead Tony's Trippel on when I visited, just as smooth and spicy—and clean—as I remember it.

Titusville has another chance at brewpub love. Matt's got a third brewery to balance, but he's up for it. "They asked me how I would manage Blue Canoe along with Voodoo," he said and snorted. "I can do a lot more than manage it, take my word for it!" Time will tell. I hope Matt remembers that it was a lack of focus that took down Four Sons. Keep an eye down the river as you paddle this canoe!

Opened: August 2008.

Owners: Keystone Brewing Company.

Brewers: Matt Allyn, Justin Dudek.

System: 7-barrel Pub Brewing Systems brewhouse, 900 barrels potential annual capacity.

2009 production: 600 barrels.

Brewpub hours: Tuesday through Saturday, 3 PM to midnight; Sunday 12:30 to 10 PM. Closed Monday.

Tours: On request, subject to brewer availability

Take-out beer: Growlers.

Food: Not quite as ambitious as the original Four Sons menu, but still interesting. Check out the appetizers: deep-fried soft pretzels, pierogies, and a wonton of the week. To fill the belly, try the hand-cut steaks, blackened grouper sandwich, shepherd's pie, substantial vegetarian items (the smoked tofu sloppy joe sounds like a winner), some tasty pizzas, and a number of mushroom dishes.

Extras: Occasional live music; see Web site for schedule. Mug club.

Special considerations: Kids welcome. Good variety of vegetarian and vegan meals available; "we will adapt meat dishes if possible; please ask."

Parking: On-street parking is pretty easy.

Lodging in the area: Knapp Farm B&B, 43778 Thompson Run Rd., Titusville, 814-827-1092 (working family farm with packages for hunters, fishers, and stable accommodations for your horse); Shady-side Hotel, 117 E. Main St., Titusville, 814-827-6923; Cross Creek Resort, 3815 William Flynn Highway, Titusville, 800-461-3173.

Area attractions: You're in the home of oil: Titusville was where Colonel Drake drilled the world's very first oil well. The **Drake Well Museum** (205 Museum Lane, 814-827-2797, www.drakewell.org) has a reproduction of that first well and pump, as well as other exhibits. **Oil Creek State Park** (305 State Park Rd., Oil City, 814-676-5915) has a number of re-created oilfield buildings with interpretive signs, plus fishing, canoeing, and picnic sites. The park also has the historic **Petroleum Centre train station**, which is a stop for the Oil Creek and Titusville Railroad (trip starts at 409 S. Perry St., Titusville, 814-676-1733, www.octrr.clarion.edu). The excursion rides are a two-and-a-half-hour trip through "the valley that changed the world," a winding, scenic journey that is always pretty, but truly gorgeous in fall foliage season. There is a bike trail in the park, and the railroad invites you to bring your bike on board if you want to shorten your trip.

Other area beer sites: If you're looking for another stop, try the **Shamrock Tavern** (310 Cooper Ave., Oil City, 814-676-0141) for some solid bar food, friendly folks, and yes, beer that's a little off the mainstream.

North Country Brewing Company

141 South Main Street, Slippery Rock, PA 16057
724-794-BEER
www.northcountrybrewing.com

I like brewpubs that dare to be different. North Country's all that: a combination of restored antique (the front two rooms date from the 1830s, one of the oldest buildings in town), log cabin in the woods, hobbit's playhouse, and eco-hideaway. Owners Bob McCafferty and Jodi Branem weren't satisfied with the difference of being a brewpub and took it further. With its determinedly restored rustic look and bold yellow paint, it doesn't fit in on Main Street at all and doesn't intend to.

Let's take a walk. Step right up and check out the Adirondack-type branch railing, the driftwood and "found" stones worked into the façade.

The brewery's right there in the window, shoe-horned into a space that was originally too small for it until they cut a little off the brewer's platform. Yes, the door does say "County Morgue," and this was the county morgue for a while (the men's room was the old embalming chamber); before that, it was a cabinetmaking business that evolved into coffinmaking.

Beers brewed: Year-round: Station 33 Firehouse Red (5 percent of sales donated to the local fire company, and it's the best-seller), Creamation Ale, McLeod's Ewe, Paddler's Pale Ale, Fruit Bowl, Stone House Stout, Squirrel's Nut Brown, Northern Lite, Paleo IPA. Seasonals: Liquid Love Stout, Sam's Harvest Ale, Jack Frost Ale, Late Night Pumpkin Ale, Catherine the Great Imperial Stout, Wee Heavy Imp Ale . . . and more one-offs coming all the time.

There was still hardwood in the space when Bob and Jodi bought it, left over from the woodworking. It wasn't wasted. Local woodworker Gregg Kristophel, a man with a real gift and a whimsical imagination, used some of it to put character in the place before it even opened. See if you can find the little mouse carved into one table leg and the little mouse footprints on the table. There's a "dragonfly" joint at the bar's corner, complete with crushed turquoise eyes (it complements the butterfly joints in the rest of the bar), and two wild, full-size carvings on the restroom doors. There's more, too, but you'll have to find them; I don't want to spoil the fun.

Peek into the dining room, where the décor pays tribute to the area's fine fishing. The upstairs is finally open, and that makes more room. There's a smaller bar here; check out the pattern on the top of the bar. Bob and Jodi did that by laying down gunpowder and firing it off!

Come on out back. There's a big patio area out here, surrounded by a fence and shaded by a huge pine tree. You'd hardly know you were in the middle of town. Concord grapevines grow over a brick archway, and there's a big stone fireplace. It's great in the summer, almost better in the fall, and one of the favorite places for private parties.

The whole place looks like something out of a movie, a movie like *Lord of the Rings*—although it's quite a bit cleaner, and with fewer edged weapons. The only thing missing is the food and the drink. We're done with the walk; let's go back to the bar and have a beer!

Sean McIntyre is the brewer here, having come out of the fall of Valhalla (it was just a Pittsburgh brewpub that closed, but "the fall of Valhalla" sounds so right in this place). I loved his beers at Valhalla, but he was a bit restricted by the space and theme there (he's somewhat restricted by space here, too; the fermentation cellar has a ceiling that's only a little over 5 feet high). Here he's wide open, and he's been making beers that fit: different, but not different by being like every other different place—really different.

How so? Sean does the big beers the geeks love, sure: imperial stouts, double IPAs, Belgian types. He does the standards that you have to have to get a broad audience in a small town: light ale, cream ale, nut brown, and a fruit beer. But he'll also have beers like Simcoe Pale, a pale ale-strength beer that's stinky with Simcoe hops, and his Honey Bear Brown, a beer made with brown malt and honey that's hellaciously smooth but delivers a ton of that brown malt flavor without being sticky. His Bucksnort Stout has a broad sweep of molasses and graham character, a spring tonic that made me forget the 2 feet of snow outside.

The Pick: McLeod's Ewe may be the punchline of a shaggy old joke, but it's also a rock-solid Scottish ale, proof that craft beer can be great-tasting and interesting without a big hop presence—taste the power of malt and yeast. I've also got to get more of that Honey Bear Brown; just amazing.

Bob and Jodi are full of amazing energy. Jodi has a real talent in the kitchen, honed by twenty years in the restaurant business. Bob is a retired archeologist who just bubbles over with ideas. The latest is farm-ing. "We're going farm-to-fork now," he said. "We take our brewer's grains home to feed the cattle at North Country Cattle Company and bring them back as burger and steaks." That's local food supply in action. The brewery is thickly involved in environmental and beautifi-cation projects in town, what Bob calls "polishing the Rock."

Slippery Rock just went "wet" for the first time in its history in 2001. Unlike other communities, it doesn't have a tradition of drinking spots that a brewpub has to fit into. North Country has had a unique chance to influence how people see taverns in this town. As a beer enthusiast, I'm proud to see the job they've done.

Opened: February 2005.

Owners: Bob McCafferty, Jodi Branem.

Brewers: Sean McIntyre, head brewer; Jake Kristophel, assistant brewer.

System: 7-barrel JV Northwest brewhouse, 1,400 barrels potential annual capacity.

2009 production: 1,318 barrels.

Brewpub hours: Monday through Thursday, 11 AM to 11 PM; Friday and Saturday, 11 AM to midnight; Sunday, 11 AM to 10 PM.

Tours: Wednesday, 4 to 7 PM; please call ahead.

Take-out beer: Growlers, for now; once Full Pint Brewing Company is in operation making North Country's beer (see page 330), there will be six-packs and cases of 12-ounce bottles, sixtels, quarter and half kegs.

Food: Sturdy fare with real beer. The menu's different, too: a frog legs appetizer; cedar-roasted salmon salad; burgers that come in a choice

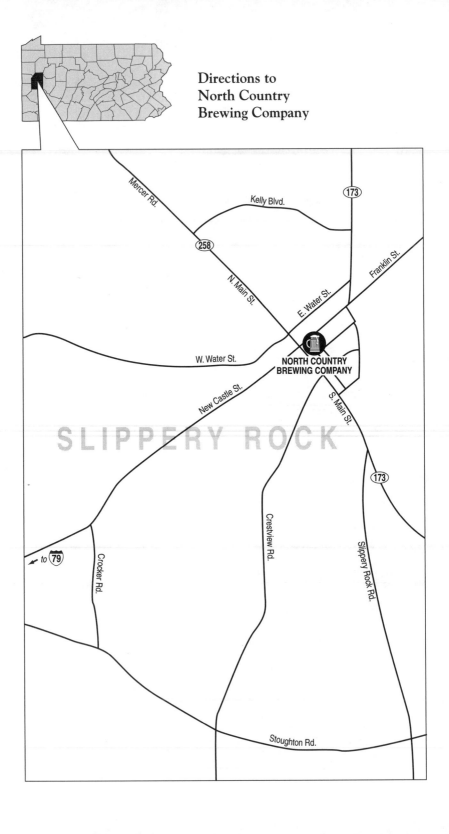

Directions to
North Country
Brewing Company

of local Angus, locally raised elk, or North Country's own beef; and many more vegetarian options than you'd expect at a place so clearly in love with meat.

Extras: Monday Night Bluegrass brings a variety of acts in every week; Tuesday features either a live band or open mike night. Free Wi-Fi available. There's also a 92-inch TV with SurroundSound for special events.

Special considerations: Kids welcome. Vegetarian meals available.

Parking: On-street parking, plus town lot across the street.

Lodging in the area: Applebutter Inn B&B, 666 Centerville Pike, 724-794-1844; Evening Star Motel, 915 New Castle Rd., 724-794-3211; Hampton Inn, 4 Holiday Blvd, Mercer, 724-748-5744.

Area attractions: Slippery Rock has a restored stagecoach tavern, the *Old Stone House* (724-738-2408, www.oldstonehousepa.org), open weekends. *Jennings Environmental Park* (at the intersection of Routes 8, 173, and 528, 724-794-6011) preserves a rare stretch of Pennsylvania prairie and presents a variety of programs throughout the year, including maple sugaring in early spring. *McConnell's Mill State Park* (Portersville, 724-368-8091) and *Moraine State Park* (225 Pleasant Valley Rd., Portersville, 724-368-8811) offer many outdoor recreation activities, including fishing, hunting, rock climbing, and Class II to Class IV whitewater boating through Slippery Rock Gorge at McConnell's Mill (and you can visit the mill itself, a restored water-powered gristmill). At Moraine, there's also camping, swimming, boating, windsurfing, biking, and hiking. If the outdoors just doesn't call to you like the indoors does, head up the road to *Prime Outlets* at Grove City (Route 208 and I-79, Exit 31, Grove City, 888-545-7221) for 140 stores' worth of shopping, seven days a week. I can smell the credit cards smoking now . . .

Other area beer sites: *B & J Coney Island* (235 Kelly Blvd., Slippery Rock, 724-794-4899) is not long on atmosphere, but they do have a nice draft selection, a beer take-out store, and sandwiches. The historic *Harmony Inn* (230 Mercer St., Harmony, 724-452-5124) is down I-79 closer to Pittsburgh, but it's more in Slippery Rock's sphere. They have a nice draft selection in an 1856 building that has been a tavern for more than a hundred years and have considered adding a brewery in the past . . . but not yet.

Beer Festivals

When May rolls around, it's time to gird your beer-drinking loins: It's beer festival season. From now till late October is the busiest time of the year for these taste extravaganzas, where you can sample a wide variety of beers from brewers large and small—even Anheuser-Busch and Miller come to the festivals now. Fests are casual and loud, educational and fun, and a chance for brewer and drinker to share some air and meet each other.

My first beer festival was about eighteen years ago at the Stoudt's Microbrewery Festival in Adamstown. About twenty microbrewers were there, set up with taps behind open tables. For a $20 ticket, we got a small glass (I still have it) to sample as many beers as we thought we could handle, along with live music from the Daisy Jug Band and a cruise down a buffet of wursts, kraut, breads, and potato salad. Brewers poured their beers; you could ask them how they made them, where their brewery was, what made their beer different, and maybe, if you'd been tipped off, ask for some of the secret beer they kept under the table. I was hooked: I wanted to go to one every weekend!

With some variation, that's how most fests go. You can probably find a local one (try www.beerfestivals.org or the calendar at www.Beer Advocate.com). Some are open sampling, some require you to buy tickets or tokens, but all of them have plenty of different beers to try.

Pick one, then hit the fest like a pro with these proven tactics: Try lighter beers first; save the darker, high-alcohol, and seriously hoppy beers for later (you don't want to blow out your taste buds too early). Get the program and make a couple notes or marks by the beers you like most—you may want to find them again. Always know where the bathrooms are.

Do some defensive drinking to keep yourself on the right side of smart. A good fest will have water available; drink plenty to clear your palate and your head (it also helps ward off hangovers the next morning). Get something to eat: Drinking big beers on an empty gut is a fast ticket to Drunksville—and the food at beer fests is usually pretty good. Most important, pace yourself so you can enjoy the whole fest and go out for dinner afterward. You'll pick up your own best practices as you go.

Once you've found out how much fun beer fests are, you can dive into one of the following, some of the best in Pennsylvania.

Stoudt's Micro Fest at Stoudt's Brewing (www.stoudtsbeer.com). One of the first, still one of the best. Stoudt's half-open architecture makes this well-ventilated festival comfortable, and a lot of regulars means the fest moves well. There are three of these through the season, with different brewers. Not a huge fest, but a great one.

Friday the Firkinteenth at the Grey Lodge Pub (www.greylodge.com). Not technically a fest—it's just a bar, and it only holds about 150 people (er . . . if that's legal), but what else can you call two dozen casks of real ale pouring by gravity right off the bar top for a happy beer geekerie? It happens every Friday the Thirteenth, and it's a different kind of crazy every time.

Taming of the Brew at the Caldwell Consistory in Bloomsburg (www.tamingofthebrew.org). This long-running small fest that showcases the small brewers from central Pennsylvania for the benefit of the local theater group might be the toughest ticket in the state: Tickets sold out in less than an hour this year.

Selinsgrove Brew Festival (www.selinsgrovebrewfest.com). This is where Pennsylvania's smallest brewers come out to play. I went last year, and I definitely plan to go again. It's a wonderfully walkable fest, a great small fest in a great small town, and Selin's Grove Brewing Company is right there when it's over.

Harrisburg Brewers Fest (www.troegs.com/brewfest). Tröegs hosts this growing fest that benefits the Cystic Fibrosis Foundation. Held on the street, it pulls in a lot of brewers from all over the country, and there's ongoing live music. I have not been, and I mean to fix that.

Kennett Square Brew Fest (www.kennettbrewfest.com). This beer festival was first held more than ten years ago to raise money for Historic Kennett Square, a civic rejuvenation project. It has since become a model for other towns and has an excellent reputation for quality and innovation.

Penn Fest and Oktoberfest at the Pennsylvania Brewing Company (www.pennbrew.com). Two great fests: Penn invites in other brewers to play in June for their Penn Fest, and you can try a lot of beers from Ohio, West Virginia, and Michigan. Oktoberfest is all theirs, and it's a blast, with music, sausage, and big glasses of Kaiser Pils.

Pints for Pets (www.pintsforpets.com). This May fest goes to the dogs: every cent of ticket sales is donated to the Central Pennsylvania Humane Society. More than 60 breweries set up stands for two sessions in the Altoona Curve ballpark; it's the biggest fest in central Pennsylvania.

Erie Fest at the Brewerie (www.wqln.org). Put on as a fund-raiser by WQLN, the PBS station that made *Pennsylvania Breweries* into a documentary . . . so maybe I'm biased, but this is a great fest, loose and happy, but not sloppy. Beer, food, and music: a tough combo to beat.

Hell with the Lid Off at Kelly's Bar and Lounge in Pittsburgh (412-363-6012). Like Friday the Firkinteenth, maybe not a classic fest, but it's sure an event, sampling a bunch of barleywines and other big beers in a cool joint. It's bound to get loud and a little boisterous—it always does—but what a great event.

Steel City Big Pour (www.constructionjunction.org). How Pittsburgh: a beer festival to benefit reuse of construction materials (is East End's Scott Smith involved in this somewhere?). Big Pour has more great ideas than any other beer festival I've ever seen, and they aren't just good the day of the fest, they keep working. A beer fest that makes you think.

Philly Beer Week (www.phillybeerweek.org). Ten days of beer events all over the greater Philadelphia area, more than six hundred of them: festivals, dinners, meet-the-brewer nights, beer trivia, brewing, tasting, lectures, pubcrawls, cooking demonstrations . . . There is a beer vibe all over town during Philly Beer Week, from the time the mayor ceremonially taps the first keg to the cluster of events all vying to be the very last event of a ten-day week that's still too short. Come. Stay. Drink.

(No Longer) Iron City
Pittsburgh

Pittsburgh has come a long way from the days of Carnegie and Frick. The steel mills are silent—and leveled—and the coke furnaces no longer loft their foul stench on the breeze. Pittsburgh went through hard, hard times in the 1970s and 1980s. The population dropped and thousands lost high-wage jobs as the American steel production industry collapsed under the pressure of subsidized overseas competition. Major regional brewer Pittsburgh Brewing—and its Iron City beer—fell into the hands of Australian investors. This city, once a symbol of American industrial might, was turning into a rusty ghost town.

I went to grad school in Pittsburgh in 1982. I treasured visits to Homestead to drink at Chiodo's Tavern. I drank my share of I.C. Light and Straub on my student budget. During that time and in subsequent visits over the next years, I watched Pittsburgh sink into a malaise as dreary as the faded old yellow brick homes peculiar to the city. I didn't know how Chiodo's would survive the demolition of the Homestead Steel Works, a massive structure right behind the bar that was a source of its business and pride.

One of the first harbingers of a turnaround was Tom Pastorius's return to town from Germany in 1985 with his idea for a microbrewery. After testing the waters by having Pittsburgh Brewing contract-brew his beer for a couple years, he started work on his restaurant and Pennsylvania Brewery. Hard work and tight budgets began to slowly pay off.

Similarly, the city started a slow return to health. Pittsburgh gradually let go of the idea that big steel would return, bringing high wages and union power with it, and started to search for its future in other directions. The citizens began to realize their strengths: smaller specialty steel industries, glass and coatings, health care, excellent universities, river trade, and tourism. Local businesses found innovative ways to compete, and employees and city government cooperated to persuade companies to stay in the 'Burgh.

Today Pittsburgh is a hardworking town with its eyes on a new future. This city of fifteen hundred bridges has built on the strengths of its past—its museums, fine architecture, and revived industries—to span the abyss left by the departed steel industry. The South Side and the Strip are bustling centers of nightlife, and the suburbs are growing and sprouting new businesses. I was happy to return to Pittsburgh, after years away, and see a cleaner, more confident city with new growth sparking all over.

But it's been a hard town for brewers. Of the seven brewers from the first edition of *Pennsylvania Breweries*—Church, Valhalla, Strip Brewing, Pittsburgh, Penn, Foundry, and the John Harvard's out in Monroeville—only Church and Penn remain, and Three Rivers had opened and closed before I got a chance to write about it.

That's right: Pittsburgh Brewing, the brewers of Iron City for more than a hundred years, finally succumbed to the fate that had been hanging over their heads for two decades. The big brick building is silent but for the racket of scrappers; brewmaster Mike Carota is making Iron City in Latrobe; and there was a proud but forlorn message on one of the trucks still parked in the lot the last time I drove by: "Thanks, Pittsburgh. From the employees and families of Iron City Brewing." Penn almost went under, too, as you'll read shortly; it was within days of fading away completely.

But though Iron City is now made in the former home of Rolling Rock—which is now made in Newark, New Jersey—and Chiodo's Tavern has been demolished and replaced by a Walgreen's, Pittsburgh's beer scene still thrives. There are other bars—new places and old ones—that keep up the spirit of this town: friendly, sincere, and openhearted. Jump in, enjoy it, and congratulate them on their success.

Go to Pittsburgh as a beer traveler, but don't miss all the other things the city has to offer. To avoid lots of repetition, I have decided to consolidate the **Lodging**, **Area attractions**, and **Other area beer sites** sections for the Pittsburgh breweries here. The entry for Rivertowne Pour House in Monroeville includes lodging and beer site information specific to that area.

Area attractions: You may want to come to Pittsburgh just to look at its architectural glories. This city is full of beautiful buildings, both industrial and residential. The Carnegie Museums house just about everything: dinosaurs, Egyptian artifacts, gems and minerals, wind tunnels and earthquake simulations, and Impressionist art. Surely something will interest you or your family. There's the **Carnegie Museum of Art** (412-622-3131, www.cmoa.org) and the **Carnegie Museum of Natural History** (412-622-3309, www.carnegiemnh .org), both at 4400 Forbes Ave., and the **Carnegie Science Center** (1 Allegheny Ave., 412-237-3400, www.carnegiesciencecenter.org), which my teenage kids still insist on visiting every time we're in Pittsburgh. Another Carnegie Museum, the **Andy Warhol Museum** (117 Sandusky St., 412-237-8300, www.warhol.org), is dedicated entirely to a famous Pittsburgh native's work. The **Frick Art and Historical Center** (7227 Reynolds St., 412-371-0606, www.frickart .org) includes the restored mansion of Henry Clay Frick, the Carriage Museum with sleighs and vintage automobiles, and the Frick Art Museum. See the Pirates or the Steelers at their beautiful stadiums, both flowing with local beer. **PNC Park** (412-323-5000, www.pittsburgh.pirates.mlb.com) is right across from downtown on the Seventh Street Bridge and an easy walk from Penn Brewery; **Heinz Field** (412-323-1200, www.steelers.com) is just downriver. They're both across from **Point State Park**, where the Allegheny and Monongahela rivers meet to form the Ohio River, a beautiful green spot right beside downtown. The 150-foot spray of the fountain is one of the largest in the country. Don't miss the **Duquesne Incline** (1197 W. Carson St., 412-381-1665, www.incline.pghfree .net), a Victorian solution to Pittsburgh's steep South Shore hills. Ride the incline's hill-hugging cable car up to the aptly named Grandview Avenue for a spectacular view of the Golden Triangle. For just walking around and having fun while maybe buying a few things, you have two great choices: the Strip District and South Side. The **Strip District** (north and south of the 2000 block of Penn Avenue) is Pittsburgh's produce and meat market. This is a busy, bustling, fun place during the day, and it steams with nightlife after dark. The **South Side** (on Carson Street around Fat Head's and Smokin' Joe's) is a younger, more fringe scene at night, but a lot of fun, and you can find some great casual food and drink here. The **Pittsburgh Zoo** (412-665-3640, www.pittsburghzoo.com) has many exotic animals, including Siberian tigers, zebras, and elephants; the PPG Aquarium, with electric eels and glass catfish; and a special kids' zoo, with a sea lion pool. For more rousing recreation, **Kennywood Amusement Park** (4800 Kennywood Blvd., West Mifflin, 412-461-0500, www.kennywood.com) is a national treasure, a well-preserved family-style amusement park, not a fancy theme park, with four roller coasters, thirty other rides, and fourteen children's rides; it was recently rated the fifth-best amusement park in the world. There's also **Sandcastle** (412-462-6666, www.sandcastlewater park.com), a water park on the Monongahela with water slides, a huge hot tub, a lazy river, and go-karts. Pittsburgh celebrates in the summer. The **Three Rivers Art Festival** (www.artsfestival.net) in June starts the ball rolling, and the **Three Rivers Regatta** highlights the Fourth of July weekend. Later in July, vintage cars crowd Schenley Park for the **Vintage Grand Prix**, and August brings the **Greater Pittsburgh Renaissance Festival** in nearby New Stanton. For further information on these events and other attractions, contact the **Greater Pittsburgh Convention and Visitors Bureau** (412-281-7711, www.visitpittsburgh.com).

Lodging in the area: When I'm in Pittsburgh, I usually stay at The Priory, a historic B&B within an easy walk of Max's Allegheny and Penn Brewery at 614 Pressley St., 412-231-3338. Other options are Doubletree Hotel City Center, 1000 Penn Ave., 412-281-5800; Best Western Parkway Center Inn, 875 Greentree Rd., 412-922-7070; Residence Inn University Medical Center, 3896 Bigelow Blvd., 412-621-2200.

Other area beer sites: One tip before we start: after you've been out till all hours, go to the "almost famous" **Primanti Brothers Bar and Grille** (www.primantibrothers.com), where you'll get your sandwich served with fries and coleslaw—right in the sandwich. It's a Pittsburgh tradition after a late night of drinking, and you may see anyone here. The menu's on the wall: roast beef and cheese, fried egg and cheese, kolbassi and cheese, fried bologna and cheese . . . and down in the corner is the note I love: "Extra cheese—25¢" In the Strip District at 46 18th St. (412-263-2142), in Oakland at 3803 Forbes Ave. (412-621-4444), on the South Side at 1832 E. Carson St. (412-381-2583), at Market Square on 2 S. Market Place (412-261-1599), and at both PNC Park and Heinz Field. A lot more locations have opened outside the city; check their Web site.

The Strip and Downtown. 6 Penn Kitchen (Sixth and Penn, 412-566-PENN) is eye-catching: outdoor marquee and lots of glass, open kitchen, chic little cocktail and craft beer bar, rooftop dining, very, very nice, and here's the kicker—it's from the Eat 'n' Park people. Really. They clean up real nice! **Kaya** (2000 Smallman St., 412-261-6565) is a cool place with a funky menu of Caribbean fusion and vegetarian dishes, great beer, and a wide selection of spirits. **Brillobox** (4104 Penn Ave., 412-621-4900) isn't in the Strip, but it's easy to get to from there, and you should: good beers and cocktails, attractive space, and funky, artsy events make it an appealing stop.

Oakland. The **Fuel and Fuddle** (212 Oakland Ave., 412-682-3473) is a clean, loud, and happy place that's a Pitt favorite. Great taps and bottles and a brick pizza oven. Just a block away is **Mad Mex** (Atwood and Bates Sts., 412-681-5656), a little rough-looking, but the fringey crowd is beer-savvy and drinks good stuff. They eat well, too: big plates of Mexican food. (Also try these other Mad Mex's: 7905 McKnight Rd., North Hills, 412-366-5656; Scott Towne Center, 2101 Greentree Rd., South Hills 412-279-0200; and Robinson Plaza II, Route 60, Park Manor Dr., 412-494-5656.) After drinking in Oakland, I usually—okay, always—wind up at **Original's** (at the corner of Forbes and Bouquet, 412-621-0435) for some fries and one of their great footlong dogs with chili, mustard, and onions. And maybe one more beer, if I'm walking.

South Side. **Fat Head's** (1805 E. Carson St., 412-431-7433) has expanded: They now have thirty-nine rotating taps, regular cask ale, and an excellent selection in bottles, and they still have the Headwiches, heart-stopping sandwiches the size of my two fists. Open wide! Across Carson is **Piper's Pub** (1828 E. Carson St., 412-381-3977), a Scottish-themed bar with a massive selection of single malts (and top-notch Irish whiskey as well) and good beer to boot: They've started a serious cask ale program that I highly recommend to you. Those two spots anchor Carson for the beer lover, but there's more. Head east, and you'll find that **Smokin' Joe's** (E. Carson and 20th Streets, 412-341-6757) has a wall o' taps going, and the bartenders know what they're pouring. Keep going upriver (which is toward Hofbräu, by the way . . .) to the **Double Wide Grill** (2339 E. Carson St., 412-390-1111), a roughly hip joint in an old garage with a no-compromises set of draft beers. (I was actually introduced to this place by Sly Fox's Brian O'Reilly; the cat gets around.) Another couple blocks . . . well, maybe you should ride instead of walk to **OTB Bicycle Café** (2518 E. Carson St., 412-381-3698), a favorite of perennial pedaller Scott Smith of East End. You'll need a ride to work off the double-fisted bar food and good craft beers. Go up the river to Homestead, close to Rock Bottom and where Chiodo's used to be, right beside the tracks, and you'll find **Blue Dust** (601 Amity St., 412-461-6220), the new "gastropub" that everyone kept telling me about, for good reason: The food was delicious, the service was smart, and the beer was kicked well up. A new regular stop for me. Much farther south, in Bridgeville (you'll have to shoot through the Tubes and run down I-279 to get there), is the **Pittsburgh Bottleshop Café** (1597 Washington Pike [PA Route 50], Bridgeville,

412-279-8191). The Bottleshop is the brainchild of Pittsburgh Brewing brewer Mark Davis, who took an empty strip plaza storefront, filled it with coolers and hundreds of bottles of beer (plus fifteen taps), staffed it with attractive young men and women, and opened the doors. The incredibly fresh pizza at **Bado's Pizza Grill** (307 Beverly Rd., Pittsburgh, 412-563-5300) would be enough for a recommendation; but they've got a well-chosen selection of beers, too. Better get over here soon. I meant to include **Amel's Restaurant** (435 McNeilly Rd., Pittsburgh, 412-563-3466) last time and forgot; my apologies, because the Meditteranean food here goes so well with the increasingly good beer they're serving. Help correct my mistake! **Barley & Hop's Bottle Shop** (5217 Library Rd., Bethel Park, 412-854-4ALE) has a well-done but limited menu (limited to meat and cheese, mostly), a comfy space with loungey style, and coolers stuffed full of hundreds of bottled beers by Tim "the Beer Geek" Santoro. Have a seat or take it with you.

North Shore. If you like German food, and Penn Brewing doesn't fill you up, get yourself to **Max's Allegheny Tavern** (537 Suismon St., 412-231-1899). Schnitzels, wursts, goulash, and sauerkraut that will make you a believer are served with a great selection of German and local beers. Not far away from Max's is the **Park House** (403 E. Ohio St., 412-231-0551), reputed to be Pittsburgh's oldest bar. It looks it: Park House has that long, narrow, "barrel house" look to it and is well worn and comfortable, with good taps of Penn beers. Over in the quiet Mexican War Streets neighborhood, you'll find a block of homes on Monterey Street that has one brightly lit doorway with an Irish flag: That's the **Monterey Pub** (1227 Monterey St., 412-322-6535). With a fine backbar, a small but solid tap selection, and a varied clientele having real conversations, the Monterey is the kind of bar I wish I had in my neighborhood; this one's a real jewel. The newest **Rivertowne** pub (337 North Shore Dr., 412-322-5000) is open on the North Shore; haven't been yet, but I've got plenty of faith that it will be as good as the others. Not on the North Shore, but up the river, is the original **Rivertowne Inn** (500 Jones St., Verona, 412-828-3707), and what a pleasant surprise this place was: a corner bar tucked in behind a supermarket plaza, with sixteen excellent taps (*not* the taps everyone else in town had, either), more than two hundred well-picked bottles, knowledgeable staff, and big, old plates of fish. You'll want to stay all night.

Shadyside and East Liberty. **Kelly's Bar and Lounge** (6012 Penn Circle South, 412-363-6012) has just gotten better and better since I first found it and now hosts beer events like the Hell with the Lid Off barleywine festival; a constant breakout spot for new East End beers. **Harris Grill** (5747 Ellsworth Ave., 412-362-5273) will do you right with a solid tap set, keep you cool in summer with a nice patio area, and mixes a mean cocktail. But folks: Tuesday is Bacon Night. 'Nuff said. The **Sharp Edge Beer Emporium** (302 S. St. Clair St., 412-661-3537) opened their first bar here, with well-made bar food and one of the best selection of Belgian taps—twenty of them—in the United States. This place alone is worth a visit to Pittsburgh, but they've expanded to a whole empire, all with twenty Belgian taps: **Sharp Edge Creek House** is downstream in Crafton (288 W. Steuben St., 412-922-8118); the **Bistro** is in the heart of Sewickley (510 Beaver St. rear, 412-749-0305); the **Brasserie** is just off Route 19 near Canonsburg (102 Gallery Dr., McMurray, 724-942-2437); and there's a new one coming to Downtown at 922 Penn Ave.

Lawrenceville and Polish Hill. One night I closed the Church and wanted one last place to go. "Gooski's," said the bartender, and I never wrote a letter to thank her. **Gooski's** is in the heart of Polish Hill (3117 Brereton St., 412-681-1658), and it is rocking, with cheap micros, a big jukebox, and a bargeload of attitude. A must-stop. The **Bloomfield Bridge Tavern** (4412 Liberty Ave., right at the downhill end of the bridge, 412-682-8611) is where you'll find great Polish food (get the pierogies or don't bother going) and a decent stash of beer, too.

Other Neighborhoods. **D's Six Packs and Dogz** (1118 S. Braddock Ave., 412-241-4666) is over in Swissvale. D's is unique: a small place with a few constantly rotating and phenomenal taps, a tiny menu of hot dogs and sausages, a small dining room and a bar . . . and more than a thousand different bottled beers back in what they call the Beer Cave. It's amazing (and the hot dogs are good stuff). You'll find East End beers at **The Map Room** (1126 S. Braddock Ave., 412-371-1955), along with a nice array of single malts, and Irish music on Sunday nights. Not far from Shadyside, you'll find the Squirrel Hill neighborhood and the **Squirrel Hill Café** (5802 Forbes Ave., 412-521-3327). The "Squirrel Cage" has changed from when I used to visit, when it was bright, loud, and young, with a broad selection of nonlocal microbrews. Now it's quieter, and older, and carries mostly local beers. Kind of like me. The Point Breeze neighborhood isn't far away, where you'll find the cleverly named **Point Brugge Café** (401 Hastings St., 412-441-3334), a beautifully set-up Belgian tribute tucked into a corner building, with one of the best-chosen small beer sets I've seen in a while; toothsome food, too. Finally, out near the airport, not near any of the breweries but simply too good, too significant to leave out, is **Bocktown Beer and Grill** (690 Chauvet Dr., North Fayette, 412-788-2333). Looking for exceptional, even rare taps? You bet. Interested in rare and vintage bottles? Tera's "Beer Library" has you covered. You want beer events? Got that (I've done one myself). Food, music, take-out beer? Look, just get on out here: If you want it, they've got it.

Pennsylvania Brewing Company

800 Vinial Street, Pittsburgh, PA 15212
412-237-9400
www.pennbrew.com

Tom Pastorius once told me a very simple truth about why he opened a microbrewery and why it brews the kinds of beers it does: "Pennsylvania Brewing exists to make beers that I like," he said. Those beers are German-style lagers, and Tom's brewery makes some of the best in the United States . . . again.

I say "again" because Pittsburgh and Pennsylvania came within a whisker of losing this treasure of a brewery. In September 2003, Tom sold a controlling interest to Birchmere Capital, a local investment group. The idea was to raise the money to expand the brand's sales area and bring all brewing in-house.

That's not how it worked out. "They started making all the strategic decisions," Tom told me recently (over lunch at Max's Allegheny; after all, if you can't eat at Penn's own table, where else would you go?). "I had a five-year consulting contract, and when it was up, they couldn't wait to get me out the door." Big mistake, guys.

By late 2008, the people from Birchmere were making noises about shutting down the brewery, going all contract, and opening a smaller brewpub

Beers brewed: Year-round: Penn Pilsner, Penn Gold, Kaiser Pils, Penn Dark, Penn Weizen, Allegheny Pale Ale. Seasonals: Oktoberfest, St. Nikolaus Bock, Märzen, Maibock, Pastorator Double Bock, Penndemonium.

in the city. Running a production brewery was too much for them, apparently. I'd wanted to go to the St. Nikolaus Bock tapping the first Friday in December for years and realized that this might be my last chance. It was all gaiety and clinking mugs in the main room upstairs, but in the Ratskeller downstairs and out in the brewery, where the cognoscenti had gathered, it was more like a wake. At least the bock was, as always, delicious.

Sure enough, brewing stopped two months later. Production was shifted to The Lion, and the restaurant only stayed open until mid-August. I remember talking to a Pittsburgh beer biz insider in November 2009 about the situation, and he just shook his head and said, "You tell me: How do you kill a successful business, a successful brand, that fast? I don't think I could have done it that fast if I'd meant to!"

With the brewery sinking fast, Tom Pastorius began to mount a financial rescue operation, pulling together investors and loans. It looked like a real long shot, and other people were making offers; "muddying the waters," Tom said later.

When I left Pittsburgh that November, I had a moment. I looked over to Penn, saw the brewery tower, and it hurt to know there was no point in driving over there. No more gleaming brewery, no more schnitzel, no more aromatic glassfuls of Dark. No more *gemütlichkeit*. I didn't give Tom's hopes of buying the brewery back from Birchmere much of a chance. I hoped for the best and knew that if it were to be done, it would have to be Tom . . . But it didn't seem likely.

Hey, I was wrong! Tom and his three investors—Linda Nyman, Sandy Cindrich, and Corey Little—pulled it off just a couple days later, taking over the brewery on November 20. There was a rush of stories in the papers (and the papers' Web sites resounded with positive reader comments; "WOO-HOO!!" pretty much summed those up), all the pieces fell into place, and the restoration began.

That was a lot of work. "They sold the kegging line, they sold the bottling line," Tom said as we walked through the cold brewery (the building's heating had broken down as well, which would keep the restaurant from opening until the spring of 2010). "For the first month, almost all I did was write checks and make apologies to suppliers."

The Pick: St. Nikolaus Bock is my sentimental favorite because of that last tapping, but that's okay—it's really good, too, one of the best bocks in the United States. It's creamy smooth, chocolaty, and just rich enough, without stepping over the line into doublebock territory. A beer hearty enough for German food, yet smooth enough to quaff. If I can pick another . . . the Kaiser Pils, to my mind, is the beer that should be the flagship. Trenchantly bitter but with enough malt to float it, deliriously drinkable and big-mug clinkable, this is a beer for talking, singing, and making friends.

But that beautiful copper brewhouse was still in place—it was mortared in place, or it probably would have been sold, too—and brewer Andy Rich was back working. The first brew was on December 3. They managed to brew enough beer for a private "We're back!" party on December 30, 2009.

They did that by brewing ale, something Penn had never done before. They have been lager specialists; only the German-inspired wheat beers they brewed were not cold-fermented. Penn's flagship, Penn Pilsner, caught on quicker with a more general audience than with craft beer enthusiasts. Lagers are underappreciated by most American beer geeks, maybe because of their association with mainstream light beers.

That's made it tough on lager craft brewers, for not only are lagers less popular, but they are also substantially more expensive to brew. They are more labor-intensive than ales, use more energy (cooling costs for the lagering), and stay in the tanks longer, which means the same amount of tankage produces less lager than ale in a year. Yet a brewer cannot charge more for lagers. The customers don't see or care about the extra costs, so they won't pay more for the beer.

What's more, lager brewers often feel that they brew to higher standards than ale brewers do. Ales are often more complex and somewhat more eccentric in character than lagers. That gives ale brewers a bit of wiggle room. Lager brewers have very little leeway; their brews are by nature cleaner, purer of essence, a simple yet subtle interplay of hops and malt. As Tom Pastorius said, "A lager brewer is hanging right out there with nowhere to hide!"

Needs must when the devil drives, though, and Penn and Pastorius are driven. "We want to double our sales," Tom said, "and we can only do that by making ales. We can make more beers; pale ales, IPAs, stouts. We will be making the same beers, plus ales." I did get a chance to taste the Allegheny Pale: It's clean (no surprise), hoppy but not overly bitter, and an easy pint to get down. I'd have another.

Whatever beer they make, Tom wanted to emphasize that this was the same Pennsylvania Brewing Company he started in 1986. "We bought the company back from Birchmere," he said. "This is not a new company; the name on the license never changed."

If you remember the crisp lager beers, they won't change; there will just be added ales. If you remember the restaurant, with the German specialties, the view of the brewhouse, and those solid communal tables in the German *gasthaus* style, that won't change, either. The Ratskeller downstairs, with its classic German service and atmosphere, the old-school horizontal lagering tanks visible? Still there. A solid presence for

Penn at PNC Park? Back on track. The only thing that's really changed is that all of Penn's brewing will be done in-house now; no more contract brewing on the big runs of Penn Pilsner. That's important today, and Tom knows it.

Eric Heinauer, the head of sales, is still there, too, and when I arrived for my visit and Eric opened the door, I knew things would be okay. If Tom and Eric and Andy are there, that's a solid core to carry over. The new partners bring strong business skill sets to the company, along with a real love for beer and new excitement. "Nothing makes new friends like buying a brewery," Linda Nyman said with a big grin. "It's better than Dale Carnegie!"

How excited is Tom Pastorius? He'd retired after working hard to build this business, only to have to come back and rescue it, and it's been a lot of hard work.

"Oh, I had about enough of retirement," he said firmly. "I'm excited to be back at it. I want to crank this place and make more beer than we ever made. I have to—I need to make some money!"

I'll let Eric have the last word. I asked him if they were still going to stick with a German theme. "Germans are the biggest ethnicity in the city, but the theme . . ." he said, and paused, ". . . the theme is Pittsburgh. We're the beer they can be proud of."

I don't think I've ever been so glad to be wrong in my life.

Opened: March 1986.

Owners: Thomas V. Pastorius, Linda Nyman, Sandy Cindrich, Corey Little.

Brewers: Tom Pastorius, Andy Rich.

System: 45-barrel Jacob Carl GmbH brewhouse, 22,000 barrels potential annual capacity.

2009 production: Not available.

Brewpub hours: Monday through Saturday, 11 AM to midnight. Closed Sunday and major holidays.

Tours: By appointment, for groups of twenty or more. (The brewery is visible from the dining room and the Ratskeller.)

Take-out beer: Six-packs, cases, quarter and half kegs.

Food: Penn makes some great authentic German food, but you can also get American food. Full lunch and dinner menus of appetizers, soups, salads, sandwiches, and entrées.

Extras: Full liquor license. Selection includes German schnapps such as Jägermeister, Killepitsch, and Himbeerngeist. Outdoor beer garden. Penn hosts the Pennsylvania Microbrewers Fest in June—a friendly, accessible fest that I highly recommend—and its own Oktoberfest the last two weekends of September. There are parties for St. Niko-laus Day (the first weekend in December) and Mardi Gras, as well as ceremonial tappings of seasonal beers; check Web site for dates.

Special considerations: Kids welcome. Vegetarian meals available.

Parking: Free off-street parking.

Church Brew Works

3525 Liberty Avenue
Pittsburgh, PA 15201
412-688-8200
www.churchbrew.com

Prepare yourself for a shock when you first walk into the Church Brew Works. At least, it was something of a shock to me the first time. Intellectually, I knew that the Church Brew Works was located in a church. As far as I'm aware, this is the only brewpub in America in such a setting.

It's in the former St. John the Baptist Roman Catholic Church, to be specific, just up the street from the now-defunct Iron City brewery in Pittsburgh's Lawrenceville neighborhood. I had actually seen the church being renovated some months before the brewpub opened. Even so, it was strange to walk into the place the first time and see a brewhouse, tanks and all, sitting right up on the altar of what was obviously, definitely, for sure a church. Don't get me wrong. I saw nothing particularly heinous about the fact that it was a brewery. I would have had the same reaction if I had found, say, a beauty salon or a McDonald's.

What's also surprising is that the people who grew up with St. John's as their church seem to be pretty happy about the brewpub in general. That's mostly because the parish had shrunk so much that

Beers brewed: Year-round: Celestial Gold, Pipe Organ Pale Ale, Pious Monk Dunkel, Millennium Trippel, and a rotating variety of stouts (Blast Furnace, Breakfast, Oatmeal, Roaster's Rebellion, Coconut Stout, Coffee Stout, Mexican Mole, Cherry Imperial Stout). Year-round bottled beers: Thunderhop IPA, Cherry Quadzilla, and Millennium Tripel. Seasonals: Burly Friar Barleywine, Bocks Au Chocolat, Absolution Ale, Penance Porter, Confessional Kölsch, What the Helles, Czech Pilsner . . . and more.

the diocese had closed it and deconsecrated the church. The building was headed for the wrecking ball when Sean Casey and other local investors bought it to convert it into the brewpub. The friends of the church, people who had been baptized, confirmed, and married there, figured that having the building and their memories intertwined with a brewpub was better than seeing the church leveled to make room for another professional building or minimarket.

Their new faith has been rewarded. The Church Brew Works has certainly brought some excitement to Lawrenceville. Colorful banners fly outside the spruced-up building. People slow down to look and then stop to have a drink (I know I do; just did it again last week).

The Pick: I really loved the Bocks Au Chocolat, and I hope they make it again: a bock made with high-grade cocoa that delivered a dry, almost dusty chocolate note that was so good with the bock. But until they do, I'm telling you to grab a Pious Monk. This beer captures what the Church has always been about: well-made, tasty, drinkable beer that's neither dull nor overwhelming.

They did a great job inside, too. The stained glass and gold decorations were retained and refurbished, as was the church's lectern, which serves as a hostess station. The ceiling is immensely high, all the way up to the organ loft in the rear. It is one of the most striking brewpubs I've ever seen.

The selection of beers ranges from good to excellent. There is a strong lager component in response to local tastes. It's no coincidence that you've got lagers here, at Penn across the Allegheny, and at Hofbräu across the Monongahela. Many Pittsburghers are of Eastern and Central European descent, and those folks do love their lagers. You can get a dunkel anytime, festbier in the fall, and Paganator doppelbock in the winter (a name I suggested during the interview, which Sean Casey grabbed on the spot and thanked me for; you're welcome, Sean).

But both head brewer Brant Dubovick and his predecessor, Bryan Pearson, made some exceptional big beers as well. Pearson's Clout Stout rocked solid with big, boozy raspberry notes, and Dubovick recently unveiled an 11 percent version of his Burly Friar barleywine that had been aged for two years in toasted oak barrels kept in the old cold-storage basement of the building; it was big but well muscled, well dosed with oak spice and vanilla. The Millennium Trippel is spritzy and rich, and very suitable for aging.

The last time I was in town, I ran into Brant sitting on the steps of the brewpub. We went inside and talked for a bit over an excellent Czech pilsner he'd made, and he told me he appreciated how I'd always praised the beers at Church for being good without relying on hops, hops, and more hops. "There's more to beer than hops," he said. "There's malt, too, and yeast." You don't stay open for this long without being right about something like that.

Sean took me around to show me what they'd been working on: expansion. There's a lot of room under the building, old storage and mechanical spaces from when it was both a church and a parochial school. They're using that room for barrel aging, bottling, and most important, more tanks.

"We've been buying bigger tanks," Sean yelled over the noise of production. "We've got a new bottling line, new six-pack holders. We're selling the champagne-size bottles in four-pack holders, getting out into the market more, playing the game to grow the business." He grinned and reminded me that we were standing in Pittsburgh's biggest production brewery. That's still a shock, with Iron City closed just down the street. (With Penn back in the swing, the claim will probably be eclipsed shortly, but Sean knew it was fun while it lasted.)

Back in the church—sorry, the pub—dinner was getting under way. The bar was busy, families, couples, and groups were sitting down to eat—a community assembling in this building again, as they did back in the days of school and parish. It does your heart good to see people going to church during the week. Church, school, and brewpub, this gathering place has been a blessing to the neighborhood.

Opened: August 1996.

Owners: Lawrenceville Brewery Inc., Sean Casey, president.

Brewers: Brant Dubovick, head brewer; Matt Moninger and Steve O'Neill.

System: 15-barrel Specific Mechanical brewhouse, 3,000 barrels potential annual capacity.

2009 production: 2,200 barrels.

Brewpub hours: Monday through Thursday, 11:30 AM to 11:45 PM; Friday and Saturday, 11:30 AM to 1 AM; Sunday, noon to 10 PM. Check Web site for winter hours.

Tours: Monday through Friday at 5 PM.

Take-out beer: Growlers; kegs by prior arrangement. Bottled Church beer (12-ounce and 750-milliliter) available at the bar and in area stores.

Food: An eclectic American regional menu that has some tongue-in-cheek beauties like the daily pierogi specials (both traditional and untraditional) and pierogi pizza on the pub menu. You'll find serious carnivore chow—filets, big pork chops, and a buffalo ribeye—matched by similarly serious vegetarian dishes: a vegan stir fry, exotic mushroom ravioli, and delicious couscous salad.

Extras: Full liquor license. Good selection of malts, bourbons, and cognacs. Mug club. Outside patio and hop garden for warm weather. Events include Oktoberfest, a Party on the Patio every Wednesday during the summer, and an anniversary party every August; check the Web site or call for dates.

Special considerations: Kids welcome. Vegetarian meals available.

Parking: Large off-street lot and plenty of on-street parking.

East End Brewing

6923 Susquehanna Street
Pittsburgh, PA 15208
412-537-2337
www.eastendbrewing.com

I owe Scott Smith. Scott got East End Brewing open just after the deadline for the third edition of *Pennsylvania Breweries*, and he was bummed. Because he was bummed, and had actually sought me out to try to get in under the line, I tried to put together an errata sheet, something to slip into the books I signed at bookstores and breweries, but it just never worked. "Next edition," I promised him, "you're in. Stay open!"

I wasn't really worried. Scott was the classic picture of the one-man brewer who was going to make it. He's a mechanical engineer, which gives him a good basis for looking at the kinds of problems a brewer runs into—the mechanical ones, that is; the regulatory ones would just have to yield to his boundless energy. He had a firm plan and an identity; two, actually. East End was going to be solidly neighborhood Pittsburgh, on the streets, and it was going to be as green and sustainable as Scott could make it.

Beers brewed: Year-round: Big Hop IPA, Black Strap Stout, Monkey Boy Hefeweizen, Fat Gary Nut Brown Ale. Seasonals and specials: East End Witte, Pedal Pale Ale, Big Hop Harvest Ale, Snow Melt Winter Ale, Literally Just a Coffee Porter, Gratitude Barleywine, Wooden Nickel Saison, Ugly American, Smokestack Heritage Porter, Toaster Imperial Stout, Bigger Hop. East End's Session Ale series has presented more than thirty sub-5 percent beers, each unique.

He started off on the right green foot with his brewing system, which he bought used from The Foundry not long after it closed. Recycled equipment and a short move: greening accomplished. More would follow . . . Almost all the brewery equipment is reused, most of it sourced locally, down to pipes, wire conduit, even the conduit hanging hardware. One pump was new, and the walk-in cooler, though used, came from Wisconsin, and you can tell those things bother Scott. The brewing is done with a single-step infusion mash; it's more energy-efficient than multistep infusion. Even the brewery building itself is recycled, set up in a deep bay of an old brick building in the rough-cut Homewood neighborhood. "I've camouflaged the brewery as an abandoned building," Scott joked at the time.

The Pick: Year-round, I'll take Fat Gary: It's my go-to in Pittsburgh bars because of its soothing malt flavor and low-alcohol sessionability. Seasonal, I'm in on Snow Melt, a delightfully estery strong ale with hints of melon and pear, a real perker-upper in the snow season. I loved Toaster, East End's fourth-anniversary celebration beer (I celebrated my twentieth anniversary with it), a rich, absolutely viscous imperial stout. If you see Scott, tell him he ought to make it again!

But as I've noticed in other places, the arrival of a brewery improved the neighborhood. I've been dropping by East End every year or so, and every time, the area looks a little better. The front door of the brewery is still battered, battleship gray and unadorned with so much as a sign, but the brewery's humming along inside. Scott's added a tasting bar up front now; before, you had to walk back the narrow hall to the brewery and take samples (and buy growlers) from a tiny bar right by the brewkettles.

He's also added tanks and a second brewer: Brendan Benson, who bought the line-cleaning business that Rivertowne brewer Andrew Maxwell was running, and then started working at East End. He's still doing both. "He's a hard worker," Scott said. "He pushes the beer forward, too."

All that success is taking the usual toll: outgrowing the building. "I'm actually getting tight on space," Scott told me at the last visit. "We're looking at an expansion in a new building, but it's not easy." For a change, it's not a money issue; it's a regulatory one. No one wants a brewery in their neighborhood, despite East End's track record.

Maybe if they drank the beer, they'd change their minds. The four regular beers have a broad range: an IPA, a beefy stout, a classic hefeweizen, and a session-strength nut brown ale. They've caught on in Pittsburgh mostly because they're simply good—how many local breweries have a popular brown ale under 4 percent?—but credit has to be given to Scott's exuberance, relentlessly self-deprecating "GOOD BEER NEWS" e-mails, and nose for offbeat events.

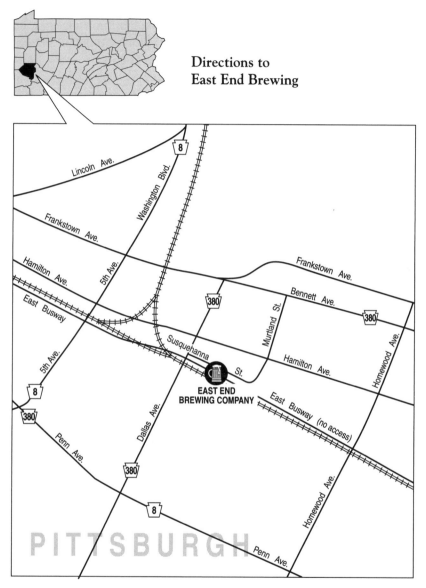

**Directions to
East End Brewing**

As an example, the annual launch of the brewery's spring seasonal, Pedal Pale Ale, since 2005 has begun with Scott hauling beer by bicycle to a surprise bar, with a free beer for everyone who rides along. That first year, there were about fifteen riders; in 2009, there were more than five hundred! The pack stretched for blocks, and Scott, helped by volunteers, hauled more than a barrel of beer to Over the Bar Bicycle Café on Carson Street. It's a big thing that started as a lark; I'd say it's like East End itself, except I'm guessing Scott's pretty serious about his business.

If you're wondering when East End is going to start bottling (beyond the small amount of big bottles they do now), don't hold your breath. Draft is much greener than bottles or cans: Kegs can be washed and reused for about forty years, and the weight is about 60 pounds less than the equivalent in bottles. That makes a pretty strong argument for a sustainable brewery to stay all-draft.

It's not just plain draft, either: Scott does some real ale as well, particularly with the Session Ale series. The Session Ales are a series of one-off beers, each different, but all low in alcohol and all somewhat experimental. (Fat Gary was once a Session Ale and got promoted to year-round.) These beers lend themselves to cask dispense, which allows the beer's flavor to stand out more. He's supplying casks regularly to Piper's Pub on Carson Street, where they're doing a serious cask ale program that you should check out.

"The Session Ales are a blessing," Scott said. "They see Big Hop out in the market, then they come by here and see all the others, and they buy growlers. A good Session Ale will sell out here in the brewery. Seasonals are huge here, too." The big bottles sell well at the brewery, especially the yearly bottling of Gratitude, a delicious barleywine that Scott does as a thank-you for brewery customers. Each bottle is wrapped in printed recycled paper, which is glued to the bottle with wheat paste, and then the bottle is neck-dipped in colored wax, a different color each year so far. It's become a huge amount of work, but he keeps doing it. It's a promise, like the promise to be sustainable, and Scott keeps his promises.

So that's East End Brewing, the oldest new brewery in this edition. You're in, Scott! Stay open!

Opened: December 2004.

Owners: Scott and Julie Smith.

Brewers: Scott Smith, Brendan Benson.

System: 10-barrel New World Brewing system, 2,300 barrels annual capacity.

2009 production: 800 barrels (est.).

Tours: Informal tours offered during growler hours only. Tuesday and Thursday, 5 to 7 PM; Friday, 4 to 8 PM; Saturday, noon to 5 PM. Check Web site; hours are slowly expanding.

Take-out beer: Growlers, specialty big bottles, kegs (call for availability). Cash or checks only.

Parking: On-street parking.

Hofbräuhaus Pittsburgh

2705 South Water Street
Southside Works Complex
Pittsburgh, PA 15203
412-224-2328
www.hofbrauhauspittsburgh.com

HOFBRÄUHAUS
PITTSBURGH

"You've brought Munich to Pittsburgh."

I'd love to argue that point, because it sounds so much like marketing. Jim Combs told me that was something one of the happy customers of Hofbräuhaus ("HOFE-broy-house") Pittsburgh told him. Jim is the head of Premier Lube, the company that runs this—what, brewpub? Beerhall? Beermusement park?—so you might expect him to oversell things a bit. But I've been to Hofbräuhaus Munich, and if you make adjustments for the riverside setting, and give the plantings time to grow, and give the traditions another few years to set in . . . this is a pretty close replication indeed.

It's not all that surprising. What Premier Lube has is not so much a franchise from the Bavarian state enterprise that owns the original Hofbräuhaus but, according to head brewer Eckhard Kurbjuhn, "a license to brew and sell beer under their name. You bring them a concept, and they approve or disapprove it. You use Hofbräuhaus glassware, use their recipes for the four house beers, and every three months, this fellow comes from Germany and tastes your beer and food." He laughed. "That's a pretty good job!"

Beers brewed: Regulars: Hofbräu Premium Lager, Munich Weizen, Light, Dunkel. Seasonals (one per month): Prussian Export, Adulterator Doppelbock, Märzen, Bavarian Wheat, German Pilsner, Bohemian Pilsner, Steelers Schwarzbier, 1810 Prince Ludwig, Weizenbock, Christmasbeer, and Zwickelbier, an unfiltered version of the Premium Lager that comes on if the seasonal runs out. Maibock and Oktoberfest are imported from the Hofbräuhaus brewery in Munich; all other beers brewed in-house.

After sampling the beers Eckhard and his two assistants have been making, I'm ready to agree, and the guy gets the food, too? Sign me up!

We were drinking hellerbock in the main beerhall, a big room that seats more than 300 people. Then there's the more restrained dining room, another 150. Go outside to the wrap-around deck, and the beer garden, and the big area down by the Monongahela, and you've got room for 1,300 people to clink steins and enjoy good German-style lager beer. They know that because they were letting that many people in, and there were still lines waiting to get in. Some days that first summer, customers were going through more than 5,000 liters of Eckhard's beer—in just one day.

The beer pours from fifty-eight taps around the building (cleaning them all takes five hours), all of them hooked to the serving tanks. There's no kegging here. "If you're going to go through 5,000 liters," Eckhard pointed out, "why use kegs?" The kitchen is huge, and about 200 people work here at full summer employment. This is the biggest restaurant in Pittsburgh.

The Pick: The Dunkel is what I have when I visit, it's what Eckhard and I drank after sampling the Maibock. It's good: clean, malty-dry in that beautiful Munich style, just a hint of chocolate, and no stickiness at the end. Perfect for the menu, or for just drinking.

The brewery keeps everyone in beer with only three brewers. You'll see it as soon as you walk in the main hall, the gleaming metal vessels sitting up above the big, hollow, square bar. It's completely automated, a showpiece for the Braukon brewery manufacturing company. Eckhard is part owner of Braukon, and he makes sure the system runs perfectly.

The four year-round beers—Premium Lager, Munich Weizen, Light, and Dunkel—are all brewed here, as are all but two of the monthly seasonal beers, which are tapped on the first Wednesday of each month. Eckhard and his crew make between 4,000 and 6,000 liters of each of the seasonal brews, but that's not always enough. "We made 6,000 liters of our Christmasbeer," he told me with a wry grin, "and we ran out on December 24!"

The Oktoberfest and the Maibock are imported from the mother ship in Germany, because "we wanted to do it right," managing partner Nick Ellison told me. Doing it right includes tapping the Oktoberfest in September, because most of Oktoberfest is in September; the sixteen days of this massive Munich festival end in October. You'd expect nothing less from the Hofbräuhaus.

The food is not limited to the German dishes that make up the original Hofbräuhaus menu. "If you want Bavarian food, you've got it," Jim Combs said, "and if you want light and healthy, we have that, too."

Finding a menu that worked wasn't the main concern; it was the tables. German beerhalls use long trestle tables, and everyone sits around the tables and shares space with their neighbors . . . and they talk.

"Would people in Pittsburgh, Americans, sit with each other?" Jim wondered. The answer is yes. And "they don't just talk to each other, they even share their food! They sing, they dance, the kids do the chicken dance. They love it!"

One of the best things about the acceptance of different types of beer taking hold in America is that places like this can brew beer, right

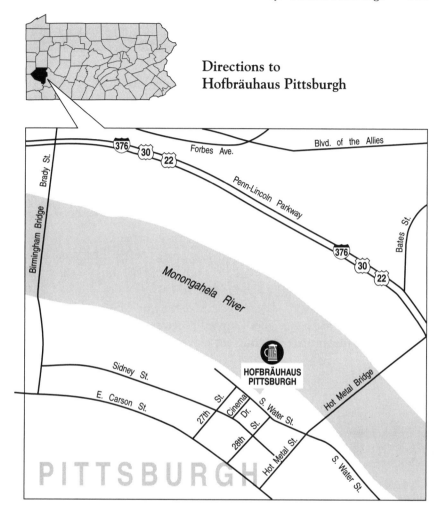

Directions to
Hofbräuhaus Pittsburgh

in the hall, and not be looked on as dangerous or strange. When you're getting a thousand people in at a time, that's proof positive that Americans are ready for more beer variety. And now I don't have to buy a plane ticket when I want fresh German beer. It's as near as the Southside Works.

Opened: March 2009.
Owners: Premier Lube LLC.
Brewers: Eckhard Kurbjuhn, head brewer; Ed Slouffman, Shawn Setzenfand.
System: 20-barrel Braukon system, approx. 2,000 barrels annual capacity.
2009 production: Not available.

Brewpub hours: Open daily at 11 AM; closing varies with amount of business, usually at 11 PM on weekdays, later on weekends.

Tours: By appointment; group tours welcome.

Take-out beer: 12-ounce bottles of Hofbräuhaus Munich beers.

Food: German-American menu, with traditional dishes like soft pretzels with obatzer soft cheese, goulash soup, assorted authentic wursts, three pork schnitzels, and Schweinshaxe (roasted pork shank); some hybrids like nachos with bratwurst and biercheese; and some straight-up American fare like pan-seared salmon, blackened tilapia, grilled chicken, and salads. Salads (which mostly have added meat) and sides are about it for vegetarians, but you can gorge on the soft pretzels.

Extras: Live music every night, all day on Saturday and Sunday; check Web site for schedule. Seasonal beer tappings on the first Wedneday of the month. Extensive outdoor dining-and-drinking area with a breathtaking view of the Monongahela.

Special considerations: Kids very welcome; they love doing the chicken dance when the bands play. Limited vegetarian options.

Parking: Limited on-site parking, but plenty of garage space within two blocks.

Rock Bottom, Homestead

171 East Bridge Street, Homestead, PA 15120
412-462-2739
www.rockbottom.com

What am I going to do, now that Joe Chiodo and his beloved bar are both gone? The tavern where I spent many happy and relaxed hours has been, in a sadly apt turn of events, bulldozed like the Homestead steel works that it served for so long, and replaced with a Walgreen's, and Joe has gone to his reward. I am bereft. Will I ever cross the Homestead High-Level Bridge to go drinking again?

Well, yes and no. No, because the bridge has been renamed (to honor the town's Negro League baseball team), so I'll have to cross the Homestead Grays Bridge. And yes, because down there, amidst all the theaters and stores and restaurants of the boomingly popular Waterfront, is Rock Bottom Homestead. That's more than enough to get me across the bridge!

You can read my rants about chain brewpubs and mall brewpubs at the entry for Rock Bottom, King of Prussia (see page 99), but you should know a little something about the mother company, too. This is now the largest brewpub chain in the country, with thirty-five Rock Bottom restaurants, all of which brew their own beer; four Chop House brewpub steakhouses; and the original Walnut Brewery pub in Boulder, Colorado. Rock Bottom is centered in Louisville, Colorado, but they have pubs all across the country, from California to Massachusetts. The chain has expanded both by opening new sites and by acquisition; the King of Prussia Rock Bottom was part of the Boston-based brew

Beers brewed: Year-round: Lumpy Dog Light Lager, Stacks Pale Ale, North Star Amber, High Level Brown, Ho'Dizzle Pale Ale. Always at least one beer on cask. Seasonals: Rotating series of wheat beers (Belgian Wit, Hefeweizen, Portland Wheat) and dark beers (Irish Stout, Cream Stout, Oatmeal Stout, Imperial Stout); Belgian Tripel, Velvet Pale Ale, Fire Chief Ale, Dunkel, Strong Scottish, Saison, Kölsch, American Dream IPA, Madame Berry Blonde, Rocktoberfest, Open Hearth Imperial IPA, Dopplebock.

moon chain, for instance, before Rock Bottom snapped the place up. The name comes from the location of the first Rock Bottom, in the first floor of what was then the Prudential Insurance building: the "Bottom" floor of "The Rock."

I've been to Rock Bottoms all across the country. If the idea of a chain is to provide the customer with a consistent product with no changes, well, Rock Bottom is a half failure, because while the menu's pretty much the same everywhere, the beer's different in every one. Do they all have a pale ale, a brown ale, a kölsch or some other light golden beer? Look around—so do 80 percent of the other brewpubs. When I stopped in at The Brewer's Art in Baltimore, one of the most different brewpubs around, they had . . . a pale ale and a brown ale. They're standard beers; people *like* them. But every brewer at Rock Bottom does them differently.

Steve Panos is the brewer here in Homestead. He's been working at other Rock Bottoms for a while now, and he's pretty happy with that freedom. "The company doesn't skimp on the brewing side," he said with a broad smile. "As long as we can hit the numbers on sales, we can make almost anything we want." There was evidence of that on the taps: a real nice, classic Belgian tripel at 9.5 percent and the Ho'Dizzle, a seriously in-the-keg dry-hopped pale ale that zinged the nose with Amarillo and Cascades (the name was a backroom brewery nickname, Steve said; someone put it up on the blackboard and it stuck).

Sales are pretty much evenly split among the regular beers, with some seasonal releases being wildly popular while they're on: Rocktoberfest, Madame Berry Blonde, and a nitro-tap Velvet Pale Ale. Over in the Sing Sing piano bar, which is part of Rock Bottom, the House Lager is the hands-down winner. They're not the most adventurous beers, perhaps, but they're well made, fresh, and tasty.

The Pick: I don't understand this, because I thought I didn't really like brown ales, but Steve's High Level Brown is sweet, smooth, lightly chocolaty, with hints of dark pit fruits, an easy-drinking pint-after-pint beer. If Ho'Dizzle is on, grab one: It's dizzying to taste this much hops flavor in a pale ale—nicely done.

That's what works for Rock Bottom. "Greg Koch of Stone Brewing in San Diego said that brewers make the beer and wait for people to catch up to them," said Kevin Reed, who is the director of brewing operations for the whole group. "In the pub business, that's not a luxury we have. We're not quite as aggressive as some of the production brewers. That's a slippery slope: Brewers like to make big beers, but if they don't sell fast enough, it's just tanks taken up. Sometimes you have to stick your toe in the water and see what brings people in the doors."

Good, fresh beer at a good price is bringing them in at Homestead. I doubt that Steve Panos will last more than fifty years like Joe Chiodo did, but while he's here, he'll be making beers you'll cross that bridge for, whatever it's called.

Opened: April 2002.

Owners: Rock Bottom Restaurants, Inc.

Brewers: Steve Panos, head brewer; Brandon McCarthy, brewer.

System: 15-barrel JV Northwest brewhouse, 2,000 barrels potential annual capacity.

2009 production: 1,300 barrels.

Brewpub hours: Seven days a week, 11 AM to midnight (or later).

Tours: On request, subject to brewer availability.

Take-out beer: Growlers and kegs (call for availability).

Food: Rock Bottom's menu really has a bit of everything, and everything I've ever had has been delicious. I particularly like their home-style favorites, like chicken-fried chicken, alder-smoked salmon, jambalaya, and barbecue ribs. Don't miss the white cheddar potatoes, a Rock Bottom signature side.

Extras: Live music on Wednesday nights; call for schedule. Trivia contests on Thursdays. Lots of TVs. Large banquet room for private par-

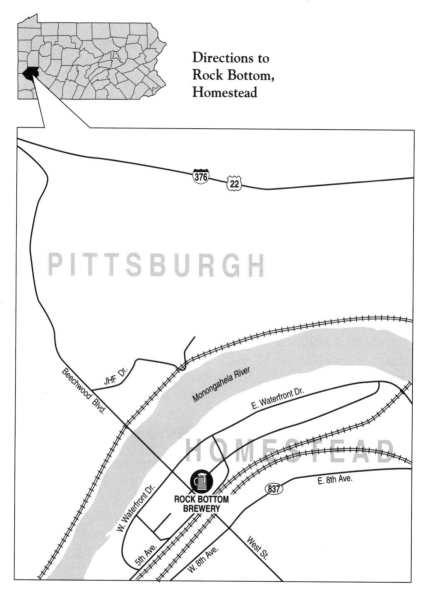

Directions to Rock Bottom, Homestead

ties and meetings. The Sing Sing dueling piano bar next door is supplied with beer by Rock Bottom.

Special considerations: Kids welcome. Vegetarian meals available.

Parking: Large on-site lot

Rivertowne Pour House

312 Center Road
Monroeville, PA 15146
412-372-8199
www.myrivertowne.com

I remember the first time I went to a Rivertowne restaurant, the one over in Verona. The first thing I liked was that when I stopped to ask a cop directions, he knew exactly where the place was and smiled: good rep. Then there was the table of four guys right inside the door being served the biggest fried fish sandwiches I'd ever seen, with sides of smoking-hot fresh-cut fries. Yum! But it was the bar in back that sealed the deal: sixteen taps of great beer (and not the same sixteen every other area craft beer bar I'd been in that trip had) backed up with an exceptionally well-chosen bottle array, good bartenders who knew the beer they were serving, and a friendly, nongeeky vibe that glued me to my seat.

"It's relaxed," agreed Andrew Maxwell. "They're not trying to be anything they're not." We were pretty relaxed, too. I was sitting at a table in Rivertowne with Andrew, his brewing colleagues Barrett Goddard and Sean Hallisey, and his new partner in the Full Pint brewery, Mark Kegg (clearly born to be a brewery partner), and we were all sampling beers. It's the hardest part of this job . . . leaving for the next appointment when you're having a great time!

Sampling beers at Rivertowne isn't easy, either. As Barrett wrote on the form I sent out requesting information for this edition, "We keep 18 beers on tap, so all the beers we brew will not fit on this page." He wasn't kidding (though he did miss the cask tap). They have seven regulars, and the other eleven taps (and the cask) may have anything: returning beer, tweaked beer, new beer. We had to try all the specials and a couple regulars; Sean even

Beers brewed: Regulars: Ultra Light Tackle, Babbbbling Blonde, Shepherd's Crook Scottish Ale, Arctic Amber, Last Chance Vienna Lager, White Lightning, Old Wylie's IPA. Specials: Yorkshire Brown Ale, Dead Head Red, Magnum P.A., Rx Pilsner, Sinister Stout, Patrick's Poison, Winter Warmer, Drunken Leprechaun, B.B. King, Crantastic . . . and that's just one week. These guys are filling eighteen taps and just brewing too many beers to list. Don't obsess; drop in and start your own list.

went over and poured me the smallest black and tan I'd ever seen, a perfect separation in a 3-ounce sampler glass.

Andrew Maxwell must be in heaven. When he was brewing over at the now-closed John Harvard's, just over the hill on the William Penn Highway, he ran as many beers as possible through the system. Rivertowne has eighteen taps, and the three brewers are filling them on a regular basis with great beers.

I was surprised to find that they had no serving tanks and were kegging everything. "It's a lot of kegs," Andrew said, "but ten beers on, eighteen beers on, it's not that much different. You just roll them through." And the other guys around the table just nodded, matter-of-factly.

The Pick: That's a lot of beers! I'm going with one of the simplest on the list: Last Chance Vienna Lager. I was very impressed with how this beer whispered to me, from the middle of a full range of tasters, and never got overwhelmed. It's a clean, malty beauty without a hitch. Second nod would go to the Arctic Amber, another malt-forward beer that was juicy and hard not to keep drinking.

"I've never been given the opportunity to do something like this," I remember him telling me when the Pour House situation came together. He was excited, and the 15-barrel JV Northwest brewhouse they got had him fired up as well. "It's gas-fired," Andrew said. "It's the nicest system I've ever touched."

Andrew is a blend of brewer—and you never forget he's a brewer—philosopher, and marketer. Take the popular regular tap, the Babbbbling Blonde. It's not just there to supply a lighter beer. "That hits a wide demographic," Andrew said. "Young, old, professional, blue collar. It is a beer to let people know that the local brewery can make beers to compete with the big brewers. It's light, but malty, and it's clean."

"Every beer on the list has a marketing purpose," he continued. "People like beer based on hopping rates, and you can hone in on what they like. Put out beers with hopping rates across the board, and you've got something for everyone." It's a grand brewpub design, and I couldn't fault him too much; with a spread like that, it's hard to think of someone not finding *something* they liked. I did, believe me.

Once the Full Pint project gets rolling (see the next entry), things will change a little. "The Rivertowne pubs will be carrying the Rivertowne beers and the other brands from North Country and Full Pint," Barrett said. "This brewery is a perfect size for here, but we can't really put it out the door, supply the others with every beer on the list."

It occurred to me after I left that if Full Pint's capacity takes the pressure off brewing the two best-selling beers at Rivertowne, that's going to give these guys a chance to brew even more beers. That put a smile on my face, and it's going to put a smile on yours.

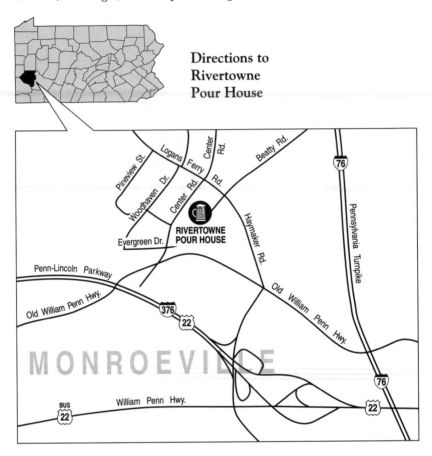

Directions to
Rivertowne
Pour House

Opened: June 2007.

Owners: Andrew and Melissa Maxwell, Joe and Amy Borow, Christian and Lisa Fyke.

Brewers: Andrew Maxwell, Barrett Goddard, Sean Hallisey.

System: 15-barrel JV Northwest system, 2,000 barrels annual capacity.

2009 production: 1,000 barrels (est.).

Brewpub hours: Monday through Saturday, 11 AM to 2 AM; Sunday, 10 AM to 2 AM.

Tours: By appointment.

Take-out beer: Growlers.

Food: Rivertowne's menu centers on seafood, but not obsessively; there's also buckets of wings, steaks, and chicken. But the fish is fantastic. "All the tuna we serve is sushi-grade," Andrew said. The big fish sandwiches—submarines—are a signature meal at Rivertowne, and you can get steamed mussels, king crab legs, Cajun catfish, salmon burgers, shrimp, fish and chips . . .

Extras: Mug club. Frequent live music or DJs on weekends; call for schedule. Dartboard. Lots of TVs.

Special considerations: Kids welcome, with a children's menu; Wednesdays are family nights, with magicians, balloons, and more. Vegetarian items on the menu, and the chefs can accommodate vegetarian requests.

Parking: Large lot across the street.

Lodging in the area: Red Roof Monroeville, 2729 Mosside Blvd., 412-856-4738; Doubletree Pittsburgh/Monroeville Convention Center, 101 Mall Blvd., Monroeville, 412-373-7300; Courtyard Marriott, 3962 William Penn Highway, Monroeville, 412-856-8680.

Area attractions: See Pittsburgh section on pages 302–04.

Other area beer sites: *Ribken's* (226 Center Rd., 412-856-3040) is just up the road from Rivertowne, a pizza joint with a jaw-dropping beer selection; take out or drink in with the beer-savvy staff. *D's Sixpax and Dogs* Monroeville branch (4320 Northern Pike, 412-856-5666) doesn't have as many beers as the Regent Square original, but it's got plenty, and it has something else: more room, more taps, and parking. Same great hot dogs, too. *Carl's Tavern* (3386 William Penn Highway, 412-823-4050) has twenty taps at reasonable prices and solid food (there's a dining room, too), all in a neatly kept bar that's clean and squared away, but not prissy. If you remember the tiny parking lot, that's expanded. It's a bit of a drive to the *Rivertowne Pub and Grille* (14860 Route 30, North Huntingdon, 412-823-2239), but it's always worth it for Rivertowne's great family and craft beer–friendly bars.

Full Pint Brewing Company

Floral Drive, North Huntingdon, PA 15642
www.fullpintbrewing.com

It usually makes me nervous to write about a brewery that isn't open yet. For a few that were coming close to opening at deadline time, but were not there yet, I decided they should wait for the next edition. There's a place in Bloomsburg that's planning to add brewing to an existing restaurant (and it looks pretty good), more nanobreweries on the model of Breaker and Copper Kettle are percolating, and a couple more ambitious ideas for production breweries are slowly coming together. But if you don't have your building, your equipment, your capital, and an experienced brewer lined up . . . a lot can happen before you open the doors.

Full Pint Brewing has the money set, a building with the brewing system already in it, and *four* experienced brewers lined up: Barrett Goddard, Sean McIntyre, Andrew Maxwell, and Sean Hallisey. If those names look familiar, well, you've seen them in previous editions . . . and in this one. All four of them are currently brewing at either Rivertowne Pour House or North Country, and plan to continue doing so, and all four are going to be brewing at Full Pint.

Just to make it more involved, they'll be making four Full Pint beers and two beers from each of the brewpubs as well, and they plan to package a variety case that will contain all eight—the only case I know of that contains beers from three different breweries. To wind up the weirdness, all four of them have already brewed on the system that's waiting to fire up in North Huntingdon; it's from the now-closed John Harvard's brewpub in Monroeville (with additional larger tanks).

Full Pint is, to the best of my knowledge, unique.

"Hey, look, it's best this way," Barrett told me. We were sitting at a table at Rivertowne, drinking beers with Andrew, Sean Hallisey, and their fifth partner, businessman Mark Kegg. "The restaurant owners run the restaurants, the brewers make the beer. The brewpubs are too small to produce this much, and new breweries are expensive. Coming

Beers brewed: Year-round: Chinookie Imperial Pale Ale, White Lightning Witbier, All-In Amber, and (for now) two Rivertowne beers, Old Wylie's IPA and Babbbbling Blonde. Seasonals: Double Triple Imperial, and many more to come.

together like this, we already have a known market for the beers from the two brewpubs; people know their names and beers. North Country needs to expand production; this solves that problem, and without spending $600,000."

The Pick: Of the four I know, I'd probably reach for the Old Wylie's IPA. It's bitter but refreshing, with a nice crisp hops finish. A lot of IPAs are sticky-bitter at the finish; this breaks clean.

But three independent businesses working together? "They all see their common interests," Barrett explained. "This can benefit all of us. We've worked together for years, just not in the same business. It's a true sense of that 'brotherhood of brewers' people talk about. And Andrew, Sean [Hallisey], and I are continuing as employees of Rivertowne."

The four planned Full Pint beers, as yet unnamed, will be an amber, a witbier, an IPA, and a fruit beer, to be joined by seasonal offerings. Rivertowne's two beers will be the Old Wylie's IPA and Babbbbling Blonde; North Country's two are the Paleo IPA and Station 33 Firehouse Red. Those are solid sellers at the brewpubs, and production here will supplement brewing at the pubs.

This reflects something I've been seeing and thinking about. With Pittsburgh and Jones closed, and bigger crafts growing by leaps and bounds, there aren't as many places for small brewers to go to have contract brewing done. Flying Dog's still doing nice work in Maryland, and The Lion will make your beer in kegs, bottles, and now cans. But I'm seeing more small brewers offering excess capacity in small batches to tinier contract brewers.

"There's a real void, with brewers closing," Andrew agreed. "This is going to work for us. We each brew our own way, for our own audience, and putting them together is going to make something special. There's nowhere else you can get one case with eight different beers from three different breweries!"

Only one more hurdle remained for Full Pint when I wrote this: a zoning issue that was being changed by a township planning commission that appeared eager to encourage this small production business. The brewery's federal and state inspections were in place, materials were waiting, power and water were hooked up. The brewers told me that they planned to start brewing the day they were legal. I think they've got a recipe that's going to work.

Full Pint's partners won all their races, jumped all their hurdles, dotted their i's and crossed their t's: The brewery opened in May of 2010. Whew! Beer is shipping in kegs and bottles; check Pittsburgh-area bars for your taste of it.

Opened: Spring 2010.

Owners: Barrett Goddard, Sean Hallisey, Mark Kegg, Andrew Maxwell, Sean McIntyre.

Brewers: Barrett Goddard, Sean Hallisey, Andrew Maxwell, Sean McIntyre.

System: 15-barrel Pub Brewing brewhouse, 5,000 barrels annual capacity.

2009 production: None.

Tours: None for now; check Web site for changes.

Take-out beer: None for now; check Web site for changes. Beers will be available at the Rivertowne pubs.

Parking: Not ready for visitors at this time; check Web site for changes.

BEERWEBS

The Web has become a great place to share beer and bar information. But as with anything else on the Web, you have to use a little wisdom. Web sites can be out of date, intensely subjective, poorly edited, and just plain wrong. Let the reader beware.

Here are the Web sites I use to find beers, bars, and beer geeks from Virginia to New York, and across the country. If I have any reservations about them, I've stated them.

Seen Through a Glass (www.lewbryson.com). This is my own Web site, which includes online updates to this and my other books, *New York Breweries, New Jersey Breweries,* and *Virginia, Maryland, and Delaware Breweries,* as well as notes on what I've been drinking, travel notes on my research trips, links to some of my other writing, and frequent comments on what's driving me crazy in the drinks business.

Liquid Diet (www.jackcurtin.com/ldo) and **Beer Yard News (www .beeryard.com).** Both of these sites are written by my colleague and good friend Jack Curtin and are great sources of well-informed news about the beer scene in Philadelphia and most of eastern Pennsylvania. Liquid Diet also comes with Jack's trademark blend of humor, rumor, liberal politics, and curmudgeonly griping. I check both several times a week.

Joe Sixpack (www.joesixpack.net). Don Russell writes the Joe Sixpack column for the *Philadelphia Daily News* and is the executive director of Philadelphia Beer Week. He also has some great Philly beer insider stuff at his site and a link to the weekly column. I tell you, this city's got so much good beer writing, it's crazy!

BeerAdvocate (www.BeerAdvocate.com). BeerAdvocate is about rating beers and talking about rating beers, which mostly doesn't interest me . . . but it is also an online community of folks who really care about the beer they drink—and the beer you drink. So the site's forums are a great place to get inside scoops on what's going on in breweries and bars. Its online directory, BeerFly, has a wide range of listings for breweries, bars, and beer stores (which are, perhaps inevitably . . . rated). Very useful site.

My Beer Buzz (mybeerbuzz.com). This Web site focuses on the beer scene in Northeast Pennsylvania (NEPA, as they call it), and it has developed in influence as rapidly as the NEPA beer scene has over the past two years. The setup is a bit different: Each brewery—from The Lion down to Breaker Brewing—and each area beer bar has a page on the site, where they can post information and the latest observations of Mister BeerBuzz about the place are also posted. A newsy and up-to-date site.

THE BONEYARD

The following breweries that were in the third edition of *Pennsylvania Breweries* are no longer open. They are, for the most part, sadly missed, but some parts of them soldier on in other breweries.

Four Sons Brewing. Four Sons closed, after a decline. Matt Allyn got back in, and you'll find the result in this edition as Blue Canoe.

Foxburg Inn. Still open but no longer brewing, which maybe isn't such a bad thing. The beer wasn't great, but the view's still tremendous.

Gettysbrew. Yes, Gettysbrew finally did close. After many years of problems with the beer and some questionable kitchen decisions, they threw in the towel.

Independence Brew Pub. Finally fell after teetering for years. Now a large sports bar; no brewery.

John Harvard's Monroeville, Springfield, and Wayne. There are no more John Harvard's in Pennsylvania. Monroeville held out the longest. The company has closed most of its outlets, but a few remain in New England and Long Island.

Johnstown Brewing. Johnstown was done in by a combination of a slipping economy and a long construction project on the main road out of town to the brewpub. It was too much to overcome.

Latrobe Brewing. See City Brewing in this edition. Belgian owner InBev sold the Rolling Rock brands to Anheuser-Busch, then sold the brewery to City Brewing. About a year later, they bought Anheuser-Busch and got the brand back, but it's still made in Newark, New Jersey.

Legacy Brewing. Less and less was heard from Legacy, and then one day their Web site was gone (as was the one for Reading Premium, a brand they had revived). There are rumors that the brands may have been bought and will be back as contract brews, but the brewery in the basement is closed.

Pittsburgh Brewing. I can't believe I'm writing this. Pittsburgh Brewing, after years of ownership changes, after years of huge debts, after finally changing its name to Iron City Brewing, closed the old Lawrenceville brewery. The brands are now being brewed at City Brewing, under the sure hand of Pittsburgh's former head brewer, Mike Carota.

Red Bell Brewing. The long, strange Red Bell story finally ended with a whimper, not a bang, when its brewpub in the Spectrum closed.

335

Red Star. Red Star lost their lease—and their way—and closed during the edits of this edition. A sad loss: the renovated train station was one of the best brewpub spaces I've seen.

Valley Forge. The new owners seemed to lose interest, and then one day it was closed.

The following breweries opened and closed between the third and fourth editions of this book.

Destiny Brewing. Opened and closed in Phoenixville in about nine months; an odd place that combined a piecemeal brewing system below with a hot dog menu sports bar above.

Hereford and Hops. This big place in Cranbury Township may just have been too ambitious, which is too bad, because they made some of their best, most ambitious beers just before they closed.

There are still a lot of copies of the second edition out there, too, so here are the places from that edition that are no longer with us.

brew moon. Became Rock Bottom, King of Prussia, when Rock Bottom bought out the brew moon chain.

Brick House. Stories abound on why Brick House suddenly closed. The only person who really knows, Joe Grigoli, left for Italy, so it's best to leave it at that.

Buckingham Mountain BC. Closed after a long downward spiral, largely unmourned. Now houses the completely different Porterhouse.

Dock Street Brewpub. An ignominious end for a grand place. Dock Street was sold to people who styled it as the Dock Street Brewpub and Mermaid Supper Club and tried to make it a brewpub by day, dance club by night. They ran it into the ground in three months. The Dock Street in this edition has some of the brewery DNA from the original: the good parts.

Foundry Ale House. Closed because of a loss of traffic during the Convention Center construction and uninterested ownership. Some tanks went to Selin's Grove.

Gettysburg Brewing Company. It was sad to see Dave Baker close up shop, a quirky, devoted man who probably kept this place open longer than was wise to do so. Beloved of the geekerie, but unable to form a steady clientele.

Independence Brewing Company. A sad, bizarre story of wasted money and wasted opportunities. Independence declined into a whimpering finish despite Bill Moore's heroic efforts.

Jack's Mountain. Brewing ended, but the place sputtered along, somewhat erratically. The brewery was removed (by Matt Allyn) in 2008.

Jones Brewing Company. Hard-headed fighting between management and labor finally did what the competition never could: Jones closed in 2002 after more than a century of keeping southwestern Pennsylvania well watered.

Mount Nittany Brewing Company. Fell off the radar without a trace. No one I've talked to is sure what happened to Mark Bloom and his dog Jed.

Mystic Brew Pub. A terribly sad loss. Terry Fies was game right up to the end, and his porter remained excellent, but there was just never enough steady trade to keep Mystic open.

Neversink Brewing. Neversink closed (largely under the weight of a recalcitrant bottling line); then reopened with a new brewer and closed again; reopened as Fancy Pants Brewing and closed again; reopened with the owners of another closed Reading brewery, Pretzel City, as Legacy Brewing . . . and has finally closed, with the equipment in the process of being sold.

New Road Brew House. Crashed and burned as a result of absolutely horrible management. Brewer Brian O'Reilly escaped to Sly Fox with his reputation intact.

Old Lehigh Brewing Company. Couldn't make it work as a part-time brewery in the back of a plumbing supply house.

Poor Henry's. Henry Ortlieb's shot at reviving his family's brewing heritage foundered, rather spectacularly, right around the same time Red Bell's big brewery crashed and Independence went down. Tough time for Philadelphia microbrewing.

Primo Barone's. Eve Martino quit brewing, and Primo couldn't find a new brewer. The restaurant is still open, but the brewery sits cold and empty.

Red Bell Brewing Company. Red Bell could be said to have sued themselves to death—much of the company's money and energy were expended in fruitless lawsuits, but they were also dissipated in projects that never worked out, like a "planned" State College brewpub and the Center City brewpub that would eventually become Independence. The big brewery was closed and the equipment sold off; the long-bruited Manayunk brewpub was open for one week (the brewhouse wound up at Abbey Wright).

Sunnybrook Beverage. Closed, then reopened as Ortlieb's Brewery at Sunnybrook, Henry Ortlieb's next project after Poor Henry's closed. Henry tried hard to make the grand old place work, with the yeoman help of brewer Bill Moore, but the brewery closed soon after Henry died in a tragic boating accident in 2004.

Valhalla. Uninterested owners and Convention Center construction killed Valhalla.

Valley Forge Blue Bell. Continuing construction on Route 202 and contractor problems tolled the bell for Blue Bell.

W. T. Hackett Brewpub. Bad management pulled the rug out from under Hackett's. The brewery remained an eerie time capsule; you could look in through the locked front door and still see the place just as it was the day it closed, down to the cheery blackboard with the day's specials. Brewer Terry Hawbaker jumped to Black Rock, a Wilkes-Barre brewpub that was open a little over a year, then landed at Bullfrog, where he has prospered.

Whitetail Brewing Company. Wade Keech was spread too thin and finally gave up on Whitetail. It has been reborn as Market Cross's brewery.

GLOSSARY

ABV/ABW. Alcohol by volume/alcohol by weight. These are two slightly different ways of measuring the alcohol content of beverages, as a percentage of either the beverage's total volume or its weight. For example, if you have 1 liter of 4 percent ABV beer, 4 percent of that liter (40 milliliters) is alcohol. However, because alcohol weighs only 79.6 percent as much as water, that same beer is only 3.18 percent ABW. This may seem like a dry exercise in mathematics, but it is at the heart of the common misconception that Canadian beer is stronger than American beer. Canadian brewers generally use ABV figures, whereas American brewers have historically used the lower ABW figures. Mainstream Canadian and American lagers are approximately equal in strength. Just to confuse the issue further, most American microbreweries use ABV figures. This is very important if you're trying to keep a handle on how much alcohol you're consuming. If you know how much Bud (at roughly 5 percent ABV) you can safely consume, you can extrapolate from there. Learn your limits . . . before you hit them.

Adjunct. Any nonbarley malt source of sugars for fermentation. This can be candy sugar, corn grits, corn or rice syrups, or one of any number of specialty grains. Wheat, rye, and candy sugars are considered by beer geeks to be "politically correct" adjuncts; corn and rice are generally taken as signs of swill. Small amounts of corn and rice, however, used as brewing ingredients for certain styles of beer, are slowly gaining acceptance in craft-brewing circles. Try to keep an open mind.

Ale. The generic term for warm-fermented beers. (See "A word about . . . Ales and Lagers" on page 27.)

Alefruit. My own invention, so far as I know. I use this term to signify the juicy esters produced by some yeasts, aromas and flavors of a variety of fruits: pear, melon, plum, peach, lemon drop, pineapple. I use "alefruit" when I can't tease out the exact fruits (or when I can but don't want to sound pretentious).

ATTTB. The federal Alcohol and Tobacco Tax and Trade Bureau, formerly part of the ATF, a branch of the Treasury Department. The ATTTB is the federal regulatory arm for the brewing industry. It has to inspect every brewery before it opens, approve every label before it is used, and approve all packaging. The ATTTB is also the body responsible for the fact that while every food, even bottled water, *must* have a nutritional information label, beer (and wine and cider and spirits) is *not allowed* to have one, even though it is a significant source of calories, carbohydrates, and in the case of unfiltered beers, B vitamins and protein. The bureau has become much more cooperative with the craft beer industry, presumably because they've recognized that it's not going away.

Barley. A wonderfully apt grain for brewing beer. Barley grows well in relatively marginal soils and climates. It has no significant gluten content, which makes it unsuitable for baking bread and thereby limits market competition for brewers buying the grain. Its husk serves as a very efficient filter at the end of the mashing process. And it makes beer that tastes really, really good. The grain's kernels, or corns, are the source of the name "John Barleycorn," a traditional personification of barley or beer.

Barrel. A traditional measure of beer volume equal to 31 U.S. gallons. The most common containers of draft beer in the United States are half and quarter barrels, or kegs, at 15.5 gallons and 7.75 gallons, respectively, though the one-sixth-barrel kegs (about 5.2 gallons), known as sixtels, are becoming popular with microbrewers.

Beer. A fermented beverage brewed from grain, generally malted barley. "Beer" covers a variety of beverages, including ales and lagers, stouts and bocks, porters and pilsners, lambics and altbiers, cream ale, Kölsch, wheat beer, and a whole lot more.

Beer geek. A person who takes beer a little more seriously than does the average person. I've been chided for using the term "geek" here, but I haven't found another one I like, so my apologies to those who object. I call myself a beer geek, if that's any consolation. Often homebrewers, beer geeks love to argue with other beer geeks about what makes exceptional beers exceptional. That is, if they've been able to agree on which beers are exceptional in the first place. A beer geek is the kind of person who would buy a book about traveling to breweries . . . the kind of person who would read the glossary of a beer book. Hey, hi there!

BMC. "Bud, Miller, Coors." Shorthand—usually derogatory—for mainstream lagers like these three brands. This has been used by craft beer enthusiasts since before it was "craft beer."

Bottle-conditioned. A beer that has been bottled with an added dose of live yeast. This living yeast causes the beer to mature and change as it ages over periods of one to thirty years or more. It will also "eat" any oxygen that may have been sealed in at bottling and keep the beer from oxidizing, a staling process that leads to sherryish and "wet cardboard" aromas in beer. Note that bottle-conditioned beer qualifies as "real ale."

Brettanomyces, or brett. A wild yeast that is generally considered undesirable in a brewhouse because of the "barnyard" aromas and sourness it can create. However, brewers of some types of beer—lambic, Flanders Red, and the singular Orval—intentionally allow *Brettanomyces* to ferment in their beer for just those reasons. Some American brewers have embraced brett, and a small but devoted group of drinkers have embraced those beers.

Brewer. One who brews beer for commercial sale.

Breweriana. Brewery and beer memorabilia, like trays, coasters, neon signs, steins, mirrors, and so on, including the objects of desire of the beer can and bottle collectors. Most collectors do this for fun, a few do it for money (breweriana is starting to command some big prices; just check eBay), but the weird thing about this for me is the significant number of breweriana collectors who don't drink beer.

Brewhouse. The vessels used to mash the malt and grains and boil the wort. The malt and grains are mashed in a vessel called a *mash tun*. Brewhouse size is generally given in terms of the capacity of the brewkettle, where the wort is boiled. A brewery's annual capacity is a function of brewhouse size, fermentation, and aging tank capacity, and the length of the aging cycle for the brewery's beers.

Brewpub. A brewery that sells the majority of its output on draft, on the premises, or a tavern that brews its own beer. Initially, Pennsylvania law forbade brewpubs to sell anything but their own beer, brewed on-premises. That law has been changed, and now brewpubs *may* obtain a tavern license and serve a full range of alcoholic beverages; not all have done so, and continue to serve only their own beer, though the brewpub license has been expanded to also allow sales of Pennsylvania wines, a nice touch. Anyone ever seen a Pennsylvania winery selling Pennsylvania beers? Just wondering.

CAMRA. The CAMpaign for Real Ale, a British beer drinkers' consumer group formed in the early 1970s by beer drinkers irate over the disappearance of cask-conditioned ale. They have been very vocal and successful in bringing this traditional drink back to a place of importance in the United Kingdom. CAMRA sets high standards for cask-conditioned ale, which only a few brewers in the United States match.

Carbonation. The fizzy effects of carbon dioxide (CO_2) in solution in a liquid such as beer. Carbonation can be accomplished artificially by injecting the beer with the gas or naturally by trapping the CO_2, which is a by-product of fermentation. There is no intrinsic qualitative difference between beers carbonated by these two methods. Brewer's choice, essentially. Low carbonation will allow a broader array of flavors to come through, whereas high carbonation can result in a perceived bitterness. Most American drinkers prefer a higher carbonation.

Case law. In Pennsylvania it is illegal to buy less than a case of beer at a beer store (or, as we call them here, "distributor"). It is also illegal to buy *more* than two six-packs of beer at a time from a bar, though you can buy two, walk out the door, and come back to buy two more. This is very confusing to out-of-staters, and it would be to us as well, if we ever stopped to think about it. Why do we have this law? The wholesalers and the beer stores did it to themselves seventy years ago. They evidently thought it would be great to sell a case at a time without having to break them open and display them. Now they can't get the law changed because the tavern owners jealously defend their six-pack sales rights, and that's making them nuts because now grocery stores are buying tavern licenses and selling six-packs. That may seem like progress, but it's really a work-around fix to a nutty law. Do us all a favor: write your state legislator and ask them to repeal the case law!

Cask. A keg designed to serve cask-conditioned ale by gravity feed or by handpump, not by gas pressure. These casks may be made of wood, but most are steel with special plumbing.

Cask-conditioned beer. An unfiltered beer that is put in a cask before it is completely ready to serve. The yeast still in the beer continues to work and ideally brings the beer to perfection at the point of sale, resulting in a beautifully fresh beer that has a "soft" natural carbonation and beautiful array of aromas. The flip side to achieving this supreme freshness is that as the beer is poured, air replaces it in the cask, and the beer will become sour within five days. Bars should sell out the cask before then or remove it from sale. If you are served sour cask-conditioned beer, send it back! Better yet, ask politely for a taste before ordering. Cask-conditioned beer is generally served at cellar temperature (55 to 60 degrees F) and is lightly carbonated. Cask-conditioned beers are almost always ales, but some American brewers are experimenting with cask-conditioned lager beers.

CIP. Cleaning in Place, or Clean-in-Place, a system to clean tanks, kettles, pipes, and other brewery equipment using a combination of cleansers in a closed-loop system, under the control of a variable amount of automation. CIP is not just a labor saver, it's a safety multiplier. It also allows you to clean parts of your system while the others remain in full operation.

Cold-filtering. The practice of passing finished beer through progressively finer filters (usually cellulose or ceramic) to strip out microorganisms that can spoil the beer when it is stored. Brewers like Coors and Miller, and also some smaller brewers, use cold-filtering as an alternative to pasteurization (see below). Some beer geeks complain that this "strip-filtering" robs beers of their more subtle complexities and some of their body. I'm not sure about that, but I do know that unfiltered beer right from the brewery tank almost always tastes more intense than the filtered, packaged beer.

Contract brewer. A brewer who hires an existing brewery to brew beer on contract. Contract brewers range from those who simply have a different label put on one of the brewery's existing brands to those who maintain a separate on-site staff to actually brew the beer at the brewery. Some brewers and beer geeks feel contract-brewed beer is inherently inferior. This is strictly a moral and business issue; some very good beers are contract-brewed.

Craft brewer. The new term for microbrewer. *Craft brewer*, like *microbrewer* before it, is really a code word for any brewer producing beers other than mainstream American lagers like Budweiser and Miller Lite. (See "A word about . . . Micros, Brewpubs, and Craft Brewers" on page 64.)

Decoction. The type of mashing often used by lager brewers to wring the full character from the malt. In a decoction mash, a portion of the hot mash is taken to another vessel, brought to boiling, and returned to the mash, thus raising the temperature. See also *infusion*.

Draft. Beer dispensed from a tap, whether from a keg or cask. Draft beer is not pasteurized, is kept under optimum conditions throughout the wholesaler-retailer chain, and is shockingly cheaper than bottled or canned beer (each half-barrel keg is over seven cases of beer; check some prices and do the math). Kegs are available in 5-, 7.75-, and 15.5-gallon sizes, and almost all are now the straight-sided kegs with handles. Pennsylvania doesn't have an ineffective and intrusive keg registration law (yet). Kegs are also ultimately recyclable, with a lifespan of forty *years*. Do like I do: Get draft beer for your next party.

Dry-hopping. Adding hops to the beer in postfermentation stages, often in porous bags to allow easy removal. This results in a greater hop aroma in the finished beer. A few brewers put a small bag of hop cones in each cask of their cask-conditioned beers, resulting in a particularly intense hop aroma in a glass of the draft beer.

ESB. Extra Special Bitter, an ale style with a rich malt character and full body, perhaps some butter or butterscotch aromas, and an understated hop bitterness. An ESB is, despite the name, not particularly bitter, especially compared with an American IPA.

Esters. Aroma compounds produced by fermentation that gives some ales lightly fruity aromas: banana, pear, and grapefruit, among others. The aromas produced are tightly linked to the yeast strain used. Ester-based aromas should not be confused with the less subtle fruit aromas of a beer to which fruit or fruit essences have been added.

Fermentation. The miracle of yeast; the heart of making beer. Fermentation is the process in which yeast turns sugar and water into alcohol, heat, carbon dioxide, esters, and traces of other compounds.

Final gravity. See *gravity*.

Firkin. A cask or keg holding 9 gallons of beer, specially plumbed for gravity or handpump dispense.

GABF. The Great American Beer Festival. Since 1982, America's breweries have been invited each year to bring their best beer to the GABF in Denver to showcase what America can brew. Since 1987, the GABF has awarded medals for various styles of beer; seventy-eight styles will be judged in 2010, with three medals for each style. To ensure impartiality, the beers are tasted blind, their identities hidden from the judges. GABF medals are the most prestigious awards in American brewing because of the festival's longevity and reputation for fairness.

Gastropub. A word I hate, because it's so awkward—it sounds like a tavern for snails—but it's useful, because it describes places that have exceptional food and make an effort to match it with good beer. Standard Tap and Monk's in Philly always leap to mind.

Geekerie. The collective of beer geeks, particularly the beer-oriented, beer-fascinated, beer-above-all beer geeks. The geekerie sometimes can fall victim to group thinking and a herd mentality, but they are generally good people, if a bit hop-headed and malt-maniacal. If you're not a member of the geekerie, you might want to consider getting to know them: They usually know where all the best bars and beer stores are in their town, and they're more than happy to share the knowledge and even go along with you to share the fun. All you have to do is ask. See the Beerwebs section for links to the better beer pages, a good way to hook up with them.

Gravity. The specific gravity of wort (original gravity) or finished beer (terminal gravity). The ratio of dissolved sugars to water determines the gravity of the wort. If there are more dissolved sugars, the original gravity and the potential alcohol are higher. The sugar that is converted to alcohol by the yeast lowers the terminal gravity and makes the beer drier, just like wine. A brewer can determine the alcohol content of a beer by mathematical comparison of its original gravity and terminal gravity.

Growler. A jug or bottle used to take home draft beer. These are usually either simple half-gallon glass jugs with screwtops or more elaborate molded glass containers with swingtop seals. I have traced the origin of the term *growler* back to a cheap, four-wheeled horse cab in use in Victorian London. These cabs would travel a circuit of pubs in the evenings, and riding from pub to pub was known as "working the growler." To bring a pail of beer home to have with dinner was to anticipate the night's work of drinking and became known as "rushing the growler." When the growler cabs disappeared from the scene, we were left with only the phrase, and "rushing the growler" was assumed to mean hurrying home with the bucket. When Ed Otto revived the practice by selling jugs of Otto Brothers beer at his Jackson Hole brewery in the mid-1980s, he called them growlers. Now you know where the term really came from.

Guest taps/guest beers. Beers made by other brewers that are offered at brewpubs.

Handpump. A hand-powered pump for dispensing beer from a keg, also called a *beer engine*. Either a handpump or a gravity tap (putting the barrel on the bar and pounding in a simple spigot) is always used for dispensing cask-conditioned beer; however, the presence of a handpump does not guarantee that the beer being dispensed is cask-conditioned.

Homebrewing. Making honest-to-goodness beer at home for personal consumption. Homebrewing is where many American craft brewers got their start.

Hops. The spice of beer. Hop plants (*Humulus lupus*) are vines whose flowers have a remarkable effect on beer. The flowers' resins and oils add bitterness and a variety of aromas (spicy, piney, citrus, and others) to the finished beer. Beer without hops would be more like a fizzy, sweet "alco-soda."

IBU. International Bittering Unit, a measure of a beer's bitterness. Humans can first perceive bitterness at levels between 8 and 12 IBU. Budweiser has 11.5 IBU, Heineken 18, Sierra Nevada Pale Ale 32, Pilsner Urquell 43, and a monster like Sierra Nevada Bigfoot clocks in at 98 IBU. Equivalent amounts of bitterness will seem greater in a lighter-bodied beer, whereas a heavier, maltier beer like Bigfoot needs lots of bitterness to be perceived as balanced.

Imperial. A beer style intensifier, indicating a beer that is hoppier and stronger. Once there was an imperial court in St. Petersburg, Russia, the court of the czars. It supported a trade with England in strong, heavy, black beers, massive versions of the popular English porters, which became known as imperial porters and somewhat later as imperial stouts. Then in the late 1990s, American brewers started brewing IPAs with even more hops than the ridiculous amounts they were already using, at a gravity that led to beers of 7.5 percent ABV and up. What to call them? They looked at the imperial stouts and grabbed the apparent intensifier: "Imperial" IPA was born. While this is still the most common usage, this shorthand for "hoppier and stronger" has been applied to a variety of types, including pilsner and—amusingly—porter.

Infusion. The mashing method generally used by ale brewers. Infusion entails heating the mash in a single vessel until the starches have been converted to sugar. There is single infusion, in which the crushed malt (grist) is mixed with hot water and steeped without further heating, and step infusion, in which the mash is held for short periods at rising temperature points. Infusion mashing is simpler than decoction mashing and works well with most types of modern malt.

IPA. India Pale Ale, a British ale style that has been almost completely co-opted by American brewers, characterized in this country by intense hop bitterness, accompanied in better examples of the style by a full-malt body. The name derives from the style's origin as a beer brewed for export to British beer drinkers in India. The beer was strong and heavily laced with hops—a natural preservative—to better endure the long sea voyage. Some British brewers claim that the beer was brewed that way in order to be diluted upon arrival in India, a kind of "beer concentrate" that saved on shipping costs.

Kräusening. The practice of carbonating beer by a second fermentation. After the main fermentation has taken place and its vigorous blowoff of carbon dioxide has been allowed to escape, a small amount of fresh wort is added to the tank. A second fermentation takes place, and the carbon dioxide is captured in solution. General opinion is that there is little sensory difference between kräusened beer and beer carbonated by injection, but some brewers use this more traditional method.

Lager. The generic term for all cold-fermented beers. Lager has also been appropriated as a name for the lightly hopped pilsners that have become the world's most popular beers, such as Budweiser, Ki-Rin, Brahma, Heineken, and Foster's. Many people speak of pilsners and lagers as if they are two different styles of beer, which is incorrect. All pilsners are lagers, but not all lagers are pilsners. Some are bocks, hellesbiers, and Märzens.

Lambic. A very odd style of beer brewed in Belgium that could take pages to explain. Suffice it to say that the beer is fermented spontaneously by airborne wild yeasts and bacteria that are resident in the aged wooden fermenting casks. The beer's sensory characteristics have been described as funky, barnyard, and horseblanket . . . it's an acquired taste. But once you have that taste, lambics can be extremely rewarding. Most knowledgeable people believe the beers can be brewed only in a small area of Belgium, because of the peculiarities of the wild yeasts. But some American brewers, Lancaster Brewing, Iron Hill, and Bethlehem Brew Works among them, have had a degree of success in replicating this character by carefully using prepared cultures of yeasts and bacteria.

Malt. Generally this refers to malted barley, although other grains can be malted and used in brewing. Barley is wetted and allowed to sprout, which causes the hard, stable starches in the grain to convert to soluble starches (and small amounts of sugars). The grains, now called malt, are kiln-dried to kill the sprouts and conserve the starches. Malt is responsible for the color of beer. The kilned malt can be roasted, which will darken its color and intensify its flavors like a French roast coffee.

Mash. A mixture of cracked grains of malt and water, which is then heated. Heating causes starches in the malt to convert to sugars, which will be consumed by the yeast in fermentation. The length of time the mash is heated, temperatures, and techniques used are crucial to the character of the finished beer. Two mashing techniques are infusion and decoction.

Megabrewer. A mainstream brewer, generally producing 5 million or more barrels of American-style pilsner beer annually. Anheuser-Busch, Miller, and Coors are the best-known megabrewers.

Microbrewer. A somewhat dated term, originally defined as a brewer producing less than 15,000 barrels of beer in a year. Microbrewer, like craft brewer, is generally applied to any brewer producing beers other than mainstream American lagers. (See "A word about . . . Micros, Brewpubs, and Craft Brewers" on page 64.)

Nanobrewer. A really tiny production brewery, roughly defined by size. There's no agreement on that definition, except "it's small." I've set my own arbitrary top limit of a 100-gallon brew size, about 3 barrels. Almost all nanobreweries are one- or two-person operations that are not their owner's primary employment. A small brew size in a brewpub is just a small brewpub.

Original gravity. See *gravity.*

Pasteurization. A process named for its inventor, Louis Pasteur, the famed French microbiologist. Pasteurization involves heating beer to kill the microorganisms in it. This keeps beer fresh longer, but unfortunately it also changes the flavor because the beer is essentially cooked. "Flash pasteurization" sends fresh beer through a heated pipe where most of the microorganisms are killed; here the beer is hot for only twenty seconds or so, as opposed to the twenty to thirty minutes of regular "tunnel" pasteurization. See also *cold-filtering.*

Pilsner. The Beer That Conquered the World. Developed in 1842 in Pilsen (now Plzen, in the Czech Republic), it is a hoppy pale lager that quickly became known as *pilsner* or *pilsener*, a German word meaning simply "from Pilsen." Pilsner rapidly became the most popular beer in the world and now accounts for more than 80 percent of all beer consumed worldwide. Budweiser, a less hoppy, more delicate version of pilsner, was developed in the Czech town of Budejovice, formerly known as Budweis. Anheuser-Busch's Budweiser is quite a different animal.

Pitching. The technical term for adding yeast to wort.

PLCB. The Pennsylvania Liquor Control Board, which enforces the Pennsylvania Liquor Code, including the infamous "case law" for beer sales, and also sells all the wine and liquor in the state. Pennsylvania is a "control state," meaning that the state occupies the place in the market that is normally taken by privately owned liquor stores. The PLCB is not always popular with consumers and retailers, but it is sometimes the only agency regulating the sanitary standards of your local taps . . . not that its agents bother to do that when there are underage-drinking sting operations to run. The PLCB is an agency seriously flawed by divergent missions: make money for the state by selling booze and simultaneously curb consumption of alcohol. Amusingly, the PLCB's Harrisburg headquarters is built on the site of the old Keystone Brewery.

Prohibition. The period from 1920 to 1933 when the sale, manufacture, or transportation of alcoholic beverages was illegal in the United States, thanks to the Eighteenth Amendment and the Volstead Act. (Pennsylvania just barely approved the measure, I'm proud to say.) Prohibition had a disastrous effect on American brewing and brought about a huge growth in organized crime and government corruption. Repeal of Prohibition came with ratification of the Twenty-first Amendment in December 1933. Beer drinkers, however, had gotten an eight-month head start when the Volstead Act, the enforcement legislation of Prohibition, was amended to allow sales of 3.2 percent

ABW beer. The amendment took effect at midnight, April 7. According to Will Anderson's *From Beer to Eternity*, more than 1 million barrels of beer were consumed on April 7: 2,323,000 six-packs each hour. Pity poor Pennsylvania: We're still waiting for the full fruits of Repeal. Ask your state legislator why you can't buy beer by the six-pack from distributors. Ask today!

Real ale. See *cask-conditioned beer*.

Regional brewery. Somewhere between a micro- and a megabrewer. Annual production by regional breweries ranges from 35,000 to 2 million barrels. They generally brew mainstream American lagers. However, some microbrewers—Boston Beer Company, Pete's, and Sierra Nevada, for instance—have climbed to this production level, and some regional brewers, like Anchor, Matt's, and August Schell, have reinvented themselves and now produce craft-brewed beer. (See "A word about . . . Micros, Brewpubs, and Craft Brewers" on page 64.)

Reinheitsgebot. The German beer purity law, which has its roots in a 1516 Bavarian statute limiting the ingredients in beer to barley malt, hops, and water. The law evolved into an inch-thick book and was the cornerstone of high-quality German brewing. It was deemed anticompetitive by the European Community courts and overturned in 1988. Most German brewers, however, continue to brew by its standards; tradition and the demands of their customers ensure it.

Repeal. See *Prohibition*.

Session beer. A beer that is low to medium-low in strength, say 3 to 4.5 percent ABV, but still flavorful, designed for what the British call "session drinking," the kind that goes on all evening through tons of talk and maybe some snacks, and doesn't leave you knee-wobbling after 4 pints.

Sixtel. A new size of keg developed in 1996, holding one-sixth of a barrel: 5.2 gallons, or about 2.5 cases. Very popular for home use (well, I *love* 'em!), and popular with multitaps as well. The beer stays fresher, and you can fit more different beers in a cold box. The word *sixtel* is of uncertain origin; it was not coined by the developer of the keg but apparently grew up out of the users.

Swill. A derogatory term used by beer geeks for American mainstream beers. The beers do not really deserve the name, since they are made with pure ingredients under conditions of quality control and sanitation some micros only wish they could achieve.

Terminal gravity. See *gravity*.

Three-tier system. A holdover from before Prohibition, the three-tier system requires Pennsylvania brewers, wholesalers, and retailers to be separate entities. The system was put in place to curtail financial abuses that were common when the three were mingled. Owning both wholesale and retail outlets gave unscrupulous brewers the power to rake off ungodly amounts of money, which all too often was used to finance political graft and police corruption. The three-tier system keeps the wholesaler insulated from pressure from the brewer and puts a layer of separation between brewer and retailer. Pennsylvania's regional brewers generally credit the state's strong three-tier laws with their survival. Recent court rulings have put the future of the regulated three-tier system in serious doubt, however, which may spell paradise or disaster for beer drinkers.

Wort. The prebeer grain broth of sugars, proteins, hop oils, and alpha acids, and whatever else that was added or developed during the mashing process. Once the yeast has been pitched and starts its jolly work, wort becomes beer.

Yeast. A miraculous fungus that, among other things, converts sugar into alcohol and carbon dioxide. The particular yeast strain used in brewing beer greatly influences the aroma and flavor of the beer. An Anheuser-Busch brewmaster once told me that the yeast strain used there is the major factor in the flavor and aroma of Budweiser. Yeast is the sole source of the clovey, banana-rama aroma and the taste of Bavarian-style wheat beers. The original Reinheitsgebot of 1516 made no mention of yeast; it hadn't been discovered yet. Early brewing depended on a variety of sources for yeast: adding a starter from the previous batch of beer; exposing the wort to the wild yeasts carried on the open air (a method still used for Belgian lambic beers); always using the same vats for fermentation (yeast would cling to cracks and pores in the wood); or using a "magic stick" (which had the dormant yeast from the previous batch dried on its surface) to stir the beer. British brewers called the turbulent, billowing foam on fermenting beer *goddesgood*—"God is good"—because the foam meant that the predictable magic of the yeast was making beer.

Zwickel. A *zwickel* ("tzVICK-el") is a little spout coming off the side of a beer tank that allows the brewer to sample the maturing beer in small amounts; it is also sometimes called the "pigtail." If you're lucky, your brewery tour will include an unfiltered sample of beer tapped directly from the tank through this little spout. Most brewers are touchy about this, as the zwickel is a potential site for infection, but with proper care, it's perfectly harmless to "tickle the zwickel." It's delicious, too: Unfiltered beer is the hot ticket.

INDEX